THE GLORY OF CHRIST
IN THE NEW TESTAMENT

GEORGE BRADFORD CAIRD

The Glory of Christ in the New Testament

STUDIES IN CHRISTOLOGY

———

in Memory of
GEORGE BRADFORD CAIRD

Edited by
L. D. HURST
and
N. T. WRIGHT

OXFORD
CLARENDON PRESS
1987

Oxford University Press, Walton Street, Oxford OX2 6DP

Oxford New York Toronto
Delhi Bombay Calcutta Madras Karachi
Petaling Jaya Singapore Hong Kong Tokyo
Nairobi Dar es Salaam Cape Town
Melbourne Auckland

and associated companies in
Beirut Berlin Ibadan Nicosia

Oxford is a trade mark of Oxford University Press

Published in the United States
by Oxford University Press, New York

© Oxford University Press 1987

British Library Cataloguing in Publication Data
The Glory of Christ in the New Testament:
Studies in Christology in Memory of
George Bradford Caird.
1. Jesus Christ
I. Caird, G. B. II. Hurst, L. D.
III. Wright, N. T.
232   BT202
ISBN 0–19–826326–0

Library of Congress Cataloging in Publication Data
The Glory of Christ in the New Testament
Bibliography: p. Includes index.
1. Jesus Christ—History of doctrines—Early church,
ca. 30–600. 2. Bible. N.T.—Theology. 3. Caird, G. B.
(George Bradford), 1917–1984. I. Hurst, L. D. (Lincoln Douglas)
II. Wright, N. T. (Nicholas Thomas) III. Caird, G. B.
(George Bradford), 1917–1984.
BT198.G54 1987   232'.09'015   87–5512
ISBN 0–19–826326–0

Set by Eta Services (Typesetters) Ltd., Beccles, Suffolk
Printed in Great Britain
at the University Printing House, Oxford
by David Stanford
Printer to the University

FOREWORD

A man of learning, powerful in the scriptures
(Acts 18: 24)

St Luke's notable description of Apollos of Alexandria will have
added meaning for those who knew the one whose memory this volume
honours, for no one came closer to embodying it in his time. When news
of George Caird's sudden and unheralded death reached two of his former students, then in North America, in the early hours of Easter Day
1984, among the flurry of emotions and thoughts which rushed to our
minds was the sad reflection that we had kept our secret too well. We
had for some time been planning a book of essays as a seventieth birthday present to our distinguished and revered teacher: so far as we
know, he remained completely unaware of the scheme. It did not take
us long, however, to agree that the work should go ahead, not now to
congratulate but to commemorate. We are equally grateful to pub-
lisher and contributors alike for their willingness to continue with the
volume in this new form.

Many of those who contributed to this work have their own tales to
tell of the kindness, wisdom, and intellectual stimulation which they
received from George Caird. We are particularly glad that Professor
Henry Chadwick has allowed us to reprint his splendid Memorial
Address, which manages to capture so many aspects of the life and
work here remembered. But in a volume of this kind it is perhaps fitting
that two of his former pupils should record their own memory of the
bracing rigour and discipline of scholarship that characterized
George's own work, together with what he expected of his pupils. It
was not unusual for a young graduate student, having written a draft
chapter of thirty pages or so, to receive eight or ten sheets of manuscript
comment (often on the back of an old agenda for a committee of the
British Academy, revealing the range of George's influence as well as
his exemplary Scottish parsimony) taking the piece apart point by
point. Seldom did misuses of a text, weaknesses in the argument, or passages which possessed something less than the lucidity for which he was
himself so famous escape his searching eye. The greatest compliment
one normally received was to have a whole page pass without
comment.

George Caird became what he was largely through hard work, but
this is not the whole story. He had that rare brilliance which becomes

apparent in early childhood and which, in his case, made a major
university chair an inevitability. And yet, unlike many distinguished
academics who might well aspire to his standards of intellectual integrity, he founded no 'school' of interpretation. Such an idea would have
utterly appalled him. He was far more interested in the quest for truth
than in the propagation of any one set of ideas, his own included. His
gift to his pupils was therefore not a set of answers but a way of thinking
and of asking questions. What he wanted most was that they—and
their pupils—should carry on with pursuing the truth from where he
left off. The best discussions with him always began with the words
'Well, it will take a lot to persuade me that what you say is right, but sit
down, let's talk about it.' Accordingly any graduate pupil who saw in
him a *Doktorvater* could do so only by adopting a rather free translation
of that singularly un-English term. To his natural children he gave his
half of the genetic package and rearing, and then stood back and
watched them, with pleasure and pride, being persons in their own
right. He did not expect them to keep thanking him or running to him
for advice. So too with his academic 'children': he wanted them, under
his watchful eye, to think for themselves. Those who habitually sought
out his time thus did so not because they were required to or because
they expected praise, but because the sheer power of his mind made
him immensely attractive. Time spent with him (whether in lecture
hall, study, senior common room, or chance meetings on the street)
always left its mark—certainly a mark of exacting scholarship mingled
with a lightness of heart at which all might set their aim. To what
extent our aim has been true may be judged partially by the essays in
this volume. One of the saddest things about it surely is that none of us
will receive ten pages of manuscript comment pointing out the ways in
which we still fell short of the ideal.

The editors believe that no volume dedicated to the life and work of
George Bradford Caird could neglect to record, at least in part, the stirring words of his friend and successor as Principal of Mansfield College,
Dr Donald Sykes. According to Dr Sykes at the funeral service held on
28 April 1984,

His outstanding and universally recognized New Testament work rested on
deep foundations of humane learning in the Classics and the Hebrew of the
Old Testament. He was at once meticulous and illuminating in all that he
wrote, going far beyond intellectual dexterity (though he always displayed
much evidence of that). He was great enough to tackle the big questions and in
his independence maintained an individual stance among competing al-
legiances. He could exercise the critical faculties of fellow scholars in their
studies, yet no less could he inspire the student who might never become

learned. For many people he was the means of making true the opening words of one of his fine hymns

> Not far beyond the sea, nor high
> above the heavens, but very nigh
> thy voice, O God, is heard.

To know George you had to hear him preach, for here became apparent one of the great strengths of his life. It was clearly the same man who conducted advanced seminars and helped graduate students to see through the complexities of their work. Many of those who went to his lectures remarked not only on the vigorous academic discipline they were invited to share, but on the direct relationship they were encouraged to see between honest probing and the preaching of the Gospel. His written works remain central and some, such as *The Language and Imagery of the Bible*, one suspects have still to make their full impact. Honours came inevitably and deservedly to George, to be quietly accepted as markers on a path stretching ahead. In human terms that path has reached its end but there will be those who will be glad to acknowledge that they could ask for nothing better than to continue a little further in the way George Caird showed them.

A multitude of friends, colleagues, and pupils who are continuing in the way of George Caird wished to be associated with this volume, but for one reason or another were prevented from contributing to it. Among these special mention must be made of John A. T. Robinson. Shortly before Robinson's death (5 December 1983) his wife wrote to the editors as follows: 'He had not only intended to write for the book but had actually done so. It did however seem best that the essay, being one of the working papers to support the Bamptons project [i.e. *The Priority of John*, delivered posthumously in the Spring of 1984 and now published by the SCM Press], should appear in the earlier volume *Twelve More New Testament Studies*. Had he lived I am sure he would have been glad to contribute an alternative essay as he much wanted to be identified with the Festschrift.' The essay in question is entitled 'The Fourth Gospel and the Church's Doctrine of the Trinity', and it begins with a lengthy and heartfelt tribute to the significance of George's writings in a number of fields, particularly New Testament Christology.

Among others who should be acknowledged, much gratitude is due to the Delegates of the Oxford University Press for their wholehearted approval of the project, and especially to Professor James Barr, who, in addition to his many suggestions, lent early support to the venture when it was being considered as a Festschrift. The staff of the OUP likewise provided constant co-operation, prompt answers to queries and invaluable advice, all of which facilitated a successful completion of the work. Mr. Andrew Saville, of Worcester College, Oxford, is to be thanked for producing the Index.

Lastly, but most crucially, the editors wish to acknowledge two women without whose love this book could not have been produced. George's mother Esther influenced him in ways which would be impossible to measure. His wife Mollie now presides over the ever-expanding family which she and George founded and apart from which he can never be understood. While the loss she suffered might have broken a lesser person, her grief did not for a moment prevent her from doing all she could to be of help to us, providing the many small but critical pieces of advice which have made this volume more an index of George's lasting influence than otherwise could have been possible. She gladly joins with the editors in thanking all those who made possible a book which we hope reflects the glory of Christ in the life and work of George Bradford Caird, in the New Testament, and in the age to come.

June 1987   L. D. HURST
                                                            N.T. WRIGHT

CONTENTS

PART III

METHODS AND THEMES

ABBREVIATIONS

AGD	*A Greek-English Lexicon of the New Testament and other Early Christian Literature*, 2nd edn, ed. W. F. Arndt, F. W. Gingrich and F. W. Danker
AHAW.PH	Abhandlungen der Heidelberger Akademie der Wissenschaften, Philosophisch-historische Klasse
AJT	*American Journal of Theology*
ANRW	*Aufstieg und Niedergang der Römischen Welt*
Apoc. Abr.	*Apocalypse of Abraham*
2 Apoc. Bar.	*Syriac Apocalypse of Baruch*
Apoc. Zeph.	*Apocalypse of Zephaniah*
Aristotle, *Phys.*	*Physics*
Asc. Isa.	*Ascension of Isaiah*
AzTh	*Arbeiten zur Theologie*
b.	Babylonian Talmud
BASOR	*Bulletin of the American Schools of Oriental Research*
BBB	Bonner biblische Beiträge
BCH	*Bulletin de correspondance hellénique*
Ber.	*Berakot*
BETL	Bibliotheca ephemeridum theologicarum lovaniensium
BGBE	Beiträge zur Geschichte der biblischen Exegese
BGrL	Bibliothek der griechischen Literatur
Bib	*Biblica*
BibB	Biblische Beiträge
BJRL	*Bulletin of the John Rylands University Library of Manchester*
BZNW	Beihefte zur *ZNW*
CBQ	*Catholic Biblical Quarterly*
CIL	*Corpus inscriptionum latinarum*
Clem., *Hom.*	Clement, *Homilies*
1 Clem.	*1 Clement*
CQR	*Church Quarterly Review*
CSCO	Corpus scriptorum christianorum orientalium
1, 2, 3 Enoch	Ethiopic, Slavonic, Hebrew Enoch
Ep. Apost.	*Epistula Apostolorum*
Ep. Arist.	*Epistle of Aristeas*
EPRO	*Études préliminaires aux religions orientales dans l'empire romain*
EQ	*Evangelical Quarterly*
ET	*Expository Times*

ETL	*Ephemerides theologicae lovanienses*
Euripides, *Bacch.*	*Bacchae*
Eusebius, *Is.*	Eusebius, *Commentary on Isaiah*
Con. Marc.	*Contra Marcellum*
Ec. T.	*De Ecclesiastica Theologia*
HE	*Historia Ecclesiastica*
FRLANT	Forschungen zur Religion und Literatur des Alten und Neuen Testaments
FRL NF	*Forschungen zur Religion und Literatur des Alten und Neuen Testaments, Neue Folge*
GCS	Griechische christliche Schriftsteller
Hag.	*Hagiga*
HNT	Handbuch zum Neuen Testament
HTR	*Harvard Theological Review*
HThK	*Herders theologischer Kommentar zum Neuen Testament*
HUCA	*Hebrew Union College Annual*
ICC	International Critical Commentary
IDB	*Interpreter's Dictionary of the Bible*
Igh., *Eph.*	Ignatius, Letter to the Ephesians
Magn.	Letter to the Magnesians
Phld.	Letter to the Philadelphians
Rom.	Letter to the Romans
Smyrn.	Letter to the Smyrnaeans
Trall.	Letter to the Trallians
Int	*Interpretation*
Irenaeus, *Adv. Haer.*	Irenaeus, *Adversus omnes Haereses*
JAAR	*Journal of the American Academy of Religion*
JBL	*Journal of Biblical Literature*
JHS	*Journal of Hellenic Studies*
JJS	*Journal of Jewish Studies*
JMES	*Journal of Middle Eastern Studies*
John Chrysostom, *Hom. on John*	Homily on John
Is. interp.	*Interpretatio in Is. 1–8*
Josephus, *Ant.*	*Antiquitates Judaicae*
Vita	*Vita Josephi*
JQR	*Jewish Quarterly Review*
JR	*Journal of Religion*
JSNT	*Journal for the Study of the New Testament*
JTS	*Journal of Theological Studies*
Jub.	*Jubilees*
Justin Martry, *Dial.*	*Dialogue*
KEK	Kritisch-exegetischer Kommentar über das Neue Testament
KNT	Kommentar zum Neuen Testament
KP	*Kleine Pauly*

LSJ	Liddell–Scott–Jones, Greek-English Lexicon
M	*Milḥāmāh*
m.	*Mishnah*
Meg.	*Megilla*
Mek.	*Mekilta*
Melch	*Melchizedek*
Midr.	*Midrash*
MT	Masoretic Text
MVAW.L	*Mededeelingen van de k. vlaamsche academie voor wetenschappen, letteren en schoone kunsten van België: letteren*
NIV	New International Version
Nonnus, *par. Jo.*	Nonnus, *paraphrase of John*
NovT	*Novum Testamentum*
NovTSup	Novum Testamentum Supplement
NTD	Das Neue Testament Deutsch
NTS	*New Testament Studies*
Origen, *Jo.*	Origen, *Commentary on John*
OTS	*Oudtestamentische Studiën*
Ovid. *Met.*	*Metamorphoses*
p	Pesher
par.	paraphrase
PG	*Patrologia graeca*
PGM	*Papyri graecae magicae*
Philo, *Abr.*	*De Abrahamo*
All.	*Legum Allegoriae*
Spec. Leg.	*De Specialibus Legibus*
PL	*Patrologia latina*
Pliny, *Ep.*	*Epistulae*
Pliny, *NH*	*Natural History*
Plutarch, *Mor.*	*Moralia*
Quest. Conv.	*Questiones Conviviales*
Pol., *Phil.*	Polycarp, Letter to the Philippians
Q	Qumran
Quidd.	*Qiddušin*
RB	*Revue biblique*
RevExp	*Review and Expositor*
RGG	*Religion in Geschichte und Gegenwart*
RHPR	*Revue d'histoire et de philosophie religieuses*
RM	*Religionen der Menschheit*
Šabb.	*Šabbat*
Sanh.	*Sanhedrin*
SBL	Society of Biblical Literature
SBS	Stuttgarter Bibelstudien
SC	Sources chrétiennes
SEÅ	*Svensk exegetisk årsbok*
SGLG	*Studia Graeca et Latina Gothoburgensia*

ShirR	*Shir HaShirim Rabba*
Sib. Or.	Sibylline Oracles
SJT	*Scottish Journal of Theology*
SNTSMS	Society for New Testament Studies Monograph Series
SoJTh	*Southwestern Journal of Theology*
SPFTM	Scripta professorum facultatis theologicae 'Marianum'
Sukk.	*Sukka*
t.	Tosepta
Ta'an.	*Ta'anit*
Tacitus, *Hist.*	*Historiae*
TDNT	*Theological Dictionary of the New Testament*
Teh.	*Tehillim*
Tem.	*Tamura*
Test. Abr.	*Testament of Abraham*
Tg. Yer.	*Targum Yerušalmi*
TLZ	*Theologische Literaturzeitung*
TRu	*Theologisches Rundschau*
TS	*Theological Studies*
TU	Texte und Untersuchungen
TWNT	*Theologisches Wörterbuch zum Neuen Testament*
TyndBul	*Tyndale Bulletin*
TZ	*Theologische Zeitschrift*
WUNT	Wissenschaftliche Untersuchungen zum Neuen Testament
Xenophon, *Mem.*	*Memorabilia*
y.	Jerusalem Talmud
ZNW	*Zeitschrift für die neutestamentliche Wissenschaft*

Curriculum Vitae

The Rev. George Bradford Caird, D.Phil., DD, FBA

Born:	London, 19 July 1917
Died:	Letcombe Regis, 21 April 1984
Married:	Viola Mary Newport of Reigate
Children:	James, John, George, Margaret

Education, Degrees, and Honours

1929–1936	King Edward's School, Birmingham (Foundation Scholar)
1936	Major Scholarship in Classics at Peterhouse, Cambridge
1939	BA (Cantab): First class in both parts of Classical Tripos, with distinction in Greek and Latin verse
1939–1943	Theology at Mansfield College, Oxford
1943	MA (Oxon)
1944	D.Phil. (Oxon): 'The New Testament Conception of Doxa'
1959	Honorary DD (St Stephen's College, Edmonton, Alberta)
	Honorary DD (Diocesan College, Montreal)
1966	Honorary DD (Aberdeen)
	DD (Oxon)
1973	Fellow of the British Academy
1981	British Academy's Burkitt Medal for Biblical Studies
1982	Collins Religious Book Award for *The Language and Imagery of the Bible*

Posts Held

1943–1946	Minister of Highgate Congregational Church, London
1946–1950	Professor of Old Testament Language and Literature, St Stephen's College, Edmonton, Alberta
1950–1959	Professor of New Testament Language and Literature, McGill University, Montreal
1955–1959	Principal, United Theological College, Montreal
1959–1970	Senior Tutor, Mansfield College, Oxford
1970–1977	Principal, Mansfield College, Oxford
1977–1984	Dean Ireland's Professor of Exegesis of Holy Scripture, Oxford, and Professorial Fellow of the Queen's College, Oxford

Professional Activities

1945–1946	Extension Lecturer in New Testament, London University
1950	Birks Memorial Lecturer, McGill University
1954	Chancellor's Lecturer, Queen's University, Ontario

1957   President, Canadian Society for Biblical Studies
             Secretary, Canadian Theological Society
1957–1962   Member of World Council of Churches Commission on
             'Tradition and Traditions'
1961–1965   Grinfield Lecturer on the Septuagint, Oxford University
1961–1966   Member of Apocrypha Translation Panel, New English Bible
1962–1965   Official Observer at the Second Vatican Council
1965   Ethel M. Wood Lecturer, London University
             Drew Lecturer, New College, London
             Commemoration Lecturer, Cheshunt College, Cambridge
1966   Congregational Lecturer, London
1967–1969   Chairman of Theological Committee of Congregational
             Church in England and Wales
1969   Birks Memorial Lecturer, McGill University
             John C. Shaffer Lecturer, Yale University
             Fall Lecturer, Union Theological Seminary, Richmond,
             Virginia
1969–1977   Reader in Biblical Studies, Oxford University
1971   Shaftesbury Lecturer
1971–1973   Chairman, Faculty of Theology, Oxford University
1972–1974   Chairman, Theology Faculty Board, Oxford University
1975–1976   Moderator of the General Assembly of the United Reformed
             Church
1977–1984   Co-editor of the *Journal of Theological Studies*
1977–1981   Member of the General Board of Faculties, Oxford University
1977–1981   Chairman, British Academy, Section III
1979–1982   Member of the Council, British Academy
1979–1980   Visitor of the Ashmolean Museum, Oxford
1979–1981   Member of Libraries' Board, Oxford University
1980   Commemoration Lecturer, Westminster College, Cambridge
1982   West-Watson Lecturer, Christchurch, New Zealand

George Bradford Caird, 1917–1984
A Memoir[1]

HENRY CHADWICK

GEORGE CAIRD was but 66 years old when he was suddenly taken from us on Easter Eve, 1984, still at the height of his powers, and the passage of time has done nothing to dull the shock and the tearing sense of loss which his death has left. We all recall his serene gentle smile, his uninhibited love of life in God's world, the at times alarming sternness of his force as a controversialist, his impassioned concern for good and accurate theology. Not a man to wear his heart on his sleeve, even those who found him hard to know quickly recognized his evident qualities of integrity, consistency, and dedicated application.

George was a Dundee Scot by origin and was properly proud of it. When his daughter Meg married a Scot, it revived his sense of having roots well to the north of Hadrian's wall. His father was a constructional engineer working in the Midlands, a man who knew how to use his hands and taught George to use his. From him George acquired great skill with tools and a capacity for making woodwork of considerable finesse. His mathematical aptitude was high, and he would work everything out on paper beforehand with each angle exactly calculated. Nothing was left to contingency or impulse or improvisation. Everything was first conceived as a whole in his mind, and, while he was self-evidently delighted, he was also less than surprised when the final product turned out just right and as intended by its creator. There was surely something of the same precision planning and total control in the way he set about his biblical scholarship.

He especially enjoyed problems which worked within an enclosed circle of rules; games like chess, and puzzles, especially when they had a logical or mathematical content. As a young man he was very useful on a golf course, and at no time of his life was he someone to challenge lightheartedly for a game of croquet or snooker. To such things he brought his rare powers of total concentration and a resolute determination to win. And these again were qualities equally apparent in his theological labours.

Though not himself a performer, he loved listening to music and

[1] This is a slightly edited version of an address originally given in St Mary the Virgin, Oxford, on 13 October 1984.

gave time and care to the support and friendship of professional musicians, many of whom, through his oboist son George, he came to know personally. It is symbolic of that side to his life that one of the greatest of our professional string quartets, the Allegri, came to his Memorial Thanksgiving to play Beethoven's deeply elegiac Cavatina. For they were close friends. So also drama was important to him, and became more so through the distinction of his son John with the Royal Shakespeare Company. Our shy, rather abstracted, and sometimes absent-minded academic, who to pupils could appear austere and even remote, achieved effortless and instant rapport with theatre people. Indeed, the theatrical touch in his own entrances and exits for lectures were a special pleasure to undergraduates. Normally he was out of the lecture-room within four seconds of the last word. He lectured as he preached almost always without a note, and for many years he held a rapt audience in the Schools for two hours a week with nothing before him but a Greek Testament, usually upside down, for he knew the text by heart.

Always thoughtful and sensitive, he was nevertheless no kind of introvert. It would have been utterly uncharacteristic of the man to worry about the state of his soul, to be consumed with the bitterness of disappointment or regret, or to wish that he had been something which he was not. Throughout his career, it was not by his own initiative that he applied for academic posts. He would allow his name to go forward for the Dean Ireland chair when friends and electors urged him to do so. He was among those scholars whose personal and professional quali-fications are such that institutions seek them out. He himself was invari-ably content with what he had, with what God had called him to do. As everyone knows, he was sublimely happy in his home, itself a micro-cosm of vigorous debate and breathtaking wit, sparkling with his wife and his three sons and his daughter, whose gifts were a source of deep joy to him. No portrait of George would be right which omitted his in-tense affection for his grandchildren. From Mollie he caught his love for bird-watching, and from his children he loved to learn about archi-tecture, drama, music, and medieval philology. His love of the country-side came out in his son James's concern for the greening of our cities.

From his school days at King Edward's, Birmingham, he acquired a first-rate education in the Greek and Latin classics, and throughout his career possessed a mastery of all the languages he needed, and of some perhaps he did not. Firsts in both parts of the Classical Tripos at Peter-house carried him on to Mansfield for ministerial training and his doc-torate. Perhaps from the influence of Leyton Richards, his boyhood minister at Carr's Lane Chapel, George was an undemonstrating but utterly determined and lifelong pacifist. So he served a three-year war-time pastorate in much bombed Highgate. In 1946 he was warmly commended by Nathaniel Micklem when an old Canadian pupil asked for the name of an up-and-coming scholar for a chair at St Stephen's College, Edmonton in Alberta. The invitation was extended. He accepted. Suddenly there was consternation in Edmonton: a member of the college staff had been studying the papers and had discovered that they had invited a man with a New Testament doctorate to occupy an Old Testament chair. An immediate cable was despatched to Dr Micklem: 'Can Caird teach Hebrew?' Back came the memorable reply: 'Yes—and if you give him an hour or two's notice, he can also teach Aramaic, Syriac, Coptic, Akkadian, Soghdian, and Sumerian.'

After four years at Edmonton he moved to be McGill's New Testament professor and also became Principal of the United Theological College at Montreal. This last post first brought him immediate experience of ecumenical dialogue with its unexpected moments of sudden joy and usually more numerous tears; an experience later to be greatly enriched by his role as observer at the second Vatican Council which he recorded in a memorable little book. Congregational principles mattered much to him as a young man, but in his maturity much less so. Although he candidly expressed to me his dissenting feeling that Anglicans had 'a fetish about bishops', he also wrote me a letter I treasure expressing his cordial, enthusiastic concurrence with the agreed statement on Eucharistic doctrine published in 1971 by the Anglican/Roman Catholic International Commission.

In 1959 he was delighted to be asked to come to Mansfield, though in financial terms it could be nothing but a very Irish rise. Of all the intellectual riches he gave to Oxford, innumerable friends have memories to record. In his college he was a splendid support and complement to John Marsh; and then as Principal he continued those wise and momentous changes which have seen the College's role in the University quite altered. He enjoyed the unreserved confidence and admiration of successive Vice-Chancellors and Registrars. Not every exact scholar is also patient with the necessities of university administration; but George was glad of his years of service on the General Board at a time when uncomfortable decisions were having to be made and when members of that august body could expect to be loved even less than usual.

But of course his greatest contribution to Oxford lay in his lectures and tutorials, carried through in a style in which, consciously or unconsciously, he continued the tradition of his Mansfield predecessors. At the centre of his work lay the question of the meaning and then of the authority of the Bible and the truth of the Gospel. Perhaps because he was so fine a classical scholar by training and first love, he had no difficulty in 'placing' the early Christian community in its ancient cultural and religious setting. More controversially he was unhaunted by fears such as are sometimes voiced, usually by theologians less familiar than he with the ancient world, that the entire ancient world-view is so incomprehensible to twentieth-century man that the Bible can only be wrapped in impenetrable obscurity and that a professor of exegesis is hardly distinguishable from a professor of divination. George believed in the perspicuity of the substance of Holy Scripture, a principle which the medieval schoolmen and the Reformation inherited from St Augustine, but one which the disciples of Rudolf Bultmann have found it notoriously hard to share.

George admired Rudolf the man but not Bultmann the scholar. His mind-set was in any event deliberately suspicious of whatever seemed fashionable; and he was disinclined to believe something true merely because it happened to be written in German. The character of his scholarly work, as also of his entire style of life, was one which did not too much care what modish people thought.

His exposition of the New Testament was grounded on the most rigorous examination of his texts, to which he brought weighty erudition, including highly detailed knowledge of the Septuagint and Apocrypha. On this foundation he could construct an architectonic, total portrait of the mind of the New Testament writers, whose diversities and polarities seemed to him subordinate not indeed to a unison but to a profounder harmony; so (one might say with the epistle to the Ephesians) the entire body, fitly framed and knit together, and at every joint interconnected, presented a tightly coherent whole. As he revealed in his fine book on *The Language and Imagery of the Bible* which won him the Collins Book Award, he could incorporate in his system quite a lot of modern linguistics and philosophy; he was at home in semantics in a way not all his theological colleagues were. In polemic he was vitality itself, his eyes shining with glee in the cut and thrust of debate and controversy, wholly without malice. Unlike Odysseus, he would use no poisoned arrows. Among his more characteristic mannerisms was the triumphant conclusion of a long argument with a rhetorical sniff or snort, somehow expressing a sense of utter finality. If his partner in debate was not fully persuaded about the strength of one or more links in the chain, he could be hard to argue with, since in such a carefully integrated whole everything appeared loadbearing, and to dislodge even one joint in the structure made one fear for the repercussions. When he was asked a question after a paper or a lecture, there would be some seconds of faintly awesome silence, hands clasped in front of his chest while his well-organized mind marshalled the relevant facts. Then there would come a crisp, articulated, coherent answer which contained within it a note of deep authority.

He enjoyed the anecdote that when James Moffatt published his modern translation of the Bible, he distributed copies to his friends with a slip bearing the words 'with the author's compliments'. Yet probably it was more true of George than of most modern New Testament scholars that he understood the task of the exegete to be not only the discernment of the author's original intention but also the elucidation and proclamation of the Gospel of God. Just as he could hardly endure sermons without intellectual content, so his lectures were truly evangelical. His dedication to the New English Bible translation was a part of this concern. The huge proportion of time and energy which he gave to the revision of this very notable version was a most significant index of his personal commitment to making Scripture immediately, or almost immediately, intelligible to our generation.

I have said too little of the rigour he used to bring to work submitted by undergraduate and graduate students. Not only were the resources of his own learning at their disposal. He made his best pupils feel that they too had something of their own to contribute, even in some of the most overworked areas of biblical study. To encounter his austerity and his patience was a discipline in itself. The austerity came into its own as an indispensable quality for the editing of a learned journal. Would-be contributors of promising material might receive many pages of carefully composed and penetrating criticism. All his own writings underwent many rewritings before he was sufficiently satisfied to publish. His remarkable commentary on the Apocalypse contains a noble acknowledgement of his indebtedness to Austin Farrer, with whose general point of view he would not have been expected to agree—other than with the principle enunciated by Farrer that probably none will be in for more surprises in heaven than expounders of the Revelation of St John. George's last years were devoted to preparing his long-awaited *New Testament Theology*, which sadly he was not able to complete. There is reason to hope, however, that his old pupil and friend Professor Hurst in California will be able to construct the remainder and see to the matter of publication.

Honours came to him, including election to the British Academy and the award of its coveted Burkitt Medal. He was constantly in demand—world-wide—to fill prestigious guest lectureships. But most of all we recall with gratitude to his Maker a man of nobility, insuppressible *joie de vivre*, which he combined with a frugal and puritan life-style, a sublime lack of self-consciousness and vanity, a simplicity of heart and single eye which were grace indeed.

HENRY CHADWICK

Bibliographia Cairdiana[1]

1950

The Truth of the Gospel, London, 1950, Oxford University Press.

1951

The Shorter Oxford Bible (with G. W. Briggs and N. Micklem), Oxford University Press.
'Christ's Attitude to Institutions', *Expository Times*, 62 (1950–1), 259–62.
The New Testament View of Life (Inaugural Lecture), McGill University Press.

1952

'Recent Articles on Biblical Interpretation', *Interpretation*, 6 (1952), 458–66.

1953

'Introduction and Exegesis to I and II Samuel', *The Interpreter's Bible*, ii, ed. G. A. Buttrick *et al.*, Nashville, 1953, 855–1175.

1955

The Apostolic Age, Duckworth Studies in Theology, Essex and London, 1955, Duckworth.

1956

Principalities and Powers, Oxford, 1956, Clarendon Press.
'The Transfiguration', *The Expository Times*, 67 (1955–6), 291–4.
'Judgement and Salvation: An Exposition of John 12: 31–32', *Canadian Journal of Theology* 2 (1956), 231–7.

1957

'Predestination—Romans ix.–xi.', *Expository Times*, 68 (1956–7), 324–7.

1959

'The Exegetical Method of the Epistle to the Hebrews', *Canadian Journal of Theology* 5 (1959), 44–51.
'Everything to Everyone—The Theology of the Corinthian Epistles', *Interpretation* 13 (1959), 387–99.

1961

'The Will of God in the Fourth Gospel', *Expository Times*, 72 (1960–1), 115–17.
'Alexander Nairne's "The Epistle of Priesthood"', *Expository Times*, 72 (1960–1), 204–6.

[1] The editors are grateful to Mrs V. M. Caird for placing at their disposal a list of Professor Caird's publications, which has been supplemented by Dr Hurst. An earlier list, published by C. H. H. Scobie, appeared in the *Bulletin of the Ralph Pickard Bell Library* of Mount Allison University, vol. 2, no. 6/7, July–August 1978.

1961–2

'He Who for Men their Surety Stood', *Expository Times*, 73 (1961–2), 24–6.
'The Kingship of Christ', *Expository Times*, 73 (1961–2), 248–9.

1962

'Samuel', *Encyclopaedia Britannica*, xix, Chicago, 1962, University of Chicago Press, 984. Reprinted 1972.
'On Deciphering the Book of Revelation' (Four Articles: 'I. Heaven and Earth'; 'II. Past and Future'; 'III. The First and the Last'; 'IV. Myth and Legend'); *Expository Times* 74 (1962–3), 13–15; 51–3; 82–4; 103–5.
'The Chronology of the New Testament', *The Interpreter's Dictionary of the Bible*, i, Nashville, 1962, Abingdon Press, 599–607.
'John, Letters of', *The Interpreter's Dictionary of the Bible*, ii, Nashville, 1962, Abingdon Press, 946–52.

1963

'Paul the Apostle', *Dictionary of the Bible*, ed. James Hastings, revised edition by F. C. Grant and H. H. Rowley, New York, 1963, Charles Scribner's Sons, 731–6.
'Paul's Theology', *Dictionary of the Bible*, ed. James Hastings, revised edition by F. C. Grant and H. H. Rowley, New York, 1963, Charles Scribner's Sons, 736–42.
The Gospel of St Luke, Pelican Gospel Commentaries, Harmondsworth, 1963. Hardback Edition, London, 1968, Adam and Charles Black.

1964

'The Descent of Christ in Ephesians 4, 7–11', *Studia Evangelica*, 2, ed. F. L. Cross, Berlin, 1964, Akademie-Verlag, 535–45.
The Unity We Seek: II. Making It Visible, London, 1964, The British Council of Churches.

1965

'C. H. Dodd', *A Handbook of Christian Theologians*, ed. Martin E. Marty and Dean G. Peerman, Cleveland, 1965, World Publishing Co., 320–37.
'The New Testament', *The Scope of Theology*, ed. Daniel T. Jenkins, Cleveland, 1965, 39–56.
'Expounding the Parables: I. The Defendant (Matthew 5: 25 f.; Luke 12: 58 f.)', *Expository Times* 77 (1965–6), 36–9.
Jesus and God (with D. E. Jenkins), London, 1965, The Faith Press.
Jesus and the Jewish Nation (Ethel M. Wood Lecture), London, 1965, University of London, The Athlone Press.

1966

The Revelation of St John the Divine, Black's New Testament Commentaries, London, 1966, Adam and Charles Black.

1967

Our Dialogue With Rome: The Second Vatican Council and After (The Congregational Lectures for 1966), Oxford, 1967, Oxford University Press.

1968

'The Development of the Doctrine of Christ in the New Testament', *Christ for Us Today*, ed. N. Pittenger, London, 1968, SCM, 66–80.

'Relations with Roman Catholics: A Congregationalist View', *Towards Christian Unity*, ed. B. Leeming, London, 1968, Geoffrey Chapman.

'Towards a Lexicon of the Septuagint I', *Journal of Theological Studies*, 19 (1968), 453–75.

1969

'Towards a Lexicon of the Septuagint II', *Journal of Theological Studies*, 20 (1969), 21–40.

'Uncomfortable Words: II. Shake off the Dust from Your Feet (Mk 6: 11)', *Expository Times*, 81 (1969–70), 40–3.

'The Glory of God in the Fourth Gospel: An Exercise in Biblical Semantics', *New Testament Studies*, 15 (1969), 265–77.

The Open Heaven by W. H. Cadman, ed. by G. B. Caird, Oxford, 1969, Basil Blackwell.

'Les Eschatologies du Nouveau Testament', *Revue d'histoire et de philosophie religieuses*, Paris, 1969, Presses Universitaires de France, 217–27.

1970

'The Christological Basis of Christian Hope', *The Christian Hope*, ed. G. B. Caird, Theological Collections 13, London, 1970, SPCK, 9–24.

'The Bible and the Word of God', *Christian Confidence*, Theological Collections 14, London, 1970, SPCK, 105–20.

1971

Christianity and Progress (the twenty-sixth Shaftesbury Lecture), London, 1971, The Shaftesbury Society.

1972

'Paul and Women's Liberty', *Bulletin of the John Rylands Library* 54 (1972), 268–81.

'Saint Paul the Apostle', *Encyclopaedia Britannica*, Fifteenth Edition, xiii, Chicago, 1972 and 1974, University of Chicago Press, 1090–4.

1973

'New Wine in Old Wine-Skins: I. Wisdom', *Expository Times*, 84 (1973), 164–8.

1974

'Charles Harold Dodd, 1884–1973', *The Proceedings of the British Academy*, 60 (1974), 497–510; printed separately, 1975, 3–16.

1976

'Eschatology and Politics: Some Misconceptions', *Biblical Studies: Essays in Honour of William Barclay*, ed. Johnston R. McKay and James F. Miller, London, 1976, Collins, 72–86, 202–3.

'Homoeophony in the Septuagint', *Jews, Greeks and Christians: Essays in Honor of*

William David Davies, ed. R. Hamerton-Kelly and R. Scroggs, Leiden, 1976, E. J. Brill, 74–88.

'The Study of the Gospels' (Three Articles: 'I. Source Criticism', 'II. Form Criticism', 'III. Redaction Criticism'), *Expository Times*, 87 (1975–6), 99–104; 137–41; 168–72.

South Africa: Reflections on a Visit (with John Johansen-Berg), London, 1976, The United Reformed Church in England and Wales, 3–14.

'The New Testament Concept of Salvation', *Tantur Yearbook* 1976–7, Tantur, Jerusalem, 19–34.

Paul's Letters from Prison, New Clarendon Bible, Oxford, 1976, Oxford University Press.

1979

The Word for Today, Sackville, NB, Canada, 1979, Mount Allison University Press.

War and the Christian, Surrey, 1979, The Fellowship of Reconciliation.

'Health', in *The Quality of Life* (Report of the British Association Study Group on Science and the Quality of Life), ed. Harford Thomas, London, 1979, The British Association for the Advancement of Science, 21–3.

'Biblical Classics: VIII. James Denney: The Death of Christ', *Expository Times*, 90 (1978–9), 196–9.

'Just Men Made Perfect', *Resurrection and Immortality: Aspects of Twentieth Century Christian Belief*, ed. Charles S. Duthie, London, 1979, Samuel Bagster & Sons Ltd., 89–103, reprinted from *The London Quarterly and Holborn Review*, 1966, 89–98.

1980

The Language and Imagery of the Bible, Essex and London, 1980, Duckworth.

1982

'Ben Sira and the Dating of the Septuagint', *Studia Evangelica*, 4, ed. E. A. Livingstone, Berlin, 1982, Akademie-Verlag, 95–100.

'Jesus and Israel: The Starting Point for New Testament Christology', *Christological Perspectives: Essays in Honor of Harvey K. McArthur*, ed. Robert F. Berkey and Sarah Edwards, New York, 1982, Pilgrim Press, 58–68.

1983

'The One and the Many in Mark and John', *Studies of the Church in History: Essays Honoring Robert S. Paul on his Sixty-Fifth Birthday*, ed. Horton Davies, Allison Park, Pennsylvania, 1983, Pickwick Publications, 39–54.

1984

'Biblical Exegesis and the Ecumenical Movement', *The Divine Drama in History and Liturgy: Essays Presented to Horton Davies on His Retirement from Princeton University*, ed. John E. Booty, Allison Park, Pennsylvania, 1984, Pickwick Publications, 203–17.

'Son by Appointment', *The New Testament Age: Essays in Honor of Bo Reicke*, i, ed. William C. Weinrich, Macon, Georgia, 1984. Mercer University Press, 73–81.

Introduction to Paul S. Minear's *Matthew, the Teacher's Gospel*, British Edition, London, 1984, Darton, Longman and Todd.

1985

Second Edition of *The Revelation of St John the Divine*, London, 1985, Adam and Charles Black, with a new preface (written 5 March, 1984).

'Perfection and Grace', in *Duty and Delight: Routley Remembered* (Memorial vol. for Eric Routley), ed. C. R. Young, R. A. Leaver, and J. H. Litton, Carol Stream, Illinois, 1985, Hope Publishing Co., 21–33.

FORTHCOMING

New Testament Theology, Oxford, Clarendon Press.

BOOK REVIEWS

Reviews published in over a dozen journals (most notably the *Journal of Theological Studies*) of over a hundred books written in English, German, French, and Italian.

MEMOIR

A memoir of George Caird by Professor James Barr appears in the *Proceedings of the British Academy*, 71 (1985), 493–521.

PART I

BACKGROUNDS TO THE NEW TESTAMENT AND ITS CHRISTOLOGY

1. Words for Love in Biblical Greek

JAMES BARR

GEORGE CAIRD was a scholar of the Septuagint as well as of the New Testament. He had a keen sense for the meanings and nuances of words, and his taste in matters of vocabulary was fastidious. He understood the danger that differences between words might be identified with theological differences. When, in the early sixties, I wrote about words for time, I took my starting-point in a note of his which, simply and economically, disproved the supposition, then influential, that καιρός and χρόνος denoted two different kinds of time.[1] Words for love are in some ways a similar case. This brief study will concentrate on the LXX: although it is in the New Testament that the term *love* becomes most central and conspicuous, it is in the LXX that much of the decisive linguistic evidence is to be found.[2]

The noun ἀγάπη is scarcely found in Greek before the LXX; and a common traditional argument suggested that it was actually coined by that version and was thus the supreme example of a word 'born within the bosom of revealed religion'.[3] Even if this argument is now less often heard, it continues to cast emphasis upon the role of the LXX in the whole matter. This is implied, or made explicit, in much modern theological discussion.

The emphasis on ἀγάπη in the twentieth century has been primarily theological in character. Nygren's influential *Eros and Agape*, made known in English from the 1930s and widely quoted, made familiar the idea of an opposition between two kinds of love, *agape* and *eros*, the former a self-giving love, the latter rather an aspiration toward, a desire

---

[1] J. Barr, *Biblical Words for Time* (London, 1962; 2nd edn., 1969), 22 f.; the reference was to Caird's *The Apostolic Age* (London, 1955), 184 n. 2.

[2] An earlier form of this essay had been delivered as one of the Grinfield Lectures in Oxford, on 17 May 1977—another link with George Caird, who had also been Grinfield Lecturer, concentrating on the vocabulary and lexicography of the Septuagint. In presenting this theme, I apologize for the brevity with which I have tried to handle the essentials of a complicated subject. A much fuller treatment is to be found in M. Paeslack's article in *Theologia Viatorum*, 5 (1953–4), 51–142. I excuse myself for returning to the same theme by pointing out that Paeslack's article is in German and in a somewhat inaccessible periodical; it is also very long, and does not focus on exactly the same questions that concern me.

[3] The phrase is Archbishop Trench's: see his *Synonyms of the New Testament* (7th edn., London, 1871), 41. In 1955 in his *Agapè, prolegomènes* (cf. below, n. 7), 32, C. Spicq virtually re-echoes Trench's judgement: 'une création propre de la religion révélée'. For a valuable recent comment, see C. C. Tarelli in *JTS* NS 1 (1950), 64–7.

for, that which was inherently desirable or beautiful. The centre of biblical religion lay in *agape*. Everyone who then knew anything about theology knew this.

Nygren himself, however, did not profess in this to be exactly describing the linguistic usage of the Greek Bible: he did not maintain that, every time ἀγάπη or ἀγαπᾶν appeared in it, it meant *agape* in his sense of self-giving love. Indeed he admitted, at least tacitly, that it did not, for he gave some attention to the use of the verb ἀγαπᾶν in a negative or unfavourable sense, in phrases like 'to love the world', 'to love the wages of unrighteousness', and the like, none of which could count as self-giving love.[4] Examples include:

John 3: 19 ἠγάπησαν οἱ ἄνθρωποι μᾶλλον τὸ σκότος ἢ τὸ φῶς
2 Tim. 4: 10 Δημᾶς γάρ με ἐγκατέλιπεν ἀγαπήσας τὸν νῦν αἰῶνα
2 Pet. 2: 15 μισθὸν ἀδικίας ἠγάπησεν

Thus Nygren was not seeking to describe all linguistic usage, but to draw the contrast between two profound theological motifs. Many now think that his account of the matter was theologically misleading in any case, and that *agape* and *eros* as motifs were not distinguished in the way he supposed; but this, whether right or wrong, is not my concern. However that may be, the effect of his book on a large public was to leave them thinking that ἀγάπη and ἀγαπᾶν formed the unequivocal designator of a particular kind of love, self-giving and self-sacrificing, quite different from the kinds of love designated by other words. *Agape* had thus become a standard word of modern theological English: few observed that ἀγάπη, ἀγαπᾶν in actual biblical Greek did not always signify *agape*.

These ideas had the effect of laying much emphasis upon the LXX as the locus where the choice of words had been made. It was widely accepted that the New Testament used ἀγάπη because it had already been used in the LXX and was thus the established term of biblical tradition. The LXX, it was supposed, had chosen this word, or even created it, out of need for a special word that would suitably express the biblical concept of love, and especially of the love of God, a word that would thus suitably correspond to the Hebrew אַהֲבָה and suitably differ from the Greek ἔρως. N. H. Snaith, for instance, in his influential work of 1944 wrote that the LXX had 'invented' this Greek word to stand for

---

[4] See Nygren's section on 'the love of the world', 155 ff. in the later English version, tr. P. S. Watson (London, 1953); from 157 we quote: 'When we are warned against love of the world, it obviously cannot be the generous, self-giving Agape-love that is meant, but only "the love of desire" or *acquisitive love*.' But, though Nygren acknowledged this, it cannot be said that his recognition of it and its implications was adequate in detail or in profundity.

the Hebrew term and that the New Testament writers thus 'found a word already to hand, with a specialized meaning already involved'.[5]

In similar terms Karl Barth, a decade later, wrote:[6]

Already here [that is, in the LXX] the only basis one can offer for the choice of the word ἀγάπη is the will at all costs *not* to speak about ἔρως in designating that which was witnessed to in the texts as 'love'. In this will were united both Hellenistic Judaism as it interpreted the Old Testament, and early Christianity as it testified to Jesus Christ.

Specification of theological content, then, is not only a major, but *the sole*, reason for the choice of words.

Similar tendencies are to be found in the magisterial work of Spicq.[7] His lengthy and devoted study seems to be influenced throughout by the conviction that the word ἀγάπη *must be* the proper and peculiar designator of a special kind of love, its proper name as it were, so that the study of this word will surely reveal the contours of this special kind of love. Again and again the evidence suggests that this is not so, and Spicq half acknowledges this, but then he starts off again on the same track, convinced that the meanings of this word will somehow lead us to a deeper knowledge of this peculiar kind of love.

All these views, then, alike emphasize the theological nature of the choice of words; they imply that if a different word had been used a different theological picture would have been created, and that awareness of this was active in the biblical writers. They are anti-Hellenistic, seeking by every means to assert the differentiation of the biblical concepts from the Greek and the importance of the vocabulary for the achieving of this.[8]

Less well known and less popularly appealing are those contrary positions which maintain that the choice of ἀγάπη, ἀγαπᾶν is not theologically motivated at all but has its basis in purely linguistic features.

One such argument came from the Belgian scholar Joly.[9] In a rather

---

[5] N. H. Snaith, *The Distinctive Ideas of the Old Testament* (London, 1944), 173.

[6] K. Barth, *Kirchliche Dogmatik*, iv/2 (Zurich, 1955), 836; ET, 737; cf. also further remarks on the following pages. Barth was one of those to criticize Nygren for his theological treatment of the question; but by his insistence upon his interpretation of the LXX and of other linguistic evidence Barth only made things worse, as seen from the viewpoint of biblical scholarship.

[7] C. Spicq, OP, *Agapè, prolegomènes à une étude de théologie néo-testamentaire* (Louvain, 1955) and *Agapè dans le nouveau Testament* (3 vols., Paris, 1958–9; abbreviated ET, St Louis, 1963–5). The earlier volume, which studies the Greek and Old Testament antecedents of New Testament usage, seems to be more serious as a linguistic study and less of a religious meditation.

[8] Spicq does not have the anti-Hellenistic animus of some of the other scholars mentioned, and he sees more of a gradual development; but on the other hand his insistence on 'new content' has something of the same effect.

[9] R. Joly, *Le Vocabulaire chrétien de l'amour est-il original?* (Brussels, 1968). C. C. Tarelli, op. cit. n. 3 above, had also and in a somewhat similar way placed biblical usage somewhere on the curve of that major long-term change, complete in modern Greek, whereby ἀγαπᾶν became the one and normal verb 'to love' while φιλεῖν as a separate verb survived only with the sense 'kiss'.

harshly anti-theological argument, in which the deficiencies of Spicq's position are severely criticized, Joly offered a quite different explanation for the rise to prominence of ἀγάπη, ἀγαπᾶν. The chief Greek word for 'love' had always been φιλεῖν, but now, he argued, this word had become increasingly specialized in the sense 'kiss' and ἀγαπᾶν moved into the vacant place of centrality as the word for love. The shift had nothing to do with theological motivations. The Bible used ἀγαπᾶν because it had already become the established verb 'to love'.

George Caird offered another non-theological explanation.[10] Far from being influenced by the theological motivations ascribed to them, he wrote, the LXX translators were 'prompted by an altogether more mundane impulse', namely 'the very close phonetic resemblance between the Greek ἀγάπη and the Hebrew אַהֲבָה'. It was not the theological meaning but the phonetic similarity that counted. This similarity had, indeed, been often noticed, but Caird's explanation accorded it a more central role than it had had before.

It must be considered uncertain, however, whether the explanation through phonetic resemblance can prevail. The great majority of LXX words that can be plausibly explained through phonetic resemblance to the Hebrew are *rare* terms: often they occur only once or twice, or they are a peculiar usage of one book or of only a few. It is easy to understand that a translator, faced with an extremely odd Hebrew word, might resort to the device of using a Greek word that was similar in form: a familiar example is δρέπανον 'sickle', used to render דָּרְבָן at 1 Sam. 13: 21, a word that occurs only twice in the Bible.[11] It is quite another matter to suppose that this was done with the frequent and basic term 'love'. I know of no well-grounded case where phonetic resemblance was the basis of choice of rendering for a common and central Hebrew term recurring one or two hundred times. The rendering βωμός for בָּמָה 'high place' is rather rare (seven cases, and only in the Prophets); the normal rendering is τὰ ὑψηλά. Similarly, σκηνή, σκήνωμα look at first sight as if they might be motivated by phonetic resemblance to שָׁכַן 'dwell'; but in fact the vast majority of cases are renderings of the common אֹהֶל 'tent', which has no such similarity. Likewise κατασκηνόω, though common, is not at all similar to any Hebrew word,

---

[10] G. B. Caird, 'Homoeophony in the Septuagint', in *Jews, Greeks and Christians: Essays in honor of William David Davies*, ed. R. Hamerton-Kelly and R. Scroggs (Leiden, 1976), 74–88; quotations from 83.

[11] Caird, 'Homoeophony', 84. I cite the example, however, only as a hypothetical one, for it is not clear that דָּרְבָן is actually the word being translated here; cf. the end of v. 20. If it is not, then the instance is not a valid one. See the recent textual discussion by P. Kyle McCarter, *1 Samuel* (Anchor Bible), 234, note on v. 20. The present writer has recently published a fresh and thorough examination of the whole idea that the LXX chose Greek words for their phonetic resemblance to the Hebrew: see *Textus* 12 (1985) 1–77.

and is to be explained rather by etymological analysis based on מִשְׁכָּן 'tabernacle' (rendered regularly by σκηνή). Even where a Greek word may seem to have some phonetic resemblance to the Hebrew, this may be accidental, and especially so if other explanations for the choice of words can be offered. And, in the case of 'love', the choice in question probably took place first in the verb and not in the noun: but it is much more difficult to say that forms of a Hebrew verb resemble any Greek word than to say it of ἀγάπη and אַהֲבָה.

The LXX evidence in fact most naturally supports the view, as regards the verb, that ἀγαπᾶν was used because it was already a normal and very natural term in the language and well established in the two connections that were most important, namely that of one person loving another like a child or a close friend and, even more, that of a human loved by a god. The LXX in this respect is one manifestation of that general rise of ἀγαπᾶν to prominence much of which is most fully documented in later writers, Josephus being the most obvious: he uses ἀγαπᾶν very much more frequently than φιλεῖν. The natural objection, that Josephus went in this direction as a result of LXX influence, should be resisted: his use of ἀγαπᾶν is very different from that of the LXX, and where it uses ἀγαπᾶν he often uses a different verb in describing the same incident. The move of φιλεῖν into the realm of 'kiss' may be a symptom rather than a cause of the same movement, for φιλεῖν was far from dead as early as this: on the one hand it was used for 'kiss' mainly within certain tenses, notably the aorist, and, on the other hand, in the original sense 'love' it is still very much alive in the New Testament and actually more strongly used there than in the LXX. Phonetic similarity may also have supported the choice in the case of the LXX, even if it was not the main influence. Basically, however, we are saying that within the LXX the choice of ἀγαπᾶν was a feature of *continuity* with contemporary usage, and not least of contemporary religious usage; the effort to portray it as a supreme example of *discontinuity* was completely wrong.

The most important factor, however, in producing the shape of the LXX vocabulary for love was another, namely the tendency of the translation to use constant equivalents: this tendency did not apply in all words but in the words for love it applied in fairly high degree. The effect of translation technique is such that LXX usage can seldom be simply defined as continuous with contemporary Greek usage or as deviating from it. It will often be continuous with it at the nodal points where the choice of terms is made, but the force of constant-equivalent renderings may well produce examples that deviate from normality in Greek. But, in essence, all this is not a result of revulsion against common Greek meanings; it is a result of the character of the LXX as a translation.

Many older treatments stressed the *weakness* and *dullness* of ἀγαπᾶν before it was miraculously transformed through its use by the LXX.[12] The LXX itself, however, gives no hint of this. It was a strong, warm, vivid and colourful term, and therefore fitted easily and naturally into the contexts of the Bible. Exactly in this regard it was stronger and also more precise than φιλεῖν, which could mean 'like', 'be friendly' as well as 'love'.

In these last paragraphs we have concentrated on the verbs. Too much attention has been paid to the specific noun ἀγάπη. Even if this noun did not previously exist in Greek and was created by the LXX translators, not too much importance should be attached to this fact in the context of the present discussion. For, in relation to ideas of love, this noun is no more than a nominalization of those same relations and emotions which in verb form were expressed by ἀγαπᾶν; no one has argued that this noun said something different about love from what the verb said.[13] Thus, even if ἀγάπη was a neologism morphologically, it was not at all one semantically; and, whatever the case with the noun, the verb ἀγαπᾶν was no neologism, for it existed in Greek as early as Homer and already in classical times was used with senses quite close to those found in the LXX and the New Testament, and this is still more obvious in Hellenistic usage.

In the Hebrew Old Testament, the verb 'love' was much more dominant than the corresponding noun (noun about forty times but verb over two hundred times). Moreover, even where a noun was used, the actual form ἀγάπη was less important in the LXX than one might imagine. In the major books it is in fact very rare. Hatch and Redpath register sixteen cases, but in one of these (2 Sam. 1: 26) the original reading is probably ἀγάπησις. Of the remainder, thirteen are in the Song of Songs or Ecclesiastes, both very literal translations and probably very late, so much so that they may not yet have existed in early New Testament times.[14] If we except these later books there are only

---

[12] Stauffer's *TWNT* article (1, 36–9) and Barth, loc. cit. n. 6 above, repeatedly use terms like 'pale', 'colourless', 'vague', 'imprecise', 'weak', 'variable', 'lacking in distinctive significance', and even 'harmless'. This arises from cherishing the contrast with *classical* Greek meanings while ignoring the likelihood that the LXX itself provides evidence of continuity with Hellenistic meanings. The idea that the word was 'filled with new content' when used in the biblical tradition is not so much wrong as a misdescription: 'new content' meant that a word, the meaning of which was already established, came to be used in a quite different set of proportions, connections, and relations—who it was who loved whom, and why, and with what effects.

[13] This is no new idea: Grimm-Thayer, 4, say of ἀγάπη: 'In significance it follows the verb ἀγαπᾶν.' But the importance of this has not always been realized.

[14] I have already pointed out this possibility in *Holy Scripture: Canon, Authority, Criticism* (Oxford,

two cases of ἀγάπη in the entire corpus translated from the Hebrew canon: 2 Sam. 13: 15 and Jer. 2: 2. In the LXX, apart from the two late books, the dominant noun for love, translating אַהֲבָה, was ἀγάπησις; this form has had little attention, doubtless because it does not appear in the New Testament. In the LXX it is widely distributed, occurring nine times in such diverse books as Samuel, Psalms, Proverbs, Jeremiah, and the Minor Prophets, plus some cases in Ecclesiasticus. Thus, among noun expressions for love ἀγάπησις is more typical of the main biblical strata than ἀγάπη is. But ἀγάπησις was of course no new creation but a long accepted word, found for instance in Aristotle. Furthermore, its presence confirms the degree of continuity with contemporary usage, for ἀγάπησις is the dominant word in the *Letter of Aristeas* (*Ep. Arist.* 44, 265, 270, but ἀγάπη 229). Here are two representative instances:

2 Sam. 1: 26 ἐθαυμαστώθη ἡ ἀγάπησίς σου ἐμοὶ ὑπὲρ ἀγάπησιν γυναικῶν
Jer. 38 (31): 3 ἀγάπησιν αἰωνίαν ἠγάπησά σε

Moreover, if we concentrate on the primary theological contexts such as the love of God for men, we note that there is practically or absolutely no case of the noun ἀγάπη in such a context within the books of the Hebrew canon, unless one so understands the references in the Song of Songs. It is rather with ἀγάπησις that these profound religious relations are expressed: so Jer. 38 (31): 3 above, Hos. 11: 4, Zeph. 3: 17, to which we may add Ecclus. 40: 20.

Thus, even if it should be true that the noun ἀγάπη appeared first in the LXX, the LXX evidence itself suggests that this new formation was semantically rather insignificant and had nothing specific to do with the expression of God's love for man or man's love for God. The fact is that the noun expression 'love' as a relation between God and man was infrequent in the Hebrew Bible. It was not in the LXX but later, and particularly in the New Testament, that this nominalization became very frequent: in the New Testament the noun ἀγάπη relates to the verb in the proportion 116:141, a ratio massively disproportionate to that found in the Old Testament.[15]

1983), 62 and notes. There are no explicit quotations of these books in the New Testament, nor, it seems, influences from their highly literalistic translation technique. This point, however, does not have to be pressed: all I need to show is that the cases of ἀγάπη in these books cannot have belonged to the earlier strata of the translation, and in these earlier strata the only examples were 2 Sam. 13: 15 and Jer. 2: 2. In any case the point is not an entirely new one: Moulton and Milligan, writing about ἀγάπη, said that the Song of Songs 'could hardly be proved to have existed for the New Testament writers' (*The Vocabulary of the New Testament*, 2).

[15] The change of ratio becomes even more extreme when we consider that a substantial number of the New Testament occurrences of the verb are in quotations from the LXX, while this is so in only one or two cases of the noun.

It is sometimes thought that the ἀγαπᾶν group was preferred because these terms did not convey an erotic or sensual connotation.[16] This is quite incorrect for the LXX. In it almost all cases of the noun ἀγάπη concern erotic love, especially if we include those in the Song of Songs: there are only a handful that are not erotic. With ἀγάπησις 2 Sam. 1: 26 refers specifically to 'the love of women'; Jer. 2: 33 is a reference to the lustful desires of Judah; and Prov. 30: 15 was surely understood in an erotic sense too. Indeed, it is likely that the use of these words in Bible translation had the effect of actually increasing their degree of erotic reference: since Hebrew used almost only one word for many kinds of love, including erotic love, the Greek translation, tending to use the same equivalences throughout, expanded the extent to which the terms were used of erotic love. Further examples will confirm this.

This brings us to the word-group ἔρως, ἔρασθαι, ἐραστής. These terms are often negative and convey disapproval. Thus ἐραστής renders מְאַהֵב, mainly in the Prophets and in a bad sense, designating the 'lovers' of an unfaithful woman. And there are some cases of ἔρως meaning desire or lust. Thus the temptress says:

Prov. 7: 18 ἐλθὲ καὶ ἀπολαύσωμεν φιλίας ἕως ὄρθρου
δεῦρο καὶ ἐγκυλισθῶμεν ἔρωτι

> Come, let us enjoy love till the morning;
> come, let us wallow in lust . . .

Here φιλία and ἔρως are closely parallel, corresponding to the Hebrew דֹּדִים and אֲהָבִים. Similarly, in Prov. 30: 15 ἀγάπησις appears in an erotic context and the next verse places in parallel with it ἔρως γυναῖκος, woman's desire or (less likely) the desire for a woman as something that is never satisfied. Thus, though ἔρως is used in disapproved erotic contexts, this in no sense sets it apart from φιλία and ἀγάπησις, which are typically used also in theologically positive relations.

More important still, the LXX evidence makes it entirely clear that they were in no way motivated by antagonism to the Greek associations of ἔρως. There is one association in which terms of this group fit well into biblical thinking, namely the context of desiring, falling in love with, and loving the divine Wisdom. Thus we have:

Prov. 4: 6 ἐράσθητι αὐτῆς, καὶ τηρήσει σε.

---

[16] Thus Trench, op. cit. n. 3 above: The absence of ἔρως, ἔρασθαι etc. is 'in part no doubt to be explained from the fact that, by the corrupt use of the world, they had become so steeped in earthly sensual passion, carried such an atmosphere of unholiness about them . . . that the truth of God abstained from the defiling contact with them; yea, devised a new word for itself rather than betake itself to one of these'. In the twentieth century theological values had changed, and it was not the sensual erotic aspect but the lofty philosophical ἔρως that came to be regarded as the enemy.

Nevertheless, for loving wisdom, as for loving the law or the commandments, ἀγαπᾶν is much more common, as we see in Proverbs or in poems like Ps. 119. In the important passage Wisd. 8: 2, terms from all three groups are combined in one sentence, in one image of the love of Wisdom:

Wisd. 8: 2 Ταύτην ἐφίλησα καὶ ἐξεζήτησα ἐκ νεότητός μου
καὶ ἐζήτησα νύμφην ἀγαγέσθαι ἐμαυτῷ
καὶ ἐραστὴς ἐγενόμην τοῦ κάλλους αὐτῆς.
εὐγένειαν δοξάζει συμβίωσιν θεοῦ ἔχουσα
καὶ ὁ πάντων δεσπότης ἠγάπησεν αὐτήν.

Far from avoiding at all costs the associations of ἔρως, the LXX very willingly and happily embraced them.

The reason why words of the ἔρως group were not much used is quite a different one from that suggested in the discussions of earlier this century. It was not because the LXX thought this group unsuitable on theological grounds—there is not the slightest evidence that the matter ever entered their minds. It was rather because the general all-purpose word for love, ἀγαπᾶν with its related nouns, already itself covered the semantic ground that the ἔρως group covered. These words already included within their range the sorts of love and loving that could also be expressed with ἔρασθαι—or so at least it seemed to them. The difficulty about ἔρως and its group was not that they designate a different sort of love from that designated by ἀγαπᾶν, but that they express only a very limited portion of the range and spectrum of love—whether good or bad, approved or disapproved—that ἀγαπᾶν normally expressed. They tended to be inchoative: they expressed falling in love, desiring, beginning to love, or they expressed unlawful lust: but ἀγαπᾶν expressed all this and a good deal more. ἔρασθαι was not really a word meaning 'to love': it simply could not have been used for most of the contexts occurring in the Hebrew Bible. It could not have been used in God's call to Abraham to 'take your son ... whom you love', which is the first case of 'love' in the Bible (Gen. 22: 2) or for God's loving the fathers of Israel (Deut. 4: 37). The whole question of contrast with ἔρασθαι was an irrelevance. There was no common and central Hebrew term which suggested or required a rendering with ἔρως, ἔρασθαι as distinct from a word of the ἀγαπᾶν group, except for מְאַהֵב = ἐραστής, 'lover'. By contrast, ἀγαπᾶν and its group were felt to fit all or almost all the contexts in which the general Hebrew אהב was used. And the tendency to use a consistent rendering favoured the use of the ἀγαπᾶν group wherever it could be used; the Proverbs translator was less attached to consistency and more to variety, hence his occasional turning to terms like ἔρασθαι.

Of this no example is more striking than that of Amnon's sick longing for his half-sister Tamar. In the LXX this was ἀγάπη. He loved her or desired her, or should we say lusted after her, ἠγάπησεν αὐτήν 2 Sam. 13: 1? By means of a trick he seized her and forced her, but after this he at once hated her, and the hatred he now had for her was greater than the love (ἀγάπη!) with which he had loved her. Similarly, in the Testament of Joseph, Potiphar's wife says to Joseph ἴδε οὖν ἀγαπᾷς με 'you see, you do love me' (7: 6)—an example, incidentally, that gives a strong impression of being colloquial usage.

This is the essential semantic point of the word-group ἀγαπᾶν: within the LXX this set of terms is theologically equivocal. We might distinguish between 'good' love (love for God, love for one's neighbour), 'bad' love (love for money, love of evil-doing), and 'neutral' love ('I love swimming' or 'I just love cheese'). As in modern English, so in the Bible, the same words may be used for 'good' and for 'bad' love. Far from designating a special kind of love, a sacrificial or a personal love, the terms are equivocal about the sort of love that is meant. Consider:

Eccles. 5: 9 ἀγαπῶν ἀργύριον οὐ πλησθήσεται ἀργυρίου
Hos. 3: 1 ἀγάπησον γυναῖκα ἀγαπῶσαν πονηρά
Zech. 8: 17 ὅρκον ψευδῆ μὴ ἀγαπᾶτε

This makes it highly improbable that the choice of these words has anything to do with a theological differentiation between one conception of love and another.

And this is not confined to the LXX, for the same is true of the New Testament. Those people who 'love' the front seats in the synagogue or at dinner have ἀγαπᾶν in Luke but φιλεῖν in Matthew:

Luke 11: 43 ἀγαπᾶτε τὴν πρωτοκαθεδρίαν ἐν ταῖς συναγωγαῖς
Matt. 23: 6 φιλοῦσιν δὲ τὴν πρωτοκλισίαν ἐν τοῖς δείπνοις

—and other instances of 'bad' love expressed with ἀγαπᾶν have been cited above. In the New Testament, then, as in the LXX, ἀγαπᾶν was theologically equivocal.

Here however there is another exception: for in the New Testament the noun ἀγάπη was theologically unequivocal. It was there that it was nominalized in such large numbers, precisely because it was a central principle of religion, and for that reason it was always 'good' love. No doubt in New Testament language 'love of money' or the like *might* have been ἀγάπη, but in fact it seems that it never was. It is this fact, in itself important and significant, that has led many to suppose that the ἀγαπᾶν group as a whole was theologically unequivocal and that this unequivocal character reached back to the origins of biblical Greek with the LXX.

Something should now be said about the φιλεῖν/φιλία group. As we have seen, φιλεῖν is commonly used with the sense 'kiss' (Hebrewנָשַׁק);[17] as a rendering of אָהֵב 'love' it is markedly less frequent than is ἀγαπᾶν. In the books of the Hebrew canon there are about eleven cases in all. Of these five or more belong to a certain class: they refer to a liking for certain foods. A typical case is:

Gen. 27: 4 ποίησόν μοι ἐδέσματα, ὡς φιλῶ ἐγώ

and there are three in this chapter, 27: 4, 9, 14, all referring to the special dainties that Isaac loved. So Prov. 21: 17, Hos. 3: 1b, and similarly Isa. 56: 10 of dogs which 'love to doze'. This 'neutral' sort of 'love'—'liking' for particular foods or habits—seems not to fit well with ἀγαπᾶν, and scarcely any cases are to be found—another nail in the coffin of the idea that ἀγαπᾶν is pale and colourless; and at times the translators abandon their usual equivalence and use φιλεῖν.

The noun φιλία is not found in any book of the Hebrew canon other than Proverbs. This has sometimes suggested to scholars that its use is a sign of Hellenistic influence. Thus Snaith wrote:[18]

The word *philia* is frequent in the Apocrypha (twenty-eight times) and twice more in Proverbs. Where, therefore, we get Greek influence rather than Hebrew influence, i.e. in the Apocrypha and in the freely-translated Proverbs, we get *philia* and not *agape*.

But closer analysis relativizes this judgement. The seventeen or so cases in 1–2 Maccabees mainly refer to amicable relations between states, for which φιλία was the normal term, often in the combination φιλία καὶ συμμαχία. This was not a Hellenization of an original Hebrew expression. In Proverbs, Ecclesiasticus, and Wisdom, although φιλία certainly occurs, it occurs in close combination with either ἀγαπᾶν or ἀγάπη. Proverbs uses φιλία as its favourite noun (about nine cases, six or so of them for forms with the Hebrew root אָהֵב), but also has ἀγάπησις at 30: 15, while for the verb it greatly prefers ἀγαπᾶν (about sixteen cases with Hebrew אָהֵב, plus some others, as against only three of φιλεῖν). Wisdom has φιλία twice, of love for God or his wisdom, but has ἀγάπη thrice and for the same reference. Moreover, it has the verb φιλεῖν only once, but ἀγαπᾶν some nine times. In Ecclesiasticus the situation is similar: though there are five cases of φιλία, there are also two of ἀγάπησις, both referring to the love of God; and in this book the standard verb for love is ἀγαπᾶν (about twenty-three cases), while φιλεῖν does not occur. The situation was thus rather like what we might

[17] And καταφιλεῖν seems always to mean 'kiss'.
[18] Snaith, op. cit. n. 5 above, 174.

expect from the literary Koine: the verb ἀγαπᾶν was familiar, but the noun ἀγάπη was slow to achieve the same familiarity. Josephus, similarly, never has the noun ἀγάπη but uses ἀγαπᾶν much more frequently than any other verb 'to love'.[19] The greater variety in Proverbs and other books came from a translation technique which emphasized consistency less. A major underlying cause for the non-use of a word like φιλία was that it belonged not only to the semantic field of 'love' but also to that of 'liking, friendship', which would come closer to רֵעַ in Hebrew; similarly with φιλός. These words *could be* more or less interchangeable with the ἀγαπᾶν group but could also denote something much less than love. The question of Hellenistic ideas and of opposition to them simply does not enter into the matter. Incidentally, φιλία, not so uncommon in the LXX, is entirely avoided in the New Testament except for the negative case of Jas. 4: 4, where I would think that 'friendship' (AV etc.) is more probable than 'love' (NEB).

This brings us back to the New Testament. We have been so accustomed to think of ἀγάπη and ἀγαπᾶν as the dominant and distinctive terms that we may fail to notice that the New Testament actually uses φιλεῖν for 'to love' in a much higher proportion than the LXX did: and this includes profound personal relations like the love for parents, the love of the Father for the Son, and the love of God for his chosen ones:

Matt. 10: 37 ὁ φιλῶν πατέρα ἢ μητέρα ὑπὲρ ἐμέ
John 5: 20 ὁ γὰρ πατὴρ φιλεῖ τὸν υἱόν
1 Cor. 16: 22 εἴ τις οὐ φιλεῖ τὸν κύριον, ἤτω ἀνάθεμα

Again, Rev. 3: 19, ἐγὼ ὅσους ἐὰν φιλῶ ἐλέγχω, is commonly taken to be a virtual quotation of Prov. 3: 12, but Proverbs uses ἀγαπᾶν while Revelation goes over to φιλεῖν. The Fourth Gospel, which has a high incidence of the verb 'to love' in strongly theological contexts, has also a strikingly high ratio of φιλεῖν in just such contexts: in addition to John 5: 20, just quoted, consider:

John 16: 27 ὁ πατὴρ φιλεῖ ὑμᾶς, ὅτι ὑμεῖς ἐμὲ πεφιλήκατε.

Jesus' love for Lazarus is twice φιλεῖν (John 11: 3, 36), although his love for Mary, her sister, and Lazarus is ἀγαπᾶν (11: 5). The disciple 'whom Jesus loved' is expressed once with φιλεῖν (20: 2), but several times with ἀγαπᾶν (13: 23, 19: 26, 21: 7, 20). Thus the incidence of the verb φιλεῖν is distinctly higher than in the LXX and closer to the proportions of the literary Koine.

This may be relevant for those places where both ἀγαπᾶν and φιλεῖν

---

[19] Cf. similarly the situation in other Jewish works such as the *Testaments of the Twelve Patriarchs* or *Joseph and Asenath*.

occur together in close juxtaposition. The most familiar is John 21: 15 ff.:

Jesus' question	Peter's answer
ἀγαπᾷς με;	φιλῶ σε
ἀγαπᾷς με;	φιλῶ σε
φιλεῖς με;	φιλῶ σε

New Testament specialists have been divided over the question whether the change of terms in Jesus' third asking, and between his questions and Peter's answers, is semantically significant.[20] The LXX evidence seems to favour the view that the shift is stylistic but not semantic, not at least in the sense that some different sort of love or conception of love is intended. There are several places in the LXX where the verb 'love' occurs twice in close juxtaposition and the translator varies the verbs in Greek:

Gen. 37: 3 f.: Ιακωβ δὲ ἠγάπα τὸν Ιωσηφ παρὰ πάντας τοὺς υἱοὺς αὐτοῦ . . .
αὐτὸν ὁ πατὴρ φιλεῖ ἐκ πάντων τῶν υἱῶν αὐτοῦ
(both verbs אהב in Hebrew)
Prov. 8: 17 ἐγὼ τοὺς ἐμὲ φιλοῦντας ἀγαπῶ
(again both verbs identical in Hebrew)

Compare also Hos. 3: 1, Prov. 21: 17. Thus the LXX displays a tendency to vary the verbs in Greek, once in a while, where the same verb occurs twice in Hebrew. This must be considered stylistic rather than semantic. It is close to the sort of variation we find in the Koine of Josephus, for example *Vita* 198, where φιλεῖν and ἀγαπᾶν are found in the same sentence referring to the same human relation. Taken together with the fact, seen above, that John elsewhere uses φιλεῖν for love in important theological senses, and that he makes other stylistic variations within the same section (βόσκειν/ποιμαίνειν; ἀρνία/προβάτια), it seems probable that no difference in the sort of loving relationship is intended. To say this is not to say that the two verbs are completely 'synonymous'. The total possible range of φιλεῖν within biblical Greek is not identical with that of ἀγαπᾶν. There is a difference of stylistic level, of associations, and of nuances. But within any one individual passage these differences do not amount to a distinction of real theological reference: they do not specify a difference in the kind of love referred to.

A word should be added about the verbal adjective ἀγαπητός. This, paradoxically, displays an array of features almost the opposite of those found in the other words for love. There a variety of different words

---

[20] I am indebted to my colleague Canon John Fenton for assisting me by kindly providing me with a survey of views in various commentaries on St John.

alike mean 'love'. ἀγαπητός by contrast means two quite different, though sometimes connectable, things: firstly 'only (child)'; secondly 'beloved'. Where translated from Hebrew, these come from quite distinct original terms. For the first, the Hebrew is יָחִיד. Here the rendering ἀγαπητός did not derive from the senses of ἀγαπᾶν that are active and typical in biblical Greek: it goes back to something in much older Greek, a sense as old as Homer in this connection, the sense of 'that with which one must be content, acquiesce'. If one has only one child, one must accept that as sufficient (LSJ). Thus in LXX times ἀγαπητός still meant simply 'only (child)': there are half a dozen cases, the best known being at Gen. 22: 2, 12, 16 in the Binding of Isaac. Such a child might in fact also be beloved, but that is not what the word said; sometimes the specification, that the child was also beloved, was added, for instance Gen. 22: 2, producing a slightly odd effect in the Greek: τὸν υἱόν σου τὸν ἀγαπητόν, ὃν ἠγάπησας—contrast also Judg. 11: 34, A text. Only one who knew the actual Hebrew would fully understand this. For ἀγαπητός is used also with the sense 'beloved', mainly translating Hebrew יָדִיד (the passive term 'beloved' comes from this root, different from that used in the active sense 'to love'). Here again there are about half a dozen cases within the Hebrew books. This sense of ἀγαπητός is, of course, directly related to the sense of ἀγαπᾶν that is normal and productive in biblical Greek.

Here again, interestingly, we have something akin to the idea of phonetic resemblance mooted by George Caird. The LXX sometimes analysed words in a way that implied that, if two words had two consonants identical in similar positions, they must be semantically connected. As it happened, יָחִיד and יָדִיד had even more than two consonants in common, they had their entire word pattern in common: they looked alike. Moreover—and this is rare for this kind of analysis—both could be, and were, quite correctly and respectably rendered by the same word in Greek. Such an occasional fortunate case may well have encouraged the belief that this sort of analysis could be carried farther.

When we have a Hebrew original we can easily separate out the two cases. In the New Testament the large majority of cases are clearly 'beloved'. At Mark 12: 6, the man has 'one' son who is ἀγαπητός; perhaps it is difficult to tell which meaning lies here—probably on the analogy of Gen. 22: 2 the meaning is 'beloved', amplifying the statement already made that he is the only child. The Lucan version, Luke 20: 13, not having the word 'one', looks more like 'my only son'. NEB hesitates and it is impossible to be sure. Similar uncertainties are found at:

Mark 1: 11 σὺ εἶ ὁ υἱός μου ὁ ἀγαπητός [and parallels].

Does it mean 'my only son' or 'my beloved son'? Was a traditional say-ing that meant 'only son' now understood as 'beloved son'? It is usually printed as if it were a quotation from the Old Testament, and if it were we could have supplied the answer, but neither Isa. 42: 1 nor Ps. 2: 7, the passages mainly referred to, contain a word close enough to lead us to an answer. The בְּחִירִי of MT at Isa. 42: 1, Greek ὁ ἐκλεκτός μου, points rather in the direction of 'beloved'. If there is really an allusion to Gen. 22: 2 then of course it would be 'only' but the sentence as a whole has no likeness to that passage. Perhaps no one knew, for the double sense of ἀγαπητός can have been clearly recognized by few; if there is doubt, the sense 'beloved', as the sense far more productive in New Testament times, is likely to have been generally understood. Ambiguity could be avoided by saying μονογενής, a word already used somewhat by the LXX, for example Judg. 11: 34, some cases in the Psalms, in Tobit, and in other books.

To sum up: the 'anti-Hellenistic' interpretation of the use of words for love in the LXX was quite wrong; there was never any real LXX evidence that favoured it. Nor is there any sign that antipathy to the theological associations of other terms such as ἔρασθαι or φιλεῖν was a factor. In particular, associations with ἔρως, far from being strongly resisted, were quite welcomed, although texts of this type were in fact few.

This does not mean that LXX usage did not effect a shift of meaning. It did; but the shift was not that from one kind of theological reference or content to another. The pattern and distribution of meanings derives from the possibilities offered by the Hebrew text translated. Thus, for instance, certain meanings which did not occur in the Hebrew אָהֵב vir-tually fell away, for instance 'to be well-pleased, contented' or 'to toler-ate, acquiesce in, be content with'. And some such changes were changes that derived from the translation techniques: such did not necessarily mean that these usages were as yet normal in the language as commonly used. It was, in all probability, because of his translation technique that the translator has Amnon 'love' Tamar (ἠγάπησεν, ἀγάπη): if he had been writing in his own words, and depending on the literary level on which he wished to write, he might well have said ἐρασθείς 'falling in love' or the like, just as Josephus did in describing the same incident (*Ant.* 7. 163 ff.); and similarly he might in many pas-sages of the Song of Songs have thought ἔρως more appropriate than the ἀγάπη that he actually used. Locutions of these kinds, being occa-sioned by the translation technique, were not necessarily reflections of what was normal in the language, nor did they go on afterwards to become normal in the language.

In its words for love the New Testament diverged farther from the patterns of the LXX than one might have supposed: there was, after all, no reason why its writers should have thought themselves obliged to reproduce the contours of the older text. Indeed, not being a translation of a fixed and older Hebrew text, the New Testament could not possibly do so. Thus we should perhaps think less of a straight line of descent from the LXX to the New Testament, and more of a line from the Koine to the latter, with influences coming also from the LXX. The New Testament used a much larger admixture of φιλεῖν in comparison with ἀγαπᾶν, and notably so in profound theological contexts. It disused φιλία in positive theological contexts. It did not use ἀγάπησις. The centrality of the noun ἀγάπη is a creation much more of the New Testament than of the LXX; and, within the New Testament, it is a creation primarily of the epistles. It is in them that its overwhelming dominance appears. In the Gospels it is still rare—rather as it is in the LXX. Mark has it not at all, Matthew and Luke only once each (Matt. 24: 12, Luke 11: 42); John is more like some of the epistles, having it seven times. The much shorter epistle 1 John has it eighteen times. Comparable, but different, relations exist with the verb ἀγαπᾶν: Mark has only one case (Mark 10: 21) apart from Old Testament quotations, Matthew and Luke have many more, but the Johannine literature, Gospel and First Epistle, has much the richest concentration.

George Caird wrote:[21]

The translation of the Old Testament into Greek opened up the possibility of a synthesis between Jewish and Greek thought; but this synthesis was not attempted by the translators, who left the fundamental nature of Judaism unchanged.

Quite so. We may add, perhaps: nor did they have to create an antithesis between the two. The existence of continuities in the meanings of Greek words, they found, did not force on them the choice between synthesis and antithesis on the theological plane. The work of translation, they seem to have found, was not dominated by that problem.

[21] Caird, *The Apostolic Age*, 27.

2 Canon and Christology

W. D. DAVIES

UNTIL very recently, when costs increased and computers threatened their dominance, the abundance and cheapness of paper and writing materials led to their almost ubiquitous use in our culture. The temptation was easy to contrast this culture with previous more oral ones in which writing was not so pervasive. But, although the Graeco-Roman and Jewish worlds of the first century, with which we are concerned, were less 'a papyrus culture' than is ours of the twentieth, this should not be over-emphasized. Those worlds were 'if not literate, literary to a remarkable degree; in the Near East in the first century of our era writing was an essential accompaniment of life at almost all levels to an extent without parallel in living memory.'[1] The reading of documents, written on papyrus or skin, was more widespread than is often acknowledged. Apparently, even in out-of-the-way Nazareth, Jesus could read, and assumed that his opponents in Galilee also could.[2]

At the same time there was a reserve about the written word among Greeks and Jews alike. This had long come to clear expression in Plato, who had urged that the invention of writing was a deceptive blessing.[3] For Plato's Socrates, so far from helping the memory, writing militates against it: it is no adequate substitute for living dialogue between teacher and taught. It is as if writing confines or even ossifies thought; at best what is written only serves as a reminder of what is already known. The profoundest truth cannot be encapsulated in writing; living thought needs the give and take of speech in dialogue. How widespread such an attitude was among the Greeks is disputed. However, though an emphasis in Plato, it was not a peculiarity of his. This attitude explains why in literary circles in Rome and Alexandria, and probably elsewhere in the Hellenistic age, 'publication' did not signify the appearance of a book or volume but was by public recitation.[4] It

---

[1] C. S. Roberts in *The Cambridge History of the Bible*, i, ed. by P. Ackroyd, C. F. Evans (Cambridge, 1970), 48.

[2] Luke 4: 15–30; Mark 2: 25, 12: 10, etc. See further Werner H. Kelber, *The Oral and Written Gospel* (Philadelphia, 1983), 78.

[3] *Phaedrus*, 274 C–275 A, in which Socrates is given the words 'You have invented an elixir not of memory, but of reminding' (Loeb translation). Compare Xenophon's *Symposium*, 3: 5, and Diogenes Laertius, 10. 12 (Loeb translation 11. 541).

[4] On 'publication', see S. Lieberman, *Hellenism in Jewish Palestine* (New York, 1962), 83–9; C. S. Roberts, op. cit., n. 1 above.

was this same attitude, along with other probably more important factors, which led in Judaism to the prohibition of the writing of the Oral Law.[5] That, like John the Baptist, Jesus did not choose to write, even though he apparently could, may be indicative.[6] For Paul his letters were a necessary but, by implication, inferior substitute for his presence (Gal. 4: 20; 2 Cor. 13: 10; 1 Cor. 11: 34). The documents of the early church were only tardily gathered together. Papias, Bishop of Hierapolis, (c. AD 60–130), makes clear this attitude in Christian circles. He explicitly preferred oral to written evidence: 'I supposed that things out of books did not profit me so much as the utterance of a voice that lives and survives'.[7]

This ambiguity towards written documents, in which writing was both widely practised and yet often distrusted, raises the question whether in the Graeco-Roman world the attitude of Jews towards their Scriptures is to be regarded as peculiar to them. By the first century, religious Jews (it should not be overlooked that doubtless most, even amongst the Jews, were not such) regarded their sacred writings—the Pentateuch (which was given pre-eminence), the Prophets, the Writings (although not all finally fixed as an authoritative canon until the end of the first century, and possibly not even then)—as not simply 'containing' but as 'being' the very words of God himself, and therefore as binding, authoritative, perfect, unchangeable, and eternal. They were conceived to comprise all that Jews know and need to know, a gateway to another, and eternal, world; they represent the eternal breaking into time; the unknowable disclosed; the transcendent entering history and remaining here, available to mortals to handle and appropriate; the divine becoming apparent. To memorize them and even to quote from them is to enter into some sort of communion with ultimate reality.[8] And, although recognized to be much in need of

---

[5] Jerusalem Talmud, *Megillah* 4. 1, 74d (with which compare *Gittin*, 66b; *Tem.* 14b): 'That which has been expressed orally [must be transmitted orally] and that which has been expressed in writing [must be transmitted] in writing.' See S. Lieberman, op cit., 87. The Talmud contains no reference to a written Mishnah. The interdiction covered Halakah and Haggadah. R. Meyers, *TWNT*, 9, 34–5 regards this interdiction as legendary and refuses to press it for the Rabbinic period. The interdiction has, moreover, been connected not with the kind of reserve toward writing found in the contemporary Graeco-Roman world, but with the fear that two laws might emerge. The interpretations of the Qumran sectarians were not immediately written down, but some time after the death of the founder. For additional caution about over-emphasizing the literary character of the Hellenistic world, see Werner H. Kelber, op. cit., 17.

[6] John 8: 6.

[7] Eusebius, *Ecclesiastical History*, 3. 39. 1–7; 14–17. It is perhaps noteworthy that, much later, on the invention of printing, Islam allowed the printing of secular books, but forbade that of the Qur'ān; so W. Cantwell Smith, *JAAR* 89 (1971), 137.

[8] See my *Setting of the Sermon on the Mount* (Cambridge, 1964), 109–90, especially 156–90. I here borrow phrases from W. Cantwell Smith, 'The True Meaning of Scripture: An empirical historian's non-reductionist interpretation of the Qur'ān', in *JMES* 1 (1980), 491.

interpretation, so that the literal was not their only meaning, the Scriptures were to be understood literally.[9] Immense care was taken to ensure that they were transmitted with strictest accuracy.[10] This Jewish attitude (though not universally held)[11] we shall examine later. At first encounter at least it is very far removed, indeed at the opposite pole, from Plato's attitude. Plato reveals little if any awareness of writings as containing divine truth, as treasures to be handed on to subsequent generations. Contrast the Library of Congress at Washington, which reminds us, each time we enter it, that books were for Milton the precious life-blood of noble spirits and for Thoreau the treasures of the wisdom of the ages; they are not simply 'reminders' but themselves of inestimable worth. Nothing of this is in Plato, nothing of the Jewish sense that in certain writings all truth is to be found, that what is needed is to excavate the inexhaustible mine of the divine revelation contained in the Scriptures and bring to light treasures that lie hidden beneath the surface.[12]

I

Are there parallels in other religious traditions to the use made of Scripture in Jewish and Christian circles? To answer this we must examine briefly a wide range of traditions and texts.[13] This much we can state: it is erroneous to regard all 'sacred texts' as necessarily and automatically 'canonical texts' such as are the Tanak and the Old and New Testaments in Judaism and Christianity respectively.

The Egyptian 'sacred texts' probably owed their sacred character to their hieroglyphic script, not to their contents: they were treated with considerable liberty in transmission, and those who read them did not thereby acquire honour as did the readers of the Torah in the Synagogue. They do not provide a parallel with the biblical canon.[14]

---

[9] Various senses of Scripture were recognized, but the literal sense remained.

[10] See B. Gerhardsson, *Memory and Manuscript*, Part I (Uppsala-Lund, 1961), 1–191; H. L. Strack and G. Stemberger, *Einleitung in Talmud und Midrasch*, 7 Auflage (München, 1982), 41–54.

[11] The compiler of the Temple Scroll at Qumran (11QTemple) could insert his own halakah in the Pentateuch. See also *b. Yebamoth*, 79a; *m. Berakoth*, 9. 5. See the chapter 'Law in first-century Judaism' in my *Jewish and Pauline Studies, Collected Essays* (Philadelphia, 1983).

[12] Compare A. Cohen, *Everyman's Talmud* (London, 1932), 132. With this also goes an emphasis on oral learning and memorizing in Judaism too; see Deut. 31: 19; Lamentations Rabbah 4: 12.

[13] In looking at the Egyptian, Near Eastern, and Semitic backgrounds, and at Hindu and Islamic sacred texts, I have no competence in the various original sources involved, and must rely on secondary works. I am particularly grateful to M. Meslin for allowing me to use his unpublished lecture, given at a colloquium at Strasbourg University in 1980 on the theme 'La Bible est-elle une livre apart?'

[14] See the mentions in Herodotus, *History* 11. 36; Clement of Alexandria, *Stromateis* 6. 4. 37, 3; Diodorus Siculus (first century BCE), *History*, 11. 4.

Somewhat closer parallels may be detected in Hinduism and Islam. The Sanskrit sacred texts were regarded as a unity, being of divine origin and possessing supreme authority, and underwent a process of something like canonization. Freedom to interpret these texts—resulting in a well-developed Tradition (*Āgama*) which came itself to possess only slightly inferior status—did not imply freedom to modify them, which would entail exclusion from the community of Hinduism. Parallels here with Judaism and Christianity are not hard to find, even though the existence of different 'sects' within Hinduism, each with its own claimed sacred texts, warns against such parallels being pressed too far. As for Islam, there are again parallels, this time between the Qur'ān with its absolute authority and the Torah in Judaism, with, again, the development of a tradition (*Sunna*) facilitating its interpretation. Despite some difference, then, there are at least partial parallels in Hinduism and Islam to the phenomena of the interpretation of the Bible as a revelation from God, the literary forms which this assumed, the development of an explicatory and supplementary tradition alongside this and the 'canonical' status afforded it, and to the influence which it has exerted on Western culture.[15]

What of the Hellenistic tradition? There is something to be said for applying the predicate 'canonical' to the role of Homer in the Greek world of the first century.[16] Even when the content of poetry was questioned, the belief that poets were 'the schoolmasters of grown men'[17] was unquestioned: and it was based on the conviction that good epic and lyric poets were inspired in a similar way to the Pythia at Delphi or such legendary figures as Bacchus and the Sibyl.[18] Like those of these, the words of the poets were originally delivered orally, only subsequently being written down and collected. As early as the seventh century BC at the Delian festival, and elsewhere, Greeks assembled to hear their minstrels recite the Homeric poems. There was a public recitation of Homer every fourth year at the Panathenic festival. This, it has been claimed, is 'analogous to the Jewish provision that once in every seven years the Law was to be read at the Feast of Tabernacles in the hearing of all Israel'.[19]

A final possible parallel to the use of the Hebrew Scriptures by Jews and early Christians comes from a later period when the dominance of

---

[15] W. Cantwell Smith has urged that the Bible has *not* influenced that culture as much as the Qur'ān has influenced Islamic life: see *JAAR* 39 (1979), 133 f.

[16] See M. Hengel, *Judaism and Hellenism*, i (ET, Philadelphia, 1974), 66.

[17] Aristophanes, *Frogs*, 1052 ff., compare 1032 ff.

[18] See Plato, *Phaedrus* 237 c–d, 244–5: *Ion* 533–5.

[19] B. S. Butcher, *Harvard Lectures*, 105, cited by James Adam, *The Religious Teachers of Greece* (Edinburgh, 1909), 9.

the epic poets had long been under attack. In the first century or two of the Christian era there was much searching for ancient authority. The impulse to appeal to tradition which surfaced at that time in the Graeco-Roman world emerged also in Judaism.[20] The appeal to the Hebrew scriptures in early Christianity is related to the same impulse.

II

But, when all this has been recognized, is the place of the Tanak in Judaism and the early Church adequately accounted for simply as the counterpart to the role played in Greece in an early time especially, but not exclusively, by Homer, and at a later date by the various philosophical traditions? The answer must finally be a qualified but unmistakable negative. There are significant differences between the approach to the Hebrew Scriptures in Judaism and early Christianity and any understanding of their ancient poets, and literary and philosophical traditions by the Greeks before and after Plato. The differences can be summarized in one word 'canon', a word very often too loosely used in comparisons between Greek and Hebrew 'sacred' texts.

A few preliminary considerations are pertinent. First, the Jews' attitude to their sacred writings induced the necessity to reproduce those texts without distortion. The Hebrew texts were transmitted with meticulous and scrupulous care. Although the evidence does not allow certainty, it is probable that such care was exercised before the first century. The texts discovered at Qumran seem to establish that the recension of the Masoretic text existed before the Christian era. Even an imperfect scroll such as 1QIsa deviates little from the Masoretic text. Contrast the care which this implies with the freer use and citation of Scripture in the *Targumim* and *Midrashim*.

This is not the place to describe the process whereby Jewish copyists, long before it was fixed by post-Talmud masoretes, ensured the preservation of the purity of the text of the Torah. There were probably pre-Christian specialists, scribes (*sopherim*) responsible for the official copying of texts.[21] These scribes were at first probably both 'copyists', in the sense of being skilled in the mechanical art of writing, and persons who knew or were schooled in the Scriptures.[22] The procedures for copying followed by the scribes probably have their parallel in the Hel-

---

[20] Butcher, ibid.: a good example is the opening section of the *Pirke Aboth*, for which see my 'Reflexions on the Aboth', in *Jewish and Pauline Studies* (Philadelphia, 1983). Diodorus Siculus, *History*, 1. 9 ff. is instructive at this point.

[21] See B. Gerhardsson, *Memory and Manuscript* (Uppsala-Lund, 1961), 43.

[22] For the situation after 70 CE, see Gerhardsson, op. cit., 51.

lenistic world, as do the rules of argumentation or of interpretation.[23]
How much Jewish scribes owed to Alexandrian textual critics is hard to
assess. As far as I am aware this question has not been seriously
addressed. There *was* certainly an indigenous scribal tradition in Jewish Palestine. The Wisdom tradition implied a writing culture long
established. The translators of the LXX could send to the Temple
authorities in Jerusalem for the best text of the Pentateuch. Most probably the translators of the Scripture into Greek were influenced by the
Alexandrian critical tradition.

Our specific concern is to discover whether the usage of Judaism in
its treatment of the texts of the Tanak points to a qualitatively different
attitude towards those texts from that found in the Hellenistic world towards the sacred texts of Greece. The Hellenistic world, particularly at
Alexandria and Pergamum, did seek to preserve its ancient texts and
the mechanical copying processes followed by Jews came to be similar
to those of the Greeks and Romans. But this insistence on the accurate
textual transmission of the Scriptures in Judaism seems to have
become, probably by the first century and certainly later, more intense,
anxious, and exacting than what we find in the Hellenistic milieu.
Alexandrian critics laboured to produce revised texts (*ekdoseis*)
especially of the poets, and commentaries upon them. It was at
Alexandria that Homer first became an object of critical study. But the
attitude of editors to the text of Homer (and, by inference, how much
more to other texts) does not suggest the 'religious anxiety' to observe
the strictest possible exactitude that is clear in the transmission of the
Scriptures in Judaism. We can probably claim with some certainty that
the work of Homeric critics such as Zenodotus (285–247 BCE), Aristophanes (*c.*195 BCE), and Aristarchus (180–145 BCE) was simply governed by a textual and literary intent and lacked the intensity that a
religious concern would be likely to have produced.

But what of the 'canons' (κανόνες) of Alexandria as they are called?
Do they not suggest that the ancient literature of Greece was elevated
to a 'canonical' status such as that achieved by the Tanak in Judaism
and the Old and New Testaments in Christianity? To answer one must
note what precisely were the concerns of the Alexandrian critics of the
third and second centuries BCE. They aimed at discriminating authentic from spurious writings and at selecting the best writers in each kind
from the enormous mass of literature which had come down to them—
good, bad, indifferent. With this end in view they prepared lists
(πίνακες) of poets: four heroic (headed by Homer), three iambic, four

---

[23] See D. Daube, *HUCA* 22, 329 ff., and his 'Alexandrian Methods of Interpretation and the
Rabbis', in *Festschrift Hans Lewald* (Basel, 1953), 22 ff.

elegiac, etc. Crates prepared lists at Pergamum in which the leading writers of prose were given the prominence ascribed at Alexandria to the epic poets.[24] To be included in these lists an author had to achieve a certain excellence in the category concerned. For this reason the lists, so it has often been held, were called 'canons' (κανόνες), and are to be understood as 'canonical'.[25]

First let it be noted that in fact the πίνακες of Alexandrian scholarship were not called 'canons'. This term is very late as a translation for the πίνακες.[26] But, in addition to this devastating lexicographical point, was the critical intention at Alexandria comparable with that which led to the canonization of the Scriptures of Judaism and Christianity? The fixing of the Alexandrian lists did reveal deep reverence, perhaps especially characteristic of the Hellenistic period, for the literary works of the ancients. But it seems that the criteria for excellence were exclusively literary: the chief responsibility for drawing up the lists was that of the two editors of Homer already mentioned, Aristarchus and Aristophanes. Their interests do not seem to have been the deeply religious ones which governed the Jews in fixing their canon. Primarily by literary discrimination, they were concerned to confirm the fame of the great authors of their people's past, not to provide a literature to govern their people in all the details of their lives in the present. The textual and so-called 'canonical' intentions at Alexandria are perhaps not to be entirely distinguished from those of Judaism and Christianity, but they certainly do not share the same dimensions as in both the latter.

III

This brings us to the question as to the purpose of the fixation of the Jewish canon of Scripture. To begin with, purely literary (as distinct from textual) criteria do not seem to have played a conscious part in the process. The concern of those who elevated the Torah, Nebi'īm and Kethūbīm to canonicity was not to recognize, confirm, or confer any literary distinction upon them. Equally the lists of Alexandria and Pergamum do not seem to have been born of a deliberate concern to

---

[24] L. Whibley, ed., *A Companion to Greek Studies* (New York, 1963), section 202, 175.

[25] L. Whibley, op. cit., 746.

[26] See R. Pfeiffer, *History of Classical Scholarship: From the Beginnings to the End of the Hellenistic Age* (Oxford, 1968), 207. Pfeiffer points out that the term 'canon' was coined for the πίνακες (repertories or lists which we should call indexes) by David Ruhnken in AD 1768. The use of it for the πίνακες was not Greek, and it was not by the ancient Greek tradition that the use of 'canon' for πίνακες was suggested to Ruhnken, but by the biblical. Eusebius, *HE* 6, 25. 3 'seems to be the earliest evidence for the canon of Scripture' according to Pfeiffer, ibid. n. 4. See further J. Barr, *Holy Scripture: Canon, Authority, Criticism* (Philadelphia, 1983), 51, and my article 'Reflections about the Use of the Old Testament in the New in its Historical Context', *JQR* 74. 2 (Oct. 1983), 105–36 (here p. 123), to which the reader is referred for fuller treatment of much in the present chapter.

meet the urgent, immediate, and continuing needs of an ongoing self-conscious religious people or community. The 'new' class of scholars engaged in editing Homer and other Greek writings in Alexandria and Pergamum were called διόρθωται, that is, 'correctors'. Jewish scribes would certainly have resented such a designation as impious: who would dare 'correct' their sacred texts? This contrasts markedly with the concern that led to the fixation of the Jewish canon, as we shall see.

But before we deal further with their concern, the other phenomenon in the Graeco-Roman world to which we referred previously again deserves attention. Does this provide, at least, a partial parallel? As we saw, in the Hellenistic age the founders of schools of philosophy came to be highly revered and their words and works cherished. There were many such schools. What particularly interests us is the attitude each school reveals to the tradition—oral and written—originated by the founder. The tradition was not regarded as of intellectual or 'philosophical' interest only. The tradition of the founder was to provide an inspiring, and normative, regulatory way of life: it provided a 'rule' or 'canon' by which the members of a particular School were to live. This scholastic 'canonization' of a teaching founder's tradition, as we shall see, approaches in part the intent behind the canonization of the Jewish Scriptures, which also were to provide a *halakah*, a way of life.[27] There is, however, an obvious difference. The canon of Judaism was to inform not simply the life of a particular school, although the interpretation of it could and did lead to the emergence of different 'schools' within Israel, but that of a whole people.

This leads to the consideration of the underlying cause for the fixation of the Jewish canon. To grasp this would help to assess how far the Graeco-Roman world offers more than formal parallels to that process.

To begin with, however much veneration for ancient texts and tradition the Graeco-Roman world reveals, it provides only a pale and partial parallel with that implied in the constant, regular, daily reading of the Torah in the synagogue. The history of the synagogue is wrapped in obscurity, but there were synagogues in first century Palestine and outside. Part of their activity was the reading and study of the Scriptures which, although not altogether formally 'fixed' as a 'canon' until the end of the first century and possibly not even then, had achieved a prominent (for reasons we shall give later we deliberately avoid the adjective 'normative') role in Jewish life. Certainly in this matter any dogmatism must be suspect, but the claim seems to be justified that by

[27] On the role of philosophy in this connection, see A. D. Nock, *Conversion* (Oxford, 1933), 181; H. Wolfson, *Philo*, i (Cambridge, Mass., 1947), 8 ff.; M. Smith in *Israel*, ed. M. Davis (New York, 1956), 80; E. J. Bickerman in *RB* 59 (1952), 49 ff.

the first century the Torah had become an ubiquitous, ever present, expression of Jewish religious life. Discussion has centred on whether the whole Torah was read annually or triennially in the first century synagogues. In any case, the lectionary activity of the synagogue in that period points to an elevation of the sacred Hebrew texts for which there is no fully adequate parallel in the Graeco-Roman world.[28]

Only recently has the nature of this elevation begun to be explored in depth. Previously the history of the canon was most often treated chronologically and factually without adequate attention either to the deep forces at work in its fixation or to the significance of the final form of the canon as such. Now it is increasingly urged that the emergence and formation of the canon in Judaism and Christianity was ultimately due to the necessity for the people of Israel, as later for the Christian Churches, to define and preserve their identity. The primary impulse behind the elevation of the Torah and the Prophets, as later of the Writings, was the felt need in the disaster of the Exile and later to re-affirm the 'story' of Yahweh's dealing with his people. That disaster made the people of Israel—for the sake of their very survival—conceive of themselves increasingly, and more and more emphatically, as a 'Chosen People', the record of whose origin and prescribed way of life and destiny they found in their ancient writings. These they revered and tried to preserve and elevate for the sake of their own continued existence. The sacred texts had become necessary to the continuing self-identity of the people of Israel; they became the book of a people and the people became a people of the book. The crises of the sixth century BCE and of the first century CE demanded the reaffirmation of Jewish identity and this was largely in part achieved through the development and ultimate fixation of the canon. The understanding of the canon thus crudely set forth here we owe especially to J. A. Sanders and Brevard Childs, who with varying emphases have called for a new canonical criticism.

And, despite the partial parallels to which we have pointed, we look in vain for a satisfactory parallel in the Graeco-Roman world. Much as the epic poets, particularly Homer and Hesiod, were revered and regarded as 'inspired', they were never regarded as 'gods', and certainly not as the voice of God, the creator of the universe. Contrast with this the Israelite view that Yahweh had spoken directly to Moses, and not only spoken to him but handed over the tablets on which he himself had written his commandments.

[28] For the synagogue, see F. Hüttenmeister in *The Cambridge History of Judaism*, iii, forthcoming. Also see Jacob Mann, *The Bible as Read and Preached in the Old Synagogue* (Ohio, 1940). According to Mann (3 ff.) the Palestinian Jewish lectionary was almost certainly triennial.

The same contrast applies to the esteem with which the traditions of the founders of the various philosophic schools were held. Some of the great philosophers *were* conceived of as having prophetic powers. But, as was the case with Homer and the poets, this did *not* connote their divinization: they were not 'gods'. But the tradition of Israel came to be directly traced to Yahweh himself, and, from the outset, its core in the Decalogue was in written form.[29] This placed the Torah outside the categories applied in the Graeco-Roman world to its ancient literature, and the interpretation of it later in Israel still further removed it from anything in the Graeco-Roman world.

This is reinforced by the way in which Homer was treated. Despite his attachment to Homer, Plato finally had to exclude him from the ideal state because he could corrupt morals.[30] The tragedians often found it necessary to correct Homeric notions of morality and of the gods. In the Hellenistic age, it is not Homer who is the teacher of the Greeks but Philosophy. The kind of criticism of Homer and the epic poets which made necessary the rise of the allegorical method in the Graeco-Roman world is not natural in their treatment of the Torah by Jews. Allegory does sometimes occur in Jewish sources but it is more native to the Hellenistic.[31] The approach of the Jews to their Scriptures (which they regarded as of direct divine origin, though they were in some circles regarded as mediated by angels[32]) was qualitatively different from that of the Greeks to theirs.

Moreover, the kind of historical circumstances which provided the impetus for the formulation and later fixation of the Hebrew canon in Judaism were absent in Greece and in Greek history. The Jewish people came to understand themselves as having been called into being through an act of Yahweh in delivering them from slavery in Egypt. With this they later connected the giving of the Torah on Mt. Sinai. The precise way in which the tradition of the Exodus and the Sinaitic tradition of the giving of the Torah came to be conjoined does not directly concern us. Those two events came to dominate the memory of Israel. Their emergence and continuance as a people were bound up with these; their ancient traditions and Scriptures centred in them; the remembrance of these two events provided them with their identity as a people. Later another overwhelming event, the Babylonian Exile,

---

[29] The accounts of the giving of the Law to Moses present problems which cannot be dealt with here.

[30] *Republic* 607 A. A sophist could even call Homer a liar and hold him up to ridicule: so Dio of Prusa, *Discourse* 11.

[31] J. Bonsirven, *L'Exégèse Rabbinique et l'Exégèse Paulinienne* (Paris, 1939) *ad rem*.

[32] Gal. 3: 19, Acts 7: 38: see my *Jewish and Pauline Studies* (Philadelphia, 1983). See also H. Wolfson, *Philo*, i. 138 ff.

engendered the necessity for the collecting of the traditions about those events and the setting in motion of the process which finally resulted in the Hebrew canon. The beginning of the formation of a canon was the means whereby Jewish identity survived the Exile in the sixth century BCE. To understand the Hebrew canon, then, well-defined, extraordinary, historical memories—of the Exodus, Sinai, and the Exile—have to be recognized as formative.

When we turn to Greek history, there are no parallels of any comparable magnitude. The Greek identity seems not to have been determined by any outstanding, spectacular historical events. If we follow Herodotus,[33] that identity was forged out of the normal processes of human interaction and exchange out of an agelong awareness of sharing in the same ethnic character, in the same religious tradition and in the same language. Greek self-awareness was mainly a *cultural* awareness, not a strictly historical one in the sense that it was, as with Israel, the product of specific, overwhelmingly significant historical events. Greeks knew no exodus at their beginnings, nor, in the course of their history, an exile like that of the Jews to Babylon. Certain Greek city states did experience exile and massive, cruel deportations, but the Greeks as a totality never faced such. When Persia threatened the existence of Greece, the threat was met and followed, not by exile, but by a period of efflorescence. It is probably significant that there is no one word for exile in classical Greek as there is in Hebrew (גולה, גלות) but rather several words emphasizing various aspects of the experience of exile. In Greek history there were famous 'exiles', such as Odysseus, but no one overwhelming 'Exile' in the Jewish sense.

Equally significant is it that, as Thucydides 1. 3 points out, the term *Hellenes* for all Greeks occurs only late and then simply to distinguish them from the barbarians: whereas the Jewish people, despite the division between the kingdoms of Judah and Israel, came to think of themselves as constituted of one people from the beginning, through the Exodus and Sinai. The Greeks never achieved such a 'politically' unified conception of themselves. The independent city states—not the land or country or people as a totality—were the foci of loyalty, but therefore *ipso facto* also of division and fratricide. Except under very great stress, such as the Persian invasion, the city states hindered the development of a unified Greek world, despite the recognition of its cultural unity. The impulse to the formation of one authoritative 'canon' to justify or preserve that unity was lacking: even reverence for Homer could not provide this. The geographical realities of Greece, as well as

---

[33] See e.g. *History* 8. 144.

Greek history, then, militated against the emergence of anything comparable to the canon of Judaism in the Classical period. In the Hellenistic period the diverse philosophical schools were also not conducive of a common Greek canon, but rather of individual 'canons' for each school. The widespread cultural Hellenic identity does not seem to have required a concentrated literary identification through a 'canon'.

We have suggested that the notion of a 'canon' of Scripture in Judaism and Christianity has no adequate or satisfactory parallel in the Graeco-Roman world. But our presentation has now to be seriously qualified. Two dangers have to be shunned: first, that of reading the role and authority of the Jewish and Christian canons, after they had been fixed, back to an earlier period; and, secondly, that of *underestimating* the variety of Judaism at the emergence of Christianity, and so of *overestimating the role of the Jewish Scriptures in Jewish life at that time*. We have emphasized the importance of the Scriptures in first century Judaism. The probable fixation of the canon at the end of that century confirms this: it recognized what was already fact. But concentration on the written Scriptures alone leads to distortion: this is why we previously rejected the word 'normative' to describe the role of the Tanak in Judaism, and simply used the adjective 'prominent'.

At this point the development of the oral law in Judaism must be emphasized. After the Persian, and particularly in the Greek and Roman periods, Jews who were in Babylon and those who had returned to Palestine confronted new cultures. They faced the new demands and complex dilemmas of those new cultures: for these the ancient Scriptures—important as they were in defining the origins and history, and safeguarding the identity, of the Jews—provided insufficient guidance. This, along with other factors, prompted a renewed development of the oral law alongside the written. Now for our purposes, contrary to what previous scholars have often asserted, it is strikingly noteworthy that the oral law of Judaism often bears little relation to the written Torah.[34] If the written Torah had enjoyed unswayed and normative authority, this is hard to understand. The strictly mishnaic collecting of oral laws, that is, without reference to Scripture, *may* have preceded the midrashic method of relating the laws to the scriptural text, which was also practised and culminated in the later *Midrashim*.[35] The two developments may have occurred side by side. Whether the mishnaic tendency was the prior we cannot ascer-

[34] Mishnah *Hagigah* 1. 8 is particularly illuminating on the connection between the written and the oral tradition. The Scribes, such as Ben Sirach, were not exegetes or midrashists, but expositors of Wisdom.

[35] See J. Z. Lauterbach, *Rabbinic Essays* (Cincinnati, 1951).

tain. But the development of the oral law was *often* apart from the written law. According to some of the Sages it came to take precedence over
the written law. This indicates that the written Law was not as all-
dominating as our treatment may have implied. There was a very rich
oral legal tradition alongside the written. This oral tradition, rooted in
long-established custom, also came to be connected with the giving of
the Torah to Moses on Mt. Sinai. This meant that it too achieved the
authority ascribed to Scripture itself.[36] The relation of Jesus, Paul, and
the early Church to the Tanak must not be isolated from this phenomenon. In confronting Judaism at the first they faced primarily not only
the written Torah, which so controls subsequent Christian thinking on
this matter, but the oral tradition, which was perhaps the more dominant in the Jewish mind.

There is a concomitant factor. As we saw, the oral law was not
always directly or indirectly connected with the Tanak. But it sometimes was. The development of the *Midrashim* points to this. This makes
clear what is obvious otherwise, that between the Tanak and the New
Testament lies a vast exegetical-interpretative activity within Judaism.
This means that in confronting Judaism the early Church, like Jesus
and Paul, faced not only both a written and oral Torah but also ways
of understanding these, that is, long-standing exegetical-interpretative
traditions. They assumed these and it was to these traditions of exegesis
and interpretation rather than to the Tanak itself in its textual nudity
that they related. Professor David Daube has long urged this. Recently
he claimed:

When dealing with the Old Testament in the New we ought to read it as it was
read by Jews of that era. The references without exception come from their
midst, are founded in their interpretation. If this often clashes with the pristine
sense (or what we take to be such) it cannot be helped. We must still stick to it.
Unless we do, we may miss parts of the New Testament message conveyed by
means of the reference.[37]

Knowledge of varied and complex interpretations of the Tanak in first
century Judaism is a necessary prerequisite for understanding Jesus',
and early Christian, engagement with it. To substantiate this claim is
not possible here, but examples of the illumination afforded by the
recognition of this approach are not hard to find. For the understanding of the use of the Old Testament in the New it matters little what *we*

---

[36] This is the implication of Mishnah *Aboth* 1. 1. See the chapter on 'The Meaning of Oral
Torah', J. Neusner, *Early Rabbinic Judaism* (Leiden, 1975), 1–33, and the forthcoming chapters by
J. Goldin and D. Zlotnik in *The Cambridge History of Judaism*, iv.

[37] In a forthcoming lecture on 'The Old Testament in the New'. See especially Mishnah
Sanhedrin 11. 3, *Yadaim* 3. 2.

understand by an Old Testament text, but what it meant *to Jews* with whom Jesus and early Christians were in debate in the first century is of primary importance: this should be one of our exegetical axioms.

Apart, then, from certain general considerations pointing to certain parallels, but even greater dissimilarities, the Graeco-Roman attitude to ancient texts helps little in our attempts to understand the early Christian engagement with the Hebrew Scriptures. We are driven to consider anew the oral tradition and the exegetical-interpretative activity within Judaism. The recognition of the complexity of the attitude to the Scriptures in the first century Judaism suggested here— especially when the mishnaic, midrashic, and exegetical-interpretative developments are given due emphasis—helps to place their use by the writers of the New Testament in better perspective. Most of them wrote when there was much freedom, and many methods were employed in the approach to the Scriptures even though they were so highly regarded. The canon was only in the process of being finally fixed for Judaism, just as the Sages had not yet codified the oral law. From this point of view the New Testament is a document from a transition period in which Judaism had not come fully to terms with either its written or oral Torah. The use of the Old Testament in the New reveals reverence and a daring freedom of exegesis: but in this it was not unique, but probably typical: it was only its Christological dimension and approach that was peculiar. Moreover, after the Hebrew canon had been fixed at twenty-two books with an unimpeachable ancestry, Christians continued to use and quote as Scripture such books as Wisdom and Ecclesiasticus, which they had received as part of the Septuagint. Owing to our familiarity with a fixed, authoritative canon, confined in Protestantism to the Hebrew Bible, it is easy to conceive of the engagement of the early Christian movement, especially before 70 CE, in too simplistic terms. They did use written Hebrew scriptures which they regarded as sacred: but these were still undefined in detail and had not yet achieved the express authority of '*The* Canon'. Above all, they co-existed with a vast tradition of oral law and subtle and infinitely varied exegetical-interpretative traditions. It is in the light of this, not of any parallels with Hellenism, that the New Testament use of the Tanak is best approached.

Despite his possibly distorting enthusiasm, the words of Josephus, who claimed what we have here reiterated, are probably near the truth.

. . . how firmly we have given credit to these books of our own nation is evident by what we do; for during so many ages as have already passed, no one has been so bold as either to add any thing to them, to take any thing from them, or to make any change in them; but it is become natural to call Jews immediately, and from their very birth, to esteem these books to contain Divine doctrines, and to persist in them, and, if occasion be, willingly to die for them. For it is no new thing for our captives, many of them in number, and frequently in time, to be seen to endure racks and deaths of all kinds upon the theatres, that they may not be obliged to say one word against our laws and the records that contain them; whereas there are none at all among the Greeks who would undergo the least harm on that account, no, nor in case all the writings that are among them were to be destroyed; for they take them to be such discourses as are framed agreeably to the inclinations of those that write them; and they have justly the same opinion of the ancient writers, since they see some of the present generation bold enough to write about such affairs, wherein they were not present, nor had concern enough to inform themselves about them from those that knew them . . .[38]

Perhaps we have been able to suggest additional reasons why classical antiquity offers no adequate parallel to 'The Canon' in Judaism and Christianity.

IV

What light may these reflections on the nature of the Jewish canon throw on the topic of Christology?

We have seen that there is no significant parallel to the 'canon' of Judaism in the first century. What has emerged is that the 'canon' of Judaism is inextricably bound up with the search for the identity and for the self-preservation and continuity of the Jewish community. But by itself the canon was not sufficient to serve this function adequately. It had to be interpreted and applied to the life of the community. This was achieved by the perpetuation and development of and obedience to the oral law. By this, among other things, the written Torah was minted down to guide the everyday living of faithful Jews. Both mishnaic and midrashic methods were applied to achieve this end. The significance of this development must be clearly recognized. Both Midrash and Mishnah involved what might be called the Judaization of the Tanak. That is, in Judaism the Tanak came to be interpreted in order to further and illuminate the self-understanding of Jews and to preserve their identity. The oral law and Midrash serve as a 'fence' around the written law and *ipso facto* around the Jewish community. The Tanak was interpreted in the interests of elevating both the significance of the Torah and of the relationship of the people of Israel as such to Yahweh. This process of Judaization has made it necessary to distinguish Israelite religion and, indeed, the religion of the Tanak, from

---

[38] *Contra Apion*, Book I, pp. 861–2 in the Loeb Translation.

Judaism. That process was more chequered before 70 CE (for example, it is doubtful whether the Sadducees ever fully succumbed to it) than later. In Rabbinic Judaism, strictly so-called, the Judaization of the Tanak, and (some go so far as to claim) its subordination to the oral Torah, reached its apogee. The developed Rabbinic Judaism which emerged after the first century gave to the oral Torah, originally an accompaniment of the written Torah, an authority equal to the latter—if not a greater one. This helps to clarify the function of the oral Torah. Probably from the time of Ezra on it evolved to make sure that the Tanak was not treated as an isolated deposit, with overweening authority, but interpreted in the interests of the community. This was why in time the oral tradition became Torah, as much as the Tanak, and according to some even more than the latter.

We suggest that the due recognition of the oral tradition as the interpretative clue to the meaning of the Tanak in Judaism is relevant to our understanding of the Christology of the early Church. We here use the term 'Christology' not in its strict traditional sense to denote the doctrine of how God became man in Christ, but in the general sense of doctrine or teaching about Christ. And as in Judaism so in the history of Christian doctrine, the centuries after the first can best illumine the latter. Marcel Simon long ago pointed to the notion of Christ as a New Torah in the Fathers. However he made no attempt to connect it with the period of the New Testament or with its documents. Later Daniélou was more receptive to such a connection and found anticipations of it in the New Testament. In *Paul and Rabbinic Judaism* we proposed that for Paul Christ had come to fulfil the role of a New Torah, although he never used that phrase. This suggestion has not been generally accepted. Apart from hesitancy expecially on the part of Protestants to apply 'legal' terms to the Lord of Grace, two reasons were advanced against it: first, the unacceptable appeal to Colossians and Ephesians, which many regard as non-Pauline or at best deutero-Pauline; secondly, the emphasis (which many regard as highly exaggerated and unwarranted) on the words of Jesus as constituting a new law. Moreover it was often confidently asserted that Paul did not think of Christ in terms of the Law, as we had implied, but of the Law in terms of Christ, who is not a new Moses in Paul. Neither of these objections is insurmountable. There are pertinent anticipations of Colossians and Ephesians in earlier indubitably Pauline epistles, and the words of Jesus—the role of which we doubtless did underline too much—do play no mean part in Paul. The role of Moses in Paul's understanding is more difficult to deal with. Here, however, we are not concerned to reassert the interpretation of Christ as a New Torah in Paul without further refinement. Let it simply be noted that in speaking of Christ as Torah we were not thinking primarily of his words as constituting Torah but of the totality of his ministry and person, his cross and Resurrection as having assumed for Paul the ultimate significance which Judaism applied to the Torah.

Such a position is simplistic and needs elaboration and refinement. The words in Torah remained authoritative for Paul: he is careful to insist that the life, death, and Resurrection of Jesus are 'according to the Scriptures'. The unchangeable 'canon' remains 'canon' for him. But just as, in Judaism, what was deemed to interpret the 'canon' became itself 'canon', so it came to pass for Paul that the life, teaching, death, and Resurrection of Jesus became the exegesis of the canon (that is, of the Tanak)—a kind of equivalent of, and hence a substitute for, the oral tradition in Judaism, as the clue to the Scriptures. When he fought against obedience to the Law, he was not primarily opposed to the Tanak but to the oral tradition which was already being elevated to the status of the written Torah. In other words, for Paul the identity of the Christian community is preserved by the tradition about Christ: he now fulfils for Christians the role of the oral law in Judaism. But once this had been recognized the further elevation of Christ to be part of the 'canon' was natural, as had been the elevation of the oral law to the same status in Judaism. Whether this stage was reached in Paul's mind we need not at this point determine. What we are concerned to suggest again is that, just as the oral Torah in Judaism implied the Judaization of the Tanak, so the elevation of the life, death, and Resurrection of Jesus by Paul led to its Christianization. Christ, we might claim, has become the 'oral tradition' of Paul, the clue to his understanding of the Tanak.

From a different angle Professor Daniel Patte has recently urged what amounts to the same thing, although he starts out not as we did from the canon and oral tradition of Judaism, but from the use of the Scriptures in Paul. I can only refer the reader to his work. For example, of Paul's treatment of Abraham he writes:

... the relation between the believers [the Christian community] and Christ is similar to that between the believers and Abraham. More generally, we may say that the relation of the believers to Christ is the same kind of relation which exists between Scripture and its fulfillments in Christ and the believers. To put it another way, the Kerygma about Christ functions in Paul as an *'oral scripture'*. This means that according to Paul's system of convictions, Christ, despite the fact that he is the Fulfillment of Scripture, *has the same status as Scripture* [our italics].[39]

---

[39] *Paul's Truth and the Power of the Gospel* (Philadelphia, 1983), 213.

A discussion of 1 Cor. 15: 3–11 leads Patte to the same conclusion: 'Indeed, for Paul, Scripture is not merely the Old Testament Scripture, but also the Kerygma about Christ, and the story of the earlier believers' experience.' It is not possible to pursue Patte's discussion but it deserves careful consideration for its Christological implications.

Outside the Pauline epistles, too, the New Testament points in other ways to a tradition, a way to be followed, which seems often to be equated with Christ Himself. This line of thought later breaks out more explicitly. In short, it is not unlikely that a consideration of Christ in the light of Torah both written and oral is still one fruitful way to approach the *mysterium tremendum* of his person.

This study is offered in memory of George B. Caird in gratitude and admiration for his scholarship, expressed with classical erudition, precision, clarity, and imagination, and no less for his human warmth and faithful stewardship as *pastor pastorum*.

3. 'Today, in Your Very Hearing': Some Comments on the Christological Use of the Old Testament

WALTER J. HOUSTON

'TODAY, in your very hearing, this text has come true' (Luke 4: 21, NEB). Essential to the New Testament understanding of Jesus Christ is the belief that in him the Scriptures are fulfilled, that the words of the prophets and the songs of the psalmists are predicated of him. The rise of the historical understanding of the Bible made this belief, like many another, difficult to hold in a naïve sense; for it was one of the chief elements in that understanding that the prophets (and others) spoke of and to their own times. Wherever the primary understanding of the Bible is historical there opens up a wide chronological and theological chasm between the seemingly contemporary intention of the Old Testament text and the equally contemporary interpretation of it in the New. But the attempt to understand Jesus without reference to the traditional expectations of his people, which he along with them saw enshrined in Scripture, has led to the inanition of Christian belief in romanticism and sentimentality.

The object of this essay, written to honour the memory of one who strove in all his work to make the Bible speak with the accents of its own time, only so that it might speak to us in our time, is to attempt to sketch out how it might be possible to understand certain strands of Old Testament expectation as pointing to Christ without letting go of their historical rootedness. It is not self-evident that the methods and insights of historical criticism limit the sphere of reference of Old Testament texts to the immediate foreground. We shall use as stimulus some recent reflections on the interpretation of texts in Isaiah and the Psalms, and end with a study of Isa. 61: 1–3, the text referred to in our epigraph.

George Caird himself, in his last book published in his lifetime, asks 'Can an utterance have more meaning in it than the original speaker or writer understood at the time?'[1] His answer is in the terms of the distinction in semantics between the sense of an utterance (what is said) and its referent (what it is said of). 'Words have the sense their speaker

[1] *Language and Imagery of the Bible* (Essex and London, 1980), 40.

intended them to have.'[2] But although a word also 'has the referent a speaker intends it to have', the reference may be of such a kind that it is 'legitimate to transfer an utterance to a fresh referent without violence to the principle that its sense is determined by the intention of the original speaker'.[3] Professor Caird compares one mode of reference to

a Situation Vacant advertisement: it describes in some detail a person whose identity is not yet known to the writer. In this category we must place the description of the servant of the Lord in Isaiah 53. The context makes it clear that the prophet believed Israel to be God's servant (e.g. 49: 3), and that he was inviting Israel to see her national sufferings in the light of his prophecy. But he was very unsure of any response. Was the servant to be the whole nation or only a remnant, to be many, few or one? The reason why modern scholars have endlessly debated these questions is that the prophet himself did not know the answers. It is as though he had published an advertisement, 'Wanted, a servant of the Lord,' accompanied by a job description. He was undoubtedly aware that many famous men, such as Moses and Jeremiah, had sat for the composite portrait he was drawing. What he could not know was that in the end there would be only one candidate for the post.[4]

In other words, such a passage as Isaiah 53 was not spoken of a particular known referent, but is in search of its referent. Hence it is legitimate to apply it to a new referent provided that that referent adequately corresponds to the sense of the passage.

There is an analogy to this approach in David Clines's study of Isaiah 53,[5] which depends not on semantics but on literary criticism, the 'new hermeneutic' of Fuchs and Ebeling, and the philosophical hermeneutics of Gadamer. Clines says that 'the original author's meaning . . . is by no means the only meaning a text may legitimately have (or create)'.[6] A text is a 'language-event' of which the key question to be asked is not what information it gives but what effect it produces; and the effect of a literary work of an imaginative kind is to create 'an alternative *world*[7] and thereby destroy the universal validity of the conventional "world"'; by 'world' is meant a 'set of principles, values, relations and perceptions' which govern a person's outlook. The reader is invited to enter the new world and, once within it, may come to see it as giving a new perspective on the known world: the two worlds coalesce, and there is, in Gadamer's phrase, a 'merging (fusion) of horizons' (*Horizontverschmelzung*).[8] Fully to enter the world of Isaiah 53, it is necessary to take up for oneself one of the roles within the drama of the

---

[2] Ibid., 56.   [3] Ibid., 58.   [4] Ibid., 57 f.
[5] *I, He, We and They* (Sheffield, 1976).   [6] Ibid., 60.
[7] Ibid., 54 (italics in the original).
[8] Ibid., 54 f.; H. -G. Gadamer, *Truth and Method* (London, 2nd edn., 1975), 273.

text, such as the role of the 'we' who undergo a radical change in their understanding of the ugly, despised servant and his acceptance of suffering; or even the role of the servant himself.[9]

Clines does not push forward his interpretation to show explicitly how it may yield a Christological sense, but it is not difficult to see how it might be done. In contemplating the figure of the servant in Isa. 53 the disciple of Jesus, drawn into that world, understands from the vantage-point of the 'we' his own world, where the unresisting suffering of Jesus has led to the glory of the Resurrection, and is enabled to say of *him* 'The LORD has laid on him the iniquity of us all.' One may also say, with due reverence, that Jesus, entering into that world, takes up the role of the Servant, fusing the horizons as he bears the role into his own world.

Thus to translate Clines's approach into the language of semantics, the original historical referent of Isa. 53, if it had one, is of no significance; indeed, it may be as meaningless to ask after its referent as in the case of a work of purely imaginative fiction. The world to which it refers is internal to itself: yet the reader who transports himself into that world may find that the sense of the text accords after all with something in his own world and enables him to understand himself and it.

A rather different approach is afforded by Brevard Childs's 'canonical reading' of the book of Isaiah and of the Psalter. According to this, the 'canonical shaping' of the book of Isaiah is intended to obliterate the particularity of the historical context of Isa. 40 ff. and present it 'as a prophetic word of promise offered to Israel by the eighth-century prophet Isaiah of Jerusalem'. The effect is that 'the message of promise became a prophetic word not tied to a specific historical referent, but directed to the future'; it has become 'fully eschatological', relating to 'the redemptive plan of God for all of history', 'offered to sinful Israel as a promise of God's purpose with his people in every age'.[10] 'The discrepancy between what happened after the exile and the prophet's eschatological description of God's will is not a criticism of the truth of the promise, but rather an indication of how little the exilic community partook of the promised reality.'[11] It is this eschatological promise addressed to a future far beyond the sixth century BC which the New Testament sees fulfilled in Christ.[12]

The same is true to a large extent of the Psalter, above all of the royal psalms. 'Although the royal psalms arose originally in a peculiar

[9] Ibid., 62 ff.
[10] B. S. Childs, *Introduction to the Old Testament as Scripture* (London, 1979), 325 f.
[11] Ibid., 327.
[12] Cf. ibid., 338.

historical setting of ancient Israel which had received its form from a common mythopoetic milieu, they were treasured in the Psalter for a different reason, namely as a witness to the messianic hope which looked for the consummation of God's kingship through his Anointed One.'[13]

Thus, according to Childs, it is the canonical shaping and setting of the prophecies and psalms that makes them receptive of Christological reference. This, however, is the level of the text which claims authority for us; the original meaning is not significant. We may note, however, that the contemporary historical references are far clearer in 'Deutero-Isaiah' than Childs suggests, and any fair reading must reckon *also* with this level.

Two main issues arise from this survey. The first is that of authorial intention. Is it really true, as Caird suggests, that the speaker's (or writer's) intention is the criterion of all aspects of meaning; or is Clines correct when he says that 'the original author's meaning is by no means the only meaning a text may legitimately have'? We must insist even against the scholar whose memory we honour that the meaning of an utterance, in any aspect, is a public matter, to be determined by recognized canons of interpretation: the subjectivity of the author does not come into it, even if it could be determined.[14] And from our own perspective we may be able to understand more of what a text means than the author could from his, as Gadamer points out,[15] though this is only true if we stand in the same tradition to some extent. The difficulties in suggesting that the character of Isa. 53 as a 'Situation Vacant' advertisement depends on the subjective uncertainty of the author about the referent are obvious. Suppose that one or other of the numerous proposals for identifying the Servant as a historical person—for example, the prophet himself[16]—were correct: this would sweep away the entire proposal. It is not the intention of the author in a subjective sense, but the openness of the text itself to alternative reference that makes it available to refer to a previously unknown referent. Moreover, what do we mean by the 'author' of a biblical passage, when it has been, like most, through at least one stage of editorial adaptation? It is the advantage of Childs's approach that it takes the ambiguity of 'authorship' seriously.

However, Clines's understanding also has its difficulties, at least if it is proposed to generalize it. The model, derived ultimately from

---

[13] Ibid., 517.
[14] Cf. Gadamer, op. cit. n. 8 above, 260.
[15] Ibid., 263.
[16] Cf. R. N. Whybray, *Thanksgiving for a liberated Prophet* (Sheffield, 1978).

Gadamer, which he is using only works well with texts which of their nature are of general reference or none—philosophy, theology, law, imaginative literature. It is as imaginative literature rather than as prophecy that Clines deals with Isa. 53; few other prophetic texts could be treated in quite the same way. Most have more obvious historical particularity of reference, and for such texts it is necessary to take into account the context of their authors, if not their intention, in order to understand them correctly.

We need therefore—and this is our second issue—a general model of the way in which prophetic language works. No account of prophecy will do which simply sees it as referring to events of the future in the same way in which one refers to events of the past. There is plenty of evidence (for example Isa. 55: 10 f.) to suggest that prophets frequently thought of their words as *creating* the realities of which they spoke. This may be seen as a magical idea,[17] but it makes much more sense to understand it performatively.[18] Prophecy is presented as the word of God and is concerned primarily with God's own actions, often explicitly and always by implication. When a person speaks of his own actions in the future we do not usually call it prediction: we may call it proposal, promise, undertaking, warning, threat, vow: all names of illocutionary[19] acts which may be seen as guaranteeing to the hearer the reality of which they speak in advance.

In such speech-acts it is not always a simple matter to apply the notion of reference. If I say to my child, 'I will make you a paper boat', neither the verb nor the object refers to anything that exists. The promises of God in the prophets may include references to existing entities such as Jerusalem or the House of David, but the *events* promised exist only in the intention of God, and how he is to fulfil his intention may be left more or less open. So Caird's 'Situation Vacant' proposal may be of wider application that at first appears, and so may Clines's; for the effect and indeed the intention of the promise may be to create a new world to which my proper response is to enter it and see how its horizon corresponds to that of my own world.

Apply this understanding now to Deutero-Isaiah, and we ask 'What is the content (since we cannot speak of reference) of these promises?';

[17] G. von Rad, *Old Testament Theology* (Edinburgh, 1965), ii. 80 ff.; R. P. Carroll, *When Prophecy failed* (London, 1979), 58 ff.

[18] A. C. Thiselton, 'The supposed power of words in the biblical writings', *JTS*, NS, 25 (1974), 283–99. 'Performative' language is defined by J. L. Austin, *How to do things with words* (Oxford, 2nd edn. 1976); in what follows I am using the word in its broader sense in which all language may be viewed performatively (ibid., 94 ff.). Cf. also Caird, op. cit. n. 1 above, 20 ff.; Carroll, op. cit., 69 ff.

[19] See Austin, op. cit., 99 ff. An illocutionary act is the act 'performed *in* saying something as opposed to the act *of* saying something'.

and we find ourselves answering on two levels. On one level one may
say that they promise the downfall of Babylon, the return of the exiles,
the regathering of the nation, the rebuilding of the city, and the recrea-
tion of its institutions. So expressed, the promises may be seen as
promptly if meagrely fulfilled. Yet apparently even the first generation
in the rebuilt city did not see the historical events they witnessed as any
proper fulfilment of the promises.[20] Understandably; for the overwhelming impression and weight of these chapters is of the promise of a
salvation of world-wide, and indeed cosmic, dimensions; they speak of
the coming of Zion's God to her as her king, the raising of Israel to
receive the homage of the nations, the transformation of the desert into
the garden of the Lord. The proclamation of the messenger in 52: 10,
'Your God is king!' (which in Hebrew is only two words), is also the
best summary of the prophet's own message. The language often strays
into the mythical, and is well argued[21] to derive from the myth and
ritual of the Jerusalem New Year festival.

How is this level to be understood? One possibility is that it is purely
symbolic: metaphor and hyperbole that 'means' no more than the first
level. Robert Carroll, in his stimulating discussion of 'unfulfilled
prophecy', discusses this possibility and dismisses it, at least as a complete answer, on the grounds that it would 'deny any cognitive content
in the oracles except the anticipation of a future', and that it is 'only
necessary because of the failure of the predictions in the first place'.[22]
Both these points seem to beg the question. What would count as the
success of such predictions?

More significant is the point that the figurative language is deployed
not to decorate a piece of good political news, but religiously, to express
in the only way in which it can be expressed the triumph of Israel's God
over all that opposes his rule.[23] It is not of course to be taken literally, as
if Deutero-Isaiah were interested in irrigation schemes in the Syrian
Desert, but its decoding goes in the wrong direction if it is taken to
stand for prosaic political expectation; rather, it stands for the power,
the reign of God already at work in and behind the political realities to
bring those expectations to pass. This mythological language is used in
the way which George Caird sees as characteristic of the use of myth in
the Bible, to express theological meaning in earthly events (or expectations).[24]

[20] Carroll, op. cit., 152 ff.; cf. P. D. Hanson, *The Dawn of Apocalyptic* (Philadelphia, 1975), 32–
208.
[21] S. Mowinckel, *He that cometh* (Oxford, 1956), 138 ff.; S. Mowinckel, *Psalmenstudien* ii (Oslo,
1922); J. H. Eaton, *Festal Drama in Deutero-Isaiah* (London, 1979).
[22] Op. cit. n. 17 above, 65 f.
[23] Mowinckel, *He that cometh*, 143.   [24] Op. cit. n. 1 above, 224 ff.

In using the transcendental language of the cult, Deutero-Isaiah has clothed the promises of God, directed though they are to a particular historical situation, in terms that permit and even demand continual reapplication. The embodiment of the reign of God in the events of the late sixth century is real; but it was not a complete embodiment, even in respect of the prosaic promises made, let alone a unique one. But the partial failure of the prophecies on the first level does not invalidate the content of the second. The assertion of the reign of God as a reality in history requires precisely that application to the whole sweep of history, with the promise of God's final triumph, that Childs sees in the canonical shaping of Isaiah. It creates a new world demanding that we enter it to transform our understanding of our own, and hence inevitably lies open to fresh understanding in terms of the events of our own world. As George Caird remarks about another myth, 'It is misleading to say that the monster *is* Rome . . . Rome is only its latest embodiment.'[25]

In understanding what is for them the supreme expression of the reign of God within the course of human history, Christians are entirely correct in seeing it as the 'fulfilment' of the Old Testament proclamations of that reign. The text can be dealt with in this way, not because it has been canonically reshaped, nor because 'not occasionally only, but always, the meaning of a text goes beyond its author'[26]—this is true in very varying degrees of different kinds of texts—nor because of any uncertainty about the referent in the mind of the author, but because of the objective and individual quality of richness and depth in the text itself.

What is true of the proclamation of the reign of God in Deutero-Isaiah is true also of the royal psalms and other more strictly 'Messianic' texts, such as Isa. 9 and 11. These texts, expressing the cultic understanding of monarchy, are saying more than simply 'may he reign justly and defeat his enemies; may there be peace in his time, and may he die in old age.' Their seemingly inflated language is used, not hyperbolically, but because they invest the king with the power to exercise on earth the eternal reign of Yahweh.[27] The performative character is quite explicit in the decrees of Yahweh quoted at Pss. 2: 7 and 110: 4: these decrees formally make the king 'Son' and 'priest', the vicegerent of God. In the king is focused the rule of Yahweh on earth, and through him flow his justice and his blessing. Among these texts the Psalms are obviously of general reference: they are intended to be used

---

[25] G. B. Caird, *The Revelation of St John the Divine* (London, 1966), 164.

[26] Gadamer, op. cit., n. 8 above, 263.

[27] Mowinckel, *The Psalms in Israel's worship* (Oxford, 1962), i. 53, 63 ff.; A. R. Johnson, *Sacral Kingship in ancient Israel* (Cardiff, 2nd. edn., 1967), 136.

of each successive legitimate occupant of the throne of David. The prophetic texts may refer to a particular member of the dynasty (for instance perhaps Isa. 9: 1–6 (Heb.)), or may express the indefinite
promise of Yahweh that a person will again exercise such power on
earth (for instance Isa. 11: 1–9).

Thus once again we find the text operating on two levels at once: it is
concerned with the visible enthronement of a ruler of the line of David,
and also with the invisible endowment enabling him to bring in on
earth Yahweh's reign of justice and peace. This is proclaimed of every
king at his accession and also probably at every New Year's festival; but
the proclamation itself, couched in mythical and idealized terms, demands a more adequate embodiment, and is capable of accommodating one far transcending the political realm.[28] The Messianic
understanding of kingship creates the figure of the Messiah as an ideal,
a situation that is always spiritually and later physically vacant, the
central figure of a new world which continues to challenge our world
and call for the response of self-involvement.

It is a commonplace that the vanishing of the power and hopes for
power of the House of David led to the tendency to emphasize the ideal,
'eschatological' aspects of the Messianic expectation.[29] But there is
another factor tending to loosen the idea of sacral kingship from its
political roots. The cultic theology of sacral kingship had perhaps never
had the field to itself in Israel, if some of the material in 1 Sam. 8, 12 is
of ancient origin, as seems likely;[30] and in the last days of the monarchy
it is strongly challenged by the coherent political theology of the
Deuteronomic school, in which the king is demystified, deprived of his
superhuman character. In Deut. 17: 14–20, not only is the king subject
to restrictions on his style of life 'lest his heart should be lifted up above
his brethren' (v. 20),[31] but more important, although he must be
Yahweh's own choice, he is not himself the agent of Yahweh's rule and
the fount of his justice: for that function has been taken over by 'this
law' (v. 18), which the king is himself subject to. It is Yahweh's commandments, not the king, that embody justice, and it is their observ-
ance by the whole people that results in blessing, as Deuteronomy
repeatedly asserts. The monarchy thus becomes, like much else, a secular rather than a sacral institution. The Deuteronomistic version of the
covenant with David as given in 2 Sam. 7 is notable for the entire absence of the mythical language characteristic of the sacral view. (Of

[28] Cf. Johnson, op. cit., 141.
[29] Mowinckel, *He that cometh*, 181.
[30] F. Crüsemann, *Der Widerstand gegen das Königtum* (Neukirchen-Vluyn, 1978).
[31] Probably the original connection of thought: A. D. H. Mayes, *Deuteronomy* (London, 1979),
274.

course, this is also true of many psalms, but we do not know their precise date or to what extent they have been adapted.)

In the Old Testament as we have it, this view of political institutions
is the normative one, and from the canonical point of view those texts
that present the ideal of sacral kingship cannot be interpreted of an
ordinary political figure. God's supreme representative on earth in the
establishment of his reign is superior to any king. Within a Bible containing Deut. 17 and Samuel and Kings, the only possible interpretation of the 'Messianic' texts is Messianic.

At the intersection of the two groups of texts that we have been considering lies the tantalizing figure of the Servant of Yahweh with which
we began. Part of the difficulty of the 'Servant Songs' is caused just by
the fact that ideas associated with royalty are here beginning to be used
to express new expectations. The cultic office of the king is the model,[32]
but the portrait is not that of a mere king. Even Eaton[33] cannot demonstrate that the king had the full range of functions attributed to the
Servant, especially in ch. 53.

Much of what I have been saying can be demonstrated from an
example: Isa. 61: 1–3, a passage closely related to the 'Servant Songs'.
It should be noted that this self-proclamation is not, as has often been
thought,[34] spoken *in propria persona* by the prophet. The nearest formal
parallel, apart from 49: 1–6, is 2 Sam. 23: 1–7.[35] The verb בשׂר is not
properly used of a prophetic announcement; in 40: 9 and 52: 7 it is used
of the dramatic characters of the watchers, not of the prophet himself.[36]
And to proclaim 'freedom to captives, amnesty to prisoners' is a performative speech-act in the political realm: it is done by one who has the
political authority to effect it. In a word it is one who announces his
investiture with Yahweh's ruling power (v. 1a) who here speaks. The
combination of the ideas of Spirit and anointing is only found in connection with the king (1 Sam. 16: 12 f., 2 Sam. 23: 1 f.)[37]

One aspect of the proclamation that has attracted attention is the
expressions and ideas that it has in common with the Pentateuchal
legislation on economic redistribution, particularly with Lev. 25. The
word דרור 'freedom' occurs besides here and in Lev. 25: 10 only in
Ezek. 46: 17, which refers to Lev. 25, and in Jer. 34 (also with קרא),

---

[32] Eaton, op. cit., 47 ff.
[33] Ibid., 84.
[34] e.g. C. Westermann, *Isaiah 40–66* (London, 1969), 365 ff.
[35] Cf. Eaton, op. cit. n. 21 above, 90, 61; Westermann (loc. cit.) compares Mic. 3: 8, but that
does not announce a divine appointment.
[36] Cf. Westermann, op. cit., 366. Why should one assume that 'Trito-Isaiah' has mistaken his
master's usage? (B. Duhm, *Das Buch Jesaia* (Göttingen, 1892), 425, quoted by Westermann.)
[37] Eaton, op. cit. n. 21 above, 90.

which is concerned with the emancipation of slaves; and the idea of a special year of grace occurs besides in Deut. 15: 1, the law of debt-remission. The Isaiah passage has been connected with that in Leviticus at least since Qumran,[38] and Zimmerli[39] has argued the case for the institution of the jubilee year as the background of the expressions here. Eaton[40] dismisses any such connection on the grounds that it fails to connect with the royal and festal features of the passage.

But in doing so he overlooks the evidence that in the ancient Near East such decrees of release and remission were typically the province of the king. The Old Babylonian kings generally proclaimed *mišarum* in the year of their accession and at reasonably frequent, though not absolutely regular, intervals thereafter.[41] These decrees provided for the remission of debts (like the Deuteronomic שמטה), the emancipation of slaves (like Jer. 34), and the return of property to its ancestral holders (like the Levitical יובל). Now it is inherently likely that the Pentateuchal laws have a prehistory, and are a development and systematization of pre-exilic practice; and it is also probable that, under the monarchy, such measures would be within the prerogative of the king as the fount of justice.[42] The Pentateuchal laws themselves are unlikely to have been in force, because of the impracticality of the fixed term (admitted in effect by Deut. 15: 9).[43] Here we have a specific legal function that has been transferred from the king to the Torah. Eaton also overlooks the point that according to Lev. 25: 9 the proclamation of the jubilee is to take place on the Day of Atonement, thus connecting it with the festal season.

Thus the suggested connection with the laws of release, so far from being at odds with the royal background of Isa. 61, supports it and is supported by it. The figure speaks as a king announcing a measure of release in the year of his accession. The passage could easily have been written for a contemporary personage (Zerubbabel?) who of course failed to fulfil its promise. But quite apart from such failure, the text itself demands a more excellent embodiment and a broader sweep of

---

[38] 11Q Melch (A. S. van der Woude, 'Melchisedek als himmlische Erlösergestalt in den neugefundenen eschatologischen Midraschim aus Qumran Höhle XI', *OTS* 14 (1965), 354 ff. (text on p. 358)).

[39] W. Zimmerli, 'Das "Gnadenjahr des Herrn"', in *Archäologie und Altes Testament: Festschrift für Kurt Galling* (Tübingen, 1970), 321 ff.

[40] Op. cit. n. 21 above, 91.

[41] J. J. Finkelstein, 'Ammiṣaduqa's edict and the Babylonian "Law-codes"', *Journal of Cuneiform Studies*, 15 (1961), 91–104; J. J. Finkelstein, 'Some new *Misharum* material and its implications' in *Studies in honour of B. Landsberger* (Chicago, 1965), 223–46; cf. M. Weinfeld, *Deuteronomy and the Deuteronomic School* (Oxford, 1972), 152 ff.

[42] Cf. Weinfeld, loc. cit.

[43] Against R. North, *Sociology of the Biblical Jubilee* (Rome, 1954), 203 ff. Cf. E. W. Davies, *Prophecy and Ethics* (Sheffield, 1981), 74 ff.

time for its fulfilment. There are three features which suggest this. The first is the greatness of the anointed one's task. It is not now a case of the release of debt-slaves and the return of families to their property, but of the release of prisoners of war (שְׁבוּיִם) and the restoration of a whole nation. The second is the depth and resonance of the themes of release and restoration, of jubilee and liberation, which cannot be limited to one historical context and cannot be adequately fulfilled in a single political adjustment. They are notions still on the political agenda of the world, as well as being deeply embedded in the religious traditions arising from the Old Testament. The third is the resumption by the anointed one of legal functions assigned to the Torah, which makes it canonically necessary to read the passage of a figure superior to the Torah.

Because of these objective features, the text is well fitted to function in the ways called for by the proposals we examined at the beginning. In the mouth of Jesus in Luke 4, a very precise function is assigned to it. 'Today, in your very hearing, this text has come true.' πεπλήρωται ... ἐν τοῖς ὠσὶν ὑμῶν: it was fulfilled as it was read. That is to say, the one for whom it was written, the one who alone has the authority to proclaim the liberation of which it speaks, has now proclaimed it, and as the words are a legal decree bringing that liberation into effect (performative language again), it is now a reality. This is the final jubilee: it involves a permanent redistribution of the unjust order of the world (compare 6: 20 ff.); and the deliverance of those who are prisoners to political forces, demonic powers (compare 13: 16), and the power of sin. Kings proclaimed jubilee; the Torah proclaims a regular jubilee; only the Messiah, as God's supreme representative, can proclaim the final jubilee. His proclamation is set out for him: it calls into existence a new world, and Jesus steps into that world in order to accept the vacant situation of Messiah, and by his faithful accomplishment of the mission fuses the horizons of that world and ours. Thus by the word uttered and the word fulfilled, the word offered and the word accepted, is God's eternal salvation wrought.

PART II

EXEGETICAL STUDIES

4. The Glory of Jesus, Mark 10: 37

JOHN MUDDIMAN

As an example of the semantic distinction between the public meaning and the private, *user's* meaning of a word, Professor George Caird was apt to quote Humpty Dumpty's famous proof of the superiority of *un*birthday presents, with its triumphant conclusion, 'There's glory for you!'[1] To a conventional linguist like Alice, *glory* could not mean 'a nice, knock-down argument'; but to a master of speech like Humpty Dumpty, *glory* means whatever he chooses. For, as it were, one person's glory is another's humiliation.

In memory of a great scholar and a generous patron of young scholars, I offer here some observations on the meanings of glory in Mark 10: 37. What was once intended as a birthday present must now, sadly, be an unbirthday present—in the most painful sense of that expression to us, but perhaps to him in the better sense, in which death is but a birthday into glory.

Discussion of the pericope on the request of James and John to sit in the 'glory of Jesus' usually centres on the enigmatic reference to baptism and cup. I propose to approach it from another direction, the meaning of glory in the evangelist's intention, general form- and redaction-critical questions and the grammar of v. 40.

(1) In the only two other places where Mark employs the word glory, it is associated with the future coming of the Son of man, but in both Mark is reluctant to predicate glory of him directly. In 8: 38 the majority text reads 'when he comes in the glory *of his Father* with the holy angels'.[2] In 13: 26 people, or perhaps the heavenly powers, will see 'the Son of Man coming on the clouds with great power and glory'. Again the glory is not specified as the possession of that figure. And if it is indeed the heavenly powers who witness the epiphany (contrast Matthew 24: 30, explicitly) the greater power and glory is more naturally that of God himself. It is noteworthy that the other synoptists

---

[1] Cf. 'The Glory of God in the Fourth Gospel: an exercise in Biblical Semantics', *NTS* 15 (1969), 265 f.; *The Language and Imagery of the Bible* (London, 1980), 38.

[2] But the minority reading of P[45] and allies may be original. The Lucan parallel (9: 26) supports the view that this text stood already in his copy of Mark. The majority reading would then need to be explained as harmonization to Matthew (16: 27). In either case, both Matthew and Luke, by abbreviation and addition respectively, seem to have reacted negatively to any suggestion in the Marcan text that angels might lend something by way of glory to the Son of man for his coming.

provide unequivocal references elsewhere to glory as the peculiar possession of Jesus.[3] If we are right in thinking that Mark displays reserve in attributing glory directly even to the future Son of man, we are entitled *a fortiori* to ask why he allows James and John to attribute it to Jesus at 10: 37 and to do so apparently without correction or comment.[4]

(2) This observation leads inevitably to a general form-critical question. The rabbinic dialogue form, with which the pericope invites comparison, is a natural pedagogic technique: the opening question or appeal of an enquirer or dim-witted student starts a conversation in which the rabbi elicits a concession by asking a counter-question on an analogous issue, and then skilfully turns it into a triumphant response to the initial inquiry. The form puts into practice the principle, 'Will your ears not listen to what your mouth is saying'. On the basis of formal similarity, the *unitary* character of the dialogues in the gospel tradition is a reasonable assumption;[5] and thus there ought to be some sort of logical connection between the component exchanges of a dialogue. However, the majority of commentators on our passage fail to indicate how the conclusion follows from the preceding discussion.

(3) Redaction-critically, the pericope is usually linked with the so-called 'blindness of the disciples' theme in Mark. There is no doubt that the evangelist has deliberately connected the pericope with the teaching on true greatness which follows it[6]—a clear example of that theme. However, this connection creates an inconsistency in the Marcan redaction, given the usual view of the pericope. If James and John are examples of the persistent blindness of the disciples, the reaction of the others to them in v. 41 is not only legitimate, it is the most hopeful sign so far in the Gospel of a breakthrough in understanding. Yet, while Jesus appears to treat the sons of Zebedee with teasing irony, he goes on to rebuke the ten with explicit severity.

(4) The grammar of the last three words of v. 40 also causes concern. An ellipse in thought and expression is normally supposed. The RSV, for example, translates: 'But to sit at my right hand or at my left is not mine to grant, but *it is for those* for whom it has been prepared.' How-

---

[3] Cf., e.g. Luke 9: 32; 24: 26 and Matthew 25: 31.

[4] The oddity of the phrase to 'sit in the glory of someone' deserves comment. Matthew's parallel (20: 21) is the more natural, 'to sit in your Kingdom (cf. also Matthew 19: 28 and 25: 31 where sitting on *thrones* of glory is mentioned). The bald expression in Mark is clearly awkward and compressed.

[5] Cf. my unpublished D.Phil. thesis, completed under Dr Caird's supervision, 'The Fasting Controversy in Mark' (Oxford, 1976), 125–43. Cf. also A. J. Hultgren, *Jesus and his Adversaries* (Michigan, 1971).

[6] James and John are referred to as the *two* sons of Zebedee already in v. 35 in order to prepare for the mention of the *ten* other disciples at v. 41.

ever, with an emphatic ἐμόν in the first clause, we expect a reference to the disposer of places not their recipients in the second.

The following sections of this paper correspond, though in a diferent order, to the problems observed above.

The inability of the pre-Easter disciples to understand Jesus was first demonstrated exegetically as a theme in Mark's Gospel by W. Wrede.[7] His references to 10: 35–40 are, however, extremely cautious. He noted that v. 38, 'You know not what you ask,' *might* be an example of the theme, but added, 'I have intentionally excluded all such passages in order to keep to what is clear, that is, to the material which is as obviously the expression of Mark's viewpoint as it is unhistorical.'[8] Recent redaction-critics, developing Wrede's insights, have been much less cautious. James Robinson simply includes our pericope in with all the other data on misunderstanding. 'The attitude which leads to Peter's theological objection to the passion (8: 32), leads also . . . to the request of James and John for places next to Jesus in his glory (10: 35 ff.), and to the anger of the other ten against them (10: 41). The disciples are throughout displaying the attitude due to the temptation of Satan (8: 33).'[9]

In an important article, J. B. Tyson pointed the discussion of the blindness of the disciples in a new direction.[10] He discerned two different aspects in it. The disciples not only misunderstand the necessity of Jesus' suffering, but also their own place in the future community. From this clue, the theory has been developed that Mark is using the blindness motif to attack, via the twelve and the family of Jesus in his narrative, the hierarchy of the Church in his own day. E. Trocmé, discussing 'the aversions displayed by the Evangelist', asks whether Mark's reservations about Peter might be due to his support of a rival faction in the early Church favouring the authority of James and John. But he immediately dismisses this possibility, since Mark is equally 'ill-disposed' towards them. 'They are treated so harshly in Mark 10: 35 ff. that Matthew preferred to ascribe their request to their mother, and Luke decided to omit the whole episode.'[11] Comparison with the paral-

---

[7] *The Messianic Secret* (ET, Cambridge, 1971).

[8] Ibid., 105. On the same page, Wrede mentions the scene at Mark 14: 29 ff., where Peter and all the other disciples protest their constancy in the teeth of Jesus' prophecy of their defection. This, he admits, is not an example of misunderstanding, but the scene is nevertheless unfavourable to the disciples, because the reader knows that Jesus will be proved right in his prophecy and that the disciples' words therefore are 'foolish deception, not to say bravado. There could be a similar idea in 10: 39,' Wrede adds, but then takes it away, 'but this is hardly very likely.'

[9] *The Problem of History in Mark* (London, 1957), 52.

[10] 'The Blindness of the disciples in Mark', *JBL* 80 (1961), 261–8.

[11] *The Formation of the Gospel of Mark* (London, 1963), 129 f.

lels is the only argument Trocmé offers for the view that James and
John are 'treated harshly' by Mark in this passage. But Matthew's version makes James and John fully a party to their mother's request on
their behalf, as 20: 22 shows, where Jesus addresses the sons over the
mother's head, with the same words as in Mark—the only element of
harshness in the passage. In fact, Matthew is happy to retain the episode in his Gospel with only slight modifications, precisely because it
does not defame unduly the sons of Zebedee, or leave them in permanent and culpable blindness. As for Luke's omission, is it plausible to
hold that he found this pericope too harsh for inclusion, but not 9: 51–
5, where James and John appear to think they have the power to incen-
diarize inhospitable Samaritan villages and need only Jesus' permission
to activate it?

The most dedicated exponent of the theory of Mark's anti-hierarchi-
cal bias is T. J. Weeden. He refers frequently to our passage, conflating
the incident with the teaching on true greatness and conveniently
ignoring vv. 39–41. For example, 'James and John importune Jesus for
the right to hold the highest positions in his glory (10: 35–7). Jesus rejects their request and in the ensuing discussion suggests that the
disciples have an entirely erroneous attitude toward discipleship.'[12]
Less immoderately, H. C. Kee interprets the passage in the same way:
'The sons of Zebedee perceive that Jesus is to play a central role in the
eschatological plan of God (10: 37), but they wrongly regard association with him as providing them places of favour and special privilege
in the new age, a confidence which Jesus tells them is *not only unwarranted
but wholly out of place.*'[13]

These examples are sufficient perhaps to illustrate the way redaction-
criticism has tended to ignore the details of Mark 10: 35–40 and to treat
it as a simple case of blindness, which Jesus equally simply rebukes.
When the text is examined closely and checked against these redaction-
critical assessments, they appear quite unconvincing. The first half of
the pericope *might* be taken their way, but the development of the dialogue in vv. 39–40, and—even more important, redactionally—the
Marcan transition to the next paragraph (v. 41) is such a serious challenge to the consistency of the Marcan redaction that we must either
admit that the evangelist has mistaken the drift of his material and
carelessly incorporated it into his Gospel, that is, we must hand the passage back to the tradition-historians, or else we have to say that we
have not yet properly discerned the significance which Mark saw in the
request for places in Jesus' glory or in Jesus' denial of his right to allo-

---

[12] *Mark–Traditions in Conflict* (Philadelphia, 1971), 62.
[13] *Community of the New Age* (London, 1977), 116 (my emphasis).

cate them. In other words, recent redaction-critics inadvertently high-light the difficulty with which I began, Mark's apparent failure here to correct or redefine the concept of glory at 10: 37.

Form-critics have analysed our pericope in several different ways. M. Dibelius held that an original paradigm consisting of vv. 35–7 followed immediately by either v. 41 or v. 42 was later added to with vv. 38–50 in recognition of the martyrdom of James and John.[14] There are several obvious difficulties with Dibelius's view. The request as it stands in v. 37 refers to places of honour in future glory, but the reply concerns positions of authority in the Church before the Parousia. If vv. 38–40 were added *after* the martyrdom of James[15] as a *vaticinium ex eventu*, there would be no reason for Jesus to be coy about prophesying their reward in v. 40. Finally, Dibelius is unclear whether he thinks the paradigm was originally free of reference to two named disciples, and that this biographical interest, foreign to a pure paradigm, was added secondarily. But it is vital to be clear about this, for it is the presence of the names of James and John in the original paradigm which alone can explain the addition of the vaticinium. One sympathizes, however, with Dibelius's dilemma. For if the names are to be included, so also must v. 41, the result of which is to leave an inconsequential dialogue element without explanation in terms of form.

R. Bultmann's view is that an original apophthegm, of the scholastic type, consisted of vv. 35–7 followed by v. 40.[16] The intervening verses are explained in the same way as Dibelius. This avoids the first two objections mentioned above. But it still leaves Bultmann undecided as to the inclusion or omission of the names, and it creates an even greater difficulty. On his view, the whole point of the pericope is the final word of Jesus in v. 40. But to fulfil that function, v. 40 would need to be unequivocal. In what kind of *Sitz-im-Leben* would an ambiguous and in-decisive apophthegm, such as Bultmann reconstructs, have circulated?

Recently, R. Pesch has argued for an original *Bittgespräch*, consisting of vv. 35–8 alone; vv. 39–40 were then added later, after the death of James.[17] The earliest form ends with Jesus' counter-question to James and John, 'Are you able to drink my cup and be baptized with my baptism?' Bultmann himself usually claimed that such dialogues as these end with a counter-question silencing further enquiry. He held back from it in this instance, because he had decided that v. 38 was part of the vaticinium. Pesch, more true than Bultmann to a Bultmannian

---

[14] *From Tradition to Gospel* (ET, London, 1934), 60.
[15] There is no evidence, apart from this passage, for an early martyrdom of John.
[16] *The History of the Synoptic Tradition* (ET, Oxford, 1963), 68.
[17] *Das Markusevangelium (HThK)* (Freiberg, 1977), ad loc.

analysis, claims that v. 38 concludes the discussion. But, surely, it cannot funtion in that way. It would not have been at all obvious in early Christian circles, participating through the Eucharist in the blood of Christ and incorporated through baptism into his death, that cup and baptism were the exclusive and incommunicable property of Jesus alone. According to Pesch, vv. 39–40 have been added later. He accounts for the difficulty mentioned above of including v. 40 in a vaticinium after the death of James in a novel way. These verses, he claims, were added, not in a traditional circle which wanted to cele-brate his glorious martyrdom, but in one which, on the contrary, wanted to distance itself from the claims to privilege made by or on be-half of the sons of Zebedee. Pesch becomes somewhat reticent here and refuses to speculate further. 'We cannot now know whether the motive of the insertion was to counteract the ascendency of the authority of John in the Church after the death of his brother.'[18] This is an interest-ing suggestion but it flies in the face of the little evidence we do have. If John 21: 22 f. alludes to the view, not shared by the final editor of the Gospel, that the son of Zebedee deserved the highest position of auth-ority, then the basis for such a claim was not at all association with the martyrdom of his brother, but, in contrast to Peter, escape from a martyr's fate and survival till the Parousia.

These form-critical approaches to our passage, which explain the second half of it as a later addition, are, for the various reasons given, unsatisfactory. They have, however, served to emphasize the ambi-guity of the reference to glory at 10: 37. Thus, we are forced back to the view, implied by the logic of the dialogue form itself, that the pericope is unitary in character. Whether this unity is the result largely of his-torical reminiscence or of consistent *Gemeindebildung* is a question I leave open.

The grammatical problem at v. 40 is basically as follows. Two different contrasts are confused in the two halves of the verse as commonly inter-preted: the contrast between Jesus and the Father, and the contrast between James and John and the other possible candidates for places on Jesus' right and left. Secondary textual variants have attempted to cope with this confusion in different ways. A number of MSS introduce an explicit reference to the Father, just as Matthew in the parallel (20: 23) has done. The contrast between ἐμόν and ὑπό or παρὰ τοῦ Πατρός, although not symmetrical in expression, provides at least the required balance in terms of thought. Alternatively, some ancient versions have tried to bring out the other contrast between the recipients of places,

[18] Ibid., 159.

construing ἀλλ' οἷς as ἄλλοις. The old Latin *k* has added a balancing *vobis* in the first clause. But asyndeton of this abrupt kind is less acceptable in Greek than in other languages.[19] The solution which I propose to this problem is that we should complete the missing element in the second clause in the way already implied by the emphatic ἐμόν in the first, and translate as follows: 'The authority to grant places on my right and left does not belong to me, but to those who have been prepared (sc. by God) to do so.' On this reading, the reference, though cryptic, is undoubtedly, in the context of Mark's Gospel, to the execution party at the cross, who, fulfilling divine preparation, dispose the places on the right and left of the crucified Christ.

In favour of this unusual interpretation I urge the following points.

(*a*) Mark has positioned our passage immediately after his third Passion prediction (10: 32–4) which alone of the three specifies the agents in the Crucifixion story, and in particular the Gentile soldiers who are to mock, spit at, and scourge Jesus before they execute him.

(*b*) The only other place in Mark's Gospel where the right and left hand places next to Jesus are mentioned is 15: 27, the Crucifixion scene. Whether or not we read the appeal to fulfilment of Scripture at 15: 28, the whole section already bristles with elements of prophecy-fulfilment in regard to the soldiers' actions and also to the motif of the kingship of Jesus, paradoxically revealed in suffering.

(*c*) The verb 'to prepare' used at 10: 40 is more appropriately applied to personal agents than to the seats of glory. It is the table at a banquet which requires preparation, not so much the seats; they simply need to be allocated! Personal agents who have a predestined role, especially those like soldiers and brides who need to be dressed for their part, may well be spoken of as 'prepared' (compare Rev. 8: 6; 7 and 15: 1).

(*d*) The verb 'to sit' is not inappropriately extended in reference to crucifixion; the small wooden peg on which a victim supported himself was known technically as the *sedile* or seat.[20]

(*e*) Finally, it is possible, given Luke 22: 24, where the dispute about greatness appears in the context of the Last Supper, that our pericope originally circulated in a Passion context in the early Church. The reference to the cup at 10: 38, in particular, should be seen alongside similar allusions in the Passion. Although he has resited the material,

[19] Another solution to the grammatical problem is proposed by M. Black, *An Aramaic Approach to the Gospels and Acts* (Oxford, 3rd edn., 1967), 114, based on a supposed mistranslation from Aramaic. He renders: 'To sit on the right and the left is not for me to grant *except* to those for whom it has been prepared.' Even supposing Black is right, we should still need to ask what Mark meant by the Greek he wrote.

[20] See M. Hengel, *Crucifixion* (ET, London, 1977), 25.

on this view, Mark does not thereby intend to underplay its paschal connotations.

If Mark intends his Christian readers to interpret v. 40 in the light of the crosses next to Jesus' own in the Passion narrative, then perhaps already at v. 37 'glory' is conceived in a paradoxical sense by the evangelist. His tradition may have spoken more straightforwardly of places in a Kingdom, as Matthew 20: 21 still does, but Mark introduces the word glory here, willing—surprisingly—to predicate it of Jesus directly, because he has in mind that special demonstration of the divine radiance which is peculiarly the possession of Jesus, revealed in his cross. Thus, it would not have been necessary for Mark to correct the misunderstanding of glory implied in the question. He takes it for granted that James and John know what baptism and cup mean, and by the time the dialogue reaches its conclusion in v. 40 they will have been told, albeit in a riddle, what seats of glory on the right and left really mean. Consistently, Mark is able to reserve a stronger rebuke in the next section for the other disciples.

As Humpty Dumpty would say: 'There's glory for you!' These observations certainly do not constitute a knock-down argument, but they point towards a solution of the unresolved difficulties of Mark 10: 35–40 with which redaction- and form-criticism are still wrestling; they offer a smoother, more natural reading of the grammar at v. 40; and they explain why Mark allows himself in just one instance at 10: 37 to refer to the glory of Jesus.

Mark makes glory mean just what he chooses, neither more nor less. Is his user's meaning of the word, frankly, incomprehensible—a case of 'impenetrability'—a word working overtime and paid extra? Or is there enough evidence in other early Christian writings for the paradox of glory in humiliation to bring the user's meaning into sufficient proximity to the public meaning to permit genuine communication?[21] St Paul, at least, would have understood him:

We impart a secret and hidden wisdom of God, which God decreed before the ages for our glorification. None of the rulers of this age understood it, for if they had they would not have crucified the Lord of glory. (1 Cor. 2: 7 f.)

[21] D. Hill, 'The Request of Zebedee's sons and the Johannine DOXA theme', *NTS*, 13 (1966–7), 281–5, hints at a similar thesis to mine. But while only Mark 10: 38–9, to which he draws attention, and not also v. 40, are included in the Marcan redefinition of glory, the similarity to the developed Johannine theme is not close.

5. 'What Doest Thou Here, Elijah?'
A Look at St Mark's Account of the Transfiguration

MORNA D. HOOKER

'THE Transfiguration is at once the commentator's paradise and his despair.' It was with these words that George Caird introduced a study of the narratives of the Transfiguration[1] in which he explored some of the ideas he had already hinted at in his unpublished Oxford D. Phil thesis on 'The New Testament Concept of Doxa'. Finding myself—as often—in fundamental agreement with his approach, though questioning some of his conclusions, it seems a fitting theme on which to offer this essay in his memory, in gratitude for the many happy and often stimulating hours we spent together, trying to hammer out the meaning of New Testament texts.

Mark's account of the Transfiguration begins with an intriguing and unusual reference to time: it took place 'after six days'. The only parallel in Mark to this precise dating is found at 14: 1, while Luke, whom one might have expected to be precise, has the vague 'after about eight days'. But six days after what? After Peter's declaration that Jesus is the Messiah (8: 29)? After Jesus' own prediction of his death and resurrection (8: 31)? Or after the affirmations about the coming of the Son of man and the Kingdom of God (8: 38 and 9: 1)? There are obvious links between the story of the Transfiguration and all three of these themes. The declaration in 9: 7 appears to be a divine confirmation of Peter's 'confession' in 8: 29—for though the heavenly voice addresses Jesus as 'Son', while Peter called him 'Messiah', the two terms stand together, rather than over against each other (compare 14: 61). The theme of suffering (8: 31) is taken up again immediately after the story of the Transfiguration, when Jesus warns his disciples to tell no one what they have seen, until the Son of man has risen from the dead (9: 9). This particular demand for secrecy suggests that the vision which the disciples have shared is of the glory which belongs to Jesus after the resurrection; this would mean that Mark intends us to see the Transfiguration as a confirmation not only of Jesus' messianic status, but of the necessity of the way of suffering, death, and resurrection which lie before him.[2] The story itself is often interpreted as a fulfilment (or a foretaste) of the

[1] G. B. Caird, 'The Transfiguration', *ET* 67 (1956), 291–4.
[2] Caird, op. cit., 291.

promise in 9: 1 about the coming Kingdom of God; but it seems more likely that Mark sees it as a prefigurement of 8: 38, which speaks of the future glory of the Son of man.[3]

The opening words of the story thus bind it closely to its context, and it is doubtful whether we need to choose between these three themes, for they belong together. But the words may well be intended to link the story with an incident quite outside the Marcan narrative altogether. In Exod. 24: 16, we read how Moses went up Mount Sinai, and how 'the glory of the Lord rested upon Mount Sinai, and the cloud covered the mountain for six days; on the seventh day he called to Moses out of the cloud'. The parallels, of course, are not exact, but if we find further echoes of the Exodus story in Mark's narrative, we shall be justified in assuming that Mark intends these opening words as a pointer to that story.[4]

Moses was accompanied by Joshua, who later succeeded him; Jesus takes three of his disciples with him—those who, in Mark's account, are closest to him—and goes up a 'high mountain'. The traditional site of the Transfiguration is Mount Tabor, which is hardly a high mountain, but the exact location is unimportant, for the mountain is the place of worship, the place of revelation, perhaps also the new Sinai of the messianic era. The statement that Jesus 'was transfigured before them' reminds us of the gulf between him and his disciples: he is revealed as sharing in God's glory, while they are the witnesses to his glory. Unlike Matthew, who refers to Jesus' face shining like the sun (Matt. 17: 2)[5] Mark does not explain in what way Jesus himself was transfigured: he refers only to the transformation of his clothes, which became whiter than any earthly whiteness. The whiteness of garments often features in apocalyptic writings which attempt to describe heavenly scenes,[6] and Mark himself describes the young man in the tomb on Easter Day as wearing white—a hint, perhaps, that he is a heavenly being. Jesus' garments are described also as 'glistening' ($\sigma\tau\iota\lambda\beta o\nu\tau\alpha$)—a word used only here in the New Testament—presumably with the reflection of heavenly radiance. The verb $\mu\epsilon\tau\alpha\mu o\rho\phi o\hat{\upsilon}\nu$ itself is an interesting one, used in the New Testament only in this story (by Mark and Matthew), in Rom. 12: 2 and in 2 Cor. 3: 18; this last passage is of particular interest to us, since it refers to Christians who with unveiled faces see (or reflect) the glory of the Lord, and are transformed into the same image,

---

[3] G. H. Boobyer, *St Mark and the Transfiguration Story* (Edinburgh, 1942), 58–61. Cf. Matt. 16: 28, which interprets the saying found in Mark 9: 1 as a reference to the coming of the Son of man.

[4] The link is made by many commentators; see, e.g. H. Anderson, *The Gospel of Mark* (London, 1976), ad loc.

[5] Exod. 34: 29 f. refers to the skin of Moses' face shining.

[6] e.g. Dan. 7: 9.

from glory to glory. This statement forms the climax of a section in which Paul has demonstrated the superiority of Christ over Moses by expounding the story related in Exod. 34 of Moses' descent from Sinai, his face aglow with the reflection of divine glory: Paul contrasts the glory which faded from Moses' face with the lasting glory of Christ. There is no necessary direct link between 2 Corinthians and Mark 9, but Mark's narrative may well have been influenced by the tradition about Moses.

The disciples see two figures talking with Jesus, and these are identified as 'Elijah with Moses'. Why should these two individuals have been present with Jesus? The traditional answer has been that they represent the Law and the Prophets: the choice of Moses to represent the Law is obvious, and Elijah is the first major prophet in the books known as 'the former prophets' in the Hebrew Scriptures. Now Matthew and Luke may well have interpreted the scene along these lines, for they have 'corrected' Mark's account and refer, as is natural, to 'Moses and Elijah', but Mark's enigmatic phrase, 'Elijah with Moses', which suggests that Moses is playing a secondary role, hardly supports this interpretation. Is there an alternative explanation of the presence of these two figures? Perhaps they were seen as suitable companions for Jesus because they both suffered on account of their faithfulness (a theme taken up in vv. 12–13): like those disciples who are prepared to follow Jesus' path of suffering, they share in his glory (8: 34–8).[7] Another link between Elijah and Moses, and one that is clearly relevant to the Transfiguration, is the fact that both of them experienced theophanies on mountains. Or again, Elijah was said to have been carried up into heaven, and was therefore one of the few people who did not 'taste death' (9: 1), and according to Jewish tradition Moses had shared a similar experience.[8] But none of these explanations of the presence of these two figures solves the riddle of Mark's phrase: why is Elijah mentioned first, when Moses was the earlier, and always remained the more significant figure in Judaism?

The explanation may well lie in the context of Mark's own narrative. The returning Elijah certainly played a part in Jewish eschatological expectation, and this tradition was already known in the first century AD, since it goes back to Malachi 3 and 4. Mark himself makes clear use of this tradition: immediately following the Transfiguration, we have the conversation between Jesus and the three disciples, in which they

[7] M. D. Hooker, *The Son of Man in Mark* (London and Montreal, 1967), 127 f.

[8] So M. E. Thrall, 'Elijah and Moses in Mark's account of the Transfiguration', *NTS* 16 (1970), 305–17; this explanation leaves us wondering why Enoch was not also present on the mountain.

ask him about the coming of Elijah, and Jesus affirms that Elijah has already come. The returning Elijah is here identified with John the Baptist, who is presented once again in the role which he regularly occupies in Mark's Gospel, as the messenger who points forward to the one who follows him, who is greater than he. But Elijah appears also in the complex of material immediately preceding the Transfiguration. Here, it is Jesus who puts the questions: asked to say what men think of him, the disciples reply that they assume him to be John the Baptist, or Elijah, or one of the prophets (8: 28): the same three suggestions have already appeared earlier in the Gospel, in the account of John's death, at 6: 14 f. It is clear that Mark intends his readers to reject these answers as wrong: John the Baptist has not been raised from the dead; Jesus is not the returning Elijah who prepares the way of the Lord—we know already from the opening verses of the Gospel what will be affirmed in 9: 13, that this is John's role; nor is Jesus 'one of the prophets'—a phrase to which we must return. Mark has thus tied the story of the Transfiguration into the popular hope for Elijah's return—a hope which he sees fulfilled in John the Baptist, who is the herald of Christ's coming. It is, then, not so strange after all that Elijah is present on the mountain, and that he is mentioned first.

But if Elijah is present as Jesus' forerunner—as the one who prepares his way and witnesses to his superiority—why is Moses there? Moses was not expected to return before the Day of the Lord.[9] In explaining why Elijah is mentioned first, we seem to have reduced Moses to the status of a mere hanger-on. At this point we need to return to the story of Caesarea Philippi, and to the third of the answers given to the question 'Who is Jesus?' He is, it is suggested, 'one of the prophets'. Like the previous two suggestions, this seems to indicate a figure returning from the past—an idea which is spelt out in Luke's version of the story, where this third suggestion is that 'one of the prophets of old has arisen'. In contrast to these assumptions, we have Peter's declaration that Jesus is the Christ, a new and unique figure, not one returning from the past. But the reply given in the earlier section of Mark, at 6: 15, varies slightly: here the third suggestion is that Jesus is a prophet in the succession of prophets, rather than one of the prophets returning from the dead. Mark's phrase may well be a deliberate echo of Deut. 18: 15, where Moses promises Israel that God will raise up another prophet like himself, in which case the speculation is that Jesus is this 'new Moses', the prophet whom God has promised to send to lead his people. But this suggestion is attributed, like the others, to popular

[9] It is sometimes suggested that some such expectation had already arisen, but the evidence is all very late.

rumour, and if Mark is indeed referring to 'the prophet' rather than to 'a prophet' in 6: 15, he presumably considers this judgement to be as inadequate as those given in 8: 28. The belief that Jesus is a prophet—whether old or new, whether the returning Elijah or the prophet like Moses—even though it springs from a desire to honour Jesus, is mistaken.

In two earlier scenes, then, Mark has already contrasted a false understanding of Jesus—that he is John, Elijah, or one of the prophets—with the truth, as yet only partially grasped. Elijah and Moses belong to the group of God's messengers who are most worthy of honour—yet Jesus is greater than they. It seems as though the traditional interpretation may have been mistaken in suggesting that Moses represents the Law and Elijah the prophets. Moses is as much a representative of the prophets as is Elijah: indeed, in Jewish thought Moses is the prophet *par excellence*, and none of his successors has lived up to him.[10] We must return to the question of the exact function of Elijah and Moses in Mark's story when we have looked at the rest of the narrative; for the moment, we note that their presence on the mountain could have something to do with Mark's belief that Jesus is *not* to be identified either with Elijah or with one of the prophets, and that they thus play a negative role.

Elijah and Moses converse with Jesus. It is only Luke who tells us the topic of their conversation—'his exodus, which he was to fulfil in Jerusalem' (Luke 9: 31). By using the unusual word ἔξοδος, Luke not only links the Transfiguration with Jesus' death, but points to a very positive and significant interpretation of that death. It is notable, too, that Luke twice (vv. 31, 32) uses the word δόξα, which is picked up in the words of the risen Christ on the way to Emmaus in 24: 26: 'Was it not necessary that the Christ should suffer these things and enter into his glory?' It looks very much as if Luke has understood the glory of Jesus at the Transfiguration as a 'preview' of the glory he obtains through suffering. Luke, however, has no reference to the conversation between Jesus and his disciples on the way down from the mountain, in which Jesus links what they have seen with his Resurrection, and then underlines the necessity for suffering. In this scene, Mark and Matthew make a link between the Transfiguration and Jesus' future exaltation similar to that made by Luke, even though the conversation they depict is different from Luke's, as is their terminology. For all three evangelists, the link with future suffering and vindication is part of their understanding of the event.

Peter's contribution is recorded by all the evangelists, and Luke

[10] Cf. Hos. 12: 14 (13); Deut. 34: 10.

agrees with Mark that he spoke without understanding. In Mark, he addresses Jesus as 'Rabbi'—a term used for Jesus elsewhere in this Gospel, but reading strangely so soon after Caesarea Philippi. Has Mark used it deliberately, to indicate the inadequacy of Peter's understanding of Jesus? In spite of his 'confession' of Jesus as the Christ, he is thinking of him still on the level of a mere teacher; however honourable the title 'rabbi' may be, it is clearly not a sufficiently exalted form of address.[11] Peter suggests building three σκηναί—tents or booths. His error is often said to be that he is premature; ignoring the predictions of suffering and death, he assumes that the End has already come—the eschatological period which will be symbolized by the people living once again in booths, like those used in the wilderness.[12] But the σκηναί Peter offers to build are for Jesus, Moses, and Elijah, not for the people in general, or even for the disciples themselves: why do they alone need booths? An alternative explanation is that Peter's mistake is that he ranks Jesus with Moses and Elijah: he thinks that he is honouring Jesus in treating him on a par with the great figures of old, and has failed to grasp that he is greater than they.[13] This solution fits the context, but fails to explain why Peter should suppose that building booths was an appropriate way of showing honour. At this point we need to consider the possible significance of these booths.

The term σκηνή is used in the LXX in a variety of ways. Its most common use is as a translation of the Hebrew אֹהֶל, meaning 'tent'—usually referring to an ordinary dwelling, but occasionally to the 'tent of meeting'. This latter structure is also termed מִשְׁכָּן in Hebrew—literally 'dwelling-place'—once again translated by σκηνή in the LXX, and usually referred to in English as the 'tabernacle'. Thirdly, σκηνή is used to translate the Hebrew סֻכָּה, which means some kind of matted construction. The plural was regularly used of the structures erected at the Feast of Tabernacles or Booths. Although these were made of plaited branches, and were used in the fields at harvest time, the explanation given to them in Leviticus linked them with the dwellings of the nomad period, which were no doubt tents (Lev. 23: 42 f., where סֻכֹּת = σκηναί is used in both verses): a custom belonging to the agrarian society is explained and justified by appeal to the wilderness experience, even though tents and booths were very different structures. This means that though Peter must be understood to be referring to 'booths'

[11] Luke, similarly, uses the word ἐπιστάτα, a vocative form which occurs regularly in his Gospel; the term indicates one who has authority of some kind. Matthew prefers the term κύριε, which is capable of bearing much more meaning than the simple polite 'sir'.

[12] So Boobyer, op. cit. n. 3 above, 76–9.

[13] R. H. Lightfoot, *The Gospel Message of St Mark* (Oxford, 1950), 43 f.

of branches, since the disciples will hardly have come equipped with camping gear, the term σκηναί can be assumed to evoke a whole range of ideas. Just as a Renaissance painter saw nothing incongruous in painting the Annunciation against a fifteenth-century Italian land-scape, so first-century Jews apparently saw no problem in portraying the tents of the wilderness period as 'booths'.

Was it then the Feast of Tabernacles, and was this why Peter wished to construct appropriate shelters for Elijah, Moses, and Jesus?[14] If so, the festival has left no other mark on the narrative—and we are again left wondering why the disciples do not plan to build booths for them-selves. Similar objections apply, as we have already seen, to the sugges-tion that the disciples might be thought to be assuming that the eschatological Feast of Tabernacles had arrived.[15] Moreover, the idea that the End was visualized as a perpetual celebration of Tabernacles has not been substantiated.[16] Professor Caird found the explanation of the term σκηναί in another of its Old Testament uses: 'The idea of the tabernacles was drawn from the story of Israel's sojourn in the wilder-ness where the tabernacle had been the shrine of the Divine glory, and Peter was proposing to build the tabernacles for three such manifes-tations of God's presence'.[17] But though both the Hebrew אֹהֶל and מִשְׁכָּן and the Greek σκηνή are used of God's tabernacle, and though Moses at least was understood to be a mediator of God's glory, Peter does not suggest building three tabernacles for the 'manifestations of God's presence': he suggests building them for Moses, Elijah, and Jesus themselves. It is true that Peter's intervention is ignored, presumably because it was considered inappropriate: but to identify the dwellings of God's glory as in any sense belonging to mere humans would surely have been unthinkable rather than merely inappropriate; such a taber-nacle could only have been for God himself.[18]

Why then should Peter wish to erect booths? Perhaps the explana-tion is basically more simple. After all, if unexpected visitors drop in, one feels obliged to entertain them in some way, to invite them in and offer them hospitality. Without house or even tent to throw open, how could the disciples show proper respect, except by building some kind of temporary shelter? And indeed, what more appropriate dwelling for

---

[14] H. Riesenfeld, *Jésus Transfiguré* (Copenhagen, 1947).

[15] This suggestion seems to have been first made by E. Lohmeyer, in 'Die Verklärung Jesu nach dem Markus-Evangelium', *ZNW* 21 (1922), 185–215.

[16] The 'promise' in Hos. 12: 10 (9) that Israel will again live in booths refers to her future punishment; Zech. 14: 16–19 is concerned with the yearly celebration of the festival.

[17] Op. cit. n. 1 above, 292. Cf. U. W. Mauser, *Christ in the Wilderness* (London, 1963), 113 f.

[18] Cf. Exod. 40: 35, where Moses is not allowed to enter the Tabernacle, because the glory of the Lord fills it.

these men of the desert than σκηναί?[19] If Jesus is included, perhaps that is because the disciples have seen him transfigured, and now realize that he belongs in the company of Moses and Elijah, as worthy of honour as they. If they require three tents rather than one, that is because the idea of 'each man in his tent' is the norm.

Peter's suggestion is foolish for three reasons. Firstly, because Moses and Elijah are not here to stay: in a few moments the disciples will see 'no-one, except Jesus'. Secondly, the reason why they are not here to stay is that, in different ways, they are Jesus' predecessors. The role of Elijah has been played out by the Baptist, whose task in all the Gospels is to act as a witness to Jesus, a sign-post who points the way to the one who follows him. Moses, also—astonishingly—is a witness to Jesus, since Jesus is the fulfilment of what was written by 'Moses and all the prophets'; the phrase is Luke's, but the belief is again common to all the evangelists. But this means, thirdly, that Moses and Elijah are in no way Jesus' equals—the truth half-grasped by the disciples at Caesarea Philippi. Moses, the greatest figure in Judaism, and Elijah, the prophet of the last days, fade from the picture as the heavenly voice draws the disciples' attention to Jesus alone: 'This is my beloved Son; hear him'. Jesus is not simply 'John the Baptist or Elijah or one of the prophets', but greater than all who came before him.

Mark attributes Peter's response to the disciples' fear—the common reaction of men and women to manifestations of God's power at work in Jesus.[20] The next verse contains further echoes of the story of Moses, to whom God spoke from the cloud which covered the mountain (Exod. 24: 15 f.; 34: 5). The words attributed to the voice also echo Deut. 18: 15, another incident concerning Moses, where he commands the people to hear the prophet whom God will raise in his place. Is Jesus here being identified with that prophet? We have already argued that Mark found that an inadequate understanding of Jesus. Moreover, what we have in the Transfiguration story is far more than one prophet commanding obedience to his successor:[21] it is the voice of God himself, commanding obedience, not to a prophet but to his Son. The combination of reflected radiance, cloud, and voice indicate that the story is to be understood as a theophany, and in this context the frequent demands in the Old Testament to hear and obey the words of God himself are more significant than the injunction to hear one particular prophet. If prophets could declare 'the word of the Lord' to his people, how much more the one who is now identified as God's beloved Son?

[19] Cf. J. Ziesler, 'The Transfiguration Story and the Markan Soteriology', *ET* 81 (1970), 263–8.

[20] Cf. Mark 4: 41; 5: 15, 33; 6: 50; 16: 8. [21] *Contra* J. Ziesler, op. cit., 267.

There is of course another important parallel with the words spoken from heaven, in the similar declaration addressed to Jesus himself earlier in the story at the Baptism. If Mark repeats the words in almost the same form, that is hardly surprising: a heavenly revelation may be relied on to remain constant. But presumably he expected his readers to remember that earlier occasion;[22] we must therefore ask what light this first story may be able to throw onto the second.

The words spoken from heaven in Mark 1: 11 form the climax of Mark's opening paragraphs. He begins by telling us that the coming of John fulfilled the prophecies that God would send a messenger to 'prepare the way of the Lord'. The description of John as a man of the wilderness, wearing camel's hair and leather girdle, and eating locusts and wild honey, suggests that he is seen as the returning Elijah. John's only function in Mark is to point the way to the one who follows him: he appears in the wilderness, to prepare the way of the Lord by preaching a baptism of repentance for the forgiveness of sins; his only message is about the one who follows him. Three times he stresses the superiority of this coming one, who is mightier than John, whose sandals John is unworthy to untie, who will baptize with Holy Spirit instead of water. John's words are followed by the arrival of Jesus on the scene, and the heavenly declaration that he is God's Son. John's function here is precisely, but far more explicitly, that of Elijah in 9: 2–13: he is Jesus' forerunner, whose task is to bear witness to him, and who must fade from the scene when his task is done; in 1: 14 he is put into prison—and 'they did to him whatever they pleased, as it is written of him' (9: 13). If the disciples, on the Mount of Transfiguration, are privileged to glimpse the glory of Jesus, and hear the proclamation of his identity, it is hardly surprising if they also glimpse Elijah, and have John's true identity explained to them.

The parallel story of the baptism thus spells out the role of John, and provides us with good reasons for the presence of Elijah on the Mount of Transfiguration, but does nothing to explain Moses' presence. We have already discovered a negative role for Elijah and Moses—their presence confirms that Jesus is not to be identified with Elijah (nor, as the ensuing conversation makes plain, with John, since he is Elijah), nor even with Moses, the greatest of the prophets (and clearly for Mark it is inconceivable that he should be a lesser prophet than Moses). But does Moses have a positive role, like that of John alias Elijah, who is the forerunner and witness to Jesus?

The conversation between Jesus and his disciples on the way down from the mountain has already supplied us with a clue about Elijah;

[22] Matthew apparently added the phrase ἐν ᾧ εὐδόκησα to Mark's second story, so bringing it into closer conformity with the earlier account.

does it offer us any guidance about Moses? Mark and Matthew are in close agreement in their accounts of this conversation, but there is one feature of the Marcan narrative which Matthew does not take up: in Mark, Jesus asks specifically what it is that is written concerning the Son of man, and links this with the fact that what has happened to the returning Elijah was also written concerning him. One of the puzzles which commentators have never solved is that of knowing where in the Old Testament such things could be supposed to be written, and since Mark does not single out any particular text, he may well be appealing to Scripture in general, rather than individual passages. If we were to press Mark to name his sources, then as far as the Son of man is concerned, he might appeal to the prophets, to the psalms, and to Daniel; Elijah remains a conundrum, unless the reference is to Jezebel's attempts on the first Elijah's life in 1 Kings. We thus seem to have possible leads in every area of the Hebrew Scriptures except for the Law, and may well wonder whether this is of any relevance at all to our original question about Moses. Surprisingly, the answer may well be 'yes', since elsewhere—both in the New Testament and in rabbinic writings—we find 'the Law' being used as a blanket term for Old Testament citations, even when the Pentateuch itself is not quoted;[23] on other occasions, appeal is made to 'Moses and all the prophets', where Moses is differentiated from the prophets, though they are joint witnesses.[24] In Mark 9: 12 f., where no particular reference is given, it would be natural to a first-century Jewish Christian to regard this as an appeal to 'Moses and all the prophets'. All this reminds us that Moses is the obvious figure to represent not just the Law, but everything that 'is written'. We must ask, therefore, whether Moses' role on the mountain-top may not be parallel to Elijah's. Elijah—in the person of John the Baptist—is the forerunner of Jesus, and witness to the authenticity of Christian claims about him. Moses, too, the first and greatest of God's prophets, is also a witness to those claims: the things which happen to Jesus—death and Resurrection—are the things which are 'written concerning the Son of man'. Moses, like Elijah, appears in the role of Jesus' sponsor.

But Jesus is greater than his sponsors—greater than Elijah, his forerunner, and greater even than Moses. We have no room here to explore the role of Moses in Mark's Gospel, and must be content with the observation that in various passages Jesus is depicted as appealing to the teaching of Moses (1: 44; 7: 10 ff.; 10: 3, 19; 12: 26, 29 ff.) At the same

[23] See John 10: 34; 12: 34; 15: 25; Rom. 3: 19; 1 Cor. 14: 21. In *b. Sanh.* 91b, Ps. 84: 5 (4) and Isa. 52: 8 are quoted as 'Torah'; similarly Zech. 12: 12 in *b. Sukk*, 51b.

[24] See Luke 16: 29, 31; 24: 27; John 1: 45; Acts 28: 23.

time, however, the Mosaic commands are set in the context of superior commands, which show Jesus acting with an authority greater than that of Moses: Jesus both fulfils the Law and points beyond it.[25] Like Elijah, Moses functions as a predecessor of Jesus, whose role is to witness to the one who is greater than he. It is appropriate, then, that these two witnesses to Jesus should be present on the mountain-top—Elijah, whose coming has restored all things, and Moses, whose writings bear witness to Christ.

Finally, we must ask whether this interpretation of the story helps us to understand the form of Mark's narrative. We have already seen that there are very clear echoes of the story of Moses on Mt. Sinai, but we have rejected as inadequate the suggestion that Jesus is being presented as 'the prophet like Moses'. Jesus is not simply in the tradition of the prophets, but the unique Son of God. Now there are several other passages in the New Testament where a comparison is made between Moses and Jesus, and on every occasion there are echoes of this same story about Sinai. The most obvious is perhaps 2 Corinthians 3, where the temporary glory of the old διακονία is contrasted with the permanent glory of the new, reflected from the face of Christians; the whole passage can fairly be described as a midrash of Exod. 34: 29–35, and the essential point is the superiority of Christ's ministers to Moses. How much greater, then, the glory of Christ himself, who is the image of God and the source of our glory (4: 1–6). Much more succinct—though nevertheless clear—is the allusion to Sinai in John 1: 14–18. Again, the passage is concerned with glory—the glory we have seen in Christ, the glory (as in Mark 9: 7) appropriate to one who is God's only Son.[26] Again, there is a contrast between Moses (through whom the Law was given) and Christ, who embodies grace and truth,[27] and who is (as in 2 Cor.) the source of blessing for Christians. Finally, there is Hebrews 3, where Jesus is said to be worthy of greater glory than Moses, since the one is a Son, the other a servant (3: 1–6); this contrast picks up the opening words of the book, in which we are told that God has spoken to his people in the past through the prophets, but has now spoken through a Son—'the effulgence of his glory'. It is worth noting, too, that in 2: 9, the glory and honour with which Jesus is crowned is said to be διὰ τὸ πάθημα τοῦ θανάτου. This same paradox of glory through death is the theme of 2 Cor. 4: 6 ff., where Paul spells out what it means

---

[25] Cf. the apparent paradox in Matt. 5, where vv. 17–20 introduce the antitheses of vv. 21–48.

[26] Here, too, the witness of John the Baptist is referred to (v. 15); but in this Gospel the identification of John with Elijah is denied (1: 21).

[27] Cf. M. D. Hooker, 'The Johannine Prologue and the Messianic Secret', *NTS* 21, (1974–5), 52–8.

for Christians to reflect Christ's glory. In John, this truth is so self-evident that the moment of Christ's death is spoken of as his glorification. And if we return to Mark 9, we find that there the glory seen on the mountain cannot be spoken of until the Son of man has been raised from the dead, and the prophecies of his suffering and rejection been fulfilled. Nor is this a 'fluke' in Mark, since on the rare occasions when he uses the word δόξα, he links it every time with the suffering and death of Jesus and his followers.[28]

Mark's account of the Transfiguration, then, presents in narrative form ideas found in at least three other New Testament writers—quite apart from the use made by Matthew and Luke of the story. The echoes of the story of Moses on Sinai remind us that the glory of Jesus is even greater than the glory of Moses. The story of the Transfiguration spells out the truths of the preceding paragraphs, 8: 27–9: 1. Jesus is not John, nor Elijah, nor one of the prophets, but a much greater figure—the Christ (or Son of God, cf. Mark 14: 61); his destiny is suffering and death, and those who wish to follow him must expect to share his fate; but his final destiny is glory—a glory which he will share with those who are loyal to him. It looks very much as though the enigma of the story may be largely due to the fact that we fail to realize that Mark is here presenting in dramatic form ideas which were part of the common beliefs of the early Christian communities.

[28] See Mark 8: 38; 10: 37; 13: 26.

6. The Transfiguration in the Theology of Luke: Some Redactional Links

ALLISON A. TRITES

GEORGE CAIRD's interest in the theology of Luke and in the meaning of the Transfiguration of Jesus is well known. Such concerns were more than evident in his Pelican Commentary on the Gospel of Luke and in the seminal article he contributed on the Transfiguration.[1] In paying a sincere and heartfelt tribute to his memory it is appropriate therefore that I dedicate these comments to one who was not only a great scholar but a student of Scripture in the deepest and most profound sense.

The Transfiguration of Jesus continues to be a remarkably puzzling episode in the New Testament. F. W. Beare claimed in 1962 that 'there is probably no other pericope in the Gospels which has received such divergent interpretations as the story of the Transfiguration',[2] while Walter Liefeld in 1974 found himself agreeing with Beare's assessment in saying that 'his comment is still valid today, for while recent studies have moved along newer paths, with perhaps the elimination of certain hypotheses, the total accumulation of theories has not thereby decreased'.[3]

The history of the interpretation of the Transfiguration is fascinating. Some exegetes, including Wellhausen, Loisy, Bultmann, and Carlston, have viewed the Transfiguration as a 'misplaced resurrection story'. Others such as Bernardin, Bacon, and Bradley have interpreted it symbolically, viewing it as illustrating theological ideas of the Early Church. With the development of Form Criticism, it was fashionable for a time to classify the Transfiguration and the Baptism as 'myths' or 'legends' (for instance, K. L. Schmidt and Martin Dibelius).

In the last sixty years it has been common to highlight its eschatological features, an approach developed by Lohmeyer, Boobyer, and Ramsey. And orthodox defenders, George Caird among them, have stoutly maintained the Transfiguration to be historical and credible.[4]

[1] G. B. Caird, *The Gospel of St Luke* (Harmondsworth, Middlesex, 1963) and 'The Transfiguration', *ET*, 67 (1955–6), 291–4.
[2] F. W. Beare, *The Earliest Records of Jesus* (Nashville, 1962), 141.
[3] Walter L. Liefeld, 'Theological Motifs in the Transfiguration Narrative', in *New Dimensions in New Testament Study*, ed. Richard N. Longenecker and Merrill C. Tenney (Grand Rapids, 1974), 162.
[4] Cf. also Donald Evans, 'Academic Scepticism, Spiritual Reality and Transfiguration', else-

Study of the Transfiguration, then, has followed the main lines of
modern biblical research.[5] Its primary concern has been to determine
the actual event behind the Transfiguration or to study the nature of
the pre-Marcan tradition. Until the last ten years relatively little attention has been given to the Transfiguration in its literary setting in each
of the Gospels. It is the purpose of this paper to direct attention to the
literary setting of the Transfiguration in Luke's Gospel and to observe
the way in which Luke relates the Transfiguration to other highlights
in the life of Jesus.

It is necessary first to observe the common elements in the Synoptic
accounts. Matthew, Mark, and Luke agree on the basic details (Matt.
17: 1–7; Mark 9: 2–8; Luke 9: 28–36). Jesus took Peter, James, and
John with him and went up a mountain. While they were on the mountain, a wondrous change came over Christ, and his garments became
white. Moses and Elijah entered the scene, speaking with Jesus. Peter
then commented to Jesus, 'it is well that we are here', offering subsequently to build three tents, one each for Jesus, Moses, and Elijah. A
cloud, however, overshadowed them, and a voice out of the cloud said,
'this is my (beloved) son. Listen to him.' From this point on they saw no
one with them but Jesus. On their descent from the mountain Jesus
charged them to remain silent about what they had seen (Matt. and
Mark), and they respected his directive and kept silent in those days
about what they had seen (Luke).

Luke's account of the Transfiguration appears to be based mainly on
Mark, but he introduces a number of significant changes. He dates the
incident about eight days after the previous scene, where Mark speaks
of six days, as does Matthew. Special attention is paid to Jesus in
prayer, a subject in which Luke is particularly interested.[6] Reference is
made to the alteration in Jesus' countenance, where the other synoptists speak directly of 'transfiguration'.

where in this volume, pp. 175–86. For summaries of the research see C. G. Montefiore, *The Synoptic
Gospels* (New York, 1968), i. 204–7; Eugene Dabrowski, *La Transfiguration de Jesus* (Rome, 1939),
113–15; U. Holzmeister, 'Einzeluntersuchungen über das Geheimnis der Verklärung Christi',
Bib 21 (1940), 200–10; C. H. Boobyer, *St Mark and the Transfiguration Story* (Edinburgh, 1942),
1–47; A. M. Ramsey, *The Glory of God and the Transfiguration of Christ* (London, 1949), 102–3;
Vincent Taylor, *The Gospel according to St Mark* (London, 1953), 386–8; W. Bundy, *Jesus and the
First Three Gospels: An Introduction to the Synoptic Gospels* (Cambridge, 1955), 306–9; H. Baltensweiler, *Die Verklärung Jesu* (Zürich, 1959), 11–18; R. Bultmann, *History of the Synoptic Tradition*,
trans. John Marsh (Oxford, 1963), 259–61; H. Schürmann, *Das Lukasevangelium* (Frieburg, 1969),
553, 564–7.

[5] Several doctoral students have recently taken up this challenge: P. R. Baldacci, 'The Significance of the Transfiguration Narrative in the Gospel of Luke: A Redactional Investigation' (Ph.D
dissertation, Marquette University, Milwaukee, Wisconsin, 1974); R. H. Gause, 'The Lukan
Transfiguration Account: Luke's Pre-Crucifixion Presentation of the Exalted Lord in the Glory of
the Kingdom of God (Ph.D., Emory University, Atlanta, Ga, 1975).

[6] See Allison A. Trites, 'The Prayer Motif in Luke-Acts', *Perspectives on Luke-Acts*, ed. C. H.
Talbert (Macon, Ga., 1978), 168–86.

Luke explicitly notes the 'glory' of Jesus, mentions the appearance of Moses and Elijah 'in glory', describes the conversation concerning his 'exodus', and refers to the sleepiness of the three disciples. He also mentions the fear of the disciples associated with the appearance of the cloud, employing the phrase 'behold, two men'.

How are these differences to be explained?[7] Two main lines of interpretation have been advanced. One suggests that Luke has access to another source.[8] A case for Lucan editing of Mark, on the other hand, is strong, since most of the changes and additions can be viewed as expressing Lucan motifs.[9] Thus, where Luke's text differs from Mark, the vast majority of the differences can be traced either to Lucan redaction or to Lucan composition.

J. A. Fitzmyer in his recent commentary on Luke 1–9 has attempted to identify the passages which belong to the Lucan redaction and those which belong to the Lucan composition:

To the former I should ascribe the following: 'about eight days' (9: 28) instead of Mark's 'six days later'; the *kai egeneto* constructions (9: 28, 29, 30); the *en tō* + infinitive constructions (9: 29, 33, 34, 36); the use of *kai idou* (9: 30), *kai autoi* (9: 36) and *eipen pros* (9: 33). Likewise redactional is the purpose why Jesus goes up on the mountain, 'to pray' (9: 28), and his experience during prayer (9: 29); the better Greek avoiding the connotation of Marcan metamorphosis; the substitution of 'Master' for 'Rabbi', the word order v. 33 (to him listen), and the title 'my Chosen One' (v. 35). On the other hand, to Lucan composition should be attributed vv. 30–33, 34b, 36bc.[10]

The whole problem is made exceedingly complex when we take into account the large number of minor agreements of Matthew and Luke against Mark. These differences have been carefully studied, and commentators have variously listed between fifteen and twenty agreements. Neirynck's[11] detailed assessment of the evidence, on the other hand, has led him to conclude that 'the examination of these data enlighten us

[7] Although some writers have argued that the Matthaean form of transfiguration story is the most original (e.g., Eugene Dabrowski, *La Transfiguration de Jesus*), it is clear that Luke for his part is working from the Marcan form of the tradition.

[8] e.g., T. Schramm, *Der Markus-Stoff bei Lukas* (Cambridge, 1971), 136–9 argues for the use of other source material. For a judicious assessment of the evidence see I. Howard Marshall, *The Gospel of Luke* (Exeter, 1978), 381.

[9] See Marshall, op. cit. This position was adopted by Hans Conzelmann, *The Theology of St Luke*, trans. G. Buswell (London, 1961), 57 n. 1. It has been cogently argued by Schürmann, op. cit. n. 4 above, i. 559–63 and F. Neirynck, 'Minor Agreements—Matthew-Luke in the Transfiguration Story', in *Orientierung an Jesus: Zur Theologie der Synoptiker: Für Josef Schmid*, ed. P. Hoffman *et al.* (Freiburg, 1973), 253–66.

[10] Joseph A. Fitzmyer, *The Gospel According to Luke (I–IX)*, 792. Marshall, op. cit. n. 8 above 381, cautiously opts for the *via media*: 'It may be best to assume that continuing oral traditions lie behind Luke's reworking of Mark's narrative, especially since some of his changes are shared by Matthew; a documentary source is very unlikely.'

[11] Cf. F. Neirynck, op. cit. n. 9 above.

more about the tendencies of the two gospels than about any source-critical relationship'.[12] This state of affairs suggests (a) that there is a deliberate restriction of Marcan material in both Matthew and Luke, and (b) there is an introduction of fresh material in both Gospels. It is, however, the particular contribution of Luke which is my concern here.

Luke's account of the Transfiguration is remarkable in what it omits and changes and in what it includes. These points will be considered in the order mentioned.

I. LUCAN OMISSIONS AND CHANGES

Luke makes no mention of the height of the mountain, though Mark and Matthew specifically refer to the retreat as a 'high mountain' (Luke 9: 28; Mark 9: 2; Matt. 17: 1). Apparently the topography of the locale was not of primary concern to the third evangelist. Luke, also, does not use the verb μεταμορφόω to describe the wonderful transformation that took place in the appearance of Christ, though this is the vocabulary adopted by both Mark and Matthew (μεταμορφώθη ἔμπροσθεν αὐτῶν, Mark 9: 2; Matt. 17: 2; compare Luke 9: 29). Perhaps, as some commentators have suggested, Luke was aware of the danger of confusing Jesus with some polytheistic pagan notions (compare Acts 14: 11, where Paul and Barnabas are acclaimed in Lystra as 'the gods' who 'have come down to us in human form'). Jesus is not to be identified in Luke's mind with one of the Hellenistic deities.[13] He is the unique bearer of the divine glory (Luke 9: 32; compare 2 Cor. 4: 7), and no *Religionsgeschichtliche* comparison of this type is appropriate or helpful.

Luke, unlike Mark, makes no reference to the detail that Jesus' clothes became 'whiter than anyone in the world could bleach them' (Mark 9: 3, NIV; γναφεύς is not a Lucan word, though it is used several times in the LXX: 2 Kgs. 18: 17; Isa. 7: 3; 36: 2). Luke also does not directly link the Transfiguration with the coming of Elijah, as both Mark and Matthew do (Mark 9: 9–13; Matt. 17: 9–13), preferring rather to connect it with the healing of the epileptic boy which immediately follows (Luke 9: 37–43a). In both cases the third evangelist sees a manifestation of the divine splendour revealed in Jesus. The 'glory' of God on the mountain-top is matched by the 'majesty' of God in the valley, where Christ meets human need. Interestingly, the noun μεγαλειότης which Luke uses here in 9: 43 is also employed in 2 Pet. 1: 17, where it is used to describe the Transfiguration of Christ.

[12] Ibid., 264.
[13] Marshall, op. cit., 383. Cf. also J. Behm on this point, *TDNT* 4, 755–9.

While Mark and Matthew both record the charge to silence which Jesus gave to the disciples, Luke notes the fact of their obedience (Luke 9: 36; Mark 9: 9; Matt. 17: 9). On the other hand, Luke, as does Matthew, differs from Mark in citing Moses and Elijah in chronological order (Luke 9: 30; compare Mark 9: 4; Matt. 17: 3).

Luke drops the closing mention of suddenness (ἐξάπινα, a New Testament *hapax legomenon* in Mark 9: 8), choosing to connect 'the journey inward' in prayer and meditation with 'the journey outward' in service 'on the next day' (Luke 9: 37). He sees a close and intimate connection between the two events and so perceives no need to use an adverb which would sever the one event from the other.

II. LUCAN ADDITIONS

The additions which Luke makes to the Marcan framework are equally noteworthy. Luke sets the story in a broader time frame, notes the purpose of the journey as prayer, and records the alteration in Christ's countenance which took place while he was praying. Luke alone refers to Moses and Elijah as appearing 'in glory', and he alone uses the striking phrase 'behold two men'. Other Lucan details are the reference to Christ's 'departure' (ἔξοδον, Luke 9: 31) as something to be accomplished in Jerusalem, the sleepiness of the disciples, and their arousal to see Christ's glory and the two men standing with him. Only Luke tells us that the Son was addressed as 'my Chosen' (ὁ ἐκλελεγμένος, Luke 9: 35).[14] Luke is also the sole evangelist who links the exit of Moses and Elijah with the eagerness of Peter to erect the tabernacles, and only he dates the healing of the epileptic boy 'on the next day' (Luke 9: 37).

It is clear, then, that the Lucan account of the Transfiguration is exceptionally interesting, both in its omissions and in its special features.[15] Whether Luke drew heavily upon another source in addition to Mark may be debated. What is not debatable is the fact that the Lucan pericope, however derived, dovetails to a remarkable degree with many other incidents in Luke-Acts. There seem to be many links between the Transfiguration and the other red-letter days in the life of Jesus. Some of these connecting features are worth exploring.

To begin, I call attention to the Baptism, where the heavenly voice calls Jesus 'my Son', the same description which is used at the Transfiguration (ὁ υἱός μου, Luke 3: 22; 9: 35). Jesus' sonship is affirmed at

---

[14] For a defence of this reading see Bruce M. Metzger, *A Textual Commentary on the Greek New Testament* (New York, 1971), 148.

[15] Cf. A. Feuillet, 'Les Perspectives propres à chaque Évangéliste dans le récits de la Transfiguration', *Bib* 39 (1958), 281–301.

the beginning of his public ministry by the heavenly voice; it is re-affirmed in the Transfiguration by the voice out of the cloud. Luke, as does Matthew, draws a parallel between these two incidents. He also uses the rare New Testament noun εἶδος only twice in his writings, once in describing the Baptism of Jesus and once in outlining the Trans-figuration (Luke 3: 22; 9: 29). In view of other indications which point in the same direction, it seems as if Luke is deliberately presenting his vocabulary in such a way that one event would recall the other.

The connection between the Baptism and the Temptation is particu-larly clear in Luke, where the prayer of Jesus is highlighted by the evangelist in both cases (Luke 3: 21; 9: 28, 29). Luke sees the Son of God commencing his public career in communion with God, and this relationship with the Father is renewed on frequent occasions, includ-ing the Transfiguration.[16]

The Spirit of God who descended at Jesus' Baptism was also present as he entered the Temptation. The similarity in language is quite unmistakable (καταβῆναι τὸ πνεῦμα τὸ ἅγιον, Luke 3: 22; πλήρης πνεύματος ἁγίου . . . ἤγετο ἐν τῷ πνεύματι, Luke 4:1). The recognition of Jesus' sonship had been a feature of the Baptism (Luke 3: 22); the son-ship is repeatedly mentioned in the Temptation (Luke 4: 3, 9; compare Matt. 4: 3, 6) and is reaffirmed later in the Transfiguration (Luke 9: 35). So each of these cardinal events in Luke's eyes sheds some light on the nature of Jesus' sonship. It is a relationship declared by the Father, tested in the crucible of temptation, and endorsed as the Son faces the suffering and shame of the cross.

Another literary feature which seems to link the Temptation and the Transfiguration is the reference to Jesus' 'glory' which is prominent in both pericopes. In the former scene the devil promises Jesus world-wide rule and acclaim, offering him complete authority and the 'glory' of all the kingdoms of the inhabited world (Luke 4: 5, 6); in the latter, the drowsy trio of disciples see Jesus' 'glory', noting also Moses and Elijah, who appear 'in glory' and converse with Jesus (Luke 9: 30, 31). Luke clearly contrasts the proffered devilish glory with the divine glory that was evident in Christ's 'glorification' (here one may use the common German term employed to describe the Transfiguration—*die Verk-lärung*).[17]

The use of δόξα in these passages is in close accord with other refer-

---

[16] Allison A. Trites, op. cit. n. 6 above, 168–86. Cf. Lindell O. Harris, 'Prayer in the Gospel of Luke', *SoJTh* 10 (1967), 59–69.

[17] Cf. E. Lohmeyer, 'Die Verklärung Jesu nach dem Markus-Evangelium', *ZNW* 21 (1922), 185–215; U. Holzmeister, op. cit. n. 4 above; H. Baltensweiler, op. cit. n. 4 above; H.-P. Muller, 'Die Verklärung Jesu', *ZNW* 51 (1960), 56–64.

ences to the divine glory in Luke's Gospel. The 'glory of the Lord' (2: 9) is evident in the Lucan Nativity story, the Palm Sunday account in Luke (δόξα ἐν ὑψίστοις, 19: 38; compare 2: 14, where the same phrase occurs), and the eschatological passages in Luke which look forward to the Son of Man's glorious Parousia (9: 26; 21: 27). In Luke's eyes it was part and parcel of the divine plan that the Christ must suffer and then 'enter into his glory' (Luke 24: 26). In his conception of *Heilsgeschichte* there was clearly a significant place for the glory of Jesus. In the Temptation Christ had been offered glory on the devil's terms and had refused it. Later he would enter the ultimate divine splendour promised to the mysterious Son of man. In the Transfiguration the privileged disciples saw a proleptic anticipation of the transcendent glory which was to be Christ's after his Resurrection and exaltation to the place of supreme majesty in the Father's presence. In other words, the Lucan redaction so skilfully presents the interconnections of these passages that their intrinsic relationship to one another may be clearly seen.

Nowhere does Luke establish a clearer redactional link between the Transfiguration and another key incident in the life of Christ than in the confession of Peter at Caesarea Philippi. Only Luke highlights the prayerfulness of Jesus on both of these occasions (προσευχόμενον κατὰ μόνας, Luke 9: 18; προσεύξαθαι . . . ἐν τῳ προσεύχεσθαι, Luke 9: 28, 29). It is also significant that the passion of Jesus figures prominently in each of these accounts, the former recording the first Passion prediction and the latter noting that the conversation of Jesus with the heavenly visitors was about the 'exodus' which he was going to accomplish in Jerusalem (Luke 9: 22, 31). While the other synoptists cite the first Passion prediction, they make no reference to the exodus theme. According to Luke, the 'Christ of God' confessed by Peter is also the one who appears 'in glory' a few days later (Luke 9: 20, 31; compare 9: 32). There is a certain numinous quality that surrounds both of these events. The disciples are sternly forbidden to disclose Jesus' true identity at the time of Peter's remarkable confession of faith (Luke 9: 21), and they act in the same fashion after the Transfiguration, telling 'no one at that time what they had seen' (Luke 9: 36).

There are also some ties which bind together Luke's report on the conditions of discipleship and his account of the Transfiguration. Both passages speak of the glory of the Son of man or of Jesus (ἐν τῇ δόξῃ αὐτοῦ, Luke 9: 26; εἶδαν τὴν δόξαν αὐτοῦ, Luke 9: 32). Both accounts refer to others who are 'standing' by (τινες τῶν ὧδε ἐστηκότων, Luke 9: 27; τοὺς συνεστῶτας αὐτῷ, Luke 9: 32). That Luke intends his readers to link the Transfiguration with both the first prediction of the Passion and the conditions of discipleship enunciated somewhat later is suggested by his opening of the Transfiguration account with an interesting reference to 'about eight days after these sayings' (Luke 9: 28).[18]

The Transfiguration is also quite carefully related by Luke to subsequent events in the life of Jesus. A tell-tale phrase, to which Professor Caird long ago called attention, is significant at this point: 'Behold two men!' (ἰδοὺ ἄνδρες δύο). This catchphrase appears to be a Lucan device which draws together a number of closely related events, for it appears in Luke's accounts of the Transfiguration, the Resurrection, and the Ascension (Luke 9: 30; 24: 4; Acts 1: 10; compare 2 Macc. 3: 26). This unique cross-referencing system helps us to see the importance which Luke attached to each of these items in the unfolding of his story and the development of his Christology.

But that is not all. Luke's account of Jesus in Gethsemane also is redacted in such a way as to recall the Transfiguration. Several illustrations will serve to make this point clear. The prayer motif is obvious and prominent in both cases (Luke 9: 28, 29; 22: 40, 41, 44, 45, 46). While the other synoptists mention Jesus' prayer on the Mount of Olives, they are not nearly as concerned as Luke with the parenetic dimensions of prayer (to which Wilhelm Ott has quite properly directed our attention[19]), nor do they refer to prayer in their accounts of the Transfiguration. It is characteristic of Luke as 'the evangelist of prayer'[20] to draw our attention to prayer as an abiding characteristic of the Christ he describes (note the suggestive use of κατὰ τὸ ἔθος in Luke 22: 39).

Another point is the drowsiness of the disciples on both occasions (ἦσαν βεβαρημένοι ὕπνῳ· διαγρηγορήσαντες δὲ εἶδον τὴν δόξαν αὐτοῦ, Luke 9: 32; εὗρεν κοιμωμένους αὐτοὺς ἀπὸ τῆς λύπης, Luke 22: 45). While both Matthew and Mark note that Christ actually caught the apostles napping (Matthew 26: 40, 43; Mark 4: 37, 40), they do not refer to the sleepiness of the three disciples at the Transfiguration. It is evidently only Luke who wishes to draw these two incidents together in this interesting way.

As Luke prepares his readers for the death of Jesus he uses several terms which recall the language of the Transfiguration. One such term

[18] Elsewhere I have suggested that audience criticism may help us to uncover the reason Luke uses the different time frame. See Allison A. Trites, 'The Transfiguration of Jesus: The Gospel in Microcosm', *EQ* 51 (1979), 70–2. It seems at this point that Luke 'wants to connect the Transfiguration with two incidents—namely, the Petrine confession at Caesarea Philippi and the declaration of the principles of discipleship given somewhat later. Both of these occasions were associated with memorable teaching imparted by Jesus, and Luke desires the reader to recall all of these sayings (Lk 9: 28)' (71–2).

[19] Wilhelm Ott, *Gebet und Heil: Die Bedeutung der Gebetsparänese in der lukanische Theologie* (Munich, 1965). For an excellent analysis and critique of Ott's views see Peter O'Brien, 'Prayer in Luke-Acts,' *Tynd Bul* 24 (1973), 111–27.

[20] A. Hamman, *La Prière*. i: *Le Nouveau Testament* (Tournai, 1959), 144.

is the verb ἀναβαίνω, employed to describe both the ascent on the occasion of the Transfiguration and the ascent of Jesus and his disciples to Jerusalem for the last time of his earthly life (Luke 9: 28; 18: 31; 19: 28; compare Mark 10: 32; Matt. 20: 17). Jesus 'went up' the mountain to pray in preparation for the role of suffering and death which awaited him. Jesus later 'went up' to Jerusalem, to suffer and die in obedience to the divine will. Luke appears to suggest a possible connection between these two events, though the link is too tenuous to be pressed.

The mention of 'Jerusalem' in Luke 9: 31 offers clearer evidence of Lucan redaction, and serves to bind together the Transfiguration with other incidents in the life of Jesus. Over and over again Luke portrays Jesus 'as moving toward the city where he was to meet his death (cf. 9: 51; 13: 22; 17: 11; 19: 28)'.[21]

From 9: 51 onward, Jesus is pictured *en route* to Jerusalem, the city that was always killing the prophets and stoning those who were sent to her (13: 34). The great journey to the city of destiny will take Christ to the cross, 'for it cannot be that a prophet should perish away from Jerusalem' (13: 33).

Despite Samaritan opposition, Jesus is 'heading for Jerusalem' (9: 53); he will not be deterred, although some Pharisees warn him to move to another location as Herod is bent on killing him (13: 31). He must 'fulfil' the divine plan in Jerusalem (9: 13).[22]

In other words, by the skilful use of certain key words and phrases Luke helps one to see the relation between the Transfiguration and other major events in the life of Christ, including the programmatic statement of the ministry in Nazareth and the post-Resurrection appearance at the end of his Gospel. Luke has presented us with a vital series of literary links which help his readers to see how closely he viewed all these events in the life of Christ.[23] On one memorable occa-

[21] Curtis Vaughan, 'The Established Facts of the Gospel', *SoJTh* 10 (1967), 31. On the journey motif in Luke see Frank Stagg, 'The Journey Toward Jerusalem in Luke's Gospel', *Rev Exp* 64 (1967), 499–512. Cf. also C. F. Evans, 'The Central Section of St Luke's Gospel', *Studies in the Gospels*, ed. D. E. Nineham (Oxford, 1957), 39 ff.

[22] The verb πληρόω is used here in connection with several other key events in Luke's Gospel such as the Nazareth sermon (4: 21) and the appearance of the risen Christ to the disciples which fulfils what is written of him 'in the Law of Moses, the Prophets and the Psalms' (24: 44). It is also very important in a number of places in Acts which speak of the fulfilment of the Scriptures (1: 16; 3: 18; 13: 27).

[23] R. H. Gause, op. cit. n. 5 above. Gause's exegetical study of Luke 9: 27–36 leads him to the following seven conclusions: 'Luke 9: 27 is predictive of the Transfiguration. There is a causative relationship between Jesus' praying and His Transfiguration. The glory in which Jesus is seen is the eschatological glory of the Son of man. Moses and Elijah are participants in the kingdom with the transfigured Jesus. Their discussion of Jesus' "exodus" brings together the themes of glory and suffering in Luke's kingdom presentation. The cloud is the Shekinah. The witness to Jesus uses the quasi-technical designation "chosen Son" as a witness to Jesus' divine sonship and a proclamation of His messianic kingship.' *Dissertation Abstracts International*, 36/7A (January, 1976), 4569–A.

sion Jesus weeps over this city when he recalls his repeated attempts to
woo and win her, declaring: 'I tell you, you will not see me until you
say, "Blessed is he who comes in the name of the Lord!"' (13: 35). As
the public ministry of Jesus draws to its close, Jesus steps across the
threshold of the Holy City and once again weeps over its blindness and
unbelief, predicting its fearful destruction as a consequence of divine
judgement (19: 41–4). Luke also connects the Transfiguration with the
Parousia. While all the synoptists use the same adjective to describe the
whiteness of Christ's garments (λευκός), Luke is the only evangelist to
tell us that Christ's clothing at the Transfiguration became as bright 'as
a flash of lightning' (9: 28, ἐξαστράπων). This seems to be a deliberate
attempt on Luke's part to link the Transfiguration with certain other
events, most notably the Parousia: 'For the Son of Man in his day will
be like the lightning, which flashes and lights up the sky from one end
to the other' (17: 24, NIV; note Luke uses the cognates ἀστραπή and
ἀστράπτουσα).[24] The fact that both events are associated with lightning
is intended to draw them together in the reader's mind. The mention of
lightning is also reminiscent of the mission of the seventy or seventy-
two[25] (Luke 10: 1–24), where the returning disciples report that even
the demons are subject to them in Christ's name. Christ, however, replies that 'I saw [note the imperfect tense of θεωρέω here] Satan fall like
lightning from heaven' (10: 18, where ἀστραπή is used again in an
eschatological context). Luke obviously sees a relationship between the
final victory of Christ and the first conquests of his fledgling disciples.
Similarly, the Resurrection of Christ which is depicted as his mighty
victory over death is described in tems of lightning (24: 4; ἀστράπτω
means 'flash like lightning'). The Transfiguration, too, was a foreshadowing of the ultimate victory, so it could also be described in similar terms. The reference to 'lightning' was thus a useful one for Luke's
purposes, helping to remind his readers of a number of the most important features in the life and work of Jesus.

Luke also presses into service the cloud terminology of the Bible,
thereby hinting at cross references to several other passages in his
Gospel (compare 12: 54). There are no less than three references to the
'cloud' in the Transfiguration pericope (Luke 9: 34 (twice), 35), and
there is a similar mention of a 'cloud' in an eschatological passage: 'At
that time they will see the Son of Man coming in a cloud with power
and great glory' (21: 27, NIV). What makes the latter passage striking

---

[24] The phrase 'in his day' in 17: 24 is textually questionable and is given a 'C' reading in the
United Bible Societies' Greek New Testament. Cf. Metzger, op. cit. n. 14 above, 167.

[25] Cf. B. M. Metzger, 'Seventy or Seventy-two Disciples?' in his *Historical and Literary Studies,
Pagan, Jewish, and Christian* (Leiden, 1968), 67–76.

is the fact that Luke has the singular form of the noun νεφέλη where both Mark and Matthew use the plural in the parallel passages (Luke 21: 27; Mark 13: 26; Matt. 24: 30; compare Mark 14: 62, and Matt. 26: 64, which also use the plural form). It appears that Luke has deliberately changed the plural form to the singular in order to suggest a link between the Transfiguration and the Parousia; the same link is apparent in his account of the Ascension, where once again a singular cloud is in view (Acts 1: 9). Apparently Luke intends his readers to see a close connection here among all three pivotal days in the life of Jesus. The Transfiguration, the Ascension, and the Parousia all have significant places in Luke's scheme of Holy History, and he tries to show these vital links to the attentive reader of Luke-Acts.

In a very real sense George Caird provided the agenda for this study thirty years ago. He wrote as follows:

... a satisfactory explanation of the Transfiguration must do justice to its connexion with the Baptism, Caesarea Philippi, Gethsemane, the Crucifixion, the Resurrection, the Ascension, and the Parousia; and with the persecution of the disciples and their share, present and future, in the glory of the risen and ascended Christ. Nor must we forget that, with all its associations, the Transfiguration had an importance of its own as a crisis in the life of Jesus.[26]

Our inquiry has tested Caird's observations with regard to the third Gospel, and has found them, not surprisingly, to be exegetically sound. There are other literary connections which bind the Transfiguration with the Baptism and the subsequent events mentioned by Caird—not to mention the Temptation, which he obviously did not explore for reasons of space. Thus, many other links exist which forge a bond between the Master and his disciples. Those who are summoned to share in his suffering and servanthood are also promised a place in his glory, both now and when he comes as the risen and ascended Lord.

Luke's Transfiguration, in short, fits admirably into his overall scheme of *Heilsgeschichte*. As I have said elsewhere,

it marks a vital stage in the revelation of Jesus as the Messiah and Son of God. ... It presents the gospel in microcosm. It points back to the Baptism [and other high points in the life of Jesus, and his disciples], and looks forward to the Cross, Resurrection, Ascension and Parousia, so it is one of those turning points which have a great interest for New Testament theology and particularly for an understanding of the kingdom of God. It looks back to the Old Testament and shows how Christ fulfills it, and it anticipates the great redemptive acts which bring the gospel story to its climax and fulfillment.[27]

---

[26] Caird, 'The Transfiguration', 292.
[27] Trites, 'Transfiguration of Jesus', 78.

7. The Interpretation of the Wine Miracle at Cana: John 2: 1–11*

MARTIN HENGEL

In a penetrating article entitled 'The Glory of God in the Fourth Gospel: An Exercise in Biblical Semantics' (*New Testament Studies* 15 (1968–9), 265–77), Professor George Caird once called attention to the important statement in John 2: 11, where for the first time it is claimed that the glory of the incarnate Logos is visibly revealed to all in a sign. He wrote as follows: 'In the Incarnation God has willed that the eternal glory of the Logos should be communicated to the man Jesus, so that others might see it and draw from it the conclusion that he was the unique Son of God (1: 14). This glory Jesus is said to have manifested in his signs (2: 11)' (269). Caird's study, typical of his work in its precision, clarity, and insight, nevertheless did not discuss the wine-miracle of Cana further in this connection. This is understandable, for he had sketched for himself a broad canvas, not to mention the feeling one gets that this miracle story continues to be something of an offence to us exegetes. In fact, one may say that the narrative of the ἀρχὴ τῶν σημείων, the first 'sign' of Jesus in the fourth Gospel, has remained until today something of a σημεῖον ἀντιλεγόμενον, although it has attracted specialists in the field again and again and has put their pens in motion so often that one might feel a certain restraint in finally setting one's own pen to work. If I do so, it is out of respect for the memory of George Caird, a biblical scholar of the first rank who was also so at home in the classics and other ancient literature that he never shrank from reopening questions from which some might understandably flee.

A recent investigation of John 2: 1–11 by B. Olsson may well be said to lay the groundwork for our study (although the significance of Olsson's work is clearly still far from being recognized). Olsson, calling it 'one of the most mysterious texts in the New Testament',[1] makes an

---

* Professor Hengel is grateful to his assistant, Ms Anna Maria Schwemer, for her intensive help in the preparation of this article. The editors also would like to thank Mr Gerhard Schmidt of the University of California, Davis, who provided the translation from the German.

[1] B. Olsson, *Structure and Meaning in the Fourth Gospel: A Textlinguistic Analysis of John 2: 1–11 and 4: 1–42*, Lund 1974), 18. Cf. in this connection below, p. 95.

effort to trace and penetrate the mysteries in a methodically and objectively impressive way.[2]

I. THE DOUBTFUL CHARACTER OF A WINE-MIRACLE

At first glance, one is puzzled by its *profane* nature, culminating in the reproach of the host, which has often caused embarrassment to interpreters: 'Everyone brings out the good wine first and then the cheap wine when the guests have had too much; but you have saved the best until now.' (2: 10, cf. below, n. 18). 'It has no analogies in the old tradition of Jesus-narratives and appears *strange* in comparison with them,' remarks R. Bultmann. For this reason he sees in the reported event only a '*symbol* of that which occurs in the total work of Jesus, in the revelation of Jesus' δόξα'. The epiphany story could only be a *picture* (*Bild*) for it'.[3]

His teacher, W. Heitmüller, had already held similar views. In accordance with Goethe's principle that 'everything that is transitory [i.e. historical] is merely a parable',[4] the evangelist understands 'the story and its facts' only as 'a shadow-reflection or an embodiment of ideas. It is history, but it has *value and significance* only because it presents higher truths, and only to that extent.'[5] In this connection it remains uncertain whether the narrative as 'production of poetic faith' derives from the evangelist himself or from the tradition of the community. That is to say, Heitmüller takes the possibility into account that the unknown poet (writer) already saw in it an unhistorical fiction: 'The question of historicity, which is for us in such a case immediately disturbing, did not exist for him in *this* sense.' Of course, the relevant moral misgivings must not be left out of account: the narrative does not

---

[2] Cf., among other things, the reviews of H. Thyen, *SEÅ* 40 (1975), 136–43; E. Ruckstuhl, *TZ* 31 (1975), 307 f.; D. W. Wead, *JBL* 94 (1975), 616 ff., who remarks in a correctly critical way: 'However, I would have preferred to see more precision in Olsson's handling of symbolism. While it seems desirable to have a uniform set of rules for the interpretation of symbolism, perhaps we should realize that this is not possible' (617 f.). R. Schnackenburg, *Das Johannesevangelium: Ergänzende Auslegungen und Exkurse*, HThK 4, 4 (Freiburg, 1984), 29: 'For the Gospel of John, the work of B. Olsson is a significant advance.' Compare this with the commentary of J. Becker, *Ökumenischer Taschenbuch Kommentar*, 4/1 (Gütersloh and Würzburg, 1979), who mentions it only as a reference to the literature; and C. K. Barrett, *The Gospel According to St John* (London, 2nd edn., 1978), does not discuss it. R. Kysar, 'The Fourth Gospel: A Report on Recent Research', *Aufstieg und Niedergang der Römischen Welt* 2, 25/3 (Berlin–New York, 1985), 2389–480 mentions it only very briefly on p. 2393, a sign that he did not recognize the significance of the investigation. J. Breuss, 'Das Kana-Wunder: Hermeneutische und pastorale Überlegungen aufgrund einer phänomenologischen Analyse von Joh 2, 1–12', BibB 12 (1976), critically discusses 'structural exegesis' (pp. 51–8), but does not take into consideration the investigation by Olsson which has the same perspective.

[3] R. Bultmann, *Das Evangelium des Johannes*, KEK (Göttingen, 18th edn., 1964), 83 and n. 4.

[4] W. Heitmüller, *Das Johannes-Evangelium: Die Schriften des Neuen Testaments* 4 (1918³), 15; Faust II, 12104: 'Alles Vergängliche ist nur ein Gleichnis'.

[5] Ibid., 58.

'contribute to the compassionate, serving love of Jesus'.[6] M. Dibelius judged it similarly.[7] As a comparison one can then at best refer only to the casting of demons into the herd of swine in Mark 5: 11–13 or to the curse of the fig tree in Mark 11: 13 f., 20 f. The narrative is admittedly not one of edification. 'If one seeks to edify the congregation far more can be said against our pericope than for it.'[8]

The critical discussion of this 'aggravating' narrative reaches much further into the past, however. D. F. Strauss had already referred to the problem of the 'appropriateness' of the miracle. He was still of the opinion that the complaint raised in antiquity (as well as in modern times) 'that it was not in accord with Jesus' stature' to be 'in the society of drunkards' and 'even to encourage their drunkenness through his power to perform miracles' is 'to be rejected as an exaggeration', since nothing can be inferred with certainty from the wine-customs mentioned in v. 10 in connection with the proceedings during the wedding. Yet, with reference to the older interpreters Paulus, Lücke, and Olshausen, he already found it quite doubtful 'that Jesus met . . . some need, as he was otherwise wont to do, but brought about a further temptation to *indulge in pleasure*; he showed himself not so much as helpful, but rather as accommodating. He performed, so to speak, a miracle in the service of luxury, rather than a really beneficent one.'[9] W. Bauer accepts this characterization of it as a luxury-miracle and compares it, among other things, with the 'deeds of the young Jesus in the childhood Gospel of Thomas'.[10]

We can, however, go back much further in this connection: according to Ephrem, the Marcionites had already derided the wedding narrative: 'They mocked the wedding meal at Cana':[11] '"Far be it from us to believe that our Lord went there!" They call the church a bride and our Lord the true bridegroom! And the symbol of the wine of the wedding feast is in their goblets, and the type of the feast is in their festivals. This is a divided doctrine, which disproves itself every time without noticing it.' In other words, the Marcionites, according to Ephrem,

---

[6] Ibid., 59 (italics mine).

[7] M. Dibelius, *Die Formgeschichte des Evangeliums* (Tübingen, 6th edn., 1971), 98: 'It strikes every reader of the Bible that this assistance is by no means necessary; it is indeed even *dubious. In any case*, it has nothing to do with the Protestant ethos' (italics mine).

[8] J. D. M. Derrett, *Law in the New Testament* (London, 1970), 244.

[9] *Das Leben Jesu* (Tübingen, 1835), 2. 224 (italics mine).

[10] HNT 6 (Tübingen, 1933³), 46. R. Pesch, 'Das Weinwunder bei der Hochzeit zu Kana (Joh 2, 1–12)', *Theologie der Gegenwart* 24 (1981), 214–25, again moves in a similar direction; he sees here a 'Geschenkwundergeschichte', which 'originally belonged to the framework of the narratives about Jesus as child or adolescent' (224), and refers as justification to the *Epistula Apostolorum* ch. 4 (15) and to the childhood Gospel of Thomas (middle of the second century) and Ps.-Matthew (Eighth/ninth centuries). The *Ep. Apost.* presupposes, of course, both the Gospel of John and that of Thomas.

mocked it only because they, struck with blindness, did not recognize the deeper, symbolic meaning of the feast, which is related to the Church and the Eucharist, but rather held fast to the external letter of the narrative.[11]

II. THE SYMBOLIC INTERPRETATION

W. F. Howard's basic observation is here valid: 'When a moral principle collides with a miracle we feel, by every Christian instinct, that it is the miracle that must go to the wall. It is not surprising, therefore, that many explain this story as *pure allegory*'.[12] The objectionable ἀτοπία of the narrative, which had already forced the narrators of the early Church to delimit it apologetically,[13] and which, of course, is perceived in a special way by the 'enlightened' modern reader, accentuates the tendency in principle to interpret it in a symbolic-allegorical way, and the results (not to say the suppositions) of exegesis remain in this connection deeply divided.

We should not, however, fall into a misunderstanding here. I am not concerned to throw doubt on the currently popular allegorical-symbolic interpretation in general; I am rather dealing with the problem of taking it as '*pure* allegory'. The latter leads, in view of the narrative to an *aporia* as much as does a one-sided clinging to an apparently simple verbal meaning and to the bare facticity of the miracle, an attitude which today can hardly be found anymore among exegetes.[14]

The seven Johannine σημεῖα refer beyond themselves to a much greater degree than do the synoptic δυνάμεις,[15] but not to ideas and

---

[11] Hymnus 47. 3 CSCO 170 (77), ed. E. Beck (Rome, 1957), 163; cf. A. Harnack, *Marcion: Das Evangelium vom fremden Gott* (Leipzig, 2nd edn., 1924, reprinted 1960, TU 45), 249 n. 1.

[12] *The Fourth Gospel in Recent Criticism and Interpretation* (London, 1931), 192.

[13] S. A. Smitmans, *Das Weinwunder von Kana*, BGBE 6 (1966), 74 ff. This concerns the historical-chronological problem of the contradiction between the forty-day temptation of Jesus in the desert and the six days between the baptism and the wedding in John. Origen already recognized the impossibility of a solution which would harmonize the contradiction: 'The fact that a historical solution to these *Aporien* shows that only a spiritual interpretation can disclose the meaning intended by the evangelist' (76). Cf. 89 ff.—a defence of Jesus' participation in a worldly wedding festival. Cf. also *Petrus Chrysologus* (d. *c*.450), Sermon 157, PL 52, 616 B/C: 'That Christ was present at the wedding was to serve as a demonstration of his power, not for the sake of pleasure. It was not an expression of human feeling, but of power. It happened for the sake of the sign, not for the sake of the stomach. It did not produce drunkenness, but revealed the deity.' Regarding the 'wine-rule', cf. 143 ff.: here the drunkenness of the guests was controversial. Theodore of Mopsuestia criticized the presentation in 2: 9 f. as inexact.

[14] Smitmans, op. cit., 37 ff. Cf. J. D. M. Derrett, op. cit. n. 8 above, 228–46, who tries with imagination *and* erudition to grasp the original historical event and recognizes the significance of the later symbolic interpretation of the evangelist in relation to his Church as well (245 f.).

[15] As Luke 11: 20 / Matt. 12: 28 shows, these also have a 'reference-character': to the presence of God's rule which is now beginning (cf. Matt. 11: 1–6; Luke 7: 18–23). A symbolic interpretation here would, of course, miss the point.

higher truth*s*, as Heitmüller thought;[16] they refer rather to *one* truth, which the Son, sent into the world by the Father, presents in his person. This results from the Christological 'monomania' of the fourth Gospel, which resists the (still popular) moralizing approach. The word σημεῖον, which John uses exclusively, brings this 'referential' quality emphatically to the fore.[17]

While the author develops this deeper significance again and again in the σημεῖα after chapter five by means of the dialogues, controversies, and revelation speeches which follow, the first two numbered Galilean miracles are merely 'told', without directly disclosing to the reader the Christological meaning behind them. He is to discover it for himself. In this context, the second miracle in 4: 46–54 clearly has a secondary significance over against the ἀρχὴ τῶν σημείων of chapter two, which is expressly referred to in connection with the second stay in Cana (4: 46). Should this be understood in such a way that, in these two cases alone, the 'sign' produced *real* faith?[18] Wholly in opposition to the later miracle stories from chapter five onward, the objectionable, vulgar conclusion of 2: 10 (which, already on the level of narration, signifies more than merely a 'humorous observation',[19] since it realistically illuminates the whole wedding festival) is in contrast to the strong pathos of the Christological conclusion of 2: 11.[20] This glaring contrast is consciously intended by the evangelist. One might actually think that he had had some pleasure in telling the miracle story, since it ends almost as a farce, in order then to conclude the whole thing with a deeply theological statement about the faith of the disciples, a state-

---

[16] Op cit. n. 4 above, 58.

[17] Only in the refusing answer of Jesus (4: 48) during the second Cana miracle does he have the Old Testament formula σημεῖα καὶ τέρατα.

[18] Cf. the double ἐπίστευσαν in 4: 50 and 4: 53; add 2: 11 in opposition to the questionable faith of the crowd in Jerusalem in 2: 23. The enumeration of the two miracles is justified by the emphasized geographical location (cf. 4: 54 and 2: 1, 11) and their meaning. It is absurd to construe an opposition to 2: 23 and 3: 2 here and to build the very questionable existence of a Semeia-source upon it. The effect of the σημεῖα of Jesus in Jerusalem to some extent 'loses its power' through the previous demand of the Jews in 2: 18 for a legitimating sign (cf. 6: 30). They do not lead to authentic faith (cf. 2: 24 f.). This explains the reproachful answer of Jesus in 4: 48, to which the 'royal official' replies with authentic faith.

[19] R. Schnackenburg, *Das Johannesevangelium*, HThK 4, 1 (Freiburg, 5th edn., 1981, 337. It is similarly interpreted by most exegetes. In reality the bridegroom is criticized!

[20] Cf. M. Dibelius, loc. cit. He sees in v. 11 an 'interpretation of the evangelist' superimposed onto the 'novella'. Bultmann, Becker, and other friends of the ominous Semeia-source must, to the contrary, at least in part attribute even 2: 11 to it. The evangelist becomes thereby a foolish editor. W. Nicol, *The Sēmeia in the Fourth Gospel*, NOVTSup 32, 1972), asserts that 'S(emeia source) would have contained v. 11a (cf. 4: 54) and probably also v. 11c (the typical miracle-theology). But in 11b φανεροῦν is a Johannine style characteristic, and δόξα also seems to be used in a typical Johannine sense, referring to the deeper meaning of the miracle (cf. 1: 14 . . .). Thus 11b is probably J.' (31.) Here it is clear that if we hold fast to a Semeia-source, we must tear this sentence apart in a correspondingly complicated way.

ment which is in the true sense of the word 'foundational' and sounds entirely different from what precedes. He is a master of dialectic and contrast and can, when he wants to, describe things in a completely realistic way.[21]

The interpretation beginning with the Valentinians and Irenaeus already shows that the narrative had been interpreted allegorically without any qualms whatever. Even more so than others, the narrative itself invites that this be done.[22] Irenaeus, *Adv. Haer.* 3. 11. 5, contrary to the Gnostic exegesis, takes the report as an actual historical event. The wine, as it was consumed first during the wedding by all the guests, and by Jesus himself as well(!),[23] was good and no one found fault with

---

[21] The 'very vulgar remarks of the master of ceremonies' (Derrett, op. cit. n. 8 above, 245), presumably gave rise to the objection of Tatian with his encratic disposition: The καὶ ὅταν μεθυσθῶσιν is missing in the Diatessaronic commentary of Ephrem (cf. L. Leloir, *Éphrem de Nisibe, Commentaire de l'évangile concordant ou Diatessaron*, 5. 8, SC 121 (1966), 110). Ephrem cites the text in a shortened form which destroys its point: 'Everybody serves the sweet wine first, and then any other wine.' Since Ephrem himself stresses in a wholly realistic way that Jesus 'gladdens the guest with sweet wine' and thereby had saved the threatened social festivities of the wedding (op. cit., 5. 9. 111, cf. also 5. 1. 107: 'The guests were drunk'), this change might well be attributable to the text of Tatian (cf. A. Smitmans, op. cit. n. 13 above, 143 f.). Already in the ancient Church a realistic exegesis, which took account of the drunkenness of the guests as wholly self-evident and for that reason excluded them as witnesses to the miracle, stood in opposition to a 'spiritual' and transposed interpretation (Smitmans, op. cit. n. 13, 144, cf. n. 3; cf. further H. Olshausen, *Biblischer Commentar über sämmtliche Schriften des Neuen Testaments* (Königsberg, 1832), 2, 70 f., and C. K. Barrett, op. cit. n. 2 above, 193, regarding 2: 10: 'There is of course no ground here for conclusions regarding the degree of intoxication of the guests at this wedding.' The interpreters of the early Church were in part closer in this connection to the real content of the narrative. In the case of a Galilean wedding, sobriety was difficult to imagine even for the one who reported it. Many examples could be given, but cf. *T. Šabb.* 7, 9 ed. Zuckermandel, line 118: 'A deed of R. Aqiba: he set up a wedding banquet for his son. In opening each amphora he said "the wine for the life of the rabbis and for the life of their pupils".' Cf. also *m. Ber.* 1, 1 concerning the sons of R. Gamaliel II, when they returned from a wedding, and *b. Ber.* 9a concerning the wedding of the son of R. Yehuda b. Levi. The pronouncements of the *architriklinos*, for which no ancient parallel has yet been found (despite H. Windisch, 'Die johanneische Weinregel', *ZNW* 14 (1913), 248–57) originates from a folk-milieu which cannot definitely be determined in terms of literary form. One could, perhaps above all, expect to find something like that in the ancient *mimus*, but of this only a very few fragments remain.

[22] The *Excerpta ex Theodoto* 65 (GCS 17. 2. 128) identify the '*architriklinos*' of 2: 9 with the friend of the bridegroom (3: 29). The bridegroom himself is Jesus as the σωτήρ (cf. Irenaeus, *Adv. Haer.*, 1. 7. 1). The friend might then correspond to the demiurge. The wedding itself becomes the image of the 'fullness of joy' and of the *anapausis* (cf. A. Smitmans, op. cit. n. 13, 207, 141 f.). For Heracleon the καταβαίνειν of Jesus from Cana to Capernaum (John 2: 12) meant the descent of the redeemer into τὰ ἔσχατα τοῦ κόσμου, i.e. the material world. 'For the Naassenes', on the contrary, 'John 2: 1–11 was an area of the darkest allegories', as W. v. Loewenich says (*Das Johannes-Verständnis im zweiten Jahrhundert*, BZNW 13, (Giessen, 1932), 66).

[23] *Sed dominus accepit de eo* (i.e. *de vino*). This idea that Jesus himself had drunk wine at the wedding probably has an anti-encratic significance (cf. his judgement of Tatian 3. 23. 8 and 1. 27. 3). Does the narrative have an anti-ascetic tendency already in John? H. Olshausen, op. cit. n. 21 above, 2. 71, suspected a conscious opposition to the asceticism of the disciples of the Baptist here (cf. Mark 2: 18 ff.): 'What a contrast this was for them (the former disciples of the Baptist), since it was the Messiah, to whom the Baptist himself had referred them, who first took them to a wedding. While John ordained them to a life of renunciation, Jesus led them to the enjoyment of pleasure. This contrast required for them an adjustment which was mediated precisely by the

it, since it had grown in a natural way as a gift of the creator (*'quod per conditionem a Deo in vinea factum est'*), 'though the wine, . . . created by the Logos from water for the use of the wedding guests, was better'.

Irenaeus is not, however, satisfied with simply setting forth the facticity of the wedding and of the miracle. That the Lord made use of an existing substance, changing the water into wine and providing drink for the wedding guests, is simply a point of reference. He *could* have provided the wine by creating it out of nothing—without water as a raw material—similar to the miracle of the loaves, when he blessed the pieces of bread and passed them out. 'Thereby he announces that the same God who created the world and commanded it to bear fruit, who put the waters in order and provided springs, likewise here gives to mankind in these last days, through his Son, the blessing of food and the merciful gift of drink.' That is to say, the 'gift' miracle of transformation, to which Irenaeus calls attention in its 'natural-historical actuality', points beyond itself to the gift of the Eucharist in the last days, as does the later feeding of the five thousand. It is precisely for this reason that Jesus must resist the urgent impatience of his mother; she— according to a 'deeper' understanding—wants to partake of the cup of the Eucharist before the time determined by the Father (*Adv. Haer.* 3. 16. 7).[24] The miraculous, creational event is for Irenaeus not an end in itself, nor simply an evidence of power; it points at the same time to the eschatological gift of Christ in the Eucharist, which becomes an actuality through the death of Jesus.

The relation of the Cana miracle to the Eucharist, in connection with the bread-miracle and the 'supper of the resurrection' (21: 9–14), with bread and fish (all three occurring in Galilee), is certainly to be taken seriously. It is still being discussed in contemporary scholarship. Consequently, Irenaeus definitely saw something that is correct, even if

miracle.' K. Barth, *Erklärung des Johannes-Evangeliums (Kapitel 1–8), Gesamtausgabe II. Akademische Werke: 1925/1926* (Zürich, 1976), 197, as an ingenious 'outsider' commands the attention of exegetes: 'Cutting through the middle between friends and foes of alcohol, the gospel says clearly and simply: He revealed *his glory*, and whoever takes pleasure in, or is annoyed by, the form in which this took place, . . . that Jesus had in this way been present without reservation, where people were enjoying themselves . . . should reflect that this presence of Jesus as well as the form of the miracle is by v. 4 most definitely placed in the shadow of the cross. If he who is here approaching his hour reveals his glory, then there is no point in weighing what is and what is not moral. . . . And if it is in his pleasure to reveal himself in a luxury-miracle, of what significance should our acclamations and protest then be?'

[24] *Properante Maria ad admirabile vini signum et ante tempus volente participare compendii poculo.* With regard to the interpretation of both passages, see the commentary of the editions by Harvey and by A. Rousseau/L. Doutreleau, SC 210 (1974), 282, 324. Regarding the Eucharist itself, Irenaeus says (*Adv. Haer.* 4. 18. 5): *'Quemadmodum enim qui est a terra panis, percipiens invocationem Dei, jam non communis panis est, sed Eucharistia ex duabus rebus constans, terrena et caelestia.'* John 2 and 6 are for him not in themselves directly 'Eucharistic' miracles, but rather Jesus points thereby to the consummation of creation in the Eucharist.

he—in the interest of the anti-Gnostic struggle and instructed by his doctrine of recapitulation—places too much emphasis on the relation between a good creation and the Cana narrative which he equated with the Eucharist. In the Gospel of John, the creation appears clearly and unambiguously in 1: 3 in an anti-gnostic sense, and the meaning of the Eucharist in the Gospel[25] is clearly stated. Moreover, Irenaeus' discovery of anti-docetic and anti-encratic components in the Cana miracle has a certain justification: this miracle simply cannot be reconciled with a dualism that denigrates body and matter.[26] Such an observation applies especially to the awakening of Lazarus from the dead, where the narrator (of the Semeia-source), according to J. Becker, moves 'to the limits of tolerability'.[27] In my opinion, the evangelist himself seeks rather—here as well as there—consciously to provoke and challenge the reader. The 'doubtful character' of both narratives, expressed by pious as well as by enlightened readers, is, in other words, *intended* by the evangelist.

III. THE SEMEIA-SOURCE THEORY AS A SOLUTION?

If therefore the opposition between concrete miracle narrative and symbolic interpretation presents a false alternative, then the question *of the scope of our interpretation and of its unambiguous criteria* must remain controversial. The time is past for attempts to 'reconstruct' the historical event. In the first half of this century attempts were still made[28] in a

[25] Ch. 6; on 6: 51–8, cf. P. Borgen, *Bread from Heaven: An Exegetical Study of the Conception of Manna in the Gospel of John and the Writings of Philo* (Leiden, 1965), 95–7; 188–92. Regarding ch. 15, 'the true vine', cf. also R. Schnackenburg, *Das Johannesevangelium, HThK* 4, 4 (Freiburg, 1984), 160. Also on 163 he says: 'Just as the verbal figure "bread from heaven", which refers in the first place to the person of Jesus (6: 51–53) and is then transposed upon Jesus' Eucharistic gift (6: 53–8), so also the understanding of Jesus as the "true vine" can awaken associations with "fruit of the vine" (cf. Mark 14: 25), which is taken during the Eucharist.' One need not be so careful— certainly more than 'associations' are awakened here! Cf. John 17: 19; 19: 34 f.; 21: 13. Regarding Jesus' 'last supper' cf. E. R. Goodenough, *Jewish Symbols in the Greco-Roman Period*, v. 1, (New York, 1956), 31–95 about bread and fish.

[26] Cf. A. Schlatter, *Der Evangelist Johannes*, (Stuttgart, 1948), 66: 'Through this narrative, John makes every idea of an ascetic opposition against the natural processes impossible. Not only through the gift of the wine ... but already through his participation in the wedding week, John removes Jesus from every form of gnosis, since gnosticism constantly sees a danger for man in natural processes.'

[27] Op. cit. n. 2 above, 4/1, 118 with reference to 11: 17, 39. This applies naturally to 2: 6–10 as well. Becker says this about the Semeia-source postulated by him, which in my opinion is a scholarly phantom. Since these objectionable tendencies are put by the evangelist in such a provocative way and for anti-docetic reasons, only he is responsible for them in the Gospel. The so-called Semeia-source is in reality only a consciously made selection from the miracle tradition within the Johannine circle, which is formed wholly from the paradoxical, dialectical-symbolic theology of the head of the school (cf. below, p. 97 f.).

[28] B. Weiss, *Das Johannesevangelium*, KEK (Göttingen, 2nd edn., 1902), 96: 'In the memory of the eye-witness with his impressions of the life of Jesus and its many miracles and in the light of the

psychologizing way to seek answers to the numerous historical questions which the artfully, not to say cleverly, constructed narrative itself abandons, and which all too easily led to the beginnings of a Jesus-novel. In their place there appeared the literary-critical, form-critical, redaction-critical, and tradition-critical hypotheses concerning the genesis and prehistory of the text. The question of the original event and its circumstances is replaced by that of the *prior strata* of the extant narrative, in which case the (in part very diverse) attempts at reconstruction, as applied to the hypothetical sources, are hardly less imaginative than the older attempts to provide an explanation.

The desire to reconstruct can here blind one's exegetical eye. This is demonstrated by numerous scholars who adopt the Semeia-source theory. In John 2: 3, they declare as original the longer, extraordinarily poorly attested reading οἶνον οὐκ εἶχον, ὅτι συνετελέσθη ὁ οἶνος τοῦ γάμου· εἶτα instead of the much better attested and simple (but perhaps more easily misunderstood) ὑστερήσαντος οἶνου, which receives the unambiguous meaning of 'when the wine gave out' only through the wine-rule in 2: 10.[29]

This is not the place to enter into a detailed discussion of the questionable Semeia-source theory and its variations. The self-evident manner with which it is presupposed by various authors does not ren-

---

meaning which it took on for his conception of Christ, the picture of that miracle of divine providence was transformed for him into this picture of a miracle of divine omnipotence.' Th. Zahn is less careful (*Das Evangelium des Johannes*, KNT (Leipzig, 6th edn., 1921): 'For the evangelist as for the reader who trusts his testimony, a wonderful coincidence of authentic human effects and human struggle for the knowledge of the divine will, on the one hand, and of a superhuman power in carrying out the known will of God, on the other hand, shows itself in this first enactment of Jesus' power as also in his last, as reported by John (ch. 11).' (160.) F. Büchsel (*Das Evangelium nach Johannes*, NTD (Göttingen, 1946), 45, goes still further: 'His disapproving word to Mary is meant seriously. The thoughts of a friendly and caring housewife, who would have liked to see a painful embarrassment redressed even in a strange house, were not his own thoughts, even considering the entirely natural qualities of his being. ... He provides assistance, because God's will has determined and given him this occasion. ...' Against this, cf. K. Barth (op. cit. n. 23 above), 194, 198.

[29] It is to be found only in the original reading of *Sinaiticus*, and, among the Old Latin, a.b.ff². j.r, eth and syr^hmg. It is an ancient correction which seeks greater precision and goes back to the second century. The reading of it^cl moves in a similar direction: *factum est per multam turbam vocitorum vinum consummari*. Sin* must then change the saying of Mary also on stylistic grounds: οἶνος οὐκ ἐστιν, similarly Tat syr^p·pal·h. Cf. B. M. Metzger, *A Textual Commentary on the Greek New Testament* (London and New York, 1971), 201; R. Schnackenburg, op. cit. n. 19 above, 332 n. 3 and C. K. Barrett, op. cit., 190 f. The shorter reading is represented by P^66.75 and all the other Greek manuscripts. At least since the two Bodmer papyri have become known, we should no longer cling to the clearly secondary, longer version. The longer version was preferred by R. Bultmann, op. cit. n. 3 above, 80, n. 6; R. T. Fortna, *The Gospel of Signs* (Cambridge, 1970), 30f.; M. E. Boismard and A. Lamouille, *L'Évangile de Jean: Synopse des quatre évangiles en Français* III (Paris, 1977), 100; H.-P. Heekerens, *Die Zeichenquelle der johanneischen Redaktion*, SBS 113 (Stuttgart, 1984), 64–6. Heekerens wants to see in the reading εἶτα λέγει a 'typical idiolect' of the Johannine redaction (65). It is that simple. Regarding the older discussion, cf. A. Smitmans (op. cit. n. 13 above, 12, n. 3).

der it the more convincing.[30] A foreign body is thereby forced into the fourth Gospel, which contradicts the great stylistic unity of the work, a point brought out by Ruckstuhl, among others.[31] How can one expect that such a theologically wilful evangelist, who according to J. Becker 'develops his theology with presuppositions other than the S[emeia] Q[uelle]',[32] should have mechanically taken over such statements as 2: 11 or 20: 30 f. (which are decisive for the construction and structure of his Gospel) from a source which was entirely theologically alien? Is even John capable of such feats? This does not mean that the author (or authors) had not made use of written sources. He knew Mark and Luke at least, presumably discussed them in the 'school', took some things over in a more or less altered way and, critical on the whole, detached himself from them. But except for the Gospels which we know already, we can *reconstruct* no written sources with sufficient certainty. The (almost naïve) trust in literary reconstruction, which is again so widespread today and which does not recognize the difference between the possible and the probable, leads more and more to games that can no longer be taken seriously.

According to R. Bultmann, who wishes to ascribe relatively little of our pericope to the redaction of the evangelist,[33] the evangelist

[30] For a more recent example see H. Köster, 'Überlieferung und Geschichte der frühchristlichen Evangelienliteratur', *ANRW* 2. 25. 2, 1477: 'John *most certainly* [italics mine] used a written source for the miracle stories, the *Semeia* (sign)-source, as well as for the passion narrative. These two sources are closely related to the sources of the Gospel of Mark.' Here everything is questionable. If assuming written sources, one would have to count Mark itself among the sources of John in the first place. The assumption of a 'sign source', however, only causes difficulties for the understanding of the Gospel. More than that, all of the source theories are everything but harmonious— cf. the extensive research reports in G. van Belle, *De semeia-bron in het vierde evangilie: Ontstaan en groei van een hypothese* (Leuven, 1975); R. Kysar, loc. cit. (n. 2 above), 2395–407, and the short overview in Heekerens, op. cit. 11 ff., who assumes a form curtailed to the three Galilean signs (2: 1–12; 4: 46–54 and 21: 1–14), completely in contrast to the comprehensive version of Becker, op. cit. n. 2 above, 1, 112–20), who wants to attribute almost the whole of the narrative material except the Passion story to a Semeia-source. For criticism cf. F. Neyrinck, 'De semeiabron in het vierde evangelie: Kritick van een hypothese,' *Academiae Analecta, MVAW.L* 45 (1983), no. 1, 1–28; cf. by the same author 'John 4, 46–54 Signs Source and/or Synoptic Gospels', *ETL* 60 (1984), 367–75. Cf. also the proposal of an 'agnosticism' toward literary-critical operations in D. A. Carson, *JBL* 97 (1978), 411–29 (esp. 428 f.).
[31] E. Ruckstuhl, *Die literarische Einheitlichkeit des Johannesevangeliums* (Studia Friburgensia 3) (Freiburg, 1951); E. Schweizer, 'Ego Eimi: Die religionsgeschichtliche Bedeutung der johanneischen Bildreden, zugleich ein Beitrag zur Quellenfrage des vierten Evangeliums', *FRL NF* 38 (1939); but already E. A. Abbott, *Johannine Grammar* (London, 1906), in the preface, x, says: 'About John, I have tried to subordinate strictly to grammatical inferences my conviction that he, too, is a master of style and phrase'; cf. also, by the same author, *Johannine Vocabulary* (London, 1905); R. Schnackenburg, op. cit., n. 19 above, 94–7; and E. Ruckstuhl, 'Johannine Language and Style', M. de Jonge (ed.), *L'Évangile de Jean: Sources, rédaction, théologie, BETL* 44 (Leuven, 1977), 125–47.
[32] Op cit., 120.
[33] Op cit., 79: Perhaps that the day is noted in v. 1, the disciples in v. 2, where they replace the brothers of Jesus—cf. *Ep. Apost.* ch. 5, where both appear—as well as 2: 12, and the ignorance of the *architriklinos* in 2: 9b and 11b from ἐφανέρωσεν.

regarded the whole narrative, as taken from the source, only as a 'symbol of the revelation of Jesus' δόξα', which makes visible to faith 'not the power of the miracle-worker, but rather the divinity of Jesus as the revealer'.[34] To the question 'to what extent may one interpret the individual strands of the narrative from the standpoint of this understanding?' he answers (in a guarded way) that 'the gift of the wine is not important, but rather the gift of Jesus himself, Jesus as revealer'. The water, in contrast to the wine, 'is an image of all that which is a surrogate of the revelation, all that by which man thinks he can live, but yet cannot live.'[35] The denial of the demand of his mother by reference to the hour has significance: 'The event of the revelation is independent of human wishes'. Accordingly the steward's ignorance (v. 9) signifies 'human blindness in the face of the person of the revealer'.[36] The question thus remains: was such an artfully constructed, exciting narrative necessary, with all its intermediary steps and with its unusually large number of actors, in order to attain this symbolic result? Could the evangelist not have said everything much more simply—less disturbingly miraculous and theologically less ambiguous? *Obviously, the prejudicial effect of the source-theory reduces the possibilities of a theological-symbolical interpretation.* This is all the more so, since an entirely different theological tendency is attributed to the author of the source from that of the evangelist. One could also ask: did the Johannine school's audience (and later the large church communities) of the second century hear this in the story, or is Bultmann's 'respectable' interpretation more related to his sermon preparations in Marburg than to the first hearers and readers of the Gospel? Put differently, is the source-theory not just as far removed from the very complex history of the origin of the Gospel (which is for us no longer reconstructable) as are the historically absurd rearrangement hypotheses in Bultmann's otherwise theologically impressive commentary?

The same problem arises in an even sharper way in the commentary of J. Becker: 'E[vangelist] therefore appropriated the S[emeia] Q[uelle] with a minimum of effort (in v. 1, 6, 9). *This is why his interpretation is hard to make out.*'[37] Becker can accordingly describe the theological significance of the miracle *for his Semeia-source* in detail: 'The glory of the miracle-worker (and hence his divinity as the one who is able to perform miracles) visible in the normally unimaginable miracle is the

[34] Ibid., 83.
[35] Ibid., 84.
[36] Ibid., 85, cf. n. 4: 'One can hardly allegorize further.'
[37] Op. cit., 1, 107 (italics mine).

occasion for the disciples to believe in him. In this way, all readers of
the source should be led to faith.' Yet *is* it a piece of writing produced in
the interest of missionary activity? What sort of naïve readers and
mission prospects are here assumed? Are they to be led to faith 'in the
divinity of the miracle-worker' by reading unbelievable *mirabilia*, of
which there were more than enough in the ancient world? This
divinity, according to Becker, becomes 'visible to everyone' in the
miracle narrative, 'so that faith in Jesus arises'. Behind this is said to
exist a competition with the cult of Dionysus and its wine-miracles.[38]
Although a bit later it is said of the source that 'the general Jewish
milieu of the narrative is beyond question' and that this source 'in a certain way [stands] closer to the Jews than to (the) Evangelist',[39] any
relation of the Cana miracle to the Old Testament and Jewish wine-
metaphors is rejected. Where and when is this Dionysus legend supposed to have been adapted to Christianity (cf. below, p. 108 ff.)? The
theological motivation of the evangelist for the incorporation of this
miracle into his strongly theological Gospel appears all the more
meagre. Becker does reject Bultmann's purely symbolic interpretation
on the grounds that the 'E[vangelist] does not mitigate the objectionably excessive miracle event' (although the question is, of course,
whether he does not *increase* it through the presumed 'additions' in vv. 6
and 9), yet the theological interest it has is limited to two points.
Together with Bultmann, Becker is of the opinion 'that it is not to the
point to attribute a deeper meaning to individual elements of the
narrative, but to understand the miracle as a whole'. He attempts this
by seeing in it a justification of 1: 51, which is due to the evangelist:
'The heavenly dimension of the messenger—just as highly mythic as 2:
1 ff. is "excessively" miraculous—is opened up.'[40] Is this whole 'excessive' effort necessary and meaningful 'for demonstrating Jesus' divine
descent and unity with the Father'?[41] This is, however, precisely *not*
expressis verbis under discussion in the narrative. What happens in it
could perhaps also be expected of a magician (cf. below p. 105 f.).

The second motif is that the 'E[vangelist] seeks with 2: 1–11 to finish
the appointing of the disciples'. But the disciples are in the narrative
only peripheral figures without any function. The appointment of disciples is precisely *not* what is being discussed. The exegesis of the ancient
Church already discussed the number of disciples present,[42] a problem

---

[38] Ibid., 1. 110.
[39] Ibid., 1. 117.
[40] Ibid., 1. 111.
[41] Ibid., 1. 112.
[42] A. Smitmans, op. cit., 89.

that has remained unsolved to this day. The actual appointment of the disciples takes place only after the crisis in 6: 66–71 and then again in 20: 19–28: only there are the Twelve mentioned (6: 67, 70; 20: 24).

In other words, the Semeia-source theory does not illuminate the interpretation of this 'mysterious' text; it obscures both it and the understanding of the whole Gospel, since the miracle occurs in a passage which is decisive for the entire work. The theory, in other words, only *displaces* the problem: what was objectionable to the old interpretation is now attributed to a *written* source. Thus all that was excessive and miraculous now appears unaltered in the source, while the profound editorial additions are attributed to the evangelist.[43] Such a procedure keeps us from taking 2: 1–11 seriously as a *Johannine* text. Heekerens justly emphasizes, at the conclusion of his (in my opinion not very convincing) book *Die Zeichenquelle der johanneischen Redaktion*, that 'an "original gospel of John", lying behind the dense and coherent web of the traditional text of John 1: 21–21: 25, . . . [is] not reconstructable'.[44]

IV. JOHN 2: 1–11 REGARDED AS A UNITY

It is the merit of the work of B. Olsson (mentioned at the beginning of this study) that it examines John 2: 1–11—in an unusually penetrating way—in connection with that 'dense and coherent web' which the *whole* fourth Gospel presents. The strength of his examination lies in that it begins by regarding the given text as a literary unity without looking for its historical connections, tradition, or redaction, but yet subjects the text itself to a detailed linguistic analysis and pays attention to its stylistic subtleties. His methods are particularly suited to the esoteric character of the Johannine 'special' language.[45] This is hardly the place to describe the 'wholistic' method of the author, which proceeds from thirty-one minute statement units and analyses these against the background of the language of the Gospel, in order then to grasp the total structure of the text through the presentation of its very different

---

[43] Cf. the procedure of W. Nicol, op. cit. n. 20 above.

[44] Op. cit. n. 29 above, 131. Cf. also his teacher H. Thyen in *Tradition und Glaube: Festgabe für K. G. Kuhn* (Göttingen, 1971), 356, and in *Kirche: Festgabe für Günther Bornkamm zum 75. Geburtstag* (Tübingen, 1980), 164: 'But such a mode of approach, which analyses the Fourth Gospel as if it were an archaeological excavation site, should not rule out the fact (that it) is equally a coherent literary work in its traditional canonical form, that is to say in the given order of texts and chapters. It is to be interpreted as a whole and not as a mere compendium of Johannine and early Christian traditions.' 'In contrast to such approaches, I regard the traditional text as "the Fourth Gospel" and therefore its last redactor as "the fourth evangelist" and creator of this work.'

[45] Op. cit., n. 1 above, 1–6 (esp. 5–6), 15–16.

reference relationships and at the end to articulate its 'message'.[46] One would only say here '*tolle, lege*', and wish that the other Johannine texts would at some time be analysed in this thorough and convincing way.[47]

The whole text shows itself as 'a symbolic narrative text with many allusive elements',[48] from which the author works out a symbolic significance or allusion for each of twenty-three concepts and formulas, differing greatly in content and intensity, but yet characterizing the whole text as symbolic.[49]

This means, however, that the evangelist attributed to the whole narrative *in all its parts* a deeper theological meaning with a view of the whole Gospel, notwithstanding whether or not he took it from the tradition or formed it editorially himself.

I would not, however, wish to go so far as does B. Lindars, whom the author cites approvingly: '*The miracle itself is unimportant* and all the interest lies in the symbolical possibilities of the event.'[50] Here a false alternative seems to be set up: σημεῖον (אות) does not mean only the symbolism of the sign, since it is at the same time a visible performance of a miracle, and one cannot declare the latter wholly inessential in favour of the former. *Without the 'deed' there is also no 'symbolism'*. Even in the case of a parable (*Gleichnishandlung*) it is always the action (*Handlung*) which is at issue at the same time. It is for this reason that the activity (*Handeln*) of Jesus during his last supper has been important for the Church. For the evangelist, the concrete deed of the incarnate Logos has essential significance: it is the ἀρχὴ τῶν σημείων of the

---

[46] Ibid., 22–7: Analysis of the statement units; 77–94: The Structure of the Text; 94–114: The Message of the Text. Regarding his procedure only a brief example from his analysis of v. 8a (54 f.) is necessary. He examines the meaning of νῦν in the general NT use of language. In connecting the imperative aorist with it (here he could also have referred to the expositions of Abbott, op. cit. n. 31 above, 319) and in connection with John, he shows that it is used here in a temporal sense and refers to the fact that the miracle has already occurred. But in the special application John gives it, νῦν is referred to the statements about the hour of Jesus (cf. v. 4), as is seen in 12: 27, 31; 13: 31; 16: 5, 22; 17: 5, 13: 'For Jn the "hour" is the great Now' (55). This is taken up again in the structural analysis in the section 'Temporal Features' (83 f.), with the result: 'The three elements of time mentioned, ἡ ὥρα μου, νῦν and ἄρτι belong together: they should ... be regarded ... that *first* the "hour" of Jesus, *then* the wine is there, the drawing, the bringing (νῦν, ἄρτι).' (84.) This is then evaluated in a summary fashion for the total interpretation (100 f.): 'I found that the *temporal relations*, unlike the spatial and logical, play an important part of our narrative ... Together they provide a striking *temporal pattern* with "*the hour of Jesus*" in centre ... This temporal structure ... draws attention to ἡ ὥρα μου in Jesus' first speech as an important key to the interpretation of the entire text' (100).

[47] The author limits himself to 2: 1–11 and 4: 1–42 only.

[48] Ibid., 114.

[49] Ibid., 113: τῇ ἡμέρᾳ τῇ τρίτῃ, γάμος, Κανὰ τῆς Γαλιλίας, ἡ μήτηρ τοῦ Ἰησοῦ, γύναι, ἡ ὥρα μου, οἱ διάκονοι, ὅ τι ἂν λέγῃ ὑμῖν ποιήσατε, λίθιναι, κατὰ τὸν καθαρισμὸν τῶν Ἰουδαίων, ἕως ἄνω, ἀντλήσατε, ἀρχιτρίκλινος, ἐγεύσατο τὸ ὕδωρ, οὐκ ᾔδει/ᾔδεισαν πόθεν ἐστίν, οἱ ἠντληκότες τὸ ὕδωρ, νυμφίον, τὸν καλὸν οἶνον, ἀρχήν, σημείων, ἐφανέρωσεν, δόξαν, ἐπίστευσαν εἰς.

[50] *The Gospel of John*, New Century Bible, (London, 1972), 123; Olsson, op. cit., 95 (italics mine).

Messiah and the Son of God (1: 41, 49) which forms the foundation and through which this Logos makes visible his hidden glory to the disciples for the first time.[51] Only because the deed actually occurred for him, can it be profoundly told again in such a way as to indicate *the whole salvific work* of Jesus and to have it refer to the paradoxical glory of the one who was elevated on the cross. Despite all the theologically reflective freedom in structuring the narrative, he does not want to write pious fiction, but to re-present what is for him a highly significant tradition from whose abundance he can consciously select[52] in a form which has his stamp and accords with *the whole*. The way we today explain the miracles which are attributed to Jesus is a completely different matter (and is in the last analysis also a dogmatic question).[53]

Keeping in mind, of course, the wealth of attempts at symbolic interpretation in a history of interpretation which spans more than eighteen hundred years, the problem which remains is to discover the deeper intention of the evangelist in saying *what* he did; further, if and how his first hearers and readers could grasp it.

Agreeing with older works by Leroy, Meeks, and others,[54] Olsson suspects that the fourth Gospel is 'a book for the *initiated*, i.e. it is addressed primarily to those who are already conversant with its substance and its special linguistic form'.[55] This is certainly on the mark in view of the history of the origin of this work in the so-called 'Johannine school' or 'community', a murky and puzzling history which is, just for this reason, portrayed today often in such fantastic ways.[56] The nearest parallel—not taken from the domain of the Greek language, however—would be the genuine Essene texts from Qumran. They have their own stylistic quality and behind them, at least in part, stands the Teacher of Righteousness, the 'Principal of the school'.[57] Yet 20: 20 f.

---

[51] 1: 14, 39, 46, 51. Note the climax.

[52] Cf. 20: 30 f.; 21: 25.

[53] Olsson, expressly stresses: 'There is no indication in the text that he himself does not regard it as historically accurate. It is presented as an occurrence in Jesus' historical situation which is a sign of something else.' (op. cit., 98).

[54] Op. cit., 97; Feine-Behm-Kümmel, *Einleitung in das Neue Testament* (Heidelberg, 12th edn., 1969), 157 ff.; A. Wikenhauser-Schmid, *Einleitung in das Neue Testament* (Freiburg–Basel–Vienna, 6th edn., 1973), 342 ff.; H. Leroy, *Rätsel und Missverständnis: Ein Beitrag zur Formgeschichte des Evangeliums*, BBB 30 (Bonn, 1968); W. A. Meeks, 'The Man from Heaven in Johannine Sectarianism', *JBL* 91 (1972), 44–72 (69 f.).

[55] Op. cit., 275, cf. 97.

[56] Olsson, 289, thus dates the analysed texts relatively early (in my opinion too early). The fourth Gospel surely got its present form only after the Synoptic Gospels, i.e. around the year 90 at the earliest. Cf. 21: 18–23: the death of Peter happened sometime earlier.

[57] Regarding the 'Johannine Community', cf. the research report by R. Kysar (op. cit. n. 2 above, 243 ff.) and especially R. A. Culpepper, *The Johannine School*, SBL Dissertation Series 26 (Missoula, Montana, 1975). For the Teacher of Righteousness and the beloved disciple, see J. Roloff, *NTS* 15 (1968/69), 129–51.

and 21: 15–17, 24 f. (cf. also 10: 16, 11: 52, 12: 20, 17: 20 ff.) point at the same time to a *universal* orientation of the fourth Gospel which is related to the greater church and which had left the esoteric circle of students behind. It would be interesting to know if, with the dissemination of the fourth Gospel to the greater church, there was a firm tradition of interpretation. This dissemination is to be dated shortly after the year 100 at the latest; one need only think of its significance for the Church of Asia Minor and of Egypt in the second century. It would also be interesting to know if Irenaeus perhaps reproduced an older tradition of Asia Minor in his Eucharistic interpretation of 2: 1–11. Since a symbolic-allegorical interpretation of the fourth Gospel immediately suggested itself (and, as our text shows, was indeed demanded), it is understandable that gnostic exegesis, as, for instance, that of the Valentinians, accepted it with special enthusiasm, despite its subtly anti-docetic character.[58]

This attempt at an almost thoroughgoing symbolic interpretation of the text, which text, as Olsson expressly emphasizes,[59] does not present a strictly composed allegory (but rather contains many central points and many different allusions) seems to me the most important contribution to our understanding of this puzzling text to have appeared in the last few decades.

Nevertheless, there are numerous questions to be asked. Since we are not dealing with a self-contained allegory, it must be emphasized that the unity of the narrative is established through the dramatically described miraculous event in its three progressive stages.[60] It is connected with surprising side-effects and maintains its effect on the reader even without the more profound 'symbolic' interpretation. We are not dealing with that which is *only* a parable. It is precisely for this reason that the fourth Gospel could be so effective, following its dissemination among the communities of the greater church at the beginning of the second century, without 'symbolic-allegorical commentary', and, at the same time, could stimulate exegetes to continually new interpretations, particularly of our narrative.

Thus the 'novelistic' and thrilling construction of the narrative is to

[58] Irenaeus, *Adv. Haer.*, 3. 11.7: '*Hi autem quia Valentino sunt, eo quod est secundum Johannem plenissime utentes ad ostensionem coniugationum suarum,*' cf. 1. 8. 5–9. 5; see also n. 22 above. The first commentary on John was written by Heracleon, a student of Valentinus, around the middle of the second century.

[59] Olsson, op. cit., 114: 'The text can *not* be described as an *allegory*. There is no consistent identification of expressions in the text with a transferred meaning. . . .'

[60] Cf. Olsson, op. cit., 98. Vv. 3–5, the lack of wine and the rebuff of his mother; vv. 7–8, Jesus' instructions; vv. 9–10 the surprising assessment of the miracle by the steward. The whole is given a frame through the theologically decisive reference to the presence of Jesus' disciples and to the effect the event has (v. 1, 2 and 11).

be taken seriously. Note, for instance, the very striking conclusion in v. 10b, with which the wedding-narrative abruptly comes to a close in order to bring about the *metabasis* of the disciples' faith. The same applies to the objectionably brief introduction in v. 3, which leaves so many questions unanswered and led to an enlargement of the text already in the second century (compare above, p. 91). In other words, the author was not only a theologian of some stature, but also an artist who can hardly take second place to the other great New Testament author, Mark. His 'irony' works on the aesthetic and theological levels (or, more precisely, on different theological levels at once).

On the other hand, the *possibilities* of interpretation (we are here faced with no necessities) accepted by Olsson seem to me still too few. A. Smitmans is correct to conclude his presentation of the more recent history of interpretation with the remark: 'The multiplicity of questions and answers, to which a report on the interpretation must address itself, is in the first place a sign of the uncertainty of this interpretation. . . . Yet, this multiplicity need not merely be a matter of uncertainty or insecurity, but could also have its basis *in the richness of the statement to be interpreted.*'[61] John 2: 1–11, and the action described as well, is an all too rich narrative. The narrative calls forth total astonishment—or annoyance. At the same time it provokes a many-sided symbolic interpretation in view of the whole salvific event told in the Gospel. One thing, at least, is clear—literary-critical slashing can only destroy this effect.

In accord with the scholarly investigations of A. Serra[62] and J. Potin,[63] Olsson has called attention to the special significance of the 'Sinai-Screen' for understanding John 1: 19–2: 11. It is unlikely, however, that the doubtless important reference to the Sinai-epiphany presents the sole key to a deeper understanding of this text. Christ as the incarnate Logos and Messiah of Israel is surely set over against the gift of the Law to Israel through Moses in an antitypical way, but there are other such keys, since the references to Sinai emerge most definitely in the framework (that is the third day in 2: 1 and the revelation of the δόξα to the disciples in 2: 11). They emerge only in a completely indirect way in the dramatized narrative itself.

By an analogy with Christ as the 'true vine' (15: 1) one could, on the basis of 2: 10, call Christ the 'good wine' (and, on the basis of 4: 10 f.,

---

[61] Op. cit., 62 f. (italics mine).

[62] Here Olsson referred back to A. Serra's essay, 'Le tradizioni della teofania sinaitica nel Targum dello pseudo-Jonathan Es. 19. 24 e in Giov. 1, 19–2, 12,' *Marianum*, 33 (1971), 1–39. In the meantime, Serra's dissertation, with its wealth of material, appeared: *Contributi dell'Antica Letteratura Guidaica per l'esegesi di Giovanni 2, 1–12 e 19, 25–7, SPFTM* 31 (Roma, 1977).

[63] J. Potin, *La fête juive de la Pentecôte: Études des textes liturgiques. I–II* (= *Lect. Div.* 65), Paris, 1971; cf. Olsson, op. cit., 102 and *passim*.

'the water of life'). The relation between the wine metaphor in the first sign and the vine in the last ἐγώ εἰμι saying is surely no accident.

The wine and the vine play an important role in connection with the Jewish expectation of the Messiah, a role that cannot be overlooked. One of the most important Messianic prophesies in Judaism was Gen. 49: 10–12.[64] It is equally instructive that the wine-cup, pitcher, grape-leaf, and grape appear frequently on the coins of the uprisings of 66–73 and 132–5, which were motivated by eschatological-Messianic considerations.[65] The Messianically interpreted blessing of Jacob in Gen. 49: 10–12 describes the eschatological ruler in Dionysiac colours:

> The scepter shall not move from Judah,
> Or the mace from between his feet,
> To the end that tribute be brought him,
> And to him go the peoples' homage.
> He tethers his ass to a vine,
> His purebred to the choicest stem;
> In wine he washes his garments,
> His robes in the blood of grapes.
> His eyes are darker than wine,
> And his teeth are whiter than milk.
>
> (Trans. *The Anchor Bible*)

To be sure rabbinic exegesis reinterpreted the wine-motif here in terms of the Torah; but must we presuppose the same one-sided interpretation for John?[66] It should be mentioned further that apocalyptic texts exist which have fantastic descriptions of the fecundity of the vine—compare 2 *Apoc. Bar.* 29: 5, 1 Enoch 10: 19 and, above all, the Papias text cited by Irenaeus (with its hyperbolics that seem absurd to us, but occur not infrequently in rabbinic and apocalyptic texts, and which also accords in some respects with the Johannine Gospel—cf. 21:

[64] F. A. Serra, *Contributi* 244–50; R. Borig, *Der wahre Weinstock: Untersuchungen zu Joh 15, 1–10* (Munich, 1967), 100, 104 f., 118. A. Jaubert, 'L'image de la vigne (Jean 15),' *Oikonomia: Festschrift O. Cullmann* (Hamburg–Bergstedt, 1967), 93–9; J. Jeremias, *Jesus als Weltvollender* (Gütersloh, 1930), 27–31.

[65] Y. Meshorer, *Jewish Coins of the Second Temple Period* (Tel Aviv, 1967), 154–69, Plates XIX–XXVIII. Prior to this, the grape can be found only in very individual cases on the coins of Archelaus and the grape leaf on procurator's coins: cf. 132, nn. 61–2; 172, no. 224, Plates VIII and XXIX. Regarding the Bar Kochba coins, see the foundational work of Leo Mildenberg, *The Coinage of the Bar Kokhba War, Typos*, 6 (Aarau, Frankfurt, Salzburg, 1984).

[66] Cf. Gen. 27: 28 f.: Isaac's blessing on Jacob; the expectation of eschatological fecundity: Lev. 26: 5; Deut. 28: 1–4; Amos 9: 13; Hos. 2: 24; 14: 8 f.; Joel 2: 21–4, 4: 18; Zech. 8: 12; Isa. 29: 17, 30: 23–6; Jer. 31: 5; Ezek. 34: 23–31, 36: 29 f.; Hos. 14: 8 (LXX diff. from MT): ζήσονται καὶ μεθυσθήσονται σίτῳ· καὶ ἐξανθήσει ὡς ἄμπελος τὸ μνημόσυνον αὐτοῦ, ὡς οἶνος Λιβάνου. To the interpretations of the Targums referred to by A. Serra (op. cit. 244 ff.) are to be added: *Tg. Jer. I* = MS. Add. 27031; as for Gen. 27: 25 cf. the Targum of the Pentateuch I Genèse, SC 245, ed. R. le Déaut, 260 f.; Add. 27031 for Gen. 27: 25; יומסא √ גנז he translates 'caché', cf. 261 n. 8: 'Rapprocher peut-être le verbe τετήρηκας de Jn 2, 10, à la lumière de Apoc. 2, 17.'

25).[67] 'Messianic-Dionysian' allusions may also be found in the Sibylline descriptions of Paradise: 'Angels lead to the light and to the carefree life, where the immortal path of the great God is and three-fold springs of *wine*, honey, and milk'.[68]

One might further refer to the messianic feast of joy, where the wine played a central role and which Jesus anticipated with tax-collectors and sinners or even in the circle of the disciples. It was not without cause that the reproach was raised against him that he was 'a glutton and a drunkard' in contrast to the ascetic Baptist.[69] The concluding remark in the Last Supper according to Mark 14: 25; Matt. 24: 29 also speaks for itself.[70]

In this context, therefore, should not the wine-miracle in John 2: 1–11 be at the same time a symbol of the 'fullness' and 'joy' which the Messiah brings? 'I have come, that you may have life and complete fulfillment ($\pi\epsilon\rho\iota\sigma\sigma\acute{o}\nu$)!' (10: 10). The motif of perfect joy follows the vine saying a number of times: 'This I have told you, that my *joy* be in you and that your *joy* be perfect [$\pi\lambda\eta\rho\omega\theta\hat{\eta}$].'[71] 'Ask and you will receive, so that your *joy* may be perfect.'[72] Origen had already emphasized this motif in his interpretation of the Cana miracle.[73]

One might also here refer to an *antitype* in the Old Testament (Jer. 16: 8 f.): 'And as for a house where there is feasting, you are not to go there either, and sit with them eating and drinking. For this is what

[67] *Adv. Haer.*, 5. 33. 3–4. On this cf. U. H. Körner, *Papias von Hierapolis*, FRLANT 133 (Göttingen, 1983), 50, 97–104. Could John 2: 6 possibly be background here for the number 6 and the *Metreten?* Cf. also H. J. de Jonge, 'BOTRYC BOHCEI: The Age of Kronos and the Millenium in Papias of Hierapolis.' M. S. Vermaseren (ed.), *Studies in Hellenistic Religion*, EPRO 78 (Leiden, 1979), 37–49. Papias, for whom the Presbyter John is the principal informant, is acquainted with the Apocalypse, 1 John (and in my opinion) also the fourth Gospel (cf. M. Hengel, 'Probleme des Markusevangeliums' *Das Evangelium und die Evangelien*, ed. P. Stuhlmacher, WUNT 28 (Tübingen, 1983), 247–51. One could *cum grano salis* call him a later 'peripheral figure' in the Johannine circle.

[68] *Sib. Or.* 2, 316–18; cf. 8, 211 f., 3, 621 f., 744 f. My emphasis. The wine stands in first place in three of the four instances.

[69] Luke 7: 34 / Matt. 11: 19.

[70] Regarding the Messianic meal, cf. H. L. Strack and P. Billerbeck, *Kommentar zum Neuen Testament*, vol. iv. 2 (Munich, 1956), 1154–9. For the fantastic size of the blessing cup, upon which David will pronounce the word of praise, cf. 1164 f.: *Yoma* 76a; *Midr. Teh.* 23 § 6; in addition cf. in n. 66 the documentation from the Targums.

[71] 15: 11. My emphasis.

[72] 16: 24; cf. the prayer of Jesus in 17: 13 and 16: 20–22.

[73] *Johannescommentar*, GCS 10, 1903, ed. E. Preuschen, 10, 38 (p. 178): $\mu\epsilon\tau\grave{\alpha}$ $\tau\grave{\eta}\nu$ $\dot{\epsilon}\nu$ $\tau\hat{\omega}$ $o\check{\iota}\nu\omega$ $\epsilon\dot{\upsilon}\omega\chi\acute{\iota}\alpha\nu$; 10, 65 (p. 182 f.): '$T\alpha\acute{\upsilon}\tau\eta\nu$ $\dot{\alpha}\rho\chi\grave{\eta}\nu$ $\tau\hat{\omega}\nu$ $\sigma\eta\mu\epsilon\acute{\iota}\omega\nu$ $\dot{\epsilon}\pi o\acute{\iota}\eta\sigma\epsilon\nu$ $\dot{o}$ '$I\eta\sigma o\hat{\upsilon}\varsigma$ $\dot{\epsilon}\nu$ $K\alpha\nu\hat{\alpha}$ $\tau\hat{\eta}\varsigma$ $\Gamma\alpha\lambda\iota\lambda\alpha\acute{\iota}\alpha\varsigma$'. $o\dot{\upsilon}$ $\gamma\grave{\alpha}\rho$ $\mathring{\eta}\nu$ $\dot{\alpha}\rho\chi\grave{\eta}$ $\tau\hat{\omega}\nu$ $\sigma\eta\mu\epsilon\acute{\iota}\omega\nu$ $\tau\grave{o}$ $\dot{\epsilon}\nu$ $K\alpha\phi\alpha\rho\nu\alpha o\grave{\upsilon}\mu$, $\tau\hat{\omega}$ $\pi\rho o\eta\gamma o\upsilon\mu\acute{\epsilon}\nu\omega$ $\mu\grave{\epsilon}\nu$ $\sigma\eta\mu\epsilon\acute{\iota}\omega\nu$ $\epsilon\mathring{\iota}\nu\alpha\iota$ $\tauo\hat{\upsilon}$ $\upsilon\acute{\iota}o\hat{\upsilon}$ $\tauo\hat{\upsilon}$ $\theta\epsilon o\hat{\upsilon}$ $\tau\grave{\eta}\nu$ $\epsilon\dot{\upsilon}\phi\rho o\sigma\acute{\upsilon}\nu\eta\nu$· 13, 391 (p. 287): $\iota\nu$' $\epsilon\dot{\upsilon}\phi\rho\acute{\alpha}\nu\eta$ $\tauo\grave{\upsilon}\varsigma$ $\sigma\upsilon\nu\epsilon\sigma\tau\iota\omega\mu\acute{\epsilon}\nuo\upsilon\varsigma$; 13, 392 (p. 288): $\dot{\epsilon}\xi$ $\mathring{\upsilon}\delta\alpha\tauo\varsigma$ $\gamma\iota\nu o\mu\acute{\epsilon}\nu o\nu$ $o\mathring{\iota}\nu o\nu$ $\chi o\rho\eta\gamma o\hat{\upsilon}\sigma\alpha$ $\epsilon\dot{\iota}\varsigma$ $\epsilon\dot{\upsilon}\phi\rho o\sigma\acute{\upsilon}\nu\eta\nu$ $\tau\hat{\omega}\nu$ $\sigma\upsilon\nu\epsilon\sigma\tau\iota\omega\mu\acute{\epsilon}\nu\omega\nu$; 13, 438 (p. 294): $\mu\epsilon\tau\grave{\alpha}$ $\tau\grave{o}$ $\lambda o\upsilon\tau\rho\grave{o}\nu$ $\dot{\eta}\mu\hat{\alpha}\varsigma$ $\epsilon\dot{\upsilon}\phi\rho\alpha\acute{\iota}\nu\epsilon\iota$ $\sigma\upsilon\nu\delta\iota\alpha\iota\tau\omega\mu\acute{\epsilon}\nuo\upsilon\varsigma$ $\alpha\dot{\upsilon}\tau\hat{\omega}$· $\kappa\alpha\grave{\iota}$ $\delta\iota\delta o\grave{\upsilon}\varsigma$ $\tauo\hat{\upsilon}$ $\dot{\epsilon}\kappa$ $\tau\hat{\eta}\varsigma$ $\delta\upsilon\nu\acute{\alpha}\mu\epsilon\omega\varsigma$ $\alpha\dot{\upsilon}\tauo\hat{\upsilon}$ $o\mathring{\iota}\nuo\upsilon$ $\pi\iota\epsilon\hat{\iota}\nu$. A. Smitmans, op. cit., 145, 281 thinks Origen's interpretation is correct. 'The wine-miracle is the beginning of the signs, "because the special sign of the Son of God is joy" (John 10: 12 GCS 10 p. 183, 2 f.)' He cites only this passage.

Yahweh of Hosts, the God of Israel, has said: See! I am going to banish
from this place—before your eyes, and in your days—sounds of mirth
and gladness, the voice of bridegroom and bride.' (Trans. *The Anchor
Bible*.) The Johannine Christ acts precisely *in opposition to* God's instruc-
tion to the prophet. For with his coming, sorrow comes to an end and
the time of joy is at hand. The witness of the Baptist (3: 29) to the over-
flowing joy of the friend of the bridegroom who hears his voice may in
this connection also be significant.

That the antithesis between the water in the stone jars—which serve
for ritual purification—and the good wine takes the antithesis in the
prologue 1: 17 further has again and again been pointed out since the
time of the ancient Church. It is tempting here to relate the plenitude
of the good wine to the gift of the spirit, 'whom God does not give ἐκ
μέτρου,'[74] which 'flows in streams'[75] and which brings to life, while the
flesh is useless (6: 63).

The reference to the Eucharist—the relation of bread and wine to
the 'flesh' and 'blood' of Christ—which become gifts of salvation
through the atoning death of Jesus (see 6: 31–58 and 19: 34 f.; compare
1 John 5: 6), of which Irenaeus knows, is likewise legitimate. The list
could easily be expanded.

I believe that John wishes to have this miracle narrative, which is
programmatic for him, interpreted in many ways—and this in the
sense of the *'multiplicity of approaches'*—so that it can be related to the
whole Gospel through a 'dense and coherent' (cf. above, p. 95) web of
references. The evangelist was, precisely because of his love of paradox
and dialectic, a richly variegated thinker, whose subtle and profound
thought is misunderstood by all the primitive, literary-critical 'master-
tailors'. This does not in any way rule out the attempt to discover the
multifaceted levels, breaks, and tensions in the Gospel or the application of sources and the assumption that heated discussions took place
in the school. Scissors are, however, in this effort not the appropriate
instrument by which to comprehend them.

This multifarious nature of the text may be seen also in the role
which the mother of Jesus plays. She not only embodies the old Israel;
she at the same time embodies the family of Jesus, which at the wrong
time makes inappropriate demands of Jesus or does not understand him
at all—a tendency which relates John to the Synoptics.[76] The nearest
parallel to Jesus' gruff rebuff of his mother (οὔπω ἥκει ἡ ὥρα μου) may
be found in the similarly structured rejection of the demands of Jesus'

[74] 3: 34.
[75] 7: 38.
[76] Cf. Mark 3: 31–5, 6: 3–6.

brothers (7: 2–8); probably they were omitted from the wedding itself quite intentionally.[77] In both cases Jesus refused to consider acting immediately (see 7: 6) for the reason that his time had not yet come,[78] although after the refusal, surprisingly, he did act (of course not publicly).[79] Jesus' reaction in chapter seven is more negative, however. In 7: 5 the faith of Jesus' brothers is directly denied by way of commentary. Over against this, the directive of Jesus' mother (2: 5) mitigates the situation and sets the stage for Jesus' action. The mother of Jesus also appears (19: 25) below the cross as a witness, while the brothers of Jesus, after their dismissal (7: 10), disappear from the Gospel.

In the same way, that at the cross Jesus entrusts his mother to his beloved disciple is an indirect affront to the brothers of Jesus, since caring for their mother was their obvious duty. Conversely, the beloved disciple, as a trusted friend of Jesus and as the one who carries out his bequest, receives a singular authority, which lends him a distinction not only over against Peter, but also over against the family relations. The latter were, according to Hegesippus, still extraordinarily influential at the time of the origin of the Gospel in Palestinian Jewish Christianity.[80] By means of the references to the family of Jesus, the fourth Gospel deals not only with the basic relation of Jewish and pagan Christians, or of the old to the new 'people of God'—a term which does not play an essential role in it; but it also addresses the relation of the Johannine group to the Jewish-Christian relatives of Jesus.[81]

These examples may suffice to show that the multiplicity of attempts at interpretation is not necessarily due to the bewilderment of the exegetes; it is intended by the evangelist himself by way of the subtle, many-levelled structure of his Gospel in the sense of a 'variety of approaches'. It is self-evident that the *introitus*, the ἀρχὴ τῶν σημείων,

---

[77] We find them instead of the disciples in the *Epistula Apostolorum* ch. 5 (ed. C. Schmidt, TU 43 (1919), p. 29). This information may be found also in John Chrysostom (*Hom. on John* 21: 1, *PG* 89, 129) and perhaps also in Epiphanius and Philoxenos of Mabug. This point stems possibly from a changed text or from the apocryphal tradition. It is certainly not original. The brothers of Jesus have intruded from 2: 12. For a treatment of the whole issue, cf. Smitmans (op. cit. 84–8).

[78] 7: 6: ὁ καιρὸς ὁ ἐμὸς οὔπω πάρεστιν.

[79] 2: 6 = 7: 10.

[80] Cf. M. Hengel, 'Jakobus der Herrenbruder—der erste "Papst"?' in *Glaube und Eschatologie. Festschrift für Werner Georg Kümmel zum 80. Geburtstag*, ed. E. Gräßer and O. Merk (Tübingen, 1985), 71–104. (Cf. Euseb., *HE* 3. 20. 6).

[81] λαός appears only on the lips of Caiaphas (11: 50 / 18: 14) and is replaced with τέκνα τοῦ θεοῦ in the interpretation. Israel appears more frequently (1: 31, 49; 3: 10; 12: 13), yet twice by way of a formula as βασιλεὺς τοῦ Ἰσραήλ in the confession or acclamation. The most important ecclesiological concept is given by the ἴδιοι (1: 11; 13: 1) in connection with the ἴδια πρόβατα (10: 3 f., 12) and with being a child of God (τέκνα θεοῦ: 1: 12; 11: 52; cf. 1 John 3: 1 f., 10; 5: 2) and points rather to the notion of the 'family of God'. Cf. also the singular passage 20: 17, where Jesus speaks of the disciples as τοὺς ἀδελφούς μου.

must play a special role here. Similar points may be made also concerning the highly varied use of titles of rank or concerning the ἐγώ εἰμι sayings. All approaches come together in this connection at the same point, in the person of Jesus and in his salvific work (and in accordance with, of course, the *secundum homines recipientes*, that is according to the understanding of the Johannine community). This *unity* in multiplicity may well be called the 'Christological monomania' of the fourth Gospel.

V. THE EXTERNAL 'COLOURING' OF THE MIRACLE NARRATIVE

I must now return to the external contours of the narrative, which is, in many ways, 'offensive' and has precious little to do with the 'Protestant ethos' of the nineteenth and twentieth centuries. Dibelius is right in this connection (compare above, n. 7). It has probably given offence from the beginning—something we should not hesitate to admit.

J. Gnilka, in his recent, brief commentary, speaks of 'the poor people's wedding of Cana'.[82] But the wedding reported by John in fact points to the opposite: the διάκονοι, that is, the slaves waiting on the tables, the ἀρχιτρίκλινος, presumably not one of the guests but the 'head slave'[83] responsible for all the arrangements of the feast, speak of an

---

[82] *Die Neue Echter-Bibel*, pt. I. (Würzburg, 1983), 22.

[83] The concept appears otherwise only in Heliodorus (*Aethiopika* 7. 27. 7) together with οἰνοχόοι and there means the head slaves who served at the table of the Persian satrap (cf. H. G. Liddell and R. Scott, *A Greek–English Dictionary* (Oxford, 1961)). In Petronius (*Satiricon* 22. 6) there is a triclinarch as the organizer of a highly questionable feast. Inscriptions testify of imperial freedmen, who administered, among other offices, that of a triclinarch of Caere (early imperial period?) (*CIL* 11. 3612), of Rome (AD 117), *CIL* 6. 1884, of Corinth (*c.* first half of the third century, Severus Alexander) (*CIL* 3. 536). Cf. *The Oxford Latin Dictionary* (Oxford, 1973), which defines it as 'a steward responsible for arrangements in the dining room'. Three inscriptions of honour for priests of Stratoniceia (Caria) in southern Asia Minor seem more revealing. At the conclusion of the enumeration of other liturgical offices (Gymnasiarch, sacrificial feasts, offerings for public buildings, etc.), expenditures for the feasts of Zeus Panamaros are listed in the Comyrion shrine. Here one reads of special, opulent banquets (τρικλινιαρχίαι; the translation of Liddell and Scott as 'directorship of feasts' is not correct in connection with these sources: in *BCH* 15, no. 144, 183 f. it says (l. 10 f.) ὑπὲρ τῶν ἑστιάσεων ... and exactly parallel to this in l. 19 ὑπὲρ τῶν τρικλιναρχιῶν; in addition, the concept appears in the plural in all three inscriptions). With regard to these banquets, the generous amounts of wine, donated by the priests, are emphasized.

(1) *BCH* 11, 1887, 383 ff. 384 ff. no. 3
       ... ἐπετέλεσαν δὲ καὶ τὰ μυ-
       στήρια τοῦ Κομυρίου εὐσεβῶς καὶ
       τοῖς μὲν ἀνδράσιν ἐν τῷ Κομυρί-
       ῳ δεῖπνα παρέσχον κατὰ τρικλει-
   30 ναρχίας καὶ τὸν οἶνον ἔδοσαν ἀ-
       φθόνως πολείταις, ξένοις, δούλοις
       . . .
   36 ... ἔθεσαν δὲ καὶ ἐν τῇ ὁδῷ
       πάσῃ ἡλικίᾳ γλυκύν τε καὶ οἶνον ἀφθόνως
       . . .

entirely different, indeed 'feudal' milieu. The six gigantic stone jars are also a sign of wealth. Such very expensive receptacles, made of soft limestone, have been found in Jerusalem. They were treasured because, unlike clay vessels, they did not become unclean for ritual purposes.[84]

The fourth Gospel puts no emphasis on the poor, in contrast to Luke (who, however, shows ambivalence in this regard). It shows rather an 'aristocratic' character: it does not hesitate to display wealth and abundance.[85] The 'luxury-miracle' of Cana stands in clear contrast to the early Christian ideal of poverty. 1 John 2: 16 f. and 3: 17 as well as 3 John thereby gain a concrete background.[86]

Miracles of gifts or provisions could in a special way raise the suspicion that magic was at work. In this regard, G. Theissen remarks that 'nothing is known of people who proposed to increase the amount of bread or change water into wine. Nothing is known of magic practices whereby such miracles could be brought about.'[87] This, fortunately,

---

This inscription is dated in the time of Marcus Aurelius by G. Deschamps / G. Cousin (*BCH* 11, 383).

(2) *BCH* 15, 1891, 185. 186 no. 130
    25   ... δόντες καὶ ὑπὲρ τῶν τρι-
         κλινιαρχιῶν ἐν αὐταῖς τῶν
         Παναμαρίων ἡμέραις ἐν τῇ
         πόλι ...

This inscription breaks off in l. 31; the donation of wine is not retained or was not mentioned.

(3) *BCH* 15, 1891, 204 no. 144: ...
         [ἔ] δωκαν δὲ κ(αὶ) ὑπὲρ τῶ[ν τ] ρικλινα[ρ]χιῶν ἐν
    20   ⟨ν⟩ τῷ τοῦ Κομυρίου κα[ιρ]ῷ πάσῃ τύχ[ῃ] κα[ὶ]ἠλι-
         κία καὶ τοῖς ἐπιδη[μ]ήσασιν ξέν[ο]ι[ς κ]αὶ
         θεατρικοῖς, προσ[απ]έδοσαν [δὲ κ(αι) ἀφ]θό-
         νως καὶ φιλοτείμω[ς]ἐν τῷ Κομ[υρίῳ] τὸν
         οἶνον.

In connection with these τρικλινιαρχίαι, we are dealing with cultic feasts, the special mark of which was a bountiful enjoyment of wine. They probably were chaired by a τρικλινάρχης. The office and the office-holder are not designated here, but it may be assumed that the priests, who were honoured there, held 'triclinarchial' offices. The matter should be investigated further. Regarding the Johannine ἀρχιτρίκλινος, one may well suspect, even with these few records, that the special form with the prefixed ἀρχι-, which otherwise is confirmed only by Heliodorus, still has a conspicuous emphasis. Also B. Olsson (op. cit., 56) came to this conclusion from a completely different direction. It is further conspicuous that the triclinarchs in Stratoniceia presupposed a large donation of wine.

    [84]   Cf. *Jerusalem Revealed. Archaeology in the Holy City, 1968–1974* (Jerusalem, 1975), 47 f., Plate 48.
    [85]   Compare the depiction of John 12: 1–8 which reworks the Anointing scene from Mark 14: 3–9. The three siblings (John 11) belong to the upper stratum, which in general plays a far greater role than in the Synoptics (cf. 3: 1 f., 4: 47 ff.; 6: 15; 18: 15; 19: 38–41). The social milieu points rather to Asia Minor, where Pliny (Ep. 10. 96. 9) complains that (even in the distant Pontus) the new superstition has reached people *omnis ordinis*, rather than to Palestine or Syria, where the great poverty of the rural communities can be inferred from the Didache.
    [86]   Regarding this problem, see W. Schäfke, 'Frühchristlicher Widerstand, iv, no. 3: Der reiche Christ', *ANRW* 2. 23. 550–6. Cf. also M. Hengel, *Eigentum und Reichtum in der frühen Kirche* (Stuttgart, 1973), 69 ff.; cf. 34 ff., 44 ff.
    [87]   *Urchristliche Wundergeschichten* (Gütersloh, 1974), 113.

can be corrected. Theissen himself refers by way of qualification to
PGM 1: 103 f., where the 'Parhedros' furnishes 'wine, bread, and whatever else you wish' to the magician, as the latter had requested. He can
even conjure up human beings (1: 98). In the Talmud, the eighty
witches of Ashkelon understand this art of 'the wishing table' and conjure up bread, meat, cooked food, *and wine* one after the other.[88]

For the opponents of Christianity, the Cana narrative could very
well be regarded as proof of the magical art of Jesus.[89]

Likewise, with the charismatic miracle worker Hanina ben Dosa, a
somewhat later Galilean contemporary of Jesus, we encounter a series
of miracles of gifts and provisions, something which is not at all rare in
the rabbinic tradition. These legends could also be regarded by non-
believers as the work of Jewish magic, which was considered as particularly effective. Thus, in time of great need, the oven filled itself with
bread and the trough with dough, the leg of the table transformed into
gold—as anticipation of the heavenly meal—and the light burned the
whole day in the sabbath-lamp, which had by accident been filled with
vinegar. The vinegar seemed to have changed into oil, and the light,
having burned the whole day, could then still serve as the Habdala
light after the end of the Sabbath.[90] A wine-miracle, on the contrary,
was out of place with this poor ascetic, who for a whole week was satisfied 'with a portion of carob-bean'.[91] There is no room in these legends
for the amusements of a profane, luxurious celebration.

The motif of transformation appears, of course, also in a completely
different context. Ephrem had already seen a connection between the

---

[88] *y. Hag.* 78a ll. 5–8: אמרה מה דהיא אמרה ומייתיא חמר ('she mumbled something and
brought wine', l. 8); par. *y. Sanh.* 23c ll. 58–60; cf. additionally M. Hengel, *Rabbinische Legende und
frühpharisäische Geschichte*, AHAW.PH (Heidelberg, 1984), 20 f. The extent to which even the Rabbis understood this art is evident in *b. Sanh.* 65b: 'R. Hanina and R. Oshaia engaged in the study
of the book of the creation (that is a book of magic), on every previous evening, and created a
'third-grown' calf which they then ate.' Magical miracles of transformation are also included: In
b.Sanh. 67b, a woman magician offers Jannai a flour drink which transforms itself into scorpions.
As punishment Jannai transforms the magician into a donkey.

[89] Regarding this problem, cf. D. Aune, 'Magic in Early Christianity', *ANRW* 2. 23. 2 (1980),
1507–57 (esp. 1524 f.). On the reproach against Jesus as magician, cf. M. Smith, *Jesus the Magician*
(London, 1978), 61–7; S. Benko, 'Pagan Criticism of Christianity', *ANRW* 2. 23. 2 (1980), 1075 f.,
1091, 1102 f.

[90] Cf. *b. Ta'an.* 24b/25a; further G. Vermes, 'Hanina ben Dosa', *JJS* 23 (1972), 28–50 (42):
'The transformation of vinegar into oil is an additional embellishment. The only parallel one can
think of without searching is the conversion of water into wine in the New Testament narrative of
the wedding feast in Cana of Galilee.' The oil miracle is basically a combination of the Elijah
miracle (1 Kings 17; 16) and the oil miracle at the consecration of the temple in 2 Maccabees 1:
21 f.—cf. *b. Šabb.* 21b; *Meg. Ta'an.* 9; cf. Billerbeck (op. cit. n. 70) 2. 539. Compare also increasing
the amount of wheat by Eleazar of Bartutha in *b. Ta'an* 24a and the magical cucumber miracle of
Eliezer ben Hyrkanos in *b. Šabb.* 68a. Cf. also the transformation of water into oil by Narcissus as
reported by Eusebius (*HE* 6. 9. 1–3).

[91] *b. Ta'an* 24b below.

Cana miracle and the miracles of Moses in Egypt. (Exod. 7–11).[92] A homily falsely ascribed to Maximus of Turin mentions 'other creative acts of power with water', among them the transformation of the water of the Nile into blood, the first of the seven (!) miracles of punishment (Exod. 7: 11–25).[93] Cassiodorus reminds us of this in connection with his interpretation of Ps. 78(77): 44; in contrast to the punishment-miracle, the nations are thereby changed—for the better.[94]

In comparatively recent exegesis D. F. Strauss has referred to this strictly antitypical context;[95] and in even more recent times it has been stressed by M. Smith and O. Betz.[96] In this way the miracle expressed not only the superiority of the Messiah and the Son of God over Moses, but his direct participation in God's creative power[97], as the interpretation of the early Church since Irenaeus (cf. above p. 89) never tired of stressing. It was precisely this that the ancient critics regarded as an indication of especially dangerous magic, in the same way that Moses was indeed admired or slandered as one of the greatest magicians.[98] The fourth Gospel articulates this reproach through the accusation in 8: 48: 'You are a Samaritan and have a demon,' which probably means 'you are a figure like Simon Magus'.[99] This ambivalence (or the doubtful character of the miracle-narrative and of the miracle-worker) speaks against the existence of a pure Semeia-source as a collection of miracles without any reference to the teaching and Passion of Jesus. Such basically sterile listings of θαυμάσια as purported ἀληθῆ διηγήματα (Lucian) concerning a θεῖος ἀνήρ were of little use as 'missionary writings' to awaken faith in non-believers. Standing at the end of the Passion and Resurrection narrative, John 20: 31 was certainly not the mechanically applied conclusion of such a document. Even for the edification of believers, it would have been appropriate only in a very qualified sense. The Johannine school with its high, theological level should not be understood in the light of the primitive-romantic milieu revealed in the later apocryphal Acts of the apostles. The later child-

---

[92] Smitmans, op. cit., 189f., 226.

[93] Ibid., 193, 225.

[94] Ibid., 225f., 240.

[95] Op. cit. n. 9 above, 2. 234.

[96] M. Smith, *Jesus the Magician*, 161, 163; O. Betz/W. Grimm, *Wesen und Wirklichkeit der Wunder Jesu*, Arbeiten zum neuen Testament und Judentum 2 (Frankfurt–Las Vegas–Bern, 1977), 128. The criticism of I. Broer, *Zur Religionsgeschichtlichen Ableitung von Joh 2, 1–11, Studien zum Neuen Testament und seiner Umwelt* 8 (Linz, 1983), 103–23, 110 n. 28, misses the point completely.

[97] Smitmans, op. cit., 187–94.

[98] On this cf. J. G. Gager, *Moses in Greco-Roman Paganism*, SBL Monograph Series 16 (Missoula, Montana, 1972), 134–61.

[99] Cf. John 7: 19; 3: 2 and Acts 8: 9–13. The history of early Christianity is characterized by the attempt to come to terms with magical practices as well as with the reproach that it, in its turn, practised them.

hood Gospel of Thomas, teeming with miracles, did not have a great effect upon the Church and was largely rejected. Practically all of the Gospels, even most of the apocryphals, are determined by the teaching and Passion of Jesus. The collections of miracles of healing were interesting as means of propaganda in places where new, miraculous cures were constantly carried out. A Semeia-source would therefore be significant at best as a 'primer' or 'stimulus' for the miracle-workers in their own group. But, while testimony of the antimontanistic Apollonius[100] even speaks of an awakening from the dead which was attributed to the Ephesian John, there is nevertheless much more to be said against such an independent document than for it.

VI. THE RELIGIOUS BACKGROUND OF THE TEXT: A FALSE ALTERNATIVE

There still remains a question concerning the history of tradition or of religion: the problem of the Dionysiac influence. The immediate dependence of the Cana miracle on the cult of Dionysus—a view held by the History of Religions school and correspondingly also found in the commentary of Bultmann—has been rejected by H. Noetzel[101] in favour of the Jewish backgrounds of this narrative. To be sure, in this view Christ is not to be heralded as 'Neos Dionysos' as the performer of a wine-miracle 'imported' from the world of the Greeks; nor was the attempt made to win over 'Dionysus initiates' to the Christian faith by means of such stories. There is no doubt that the narrative has a Jewish-Palestinian background and this is clear on the basis of its location and circumstances.

W. L. Knox, in a brief reference, and Morton Smith, extensively, have called attention to a Phoenician Dionysus saga of the second half of the second century.[102] It occurs in the novel *Leucippe and Clitophon* by the otherwise unknown Achilleus Tatius. Smith has thereby brought to light something like a missing link.

It happened at that season to be the festival of Dionysus Lord of the Vintage; for the Tyrians claim him as their own proper deity, singing on the subject Cadmus' myth [μῦθον], which they relate as the origin of the festival; 'and this is it. In early days men had no wine; [all the vines] ... were derived from

---

[100] Eus., *HE* 5. 18. 14.

[101] *Christus und Dionysos*, *AzTh* (Stuttgart, 1960).

[102] W. L. Knox, *Some Hellenistic Elements in Primitive Christianity* (London, 1944), 60 n. 1. Morton Smith, 'On the Wine God in Palestine (Gen. 18; Jn 2 and Achilles Tatius)', *J. W. Baron Jubilee*, vol. ii (1975), 815–29; cf. by the same author *Jesus the Magician*, 120, 163, 200. The most recent investigation of I. Broer (op. cit. n. 96 above, 103–23) does not contribute essentially anything more to the matter.

Tyrian vines, the original mother of all wines being a plant of their country. There was a certain shepherd noted for his hospitality . . . Dionysus once paid a visit to this herdsman, who set before him the produce of the earth . . . *their drink was the same as that of the oxen, since vines did not yet exist.* Dionysus thanked the herdsman for his kindly cheer, and pledged him in a friendly cup; but his drink was wine. The herdsman, drinking of it, danced for joy [ὑφ' ἡδονῆς βακχεύεται], and said to the god: 'Where did you get this purple water, my friend? Wherever did you find blood so sweet? For it is not that water which flows on the ground—that, as it descends into the midriff, affords but a faint pleasure, while this delights the sense of smell before ever it reaches the mouth; when you touch it, it is cold, but it leaps down into the belly and there, far down, lights up the fires of delight.' 'This,' said Dionysus, 'is *harvest water,* the *blood of the grape*'[103] then the god led the herdsman to the vine, and took hold of the clusters and squeezed them; and then, pointing to the vine, 'Here is your water,' said he, 'this is its source.' That is the way in which wine came to men, as the Tyrian story goes.[104]

This Phoenician etiological saga describes viticulture as a gift of Dionysus to the Tyreans. As in the case of writing and other gifts of culture, the Greeks also got it from the Phoenicians.[105] The parallel between this story and the Phrygian saga of Philemon and Baucis is striking; there Zeus and Hermes (among others) likewise perform a miracle, with the exception that the two hospitable and poor old people are favoured with an increase in the *volume* of wine rather than with a transformation into wine, a fact which they recognize with much consternation.[106]

[103] αἷμα βότρυος; cf. Gen, 49: 11; Deut, 32: 14; Ecclus. 39: 26.

[104] 2. 2. 1–6. Text according to the edition: *Achilles Tatius: Leucippe and Clitophon,* ed. E. Vilborg, *SGLG* 1 (1955); translation according to the edition by S. Gaselee, *Achilles Tatius,* The Loeb Classical Library (London–Cambridge, revised and reprinted 1969). For the dating of the novel: *Achilleus Tatios: Leukippe und Kleitophon,* K. Plepelits, BGrL 11 (1980), 7–16: third quarter of the second century (16). The novel-like narrative itself takes place in Sidon. In 2. 3. 3 a crater is described with a representation of Dionysus as a vintner: ἵνα τὴν ἄμπελον . . . γεωργῇ; cf. John 15: 1, likewise the motif of friendship and joy in 15: 11 ff.

[105] On this see K. Plepelits (op. cit. n. 104 above, 226 f.): 'Prior to the narration of the Tyrean legend, the corresponding saga of Icarius is here briefly considered. The saga was generally well known. Icarius was a shepherd. . . . He took the wine-god Dionysus in as a guest. Dionysus was still unknown in Greece at the time of Icarius. In gratitude, Dionysus presented him grape-vines and the knowledge of wine production. . . . It is clear what is meant: the legend that I will now tell is so similar to the Attic saga of Icarius that it seems to have come from Attica. Nevertheless it is an original Tyrean legend.' In the Icarius narrative, however, it is the very transformation motif of water to wine that is missing. Cf. H. Hunger, *Lexicon der griechischen und römischen Mythologie* (Vienna, 6th edn., 1974), s.v. Ἰκάριος.

[106] Ovid, *Met.* 8, 679–83:

> Interea totiens haustum cratera repleri
> Sponte sua per seque vident succrescere vina;
> Attoniti novitate pavent manibusque supinis
> Concipiunt Baucisque preces timidusque Philemon
> Et veniam dapibus nullisque paratibus orant.

In the Phoenician shepherd-Dionysus narrative we have, in all probability, a Greek interpretation of an older Phoenician-Canaanite myth (and, by analogy, in Philemon and Baucis that of Phrygian myth).

In Ugarit and the Amarna Letters we already encounter a god *Tiršu*: 'He signifies inebriating drink or its effect.' In this regard we can hardly separate the name of the god from the material thing.[107] Along with this, the wine was also connected with El (and Baal).[108]

Morton Smith, who refers to the manifold connections of Dionysus to Palestine, Phoenicia, and southern Syria during Hellenistic times, mentions the south-Judaean hero אֶשְׁכֹּל as a possible wine divinity.[109] Herodotus had already identified the Egyptian Osiris with Dionysus. He was also of the opinion that the Phoenician Cadmus and his companions had brought the cult of Dionysus to Greece.[110] Moreover, the Arabic god Orotalt is said to be none other than Dionysus (3.8.3). The Greeks later connected the wine-god with the Arabic Dusares (who still retained his own character, it should be added).[111]

Not even Yahweh escaped this fate. It may well be that in early Hellenistic times hellenized Jews also participated in this long enduring interpretation.[112] Tacitus vehemently rejects the identification,[113] while Plutarch readily discusses it.[114]

Raphia, Damascus, and Scythopolis (Beisan), bordering on northern Galilee, traced their founding to Dionysus. Scythopolis regarded itself as Nysa and as the God's place of birth and upbringing. The grave of his nurse was located there.[115] Apart from the cities mentioned, Diony-

---

[107] H. Gese *et al.*, *Die Religionen Altsyriens, Altarabiens und der Mandäer*, RM 10. 2 (Stuttgart, 1970), 111. Gese refers to M. C. Astour, *Hellenosemitica* (187), who sees in the word θύρσος a derivation from the name of this god. Cf. P. Cornelius Tacitus, *Hist.* 5. 5 (*Wissenschaftliche Kommentare zu griechischen und lateinischen Schriftstellern*), commentary by H. Heubner and W. Fauth (Heidelberg, 1982), 89.

[108] S. P. Xella, 'Studi sulla religione della Siria Antica. 1 El e il vino (RS 24. 258), *Studi Storico Religiosi*, 1. 2 (1977), 229–61 (notice by Dr B. Janowski); for Baal cf. Hos. 2: 7, 10; cf. 4: 11 f.

[109] M. Smith, op. cit. n. 102 above, ii, 826 f.; cf. Gen, 14: 13, 24 and Num 13: 23 f.

[110] 2. 49. 3.

[111] C. Colpe, *KP* 2, 184 f.

[112] M. Smith, op. cit. n. 102 above, ii, 822 ff.; M. Hengel, *Judentum und Hellenismus*, WUNT 10 (Tübingen, 2nd edn., 1973), 546 ff. at the time of Antiochus Epiphanes.

[113] *Hist.* 5.5.

[114] *Quest. Conv.* 4. 4. 4–6, 2 (*mor.* 669c–672b) with commentary in M. Stern, *Greek and Latin authors on Jews and Judaism*, i (Jerusalem, 1974), 550–62 (no. 258).

[115] E. E. Schürer, G. Vermes, F. Millar, *The History of the Jewish People*, II (Edinburgh, 1979), 51. 143; Raphia and Damascus according to Stephanus Byzantinus; for Scythopolis cf. Pliny, *NH* 5. 18. 74: 'Scythopolim antea Nysam, a Libero Patre sepulta nutrice ibi Scythis deductis.' In more detail still, *Solinus*, ed. T. Mommsen (Berlin, 2nd edn., 1885), ch. 36. Dionysus appears on the coins of Scythopolis; cf. especially G. F. Hill, *Catalogue of the Greek Coins of Palestine* (Bologna, 1965), 76 ff., and H. Kienle, *Der Gott auf dem Flügelrad: Zu den ungelösten Fragen der 'synkretistischen' Münze, BMC Palestine S. 181, Nr. 29*, Göttinger Orientforschungen, Ser. VI vol. vii (Wiesbaden, 1975).

sus appears in Palestine during the period of the emperors also on the coins of the cities of Caesarea and Aelia Capitolina.

It is in many ways possible that motifs of Semitic vegetation and wine divinities (who in Hellenistic times were clothed in the vestments of Dionysus) had penetrated Judaism since early antiquity. This was true also of festivals[116] as well as of miracle-stories and haggadic legends. For example, the Haggada reports a miraculous provision of wine at the meal of Isaac before the blessing of Jacob in Gen. 27: 17, which mentions only the 'delicacies' prepared by Rebekah, with the wine mentioned only later (27: 25).[117] 'and who brought him wine? Michael brought him wine from out of the Garden of Eden. Our teachers said: you find no blessing of wine outside of this one and the one of Abraham . . . (Gen. 14: 18).[118]

Regarding the water which Moses struck from out of the rock, R. Eleazar of Modaim taught that Moses said to Jethro: 'In the waters of this well, which God has given us, we have the taste of new wine, the taste of milk, the taste of honey, that is, the taste of all the sweet drink in the world.'[119] Pliny, *Natural History*, 2. 106. 231, on the island of Andros said that 'a spring with the taste of wine flows in the temple of *Liber Pater* always around the ninth of January'. With its adaptability and its persistence, the desert miracle was far superior to that of Dionysus.[120] One could hardly doubt that this haggadic motif stems from the Dionysiac world of ideas and imagination. The same holds for the milk and honey springs in the Messianic kingdom of the Sibyllines (cf. above p. 101).

And finally, the Midrash to Num. reports that the grapes which the messengers had brought back with them were gigantic and that the wine was sufficient for all the sacrificial libations of Israel during the forty years of wandering through the desert![121] According to R. Levi, following R. Jochanan, the wine came from the well which accompanied Israel, 'out of which came most of their refreshments'.

---

[116] Cf. M. Smith, op. cit. n. 102 above, ii, 827 and n. 44.

[117] On this cf. also P. Xella, op. cit. n. 108 above, 241, in regard to Gen. 27: 25, who presents in detail the background of this special banquet מַצְעָם in terms of the history of religion.

[118] *Tanch B, Bereschit*, Section 3, §16; in more detail still *Tg. Yer.* 1 on Gen. 27: 25; 'And he ate and had no wine; but an angel prepared it for him from out of the wine whose grapes had been preserved since the days of the beginning of the world. And he gave it into the hand of Jacob, and Jacob brought it to his father, and he drank.'

[119] *Mek. Exod.* 18: 9, ed. Lauterbach 2. 174 f.

[120] Cf., however, already Euripides, *Bacch.* 704–7: a woman strikes the rock with the thursos and water flows; another strikes the green, fruitful earth and a wine-spring appears; another divides the earth with a finger and they 'had plenty of milk'; and at the same time honey flows from the thursos-staff in streams. On this cf. also Goodenough, op. cit. n. 25 above, vi. 185.

[121] *ShirR* 4. 12 § 3 (for 4: 13).

Such wine hyperbolics are to a certain degree a foreshadowing of the plenitude foretold in the apocryphal texts concerning Paradise. The Jewish Haggada could very well enter into competition with the cult legends of the Greek wine-god, no matter from what sources it was fed: Canaanite, Dionysian, or its own.

Thus, to make a long story short, the old opposition, here Dionysus, there old Israel and Judaism, had basically become obsolete as concerning the wine-tradition. The motifs swapped back and forth over contiguous borders even in the small Jewish territory of Palestine, 'Dionysus' had been at home in Palestine for a long time. No matter how rigorously Judaism had marked off its veneration of God from 'alien worship' (especially since the time of the Maccabees), there could arise cult-motifs from alien spheres in Palestinian Judaism as well as in early Christianity. One need not necessarily have to speak of a pagan influence, directly and consciously taken over, or of missionary adaptation. In this context the Palestinian 'Dionysus' is again impressed wholly with the stamp of the old Semitic vegetation-deities. Tyre, Sidon, and Scythopolis bordered on Galilee. The motif of the transformation of water into wine could have already penetrated in the popular Haggada of the Galilean rural population long before the first Christian narrative about a wine-miracle began circulating. Since the OT-Jewish miracle tradition had included multiplication and transformation miracles in great numbers, and since the wine symbolism played an important role even for the temple cult and the eschatological expectations, a transformation of water into wine would hardly have been seen as an alien element. It was as suitable for the Messiah of Israel as it was for the pagan god.

8. Is John's Christology Adoptionist?

FRANCIS WATSON

'AND the Word became flesh and dwelt among us': this statement has rightly been seen by many commentators as the climax of John's prologue and the key to the Gospel as a whole.[1] The eternal, divine Logos, who was with the Father in the beginning and through whom the universe was made, enters human history as a man. Ever since the acceptance of all four Gospels as canonical, it has been traditional to understand John 1: 14 as a reference to the conception and birth of Jesus, as recounted by Matthew and Luke. While the latter evangelists tell us of the miraculous event through which this conception and birth took place, John locates the real miracle not in Jesus' lack of a human father but in the Incarnation, the becoming man of the *logos* who is also *theos* (1: 1). John (so it is said) takes us behind the scenes and shows us what was really happening in the beginning of the life of Jesus of Nazareth.

This harmonizing of John with Matthew and Luke is very ancient. It is to be found already in the so-called *Epistula Apostolorum*, which may date from the mid-second century AD: 'We believe that *the word*, which *became flesh* through the holy virgin Mary, was carried (conceived) in her womb by the Holy Spirit, and was born not by the lust of the flesh but by the will of God, and was wrapped (in swaddling clothes) and made known at Bethlehem . . .'[2] But one wonders whether such harmonizing is legitimate. John shows absolutely no interest in the circumstances of Jesus' birth and no knowledge of the synoptic traditions at this point. 1: 13 should not be understood as a tacit reference to the virgin birth; it simply refers to the contrast between natural birth and birth from above discussed again in 3: 3 ff.[3] In 6: 42, the crowd's claim

---

[1] E.g. R. Bultmann, *The Gospel according to John* (ET, Oxford, 1971), 64; C. H. Dodd, *The Interpretation of the Fourth Gospel* (Cambridge, 1953), 285, 294 f.

[2] *Ep. Apost.* 3; E. Hennecke (ed.), *New Testament Apocrypha*, (ET, London, 1963), i. 192 f.

[3] Against E. C. Hoskyns and F. N. Davey, *The Fourth Gospel* (London, 1940), 164 ff.; C. K. Barrett, *The Gospel according to St John* (London, 1955), 137 f.; J. N. Sanders and B. A. Mastin, *The Gospel according to St John* (London, 1968), 79. The singular reading in some Latin authorities ('qui . . . natus est') is reflected already in *Ep. Apost.* 3, quoted above, and accepted by A. Loisy, *Le Quatrième Évangile*[1] (Paris, 1903), 174 ff., and others; this would then be an explicit reference to the Virgin Birth. But the plural is found in all the Greek MSS, and should probably be accepted (so B. M. Metzger, *A Textual Commentary on the Greek New Testament* (London/New York, 1975), 196 f. and most recent commentators). The singular reading reflects a desire to assimilate John to the Synoptics.

to know Jesus' father and mother is not refuted. In 7: 41 f., the crowd rejects Jesus' claims because he comes from Galilee not Bethlehem.[4] If Jesus' birth as the moment of divine incarnation is as important for John as is usually thought, it is strange that he completely ignores it and appears to know nothing of the beliefs held in other parts of the early Church.[5] We therefore cannot be certain that for John the descent of the Son of God from heaven (3: 31; 6: 38, 58; 8: 14, 23) has as its goal the conception and birth of Jesus. It is the purpose of this article to argue that there is another possibility: *that the union of the Logos or Son of God with Jesus of Nazareth took place in the descent of the Spirit at his Baptism.*[6] If this is correct, then John's Christology must be seen as 'adoptionist'.[7]

I

That was the view of Johannine Christology taken by A. Loisy. In his *Le Quatrième Évangile* (of which the first edition was published in Paris in 1903), Loisy opposed Holtzmann's claim that the evangelist's theology of the Logos in effect makes the traditional motif of the descent of the Spirit superfluous. He claims that the incarnation of the Logos is to be identified with the descent of the Spirit: 'L'union permanente de l'esprit divin à l'humanité de Jésus fait le Christ et constitue sa filiation divine; elle est le mode ou, si l'on veut, le symbole de l'incarnation.'[8] Thus, what took place at Jesus' Baptism was 'l'adoption de cette humanité par la personne divine du Verbe'.[9] For that reason, nothing is said about Jesus before the descent of the Spirit. Although Church

[4] This is sometimes seen as an example of Johannine irony: the crowds do not know what the evangelist and his readers know, that Jesus *was* born at Bethlehem (so Sanders and Mastin, op. cit., 216; R. E. Brown, *The Gospel according to John* (London, 1971), i. 330). But Johannine irony occurs not when people lack information, but when they misunderstand a statement about the heavenly world because their minds are bounded by earthly realities (John 3: 3 ff., 6: 52 ff., 7: 34 ff., etc.); Bultmann, op. cit., 63 n.

[5] The only other possible Johannine reference to the Virgin Birth is in John 8: 41, where the Jews' statement, 'We were not born of fornication', has sometimes been understood to reflect the Jewish charge that Jesus was illegitimate (so Hoskyns op. cit., 392 f.; Barrett, op. cit., 288; Brown, op. cit., i. 357). R. Schnackenburg's arguments against this view are convincing (*The Gospel according to John* (ET, London, 1966–82), ii. 212).

[6] Unlike the Synoptics, John does not explicitly refer to Jesus's Baptism as the occasion for the descent of the Spirit. But 1: 31 implies that the evangelist was familiar with this tradition: 'For this I came baptizing with water, that he might be revealed to Israel'. There is thus a link between baptism and the revelation of the Son of God to John through the descent of the Spirit, and the link must surely be that Jesus was revealed as the Son of God at his Baptism.

[7] This term was first applied by Harnack to Christologies in which Jesus is an ordinary man who undergoes a fundamental change of status when the Spirit descends at his Baptism.

[8] Op. cit. n. 3 above, 230.

[9] Ibid., 232.

tradition has tried to assimilate John to Matthew and Luke, he is in this respect closer to Mark.

Loisy did not work out his suggestion in detail, and it apparently made little impact in subsequent scholarship; it is dismissed cursorily by Bultmann[10] and by Hoskyns.[11] However, this view was revived (without explicit reference to Loisy) by R. H. Fuller, who argued in an article published in 1976 that, according to John, 'Jesus became at his baptism the incarnation of the preexistent logos'.[12] He claims that, in the pre-Johannine hymn underlying John 1: 1–18, σάρξ in v. 14 originally referred to the whole earthly history of Jesus; but in the present context, after the addition of the passages about John the Baptist in vv. 6–8, 15, it refers to the descent of the Spirit at Jesus' Baptism.[13] Fuller acknowledges that this Christology is 'shockingly suggestive of adoptionism', which he understands as 'a denial of the divine initiative'.[14] But he relativizes this by referring to John 18: 37 ('For this I was born, and for this I have come into the world . . .')[15] and Luke 2: 40, 50 (which refer to Jesus' growth in wisdom).[16] He concludes: 'God raised up a man who was at each stage of his historical growth being perfectly prepared to incarnate the divine logos in his human history'.[17] Thus, his argument is that Johannine Christology has certain affinities with adoptionism, but he draws back from the conclusion that this Christology is genuinely adoptionist.[18] The present article will argue for the latter conclusion.

The main evidence for this view is to be found in 1 John. (Although modern scholars rightly emphasize the differences between the Gospel and epistles of John, it is reasonable to suppose that theological views found in the epistles *may* also be found in the Gospel.) It is probable that the epistles are combatting a form of docetic Christology: 'Many deceivers have gone out into the world, men who will not acknowledge the coming of Jesus Christ in the flesh' (2 John 7; see also 1 John 2: 22,

[10] Ibid., 62 n.

[11] Ibid., 184.

[12] 'Christmas, Epiphany, and the Johannine Prologue', in M. L. Engle and W. B. Green (eds.), *Spirit and Light: Essays in Historical Theology* (New York, 1976), 63–73, 69.

[13] Art. cit., 66–9.

[14] Ibid., 64, 70.

[15] If John 18: 37 is indeed the one reference in the Gospel to the birth of the human Jesus, then this makes it hard to argue that the evangelist's theology is consistently adoptionist. But the order of the phrases suggests that γεγέννημαι refers to the 'birth' of the pre-existent Logos, i.e. his coming into being. This interpretation is confirmed by the use of μονογενής in 1: 18 and 3: 16 and by the constant reference to Jesus as the 'Son' of the 'Father'.

[16] Art. cit. n. 12 above, 70.

[17] Ibid.

[18] According to R. E. Brown, *The Epistles of John* (London, 1983), 77, Fuller subsequently modified his position in 'New Testament Roots to the *Theotokos*', *Marian Studies*, 29 (1978), 46–64.

4: 2 f.). The common view of their error is that, as C. H. Dodd puts it, 'They would not confess the reality of the Incarnation';[19] in other words, they thought that Jesus Christ's humanity was a mere illusion. But some early forms of docetism seem to have been more concerned with Jesus' death than with his humanity as a whole. The point at issue was whether the union between the human Jesus of Nazareth and the divine Christ (or Logos, or Son) was permanent and complete, or whether a separation between them took place at the Crucifixion, so that the divine element did not share in suffering. It is this view that 1 John 5: 6–8 seems to oppose: 'This is he who came by water and blood, Jesus Christ, not with the water only but with the water and the blood. And the Spirit is the witness, because the Spirit is the truth. There are three witnesses, the Spirit, the water, and the blood; and these three agree.'[20]

The references to the Spirit here have nothing to do with the descent of the Spirit at Jesus' baptism; they concern the Spirit's present function of bearing witness to the truth within the congregation (see 4: 2, 6; 2: 20, 27).[21] The vital phrase is in v. 6: 'Not with the water only but with the water and the blood'. The author agrees with his opponents that Jesus Christ 'came by water'—an obvious reference to Jesus' baptism. But they disagree about whether he 'came . . . by blood'; they disagree in their interpretation of the Crucifixion. The precise meaning of this passage would remain hopelessly obscure, were it not for the information provided by other texts. According to one widespread early Christology, Jesus was an ordinary man, born of Joseph and Mary; at his baptism, the Christ or Logos descended upon him, but left him again prior to the Crucifixion.[22] If this is the correct background to 1 John 5: 6–8,[23] it would mean that the author is opposing the denial that

---

[19] *The Johannine Epistles* (London, 1946), 99. This view is rejected by Brown, *Epistles*, 505 (cf. 76 ff.): 'The issue is not that the secessionists are denying the incarnation or the physical reality of Jesus's humanity; they are denying that what Jesus was or did in the flesh was related to his being the Christ, i.e. was salvific.'

[20] In the light of this passage, it is likely that the heretics who denied 'the coming of Jesus Christ in the flesh' denied not the reality of the Incarnation in general, but the reality of Christ's *sufferings*. σάρξ (2 John 7, 1 John 4: 2 f.) is linked specifically with the death of Jesus in John 6: 51 ff., Ign. *Rom.* 7. 3, *Phil.* 4, *Smyrn.* 7. 1. Polycarp links 1 John 4: 2 f. with a condemnation of 'whosoever does not confess the testimony of the cross' (Pol. *Phil.* 7. 1).

[21] So R. Bultmann, *The Johannine Epistles* (ET, Philadelphia, 1973), 10; J. L. Houlden, *A Commentary on the Johannine Epistles* (London, 1973), 127.

[22] This Christology is attributed by Irenaeus to Cerinthus (*Adv. Haer.* 1. 26. 1) and perhaps to Carpocrates (1. 25. 1), and variants of it are found among the Valentinians (1. 7. 2, 1. 30. 12–14). Cf. the Nag Hammadi *Gospel of Philip*, where the Virgin Birth is denied (2. 55. 23–6, but contrast 71. 18–21), Jesus is revealed at the Jordan (70. 34–71. 3), and the Lord leaves him before his death (68. 26–9).

[23] So Dodd, *Epistles*, 130; Bultmann, *Epistles*, 80; Houlden, op. cit., 126; R. Schnackenburg, *Die Johannesbriefe*² (Freiburg/Basel/Vienna, 1963), 258.

the divine element in Jesus Christ was subject to suffering. But it would also mean that the author has no quarrel with the view that the divine element became united with Jesus of Nazareth at his baptism. Bultmann is therefore only partially correct when he claims that 1 John 5: 6 'obviously contradicts the gnosticizing view that the heavenly Christ descended into Jesus at his baptism, and then abandoned Jesus again before his death'.[24] The author clearly contradicts the latter view, but he just as clearly affirms the former: the heavenly Christ *did* descend onto Jesus at his baptism. It seems that the author rejects his opponents' docetic understanding of the Crucifixion but affirms their adoptionist understanding of Jesus's baptism.[25] If that was the view of the author of 1 John, it is at least possible, and perhaps probable, that the same view was held by the evangelist.

II

We must now survey some of the evidence for the early existence of this adoptionist and docetic Christology. We shall confine ourselves to material which is historically and geographically close to the Johannine circle.

(1) *The Evidence of Irenaeus*

In his work against heresies (1. 26. 1), Irenaeus describes the views of the heretic Cerinthus as follows:

He represented Jesus as having not been born of a virgin but as being the son of Joseph and Mary according to the ordinary course of human generation, while he nevertheless was more righteous, prudent and wise than other men. Moreover, after his baptism, Christ descended upon him in the form of a dove from the Supreme Ruler, and then that he proclaimed the unknown Father, and performed miracles. But at last Christ departed from Jesus, and that then Jesus suffered and rose again, while Christ remained impassible, inasmuch as he was a spiritual being.[26]

---

[24] *Epistles*, 80; also Dodd, *Epistles*, 130.

[25] According to Brown (*Epistles*, 577 f.), 'the water only' refers to the secessionists' view of the coming of Christ upon Jesus at his Baptism, whereas 'water and blood' represents the author's emphasis on the death of Christ, when water and blood poured out of his heart (cf. John 19: 34 f.). But there seems no reason to deny that 'water' means the same thing in the two phrases. 'Not with the water only' is a concession as well as a denial; elsewhere, Brown admits the possibility of this (op. cit., 67). As regards John 19: 34 f., this passage and 1 John 5: 8 should be interpreted in the light of 1 John 5: 6, the least obscure of these three passages linking 'water' and 'blood'. Many scholars think that the former two passages refer to the sacraments (Hoskyns, op. cit., 635, Bultmann, *Gospel*, 677 f., Barrett, op. cit. n. 3 above, 463; Schnackenburg, *Johannesbriefe*, 261 f., Bultmann, *Epistles*, 80 f., Houlden, op. cit. n. 21 above, 128). But 'blood' is not a natural description of the Eucharist, and if there is a sacramental reference at all in John 19: 34 f. and 1 John 5: 8, it must be understood in terms of 1 John 5: 6: the 'water' and 'blood' of the sacraments attest the fact that Jesus Christ 'came by water and blood'.

[26] *Ante-Nicene Fathers*, i (American edn., repr. Grand Rapids, Michigan, 1975), 352.

According to Epiphanius (*Adv. Haer.* 51), the 'Alogoi' claimed that both the Revelation and the Gospel of John were in fact the work of Cerinthus. Dionysius of Alexandria spoke of 'some before us' who argued that Cerinthus was the author of Revelation (Eusebius, *HE* 8. 25. 1–2). Irenaeus recounts the apocryphal story that the apostle John fled from the public baths at Ephesus when he learnt that Cerinthus was there (*Adv. Haer.* 3. 3. 4). This story may have arisen from the need to combat suspicion about the close relationship between Cerinthus and the Johannine literature. Perhaps it is for the same reason that Irenaeus insists that John wrote his Gospel specifically to oppose Cerinthus (3. 11. 1). These passages confirm the possibility of a link between Johannine Christology and that of Cerinthus.[27]

After describing the views of Cerinthus, Irenaeus turns to the Ebionites, and says of their Christology: 'Their opinions with respect to the Lord are similar to those of Cerinthus and Carpocrates' (1. 26. 2). Elsewhere, however, he attacks them only for their denial of the Virgin Birth (3. 21. 1, 5. 1. 3), and not for holding that before the Crucifixion 'Christ departed from Jesus', as Cerinthus claimed. Irenaeus describes the Ebionites as Jewish Christians who continue to observe the law of Moses and reject the apostle Paul (1. 26. 2). They would have shared the belief of earlier Jewish Christianity that the Spirit descended on Jesus at his Baptism (compare Mark 1: 10). But none of the heresiologists give us reason to suppose that they shared Cerinthus's docetic view of the Crucifixion.

So it seems likely that Cerinthus derived his adoptionism from Jewish Christianity, but not his docetism. But it is possible to surmise how the latter grew out of the former. On the Jewish Christian view, the descent of the Spirit onto Jesus is seen as his endowment with divine power. But on Cerinthus's view, this divine power is hypostatized; it becomes a divine *being*, called 'Christ'. The descent of the Spirit onto Jesus becomes the union of divinity with humanity. This leads inevitably to the question of the divine passibility: when the human Jesus suffered, did the divine Christ suffer too? Cerinthus thought not, no doubt under the influence of the a priori belief that it is impossible for the divine to suffer,[28] and this led to his view that Christ left Jesus prior to the Crucifixion. 1 John therefore represents an intermediate stage between the Christology of Jewish Christianity and that of Cerinthus. The hypostatization of the divine power which descended on Jesus has taken

---

[27] John's Gospel seems to have been highly valued by heretics and regarded with suspicion by catholics during the earlier part of the second century; on this, cf. M. R. Hillyer, 'The Gospel of John in the Second Century' (diss., Harvard, 1966); E. H. Pagels, *The Johannine Gospel in Gnostic Exegesis*, SBL monograph 17 (Nashville/New York, 1973).

[28] Pagan parallels are cited in M. Hengel, *Crucifixion* (ET, London/Philadelphia, 1977) 15 ff.

place (1 John 1: 1), but the author rejects the view of Cerinthus that the union between divine and human in Jesus Christ was impermanent.[29]

Thus Cerinthus's modified form of Jewish Christian Christology seems to be the view attacked in 1 John 5: 6–8; but although the author attacks the docetic view of the Crucifixion, he has no quarrel with his opponents' adoptionism. His view was therefore that the man Jesus and the divine Christ were united in the descent of the Spirit at Jesus's baptism. This raises the possibility that the same Christology is present in the fourth Gospel.

(2) *The Evidence of Ignatius*

The docetism opposed by Ignatius is again concerned primarily with the Crucifixion, and not with the more general question of Jesus Christ's humanity. In *Magn.* 9. 1, Ignatius speaks of the saving power of Christ's death 'which some men deny'.[30] *Trall.* 10. 1 speaks of some who are 'without God' and 'unbelievers', who say that 'his suffering was only a semblance'. The same language is used in *Smyrn.* 2. 1, and *Smyrn.* 5. 3 requires that such people should 'repent concerning the passion'. It is possible that this form of docetism is identical to that of Cerinthus. But, according to Irenaeus, Cerinthus affirmed the physical Resurrection of Jesus, whereas the heretics opposed by Ignatius did not. Thus, in *Smyrn.* 3. 1, in opposition to the heretics, Ignatius asserts that Jesus 'was in the flesh even after the Resurrection'. This suggests that these heretics maintained the unity of Jesus Christ, unlike Cerinthus, but claimed that he only appeared to suffer and that in his risen form he was no longer a being of flesh.

For our purposes, however, the most important parts of Ignatius's evidence are the indications that the heretics he opposed shared the adoptionism of Jewish Christianity and of Cerinthus. In *Eph.* 19. 1, Ignatius writes: 'And the virginity of Mary, and her giving birth were hidden from the Prince of this world, as was also the death of the Lord.' Here, the virginity of Mary and the birth and death of the Lord are presented as esoteric truths known only to real Christians. Thus,

---

[29] Brown argues that Cerinthus was considerably later than the Johannine literature. Irenaeus speaks of the Nicolaitans as having proclaimed their errors a long time before Cerinthus; the Nicolaitans are mentioned in the Johannine literature (Rev. 2: 6, 15), and Cerinthus must therefore have been much later (*Epistles*, 65). But Irenaeus dates the Nicolaitans early because he thinks that they were founded by the Nicolaus of Acts 6: 5 (*Adv. Haer.* 1. 26. 3); in other words, he places them in the earliest years of the Church's existence. There is therefore no reason to date Cerinthus much later than AD 100, and this is confirmed by the comparatively primitive nature of his system.

[30] Here, speaking of the Lord's Day, Ignatius writes: ἐν ᾗ καὶ ἡ ζωὴ ἡμῶν ἀνέτειλεν δι' αὐτοῦ καὶ τοῦ θανάτου αὐτοῦ, ὅν τινες ἀρνοῦνται. It seems better to take ὅν to refer to 'his death' (Lightfoot) than to 'him' (K. Lake). In other quotations from Ignatius, Lake's translation (*The Apostolic Fathers*, i (Loeb Classics, London, 1925)) has been followed, except where specified.

Ignatius praises the church at Smyrna because in contrast to the heretics they are fully persuaded that the Lord is 'in truth of the family of David according to the flesh, God's Son by the will and power of God, truly born of a virgin . . .' (*Smyrn*. 1. 1). So the heretics did not only deny Jesus Christ's sufferings and his physical Resurrection; they also denied the Virgin Birth. It is very probable that like Cerinthus they did so because they held that it was at Jesus's baptism that the union between the human Jesus and the divine Christ took place. Thus, in close proximity to the two passages quoted above, Ignatius gives his own interpretations of the Baptism of Jesus. In *Eph*. 18. 1, he refers ironically to the unbelieving heretics as 'the wise' and 'those who are called prudent', and then continues in 18. 2: 'For our God, Jesus the Christ, was conceived in the womb by Mary according to a dispensation, of the seed of David but also of the Holy Ghost; and he was born and was baptized that by his passion he might cleanse water.'[31] In *Smyrn*. 1. 1, Ignatius again links the Virgin Birth with an explanation of the Baptism of Jesus: he speaks of 'our Lord' as 'truly born of a virgin, baptized by John that all righteousness might be fulfilled by him' (alluding to Matt. 3: 15). The reason why he makes this link is presumably that the heretics denied that the union between God and man took place through a virgin birth, asserting that it happened when the divine Christ descended onto the human Jesus at his Baptism. For this reason Ignatius affirms the truth of the Virgin Birth and is forced to give an alternative explanation of Jesus's Baptism. Like Cerinthus, the heretics opposed by Ignatius combine a docetic view of the Crucifixion with the adoptionism of Jewish Christianity.[32] Against this background, it becomes quite comprehensible how the author of 1 John could have attacked his opponents' docetism but shared their adoptionism. This leads one to ask whether the Christology of the Gospel of John is also adoptionist.

III

There are two features of the Gospel of John which appear to make it likely that the evangelist's Christology is adoptionist: the first is the portrayal of John the Baptist and the second concerns the Johannine Christ's claim to have come down from heaven.

---

[31] Lightfoot's translation (*The Apostolic Fathers* (London, 1891)); Lake translates τῷ πάθει as 'by himself submitting'.

[32] They are usually referred to simply as 'docetists' (e.g. by W. R. Schoedel, 'Theological Norms and Social Perspectives in Ignatius of Antioch', in *Jewish and Christian Self-Definition*, ed. E. P. Sanders, i (London, 1980), 30–56. But they are also 'adoptionists'.

(1) As was noted above, John has nothing to say about the birth of Jesus. He challenges neither the view that Jesus was the son of Joseph and Mary (6: 42) nor the view that he came from Galilee and not Bethlehem (7: 41 f.). If he believes that the conception and birth of Jesus constituted the process by which the Logos assumed flesh, it is very odd that he has nothing at all to say about it. For him, the significant history of Jesus Christ begins with the witness of John the Baptist (1: 6–8, 15, 19 ff.). Many commentators have suggested (probably rightly) that the evangelist is involved in controversy with followers of John the Baptist. But it should be noted that the evangelist is not only concerned to deny that John was 'the light' (1: 8) or 'the Christ' (1: 20). Unlike the other evangelists, he regards John as of quite crucial significance as the unique witness to Jesus Christ. One possible reason for this unique status is that John is the only one who witnesses the descent of the Spirit onto Jesus:

And John bore witness, 'I saw the Spirit descend as a dove from heaven, and it remained on him. I myself did not know him; but he who sent me to baptize with water said to me, "He on whom you see the Spirit descend and remain, this is he who baptizes with the Holy Spirit'. And I have seen and borne witness that this is the Son of God.' (1: 32–4.)

The evangelist does not explicitly identify the descent of the Spirit from heaven with the descent of the Logos from heaven. In John 1 and elsewhere, he is working with old Jewish Christian tradition, to which the idea of a second divine hypostasis is foreign. But our examination of the Christology of Cerinthus has shown that belief in a second divine hypostasis could be closely connected to Jewish Christian adoptionism. The fact that the narrative of the fourth Gospel begins with the Baptist's witness to the descent of the Spirit onto Jesus suggests that the same adoptionism is present there. For this reason, the Baptist's witness is unique, superior even to that of the apostles: he alone saw the supreme event in which divinity and humanity became one.[33]

This interpretation is confirmed by two further points: (i) 1: 32 speaks of the Spirit καταβαῖνον . . . ἐξ οὐρανοῦ; elsewhere in the Gospel the Son is described as ὁ ἐκ τοῦ οὐρανοῦ καταβάς (3: 13) and ὁ καταβαίνων ἐκ τοῦ οὐρανοῦ (6: 33, compare 6: 38, 41, 42, 50, 51, 58, where similar language is used). The parallel between 1: 32 and these explicitly Christological passages suggests that the traditional idea of the descent of the Spirit from heaven is identified in Johannine theology with the

---

[33] Brown claims that the secessionists could have derived their view of the descent of Christ onto Jesus at his baptism from their reading of John 1 (*Epistles*, 77 f.).

descent of the Son of God from heaven. (ii) This interpretation of John the Baptist is attested by the Nag Hammadi literature.[34] In *The Testimony of Truth* (9. 30. 19–28), we read: 'But the Son of Man [came] forth from Imperishability, [being] alien to defilement. He came [to the] world by the Jordan river, and immediately the Jordan [turned] back. And John bore witness to the [descent] of Jesus. For he is the one who saw the [power] which came down upon the Jordan river . . .' The reference here to John the Baptist's witness may well derive from the Gospel of John, and this would then be evidence that some people interpreted John 1 in an adoptionist sense.

(2) Again and again the evangelist tells us that the Jews reject Jesus' claim to have come down from heaven and to possess a unique filial relationship with the Father. For them, the claim of a man to be God is incomprehensible and indeed blasphemous (10: 33, 36, 5: 18). Jesus claims to have 'descended from heaven' (3: 13), and is thus able to speak of what he knows and to bear witness to what he has seen, but they remain incredulous and uncomprehending (see 3: 11). It is this Christology which has led to the break between the Johannine community and the synagogue (9: 22, 33 ff.).

How is John able to portray Jesus in this way? The problem is solved if we regard his Christology as adoptionist. In *The Second Treatise of the Great Seth*, we read (7. 51. 20–52. 10): 'I visited a bodily dwelling. I cast out the one who was in it first, and I went in . . . And I am the one who was in it, not resembling him who was in it first. For he was an earthly man, but I, I am from above the heavens . . . I revealed that I am a stranger to the regions below.' Here we have a clear example of an adoptionist Christology. Jesus is at first an ordinary man, but when the Christ comes, his human mind is suppressed; the heavenly Christ now dwells in his body and speaks through him. The content of his message is simply that he is 'a stranger to the regions below', that he is 'from above the heavens'. This Christology has affinities with a widespread contemporary view of inspiration: man in his natural state consists of body and mind, but when inspiration occurs, the mind is banished and the Divine Spirit becomes united with a human body.[35] But what is far more important is that the claim to have come from above is only made possible by an adoptionist Christology in which a divine being from the

---

[34] *The Nag Hammadi Library*,[2] ET, ed. J. M. Robinson (Leiden, 1984).

[35] For example, Philo writes in *Spec. Leg.* 4. 49 (Loeb translation): 'No pronouncement of a prophet is ever his own; he is an interpreter prompted by Another in all his utterances, when, knowing not what he does, he is filled with inspiration, as the reason withdraws and surrenders the citadel of the soul to a new visitor and tenant, the Divine Spirit, which plays upon the vocal organism and dictates words which clearly express its prophetic message'. This view derives from Apollonian manticism; see *A Theological Dictionary of the New Testament*, vi. 345–52.

heavenly world descends and becomes united with an already existing human being. This may well shed light on Johannine Christology.

If this is the case, Johannine Christology rests on the presupposition that, before the descent of the Spirit, Jesus of Nazareth is an ordinary man, born of human parents. But with the descent of the Spirit, his human mind is set aside, and the divine Logos or Son enters and becomes united with his human body. From now on, the words of Jesus are the words not of an ordinary man but of the divine hypostasis who dwells within him. Thus he can say: 'I have come down from heaven, not to do my own will, but the will of him who sent me' (6: 38). The Jews cannot understand how Jesus can say, 'I am the bread which came down from heaven', because they mistakenly regard him as the ordinary man whose parents they know (6: 41 f.). They are unaware that in the human body of Jesus there now dwells the divine Logos or Son, who can truly claim to have come down from heaven. Similarly, in 8: 58 Jesus says, 'Truly, truly I say to you, before Abraham was, I am.' The Jews again regard these as the blasphemous words of an ordinary man madly claiming to be divine, and so they attempt to stone him (8: 59). What they do not realize is that the one speaking is not a mere man but the Son of God who has clothed himself with a human body.[36]

Within the confines of a short article, it is obviously impossible to work out this interpretation of Johannine Christology as adoptionist in detail. But the evidence presented here suggests that this hypothesis is as least worthy of serious consideration. The most natural interpretation of 1 John 5: 6 indicates that the author and the secessionists both took an adoptionist Christology for granted. The existence of such a Christology can be confirmed from material historically and geographically close to the Johannine community: Irenaeus's account of Cerinthus and Ignatius's attacks on his opponents. The portrayal of John the Baptist in John 1 and the evangelist's Christology as a whole suggest that he too regards the descent of the Spirit as the moment of the Incarnation of the Son of God.

If this is correct, we must revise our conceptions about 'high' and 'low' Christology in the New Testament, since Johannine Christology

---

[36] According to Bultmann, the Jews expect the Revealer to come 'as a hero or θεῖος ἄνθρωπος, as a miracle worker or mystagogue . . . Men want to look away from the humanity, and see or sense the divinity, they want to penetrate the disguise . . .' (*Gospel*, 63). They take offence because 'the Revealer is nothing but a man' (62), and 'it is in his sheer humanity that he is the Revealer' (63). But surely it is the evangelist's purpose that we *should* view Jesus as a miracle worker and mystagogue, and that (unlike the Jews) we *should* penetrate the deceptive veil of humanity in order to perceive the divinity within. E. Käsemann is nearer the truth when he describes Jesus in John as 'God descending into the human realm and there manifesting his glory' (*The Testament of Jesus* (ET, London, 1968), 13).

has always been regarded as an example of the former and adoptionism of the latter. Adoptionism is often seen as 'a denial of the divine initiative' (Fuller).[37] But it is not that, any more than Matthew and Luke deny the divine initiative by teaching that an already existing human being was chosen to be the mother of Jesus Christ. The question at issue is simply when the divine initiative began. Perhaps one should distinguish instead between low and high *adoptionist* Christology. In the former, the human Jesus of Nazareth is still of central importance, and his endowment with the Spirit gives him a unique role in salvation-history and enables him to perform works of power. In the latter, the emphasis is on the divine Logos or Son, who enters the body of Jesus of Nazareth at his baptism and through him announces his own heavenly origin and the promise of salvation.

No doubt Johannine Christology, interpreted in this way, seems crude and even offensive to our modern sensibilities. But this interpretation at least has the merit of simplicity and clarity, which is more than can be said for most other views.

[37] Art. cit. n. 12 above, 70.

9. *Ecce Homo!* Irony in the Christology of the Fourth Evangelist

GEORGE JOHNSTON

I

IN a classic story in his *Lives* of eminent artists Giorgio Vasari tells how Donatello made a lovely wooden crucifix. He believed that he had produced a work of rare beauty and piety and sought the opinion of his dear friend Filippo Brunelleschi. Filippo looked, and smiled enigmatically. Pressed by the sculptor to speak his mind openly, he told Donatello, 'You have put a ploughman on the Cross, not a Christ whose body was the most delicate and most perfect.' Donatello was discomfited. 'Carve one yourself, then,' he said. Filippo did so, and one day he arranged that Donatello would go to Brunelleschi's house alone after they had been out shopping for eggs and cheese and other provisions. So Donatello went in, saw the carving done by his friend, and was dumbfounded. He was so amazed that he spread out his hands and let his apron fall loose. Whereupon, of course, he spilled the cheese and the eggs in pieces on the floor. When Filippo arrived he said to him, 'It's for you to make Christ, for me to make ploughmen!'[1]

The story illustrates the dilemma of artists, historians, and theologians who hold the orthodox Catholic faith in Christ as God incarnate. How are they to do justice to the doctrine of the divine presence in a Jew who was born in Palestine during the latter years of Herod the Great? Brunelleschi objected to a peasant Jesus, yet the records speak of a Nazarene family that must have been sociologically close to the level of peasants. Joseph was a carpenter (Matt. 13: 55), as was Jesus (Mark 6: 3). When he began to preach, his townsfolk and his relatives were amazed and worried (Luke 4: 22; Mark 3: 31–5; compare Luke 14: 26; John 7: 5): for people were saying, 'He is beside himself' (Mark 3: 21). Yet for all the evangelists Jesus is 'God's beloved Son'. St Paul calls him God's Son, descended from David according to the flesh (Rom. 1: 3) and God's own Son (Gal. 4: 4; Rom. 8: 32). The seer of Revelation acclaims him as 'the root and the offspring of David, the bright morning star . . . the Alpha and the Omega' (Rev. 22: 13, 16; compare 1: 8,

[1] Giorgio Vasari, *Lives of the Most Eminent Painters, Sculptors, and Architects*, trans. G. Du C. De Vere, ed. R. N. Linscott (New York, 1959), 85 f.

where it is the Lord God who is the Alpha and Omega). Not much later, Ignatius of Antioch describes the Christ as the 'one Physician, who is both flesh and spirit, born and yet not born, who is God in man [v. l. in flesh], true life in death, both of Mary and of God, first passible and then impassible, Jesus Christ our Lord' (*Eph.* 7. 2). Again, he 'was of the family of David, and of Mary, who was truly born, both ate and drank, was truly persecuted under Pontius Pilate, was truly crucified and died in the sight of those in heaven and on earth and under the earth' (Ign. *Trall.* 9. 1; compare *Smyrn.* 1. 1–2; 1 *Clem.* 36. 4; 59. 4).

The *floruit* of the fourth evangelist must have been close to that of John the seer, exiled to Patmos, and not much earlier than that of Ignatius. His faith, and that of his Church, is no doubt to be looked for in the maximal Christological statements of his Gospel-book. Hence, for him, Jesus Christ is Son of God (20: 31 and *passim*), Lord and God (20: 28), the Logos that existed in the beginning as God in personal union with God (1: 1, 18). The book was written to deepen and/or produce a life-giving belief in this Son of God, so that as a literary artist the author had to find a way to present God in a man. The irony of the situation becomes evident when John's 'camera' pans from Pilate's *Ecce Homo* (19: 5), lighting up before our eyes a battered, bleeding Jesus crowned with thorns and arrayed in the purple robe of royalty, to the radiant unearthly Lord who greets his disciples after the Resurrection with 'Peace' and bids Thomas not to be faithless but believing (20: 26 f.).[2]

Both pictures are in John, yet we are bound to ask what happens to the *Homo* if the other is the dominant presentation. Are readers meant to see and hear throughout the Gospel only a divine, incomparable, Spirit-filled Christ? Has the peasant of Galilee been transfigured from the start—and in the process been lost?

It is the purpose of this essay to examine this question once more, using a single verse as a clue. This is not only for my own satisfaction, and in tribute to a truly great biblical theologian, George Caird. It is because incarnational doctrine is again under fire and can never be kept off centre stage.

II

The key verse is 17: 5 in the royal prayer: 'And now, Father, glorify thou me in thy own presence with the glory which I had with thee before the world was made.'[3]

---

[2] This Christ is shown in the marvellous *Anastasis* wall-painting in the church in Chora, Istanbul: see John Beckwith, *Early Christian and Byzantine Art* (London, 1970), Illustration no. 279.

[3] The textual and translation problems are discussed by A. Laurentin, *DOXA* i (Paris, 1972), 19–31. See also Ernst Haenchen, *John* 1, Hemeneia Commentary (Philadelphia, 1984), 130.

The speaker is called 'Jesus' in 17: 1 and that causes misconceptions. For in this Gospel Jesus appears to be one who travels, talks, heals, debates, suffers, and dies. As this person, he is the 'flesh' of 1: 14, and he has a mother (2: 1). Hence this human being had a beginning in time; he was once an embryo in a womb. So we cannot be expected to regard the speaker of 17: 5 as claiming that *as Jesus* he pre-existed the creation and shared the eternal divine glory.

In fact the speaker is 'the Son'. He has fulfilled his Father's commission to reveal him and to save his people (3: 16–21; 5: 43; 7: 16; 8: 26, 42; 10: 25–30). But the prayer is not the precise words of the Saviour in the upper room, remembered and recorded by the men who heard it. Rather, as many commentators would agree, it is a Johannine compilation. It *may* include reminiscences of Jesus' prayers; it may also echo an ecclesiastical liturgy, for example in the verse 3 that looks like a gloss if said by the Son. The prayer is not a poem nor a hymn, but it should not be interpreted in the most prosaic manner. There is a mystical aura to it, and one approaches with wonder, shoes removed (as it were) because this is holy ground. The Son is Jesus Christ, the Church's Lord, and the evangelist expresses the community's belief that its Lord still lives, that he lives in the magnificence of eternal glory by the side of his Father (whatever such an image can mean).

It is clear, on the other hand, that 17: 5 implies very real awareness of a sea-change in the Son's circumstances. The Logos *had become flesh*! This need not mean, of course, that an eternal Being had been transmuted into a mortal temporal creature; but things could never be the same again in the life of the Godhead, once the Logos had entered into this strange reality. So as he prays, the incarnate Son, John must want us to appreciate, is not in exactly the same glorified state as he had been before the creation of the world. And if that is the case, then we must consider what implications are to be drawn in respect of the author's intention in telling the Jesus-story.

For this reason I have to dissent from the judgement of Dr Caird's teacher, W. H. Cadman, who strenuously objects to reading 17: 5 as meaning that the Logos-Son had relinquished his pre-existent glory. He had retained it, Cadman argues, and manifested it in his historical life.

The speaker is not the Logos but the Logos incarnate, the man Jesus, who can claim to have had glory before the world was because he has accepted what God has willed—His total identification with the Logos. It would be equally mistaken, however, to think that Jesus is praying to be Himself endowed with the eternal glory of the Logos. This He has already possessed in virtue of the Incarnation: throughout His earthly life He has been in the bosom of the

Father (i. 18), in heaven (iii. 13), in the Father (x. 38; xiv. 10) . . . (xvii. 5) is a prayer to be received into the presence of God not merely as man, but as the inclusive representative of humanity.

Jesus and his beloved friends, says Cadman, constitute a unity, and the friends are to share the glory and the love eternally, as 17: 22–6 show.[4]

Without going into the details of this position, let me simply observe that this makes Jesus' life in two worlds a real oddity. It certainly prevents us from understanding in ways that make sense Jesus' human nature, his intelligence and knowledge, his being a first-century person. It leaves the door wide open to a form of docetism; and the issue is precisely whether John the evangelist was a naïve docetist. It is one thing to portray a human life lived in communion close and intimate with God; it is quite another thing to regard even the life of a great saint as one that publicly shines with the radiance of eternity.

As I read it, John 17 summarizes the theology of the fourth Gospel. This states, paratactically and not in systematic philosophical language, that the Father known in and through Jesus is God the Holy One, unseen, lover of the world, source of life, and one who satisfies petitions made in the name and spirit of Christ.[5] God's icon is his Son, whom he commissioned to be his representative, to teach the truth, and to deal with sin.[6] God has sent the spirit of truth as his other representative or *paraclete*, to empower the disciples, to convict the world of sin, and above all to keep alive the witness to Jesus, the mission of Jesus, the meaning of Jesus' ministry in all its significance.[7] This spirit was given only after Jesus had been glorified (7: 39), which in John means after the Crucifixion.

As we have said, none of this is elaborated in technical theological discourse. For, like all the Gospels, John's is a Passion story with a prelude; and the author has subtle ways of hinting at the dénouement from the beginning (1: 10 f.).

The question is whether John has provided, as still a few modern scholars think, the most primitive, apostolic, literally accurate, and therefore trustworthy account of the events that were accomplished once upon a time in Galilee, Samaria, and Judaea; or whether his book is disguised as history, because his Logos is only a god disguised as a Jew. In recent studies Ernst Käsemann's *The Testament of Jesus* stands out as a brilliant and provocative statement of the latter judgement.[8]

---

[4] W. H. Cadman, *The Open Heaven*, ed. G. B. Caird (Oxford, 1969), 206; cf. 138, 144, 172.
[5] 17: 11; 1: 18; 5: 37; 3: 16; 5: 26; 15: 16; 16: 23 f.
[6] 1: 18; 8: 19; 10: 38; 14: 7, 9 f.; 1: 29; 15: 22.
[7] 14: 26; 15: 26 f.; 16: 7–11; 20: 22.
[8] (London, 1968), 26.

He categorizes John's Christology as given 'only in the form of a naïve docetism', but he pays very little attention to 17: 5 (it fails to get into the index of the English version). The orthodox view is closer to the former position, and it often leans far back on the teaching of Irenaeus of Lyons and the great work of Origen of Alexandria, who link John 17: 5 to Phil. 2: 7 f., where he who was in the form of God 'emptied himself, taking the form of a servant, being born in the likeness of men. And being found in human form he humbled himself and became obedient unto death . . .'[9]

I propose to take 17: 5 quite seriously as a Johannine pronouncement that once the Logos-Son had been glorified, sharing the radiant splendour of the Father, but at the crisis of his life on earth he ascends in prayer, doubtless in a profound spiritual communion, seeking the *restoration* of what had been abandoned. To do this requires my own immediate fresh rereading of the Gospel, to see if it does indeed present an unglorified Lord at his work. We shall have to account at the same time for references to 'glory' and 'manifested glory' in such texts as 1: 14; 2: 11; 5: 44; 7: 39; 8: 54; 11: 4, 40; 12: 16, 23, 28; 13: 31; 14: 31; 16: 14; 17: 1, 4. Limitations of space will preclude an exhaustive commentary on all those texts; it will be enough if we can show important signs of the Lord without his eternal glory.

III

My thesis begins from the recognition that the orthodox, Catholic view of Jesus Christ as the incarnate Son of God is the setting for John's presentation of the incarnate life. For this evangelist and his Church, the icon of the Father must be framed unmistakably in divinity, and yet the face of the icon is a Jewish face. We must start from there.

Jesus is depicted as a Jewish male who breaks the convention about conversing with a female Samaritan of ill-fame (4: 9). When he did this, he was thirsty—really thirsty, beside a well that had then and still has delicious water.[10] Surely it is gratuitous to dismiss this encounter as a fictitious recognition and disclosure scene invented by an early Christian Defoe.[11]

As was noted above, Jesus had a mother, though, unlike Ignatius,

---

[9] See, e.g. B. F. Westcott, *The Gospel According to John* (London, 1882), 240–1; Leon Morris, *Studies in the Fourth Gospel* (Grand Rapids, 1969), 283–92; Origen, *de Principiis*, 3. 5. 6; A. Laurentin, *DOXA*, i, 60 f. and *DOXA* ii *passim*.

[10] I have tasted it!

[11] Westcott, op. cit., 66, happily declares that this section 'bears evident traces of being the record of an eye-witness'. That may be going too far.

John for some reason never bothers to give her name (2: 1–4; 19: 25–7); but it may be inferred that she was Jewish.

What is more significant is that Jesus had an earthly Jewish father called Joseph. Philip of Bethsaida, a new disciple, tells Nathanael that Jesus of Nazareth, Joseph's son, is the predicted Messiah (1: 45; specific references to the predictions of the Hebrew scriptures are not provided even at 5: 39–47). If one may say so, it is a Lucan point of view that makes conservatives like Westcott comment that Philip is simply using the name by which Jesus would be commonly known: his ID card said 'son of Joseph' (op. cit., 26; Luke 3: 23; 4: 22; compare Matt. 1: 18–23). Bultmann is to be preferred when he notes that 'the Revealer is nothing but a man'.[12] Yet, *pace* Bultmann in his *Theology of the New Testament*, this also means that Jesus' life on earth as the son of Joseph was indeed and remains 'an item of the historical past', just as Julius Caesar's or Muhammad's or our own lives fall into that category. For that is what it means to live a truly human life in time.[13]

Again, at John 6: 42, when Jesus has grandiloquently claimed to be bread which has descended from heaven, the Jews mutter, 'Isn't this man Jesus, the son of Joseph? Don't we know his father and mother?' They do indeed.

I propose that this identification should be accepted as matter of fact for the fourth evangelist. I am convinced that John (whoever he was) intends us to observe the irony that Joseph's son is the Son of God. How this can be, and just how far we are to define it ontologically, John does not tell us; unless 3: 34; 6: 43; 7: 39; 10: 36; 15: 26 and 20: 22 are intended to teach that Jesus was the perfectly inspired man, prophet, Messiah, and agent of the most holy Lord God.[14]

In the fourth Gospel, then, Jesus is a Nazarene, a teacher, healer, and wonder-worker who fulfilled his mission in Galilee, Samaria, and Judaea during the terms of office of Pontius Pilate and Caiaphas. He is Donatello's ploughman. In ch. 9 we have the very dramatic story of a man born blind whom Jesus healed. The stages in his recognition of who this Jesus is are given in verses 11, 17, 33 and 35–8: Jesus is first a prophet, then a man who must have come from God, and finally he is the Man (lit. 'Son of Man'). Now, John the Baptist too had been sent from God (1: 6), and no one, I think, has suggested that he was the mythical figment of a Christian imagination. Nor were the great prophets of Israel docetic spokesmen for the Lord Yahweh. No more

---

[12] *The Gospel of John* (Oxford, 1971), 62.

[13] *Theology of the New Testament*, ii (New York, 1955), 49.

[14] As a rule, systematic theologians do not take kindly to any definition of the person of Christ in terms of a man inspired by the Holy Spirit.

was the final Messianic prophet a mirage for our evangelist. John displays to us a man.

Another comment from Bultmann may be cited, because it makes the point admirably: the offence of the Gospel is that people want a recognizable revelation.

The Revealer—although of course he must appear in human form—must also in some way appear as a shining, mysterious, fascinating figure . . . His humanity must be no more than a disguise. . . . All such desires [to see 'the divinity'] are cut short by the statement: the Word became flesh. It is in his sheer humanity that he is the Revealer. . . . the δόξα is not to be seen *alongside* the σάρξ, nor *through* the σάρξ as through a window; it is to be seen in the σάρξ and nowhere else. . . . The revelation is present in a peculiar *hiddenness*.[15]

I should prefer to define the revelation as one that lacks 'glory' (whatever is said in various comments that seems to contradict this!), but it will be perceived in the halo of the divine *shekinah* after the death of Jesus through the witness of the Paraclete in the life of the Church.

During his historical life, then, Jesus according to John 1: 11; 3: 19 f.; and 7: 35 f. is expressly rejected as God's agent. His enemies persecuted him and planned to kill him (5: 16–18, 10: 31), for they understood the menace to them in his claims for himself. They had no illusions about his actual successes (7: 45–52; 11: 47–53). When the plans came to fruition, there was a real corpse on a cross (19: 30 ff.). Until that moment Jesus was dubbed a madman, a demoniac, a sinner, one who led people astray—what an unglorified Christ that is! Crowning insult, he is called a 'Samaritan', that is, an alien and a heretic. He is beyond the pale, and not even a quite respectable ploughman (7: 7, 12, 20; 8: 48; 9: 24; 10: 20). People in general ('the world') hated him because he exposed evil, hypocrisy and godlessness (15: 18–22).

It is ironical that out of this enmity and conspiracy God was to congregate his scattered spiritual children, since Jesus' death, though truly concerted by enemies, was to be providentially transformed into a vicarious act of atonement, a deed that would save the nation of Israel (11: 50–3). The cross would draw all people to him as the Lamb of God and the Saviour of the world (1: 29; 4: 42; 12: 32). John was free to record this interpretation of what Jesus' death means for all humanity simply because he had seen the congregation take shape in the Roman Empire despite the continuing hostility of Jews and others (12: 42 f.; 17: 20; compare 9: 22; 16: 2 f.).

Another motif in the portrait of the unglorified Christ is that he is a

---

[15] R. Bultmann, *Gospel of John*, 63, with a reference to H. Clavier's 1955 article in the *RHPR* on the paradox of the Johannine Christology.

focus of controversy as the prophet who was to come and therefore, per-haps, the prince of Israel (4: 19; 6: 14 f.; 7: 40; 9: 17; 1Q Testimonia; Acts 3: 22; Deut. 18: 15). It was proverbial that prophets were not acceptable among their own folk, with Isa. 6: 9 f. as the key passage (Mark 4: 12; 8: 18; Luke 4: 24; John 12: 38–41). But, though their word might be disobeyed or ignored, no one doubted the physical reality of their presence. Similarly Jesus is a preacher in that Israelite prophetic tradition. In many texts he is described also as a teacher, sometimes as rabbi, and sometimes with a Greek equivalent (1: 38, 49; 3: 2, 26; 4: 31; 6: 25; 9: 2; 11: 8, 28; 13: 13 f.; 20: 16; compare 8: 4). It is true, and lamentable, that John gives very little of the public teaching in spite of Jesus' retort to the High Priest, 'I have spoken openly to the world; I have always taught in synagogues and in the temple, where all Jews come together; I have said nothing secretly' (18: 20 f.). The reason is that the framework of his narrative is a series of polemical confronta-tions in which the basic subject is the Messianic status of Jesus; doubt-less a topic of special interest and debate in the area from which the fourth Gospel comes. And chs. 13–16 are dense with private teaching to his closest friends and disciples. Presumably John means that Jesus did not pass on in private an esoteric sort of teaching that would not cohere with what was delivered in public.

I do not believe that it can be demonstrated that this Johannine material is all authentic, yet it may be argued that sentences within it read strangely if the evangelist was simply a historical novelist of a kind or, what is worse, was Käsemann's docetic heretic. Consider, for example, 13: 8, 'If I do not wash you, you have no part in me'; 13: 15, 'I have given you an example, that you also should do as I have done to you'; 13: 20, 'he who receives any one whom I send receives me; and he who receives me receives him who sent me.' Reference should also be made to the new commandment (13: 34 f.), the 'peace' of the Lord (14: 27), and the warning about persecution and the scattering of the disciples (15: 20; 16: 32).

Few though the teaching locales are—in the synagogue at Caper-naum, beside Jacob's Well, and in the Temple at Jerusalem—and few though the authentic sayings, still we can garner enough to depict a flesh-and-blood Master (13: 13). His pupils appreciated, but only in partial degree, that he was indeed the mediator of divine truth and the human pointer to the ultimate reality of God (1: 14a, 17b). Peter speaks in the Johannine idiom (6: 68 f.) when he voices at a certain stage in the disciples' pilgrimage of faith a quite genuine belief: 'You have the words of eternal life . . . you are the Holy One of God.' And yet the disciples were obtuse, prejudiced, conventional in their views of

Messiah and the new age. Philip and Thomas mirror their incredulity, Peter their weakness (13: 38; 14: 5, 9; 16: 32; compare 11: 1–16). Judas is the traitor who found Jesus in a familiar haunt and watched the arrest (6: 70 f.; 13: 2, 27–30; 18: 2 f., 5). Jesus is seized, bound, tried, and condemned as a spurious king. In spite of the grand gesture of 18: 6, this Jesus (whatever else he may be for the fully developed faith of the Church that is reflected often in this Gospel) is a peasant-king, an unglorified Christ. ECCE HOMO!

And that is why it is remarkable that Käsemann fails so signally to take seriously certain 'features of the lowliness of the earthly Jesus in the Fourth Gospel'. For him they seem merely to represent 'the absolute minimum of the costume designed for the one who dwelt for a little while among men . . .' Because the Son is obedient to the Father 'it cannot be denied that we meet here the tradition of a christology of humiliation as known to us through Phil. 2. 7 f.', but this must not be employed as the basis for the Gospel's doctrine of Christ as a whole.

Obedience is the form and concretion of Jesus' glory during the period of his incarnation . . . The disguise, the hiding, of a divine being in lowliness may appear paradoxical, but it is not really paradoxical at all. . . . Lowliness in John is the nature of the situation, of the earthly realm which Jesus entered. In entering it, he himself is not being humbled. He retains the glory and majesty of the Son until the cross.

Hence the real definition of his obedience is not service to God, for it is the result of his glory 'and the attestation of his glory in the situation of the earthly conflict'.[16]

The logic of such a position, if it was really held by the fourth evangelist, surely leads to a denial that Jesus Christ, the Son of God, the Word made flesh was ever put to death. You cannot kill glory of the kind described by Ernst Käsemann. The flesh of the son of Joseph was by no means just a temporary costume for a piece of play-acting. Of course there was a glory about the earthly life of Jesus, as there is about the life today in Calcutta of Mother Teresa, as she does so much that is beautiful for God. John and the Church in the centuries that followed could not escape trying to show the God in the Man, the eternal love in the world of imperialism and religious hypocrisy. They did believe in an incarnation. And yet they also knew Jesus as the peasant Jew who was at heart humble and obedient, the servant of his disciples as much as the servant of God. Even if one does not accept a theology of incarnation as the best way to understand the significance of Jesus of Nazareth, one has to do justice to the plain signs of the unglorified Christ in John's book.

[16] *The Testament of Jesus*, 10–12, 18 f.

IV

Humiliation is a central feature in the portrait of Jesus in the fourth Gospel. He is the *Homo* who could be humiliated by the mob, the soldiers, the priests, and Pilate himself. He is unmistakably a peasant Christ in the narrative of his Passion. But it has already been conceded that the border within which the icon of Jesus is shown is far more wonderful. I look on the Gospel as a treasure comparable to the marvellous illuminated Gospel-books that issued from Irish and Northumbrian *scriptoria* in the eighth and ninth centuries: Durrow, Lindisfarne, Kells, and Lichfield. It is enshrined in a magnificent cover with a cross decorated in precious jewels. Within the brilliant border one sees vine scrolls of heavenly beauty, and there are 'Carpet Pages' studded with signs of godly beauty, symbols of love and faith, all of them proclaiming Christ as the Way and the Truth and the Life; Christ the Light of the world, the Good Shepherd, and the Son of Man whose human existence is a Bethel where angels play on Irish ladders, running up and down between heaven and earth. O, the glory of it! The icon names Jesus as the Christ who has ascended to the Father and who reigns now and for ever from heaven (20: 17b). It is altogether theological and confessional, it is orthodox and catholic: admitted. Yet in no way should the splendour hide from our eyes the humiliated Jesus who hung upon a cross in the sight of his mother and his friends.

Barnabas Lindars would explain the Johannine picture of the Son of Man as due to

the fusion of two originally distinct concepts, the descent of wisdom and the ascent of the Son of Man. The pre-existent Wisdom did not have a glory like that of the Son of Man in his enthronement in Dan. 7 . . . But this is how John thinks of the glory of the Son of man. It is a matter of intimate personal relationship, rather than splendid robes and royal state. In the final reckoning, it can only be expressed in terms of love (verse 24).[17]

Raymond Brown regards the royal prayer as an independent composition added by the redactor along with chs. 15 and 16, and he maintains that 'the Jesus of the Last Discourse transcends time and space, for from heaven and beyond the grave he is already speaking to the disciples of all time.'[18] As C. H. Dodd used to say, the prayer is itself the Ascension, and its fulfilment is made possible by Christ's laying down his life for his friends.[19]

I can fully accept the substance of such insights into the full doctrine

---

[17] *The Gospel of John: New Century Bible* (London, 1972), 520 f. Cf. Cadman, *The Open Heaven*, 40.
[18] *The Gospel According to John*, ii, 747.
[19] *The Interpretation of the Fourth Gospel* (Cambridge, 1953), 419, 423.

of the fourth evangelist, since he is so obviously dazzled by Easter brightness and he writes as a participant in the mission and ministry of the Paraclete. Let me quote a wise summary by Franz Mussner:

The identity of the historical and the glorified Christ is, from the ontological point of view, given by what Jesus Christ himself was. This does not mean, of course, that John had no idea of the contrast between the operation of the earthly Jesus and that of the risen Christ (cf. E. Haenchen in *TLZ* 89 [1964], pp. 893 f.). For the Church the identity of the historical and the glorified Christ became evident and conscious by the operation of the Paraclete.[20]

What I now wish to argue for is that certain Johannine texts belong to the border and not to the actual icon of Jesus itself. They express the faith of John and his contemporaries and should not be transferred *simpliciter* to the portrayal of the historical Jesus. It was of decisive importance to John that the Son of God he commends to his readers is the Jesus who lived and died long ago.

Thus the 'we' of 1: 14 are Catholic believers in the Johannine community towards the end of the first or beginning of the second century. The 'glory' they have seen is not some splendour of the Lord in his flesh; it is rather the radiance of his eternal Sonship, confirmed by his Resurrection and the subsequent history of his 'presence' with the Church. 7: 39 shows quite decisively that this was in the evangelist's mind as he wrote (or edited his traditions). Compare 2: 22 and 12: 16.

To say, after the first Cana miracle (2: 11), that Jesus manifested his glory and that his disciples believed in him, cannot mean that the wedding company or the disciples actually had a vision of the divine Logos/Son. The event was a sign, and signs were not revelations open to the general public. 'Belief', too, must be taken with a grain of salt. When we examine the total picture in John, say at 2: 23; 4: 39; 7: 31; 7: 39; 9: 38; 11: 45 and 12: 42, we are bound to interpret John as showing timidity, hesitation, half-formed faith. The 'real thing' awaited Easter and the work of the Spirit; and even after that, if one accepts the thesis of J. Louis Martyn, the hesitation and fear of 12: 42 may well refer to contemporaries of the evangelist who still belonged to Jewish synagogues.[21]

5: 36–47 provides a classic example of a developed Christian apologetic in the face of Jewish rejection of the Church's *kerygma*. 'Glory' in v. 41 means 'recommendation', and in 44 it means 'praise'. Like Moses before him, Jesus represents God and calls God 'Father'.

8: 54, 'If I glorify myself, my glory is nothing; it is my Father who

[20] *The Historical Jesus in the Gospel of St John* (London, 1967), 109 f., note 16 to section VII.
[21] *History and Theology in the Fourth Gospel* (New York, 1968).

glorifies me, of whom you say that he is your God,'[22] belongs to the same line of defence of Jesus as Israel's true teacher. The 'glory' will be referred to again several times (in the noun or the verb), but always the time is postponed until the actual event of the Crucifixion which for John is the real exaltation of Jesus; it leads to his triumph, and it is to be understood only in the sunshine of Easter visions and the ecstasies of spiritual graces (see, for example, 12: 23; 13: 31; 17: 1).

On 11: 40 Lindars may be quoted:

The miracle will prove that Lazarus' fatal illness was 'for the glory of God', because it will be a practical demonstration that Jesus is God's agent to give the Resurrection and the Life, the eternal salvation of mankind. It will also be a symbolic anticipation of Jesus' own Resurrection, in which God's glory is supremely made manifest. From this point there is no further mention of Jesus' emotion.[23]

14: 13 states Johannine theology: the divine response to Christian prayers offered in the Son's name continues to reveal to the eyes of faith the wonder of God the Father.

16: 14, the Paraclete 'will glorify me': what the Spirit does for disciples in the Church and through them in the world always refers back to the Christ who came, died, and rose again. It is this Christ whose reputation is magnified, whose union with the Father in eternal love is confessed and praised, whose position as world-Saviour is proclaimed. The Spirit is the Spirit of Christ (15: 26).

17: 4, 'I glorified thee on earth': Jesus' lifelong obedience, his revelation of the reality and truth of God, his display of the divine grace and love, all redound to the praise and honour of the Father. Jesus 'glorified' God, and it is God who remains the ultimate source of the glory that is to be granted to the Son and to the Church. I can find no trace in John of the concept of the *perichoresis* (the circuminsession), for his theology is not yet an articulated doctrine of the eternal Trinity.

V

It is not the purpose of this essay to defend the profound Logos/Son Christology of John's Gospel, nor to suggest that it is necessarily the most adequate predicate for those who still wish to be the pupils and representatives of Jesus. What I propose is that radical critics like myself who cannot accept the apostolic authorship of John nor its early date need to re-evaluate the portrait of the incarnate Lord. We have

[22] The Bodmer papyri read 'our God', and this is accepted by R. E. Brown, *John*, i. 359.
[23] *The Gospel of John*, 400.

tended to dismiss Jesus' tears at the grave of Lazarus because of the delay noted at 11: 6. 'Lazarus had to die. Let him die, so that the Son and God himself may be glorified!' Jesus could not have said that; but the Johannine Jesus does so, speaking out of the orthodox border; and he is painted like that out of an excess of zeal by John or his source. Yet even John's Jesus must have loved and wept and experienced distress as he lived in the flesh of our humanity (11: 3, 33, 35; compare 12: 27; 13: 21). The Lazarus story remains incredible and the conqueror-frame of the icon tends to drown out the peasant Jesus. (Elsewhere in the Christian literature of the first century the emotion of Jesus is made evident: Mark 14: 33; Phil. 2: 8; Heb. 5: 7 ff.)

We need to underscore in the Passion narrative (John 11: 55 ff.) the signs of the unglorified Lord. He is bound and beaten (18: 22); he is crowned and garbed as a king but hailed in cruellest mockery (19: 1–3). Joseph of Arimathea and Nicodemus buried the corpse of Jesus in a garden tomb (19: 38–42). When Mary meets the risen Christ in the same garden, she is put off with the *Noli tangere*: 'do not cling to me, for I have not yet ascended to the Father' (20: 17). Bultmann may be right to find here some criticism of a naïve Easter faith that was dependent on physical sight and touch. 'The real Easter faith ... consists in understanding the offence of the cross; it is not faith in a palpable demonstration of the Risen Lord within the mundane sphere.'[24] Yet the same narrative is beyond all question a recognition scene. Mary did not know the Lord until he spoke her name, 'Miriam', in the old familiar Aramaic.[25] She responds likewise with *Rabbouni*, 'my teacher'. Dare we call this the peasant tongue? Jesus is the teacher who had talked colloquially with his students, and it is he whom Thomas adores as *Dominus et Deus meus*, 'my Lord and my God' (20: 14, 16, 28). We may cite St Paul's insistent claim in 1 Cor. 9: 1, 'Have I not seen *Jesus our Lord*?' and 15: 8, 'he appeared also to me'. The Christian affirmation is that Jesus was recognized as the Lord; that he is the icon of God (2 Cor. 4: 4), the Man in whom God has shone so that his beloved see 'the light of the knowledge of the glory of God in the face of Christ' (2 Cor. 4: 6). Neither Paul nor John was a naïve docetist, and we must not be persuaded by Käsemann to the contrary in the case of John.

John did not in fact produce a theological formula like that of the *Tome of Leo* or the Council of Chalcedon. It is not legitimate to read his Christology as if it were a statement of 'divinity' conjoined with 'humanity' in a single personality (πρόσωπον), any more than his language in

---

[24] *The Gospel of John*, 688.

[25] 20: 16 where the best MSS read 'Mariam'. This is Jewish Aramaic. Brown's note may be consulted: ii. 990 f. Jesus must have used a familiar form of the name.

15: 26, 'the Spirit of truth, who proceeds from the Father', should be taken quite literally as an inspired secret about the intra-trinitarian life of the Father, the Son, and the Holy Spirit.[26] John is far more an artist-theologian than a patristic scholar! To some extent he is, as R. H. Strachan tried to show, a dramatist. He is full of wonder that the man of Nazareth, the 'Nazoraean' (if that is what this strange word means), the son of Joseph, teacher and Lord of the Church, the revealer of God, had been the kind of Master who could stoop to a slave's duty by washing the feet of unreliable disciples and who had left those same persons, except Judas, to carry on his mission and eventually to share his glory (17: 14–23). What John and his Church could never abandon (compare 1 John 2: 22; 4: 2 f.) was the certainty that they had seen the meaning of God and had found their salvation in a Jew called Jesus. He had been crucified at a specific time and place, but he lives for ever in God, 'beside his Father', in a love that flows out creatively and redemptively to bless the world and all the people in it, to encourage the communion and the spiritual unity of the Church on earth, to which all his dear children are finally to belong.

[26] The tyranny exercised by John's vocabulary over patristic pneumatology and that of those orthodox scholars who accept that as dogma is well illustrated in the three volumes of Yves Congar, *I Believe in the Holy Spirit* (London, New York, 1983 (French original, 1979 and 1980)).

10. Reflected Glory: 2 Corinthians 3: 18

N. T. WRIGHT

THE third chapter of Second Corinthians is all about glory. But what precisely does it say about this glory? And how does glory, as a theme, fit within the overall argument of the wider unit (2 Cor. 2: 14–4: 6, or indeed 2: 14–6: 13)? In particular, what does Paul mean by the verse (18) with which ch. 3 reaches its triumphant conclusion? Has he 'proved too much' at this point?[1] Do Christians 'reflect', or 'behold as in a mirror', the glory of the Lord? If the latter, what is the mirror? And what is the 'glory' itself? There is no agreement on any of these points.[2] This is just the sort of verse (and section) that George Caird loved to expound.[3] Though I cannot tell what he would have thought of my central argument, I am confident that he would have enjoyed having the questions opened once again, and am therefore happy to dedicate these reflections to his memory.

I

It is now generally agreed that the overall theme of the section of which 3: 18 forms a central part is Paul's defence, not of his apostolic ministry in itself, but of the particular style or character of that ministry.[4] It is a ministry of sincerity (2: 17), of confidence (3: 4), of glory (3: 8–11), of

---

[1] So C. K. Barrett, *A Commentary on the Second Epistle to the Corinthians* (London, 1973), 126, quoting Lietzmann.

[2] Among recent literature on the subject, see Barrett, op. cit.; J. -F. Collange, *Énigmes de la Deuxième Épître de Paul aux Corinthiens*, SNTSMS 18 (Cambridge, 1972), 114–25: V. P. Furnish, *II Corinthians*, Anchor Bible (New York, 1984), with extensive bibliographical listings; W. C. van Unnik, '"With Unveiled Face", an Exegesis of 2 Corinthians iii 12–18', *NovT* 6, 1963, 153–69 (reprinted in his *Sparsa Collecta*, i, *NovT* Supplement 29 (Leiden, 1980), 194–210); J. D. G. Dunn, '2 Corinthians III. 17—"The Lord is the Spirit"', *JTS* NS 21 (1970), 309–20; C. F. D. Moule, '2 Cor. 3: 18b, καθάπερ ἀπὸ κυρίου πνεύματος', in *Neues Testament und Geschichte*, Cullmann FS, ed. H. Baltensweiler and B. Reicke (Tübingen, 1972), 233–7; C. J. A. Hickling, 'The Sequence of Thought in II Corinthians, Chapter Three', *NTS* 21 (1974–5), 380–95; A. T. Hanson, 'The Midrash in II Corinthians 3: A 'Reconsideration', *JSNT* 9 (October 1980), 2–28; M. D. Hooker, 'Beyond the Things That Are Written? St Paul's Use of Scripture', *NTS*, 27 (1980–1), 295–309; E. Richard, 'Polemics, Old Testament, and Theology: A Study of II Cor., III, 1–IV, 6', *RB*, 88 (1981), 340–67; J. Lambrecht, 'Transformation in 2 Cor. 3, 18', *Biblica* 64 (1983), 243–54.

[3] See, for example, his 'Everything to Everyone: The Theology of the Corinthian Epistles', in *Interpretation*, 13 (1959), 385–99, at 391 f. The passage also featured, of course, in his doctoral thesis (234 ff.).

[4] See, among recent commentators, Barrett and Furnish, ad loc.

great παρρησία (3: 12), and one in which the minister need not lose heart (4: 1, 16). This theme falls, in turn, within the wider argument of the chapter: that Paul does not need 'letters of recommendation', because the Corinthian Church is itself his 'letter' (3: 1–3). The idea of 'commendation' is a major theme, in fact, in the letter as a whole (as it stands, that is without taking sides at present in the debate on the unity of the letter): see 4: 2, 5: 11 f., 6: 4, 10: 12, 18, 12: 11. These arguments form the basic structure of the passage, within which the rest of the complicated discussion must find its place. (The nature of Paul's ministry continues as the main subject right through to 6: 13: this is clear from 5: 11–15, where verse 12 in particular echoes ch. 3 at several points, and from 5: 20 f., 6: 1–13.) Paul's defence of the character of his ministry includes as one important feature the demonstration that the human weaknesses and frailties which characterize it do not undermine its credibility but, on the contrary, reveal precisely its Christlike character (4: 7–12, 16–18, 6: 3–10). This theme is strengthened further by Paul's emphasis that he is not sufficient of himself to be a minister of Christ, and that his 'sufficiency' is from God (2: 16; 3: 5–6).

If the main thrust of the argument is thus a defence of Paul's ministry, both in that he does not need 'letters of recommendation' and in his paradoxical apostolic boldness and confidence, the main weapon with which he begins this thrust is the concept of the new covenant. Though mentioned explicitly only in 3: 6, this is clearly in mind in the language of 3: 3, with its echoes of Ezekiel 36 and Jeremiah 31, and it dominates the subsequent discussion (3: 7 ff.). Paul's 'sufficiency', which comes from God, consists in this: that he is a minister of the new covenant, which operates by means of the Spirit's work in the hearts of his hearers. The two conclusions Paul draws from this within the present argument are (1) that the Corinthians are themselves, because of the Spirit's work, his 'letter of recommendation' (3: 2 f.), and (2) that he himself can be bold, can speak the truth in Christ without fear or reserve: 'because we have this hope, we use great boldness' (3: 12).[5] Both of these, I shall suggest, are present in the climax of verse 18, and to recognize this is to achieve fresh understanding of that verse.

It is in this light that the difficult discussion of Moses and his veil may be understood (3: 7–16). Although it is sometimes suggested that Paul's opponents were already using Moses as a model of true ministry (and contrasting him with Paul, to the latter's disadvantage), such explanations are not needed if we recognize the importance of the covenant

---

[5] Hanson, op. cit. n. 2 above, 23 sees the second of these points, but for the first he substitutes 'it is a ministry which is centred on Christ'—an idea which he has, I believe, imported into the context: see below.

theme throughout the passage.[6] The argument falls naturally into two sections, 3: 7–11 and 3: 12–18.

It is not difficult to assess Paul's purpose in 3: 7–11.[7] He wishes to argue that his ministry possesses δόξα, glory—presumably to counter any suggestion that an itinerant preacher with a poor speaking style and a prison record is not fit to be an apostle of the Lord of glory. He argues, not by means of demonstration ('what I mean by glory is *x*: you can see that I possess *x* because . . .') but, in the first instance, with an *a fortiori*: the ministry of the old covenant had δόξα, so that of the new must have even more.[8] He makes this point in three different ways. (1) The ministry of the old covenant was that of the 'letter', written on stone, and was a dispensation of death (Paul is obviously picking up the themes of vv. 3, 6): that of the new is of the life-giving Spirit (vv. 7–8: compare Rom. 8: 10, 1 Cor. 15: 45). (2) The ministry of the old covenant was one of condemnation (Paul does not here say why this is so, nor does he substantiate the previous claim that the old dispensation was one of death): that of the new is one of justification (v. 9).[9] This point is then amplified in v. 10: it is as though, by comparison, the old has come to have no glory at all. (3) The old covenant was destined to be abolished: the new is destined to remain. Thus, if Paul's readers acknowledge that he is a minister of the new covenant, they must see that his ministry possesses δόξα, however surprising that may be.

It is within this (of itself quite clear) argument that Paul refers to the glory of Moses' face. In v. 7, by way simply of indicating how great Moses' glory was as a minister of the old covenant, he writes that his glory was such 'that the Israelites could not look steadily at the face of Moses, because of its glory—which glory was to pass away' (my translation). The reason why the Israelites could not look at Moses was not, here, because the glory was passing away, but because it was at present so bright. The reference to its impermanence (τὴν καταργουμένην) is simply introduced as a foretaste of Paul's third *a fortiori* (v. 11), much as his reference to the 'ministry of death' (v. 7) is a foretaste of the second *a fortiori* (v. 9).

So far, so good. The final paragraph, however, is of course the most problematic. Almost every verse presents fresh difficulties. What was it that the children of Israel were not supposed to look at (τὸ τέλος τοῦ

---

[6] In connection with the debate over Paul's opponents in this passage, see now the wise comments of Furnish, 242–5. We do not need elaborate hypotheses, either of the theology of Paul's opponents or of the textual prehistory of our passage, to make sense of the argument.

[7] Despite Richard, op. cit. n. 2 above, 358, who sees it as a 'parenthetical clarification' of v. 6.

[8] So Caird, 'The New Testament Conception of Δόξα', unpublished D.Phil. (Oxon.) Thesis, 1944, 236 ff.

[9] Although justification is not normally associated directly with covenant theology, I shall elsewhere advance arguments to show that, for Paul, it should be.

καταργουμένου, v. 13)? Why does Paul suddenly mention their hardness of heart, and how can he move the veil from Moses' face to their understanding (v. 14) or to the hearts of his Jewish contemporaries (v. 15)?[10] Is v. 16 an adapted quote from Exod. 34: 34, or is it a general statement? Does 'the Lord' in v. 17—and in v. 18—refer to the Spirit *as* Lord, to Yahweh as Spirit, or to Jesus—or, by implication at least, to more than one of these three? Finally, in v. 18, what precisely does κατοπτριζόμενοι mean (looking intently? seeing as in a mirror? reflecting?): why does Paul say that 'we are being changed into *the same* image'? The same as what? Must ἀπο δόξης εἰς δόξαν remain ambiguous and perhaps rhetorical, 'from glory to glory'? And how can we cope with the final four words, καθάπερ ἀπὸ κυρίου πνεύματος? How do they fit into the overall thought?

To analyse, let alone to answer, all these questions would require a longer article than this. I propose to look at the problems of v. 18 in particular: and one of the ancillary arguments for the position I shall adopt is that it goes with a way of reading vv. 12–17 also which at least suggests plausible answers to the questions raised by those earlier verses.

II

We may begin by repeating a point which, though it should be quite obvious, is often forgotten. The argument, as we have seen, is twofold: it concerns the 'letter of recommendation' written in the hearts of the Corinthians and, within that, the nature of Paul's ministry. Having established that this is a ministry of the new covenant, which involves the writing on the heart by the Spirit (vv. 1–6), and having argued that, precisely as a new covenant ministry, his work has δόξα far exceeding that of Moses, Paul is now making the further point that, 'because of this hope',[11] he is able to use much παρρησία, freedom of speech. This is the specific point of the new section: Paul can be bold in his dealings with Christians. He has no need to veil the glory: he can let it be clearly seen. If this is his main point, his conclusion is obviously v. 17b: where the Spirit of the Lord is, there is freedom—freedom, that is, not in the vague sense of release from any constraints at all: not even in the more precise sense of freedom from the law, though that idea is both thoroughly Pauline and quite closely related to the present passage:

---

[10] Or for that matter his pagan ones, or perhaps to the gospel (4: 3–4).

[11] i.e. the hope of life, guaranteed by the gift of the Spirit in the present, as in v. 5. He does not say, as one might have expected, because of this ministry: this shows that the δόξα in question is eschatological, as in Rom. 8: 30.

rather, freedom in the sense of freedom of speech, boldness, openness, and honesty in proclaiming and defending the gospel (compare 2: 17, 4: 1 f.).[12]

It then becomes apparent that the main contrast in the passage is not that between Paul and Moses, but that between the Christians—even those in Corinth!—and the Israelites, both of Moses' day and of Paul's.[13] Paul can use boldness not because he is different from Moses but because those who belong to the new covenant are different from those who belong to the old. This is the point of vv. 14 f.: Moses had to use the veil, because the hearts of the Israelites (unlike those of the new covenant people: this is the point of the ἀλλά, 'but', at the start of v. 14) were hardened. The Israelites come, that is, in the category indicated in vv. 3, 6: they are those who belong to the covenant on tables of stone, the covenant of the 'letter'. The argument is not so much allegorical, or even (as current fashion would have it) 'midrashic', but follows the line of thought in Gal. 3: 15–22, or even Mark 10: 2–9. Difference in style of ministry is occasioned by difference in the spiritual condition of the hearers: Paul's overall point is that his boldness is correlative to the new covenant membership of the Corinthians, whereby they are themselves his 'letter of recommendation'. This shows that vv. 14–15 are not an aside, but a development of Paul's main point.[14] It also explains, incidentally, why Paul's argument in vv. 7–11 does not result in his having to wear an even thicker veil, to hide the even greater glory.[15]

Christians, then, are those upon whose hearts the Spirit of the living God has written the 'letter of recommendation', so that they can be known and read by all (vv. 2–3). Paul's ministry is therefore a ministry in which God equips him by the Spirit to minister to those who are receiving the Spirit (vv. 5–6), and who, as he will now show, are able to look upon the glory with unveiled face. Although we cannot here go into the detail of the problematical verses 13–14, from this perspective

[12] So, rightly, Furnish, 277, against, e.g. Hickling, op. cit. n. 2 above, 394: though Furnish obscures the issue with the alleged parallels from Philo, which give a quite different sense of both 'freedom' and 'boldness' from that which Paul here develops. Dr George Johnston suggests to me that ἐλευθερία here may be another 'Exodus' motif. For the background of παρρησία see the various articles of W. C. van Unnik, who argues that the Semitic background of the word points of itself to the idea of 'barefacedness'. Whether or not this will stand, there is clearly a very close link between v. 12 and vv. 17–18.

[13] So R. Bultmann, *Der Zweite Brief an die Korinther*, ed. E. Dinkler (Göttingen, 1976), 93 f., Furnish, 213–14, against, e.g. Caird, ad. loc., and Hickling, 393, who thinks that Moses is contrasted with the Christians; or Richard, op. cit. n. 2 above, 364 n. 82, who makes the extraordinary claim that Paul makes Moses 'a precursor of his Christian rivals and the antithesis of the true Christian minister'. So, too, J. Jeremias is not strictly accurate when he says (*TDNT* 4. 869 n. 230) that here 'Moses represents the OT community': rather, he stands over against them. He alone could look at the divine glory with unveiled face, as a *precursor* of the Christian in 2 Cor. 3: 18.

[14] *Contra* Furnish, 233, 236, 243.

[15] *Contra* Hooker, op. cit. n. 2 above, 297 f.

it seems that Furnish (203) is correct in seeing that vv. 7, 13 speak, not of a glory which gradually fades from Moses' face, but of a glory which, because it is part of the old covenant, is to be annulled as is that covenant.[16]

It is in this light that the direction of thought in vv. 16–17 becomes comprehensible. Paul desires to show that the new covenant people whom he has described briefly in vv. 1–3, 6 are capable of receiving the glory of that new covenant, and therefore that the appropriate style of new covenant ministry is boldness as opposed to a veiled secrecy. To this end he uses Exod. 34: 34: not as an exact quotation, but as a deliberate allusion, in order to make the transition between Moses, who in the Exodus narrative was the one who went back into the presence of the Lord and so removed the veil, and the people, *whether apostles or their hearers*, who now possess the freedom which allows 'boldness'. Paul certainly desires that the Exodus passage should still be in mind, otherwise he would surely have added τις to make it clear that the subject of ἐπιτρέψῃ is no longer 'Moses', but 'one' or 'someone': and this means that ὁ δὲ κύριος at the start of v. 17 can bear its natural anaphoric sense: '"the Lord" here refers to the Spirit'.[17] Equally, Paul certainly desires that the quotation/allusion should do more than merely refer to Moses himself, as is clear from the alterations he has made. Specifically, he wants to include a reference to all those who 'turn to the Lord' and therefore possess 'freedom'. V. 17, therefore, draws on the categories of vv. 1–6, in the light of the discussion of Moses in vv. 13–16, to provide a QED to Paul's statement in v. 12. 'The reason we have boldness is this: you, unlike the Israelites before whom the glory (even of the old covenant) had to be veiled, possess the Spirit because you are within the new covenant, and you are therefore able to bear the bold, direct revelation of God's glory.'

If this exegesis is correct—and it seems to make very good sense of an otherwise difficult passage—it raises a possibility for the interpretation of v. 18 which has not, to my knowledge, so far been explored. Paul is dealing not merely with his own ministry but with the state of heart of his hearers. This is clearly reinforced by the 'all' which emphasizes that the 'we' at the start of the verse is not merely the 'royal we', or 'Paul and his fellow-workers', but refers to each Christian.[18] This, and not a self-reference, is Paul's main point.

There is general agreement that linguistic evidence favours the

---

[16] *Contra*, e. g. Hooker, 291, 303–4: see the discussion in Hanson, 13 f.

[17] See the works of Dunn and Moule cited above n. 2, against Furnish, 210 ff. Furnish is right, however, to reject the Christological interpretation of, e.g. Hanson (see below).

[18] The omission of πάντες in P46 may safely be ignored.

meaning 'behold as in a mirror' for κατοπτριζόμενοι.[19] But the question, the lack of satisfactory answers to which has driven scholars to seek less frequent meanings, is—what is the mirror? I suggest that the 'mirror' in which Christians see reflected the glory of the Lord is not, in this passage at any rate, the gospel itself, nor even Jesus Christ. *It is one another.* At the climax of Paul's whole argument, he makes (if I am right) the astonishing claim that those who belong to the new covenant are being changed by the Spirit into the glory of the Lord: when they come face to face with one another they are beholding, as in a mirror, the glory itself.[20] Though the verb could therefore have its alternative sense of 'reflect', since the one in whom the glory is seen as in a mirror could himself be said to be 'reflecting' the glory, that is not the point Paul is making.[21] Unlike the Israelites, those in the new covenant can look at the glory as it is reflected in each other. This is the final proof that the Corinthians themselves are Paul's 'letter of recommendation'. And, if this is so, 'the Lord' in the phrase 'the glory of the Lord', the object of κατοπτριζόμενοι, need not be identified as either 'God' or 'Christ', but may, perfectly consistently within the thought of the chapter as a whole, refer to the Spirit. It is the peculiar glory of the Spirit that is seen when one looks at one's fellow Christians.

V. 18, if this is correct, thus picks up quite precisely the thought of vv. 1–3. It does not 'prove too much',[22] or introduce 'an entirely new idea',[23] or leave behind the purpose of the earlier part of the chapter.[24] The new covenant people are a letter, written by the Spirit, to be known and read by all—'a letter of Christ, ministered by us' (v. 3). The 'turning to the Lord' spoken of in the allusion to Exod. 34: 34 is a turning to, an openness towards, the Spirit—who is operative in the ministry of Paul and also in the new covenant community. The phrase need not be taken in the general sense of 'turning to Christ', that is, becoming a Christian, though this is no doubt implied. It is more specific: when one looks at the work of the Spirit, the veil is unnecessary. It is taken

[19] For the alternative, 'reflect', see, e.g. W. L. Knox, *St Paul and the Church of the Gentiles* (Cambridge, 1939), 131 ff. (See the discussion in Collange, op. cit. n. 2 above, 116 ff.) Our argument renders this solution unnecessary.

[20] Lambrecht (op. cit. n. 2 above, 250) seems to want to include this possibility as an extension of his main point that the gospel is the mirror in question. But his argument is very vague at this point: and his suggestion that this 'seeing' is itself indirect is hardly compatible with the main emphasis of the passage.

[21] *Contra* Van Unnik. op. cit. n. 2 above, 167. Caird, in both of the works already cited, argued that 'reflect' makes better sense of the passage as a whole and in particular its underlying Christology. I submit that these arguments point more to 'behold', not in the sense that Caird rightly rejected (a contrast between Moses and Jesus), but in a sense consonant with his main emphasis (that Paul and the Corinthians are being changed into the glory of God).

[22] See above, n. 1.

[23] Furnish, 238.

[24] *Contra* Hickling, 393.

off—this is the point of the passage—not in private communion with God, but in the boldness with which Paul proclaims the gospel to the Corinthians.

Two different emphases in ch. 3 as a whole come, therefore, to full expression in verse 18. (1) The Christians in Corinth are Paul's 'letter', because the Spirit has written the new covenant on their hearts through his ministry: it is this that is expressed in 'we are being changed'. (2) Paul's ministry is 'bold', 'unveiled': 'we all, with unveiled face, behold as in a mirror the glory of the Lord'. What is the logical relation between these two? It is possible to let the emphasis fall on (2), translating in some such way as: 'it is *as we behold* the glory of the Lord as in a mirror—that is in one another—that we are being changed . . .'. This would emphasize the participle κατοπτριζόμενοι rather than the indicative μεταμορφούμεθα, and it may be for this reason that P46, partially supported in A and elsewhere,[25] reverses the grammatical order, exchanging the participle and indicative and reading κατοπτριζόμεθα οἱ τὴν αὐτὴν εἰκόνα μεταμορφούμενοι κτλ. This throws the weight of the sentence even more clearly in this direction: 'we all, with unveiled face, behold the glory of the Lord—we, that is, who are being changed into the same image from glory to glory'. The participle could then have explanatory force: it is precisely because 'we are being changed . . . into glory' that 'we all behold the glory of the Lord as in a mirror' in the course of Christian ministry.[26]

The majority reading, however, seems to throw the weight of the sentence on to the indicative μεταμορφούμεθα: and this is probably to be preferred. It is here, after all, that we find the climax of the underlying discussion: Paul does not need 'letters of recommendation' because he and the Corinthian Church alike are being 'changed' so that they, the Church, *are* his 'letter'. The relation between the two verbs is therefore straightforward, even though the meaning is striking: it is as we behold the glory in one another that we are being changed into the same image. The parallel with Moses is that, just as Moses gazes at the Lord, with the result that his face is changed, so Christians gaze (as in a mirror) at the Lord, the Spirit—in one another: and so they are changed, as the Spirit writes the 'letter', the new covenant, on their

---

[25] e.g. in some occurrences of the phrase in Origen.

[26] This reading cannot be lightly dismissed. It explains the other readings well: κατοπτριζόμεθα οἱ could easily have been contracted into κατοπτριζόμενοι, which yields the odd reading in A (and 614, a thirteenth-century minuscule) of two participles without a main verb. Having arrived at that reading, one of the natural corrections open to a scribe would be to turn μεταμορφούμενοι into μεταμορφούμεθα, particularly in view of the greater patristic interest in transformation, even deification, than in the boldness of apostolic ministry. Finally, the reading of the ninth-century MS 33, which has both verbs in the indicative, can be explained as a copying error from either source.

hearts. The reading of P⁴⁶ may, perhaps, have come about through a scribe's being so taken up with argument (2) as to forget the underlying argument (1).

One of the strengths of the view of v. 18 I am proposing is the sense it is able to make of the otherwise troublesome phrase τὴν αὐτὴν εἰκόνα, 'the same image'.[27] On the one hand, the word εἰκών is introduced suddenly: although Paul will make an important further use of it in 4: 4, that seems insufficient to explain why he brings it in here, especially since the uses are not quite the same. It seems much better to take it very closely with κατοπτριζόμενοι, understood as I have suggested, that is 'beholding as in a mirror'. That which one sees in a mirror is an εἰκών, a reflection.[28] Of course, Paul is quite well aware of the other overtones that might be heard (of Gen. 1: 26, for instance) in what he is saying: but his present use is simply part of the overall metaphor of this particular verse (so Barrett, Furnish). On the other hand, the force of τὴν αὐτήν, 'the same', at last becomes clear. Paul is not saying that one is changed into the same image as Christ. He is asserting that Christians are changed into the same image as each other. This is why he can be so bold: he and his audience have this in common, that each of them is being changed into the same image, and so is able to behold the glory of the Lord reflected in the other.[29]

The rest of the sentence presents less of a problem, though of itself it is still ambiguous enough.[30] Although ἀπὸ δόξης εἰς δόξαν could simply mean 'from one degree of glory to another', the thought of the verse as a whole, and the ἀπο- phrase which immediately follows, suggests that ἀπὸ δόξης refers to the source of the glory, that is the Spirit who is producing it in Christian lives, and εἰς δόξαν to the resultant glory which is actually possessed by believers.[31] The final phrase, καθάπερ[32] ἀπὸ κυρίου πνεύματος, then has the force of a 'that is': 'from glory to glory—that is to say [*or* as one would expect] from the Lord, the Spirit'. Our earlier suggestion about 'the glory of the Lord' leads us to the view of this phrase which takes the two words in apposition—'"the Lord", that is the Spirit'. The chapter has come full circle. The Spirit (who is not to be separated in a Marcionite fashion from the Lord with whom Moses

---

[27] See Furnish, 215, discussing, among other things, the apparently awkward accusative.

[28] e.g. Euripides, *Medea*, 1162, Plato, *Republic*, 402 B. I am not persuaded that Wisdom 7: 26 forms part of the intended background to this verse: εἰκών is the only word in common between the two passages. This is not, of course, to say that 'Wisdom' ideas are totally absent from the passage, or that Paul does not make use of such themes elsewhere.

[29] This solution is similar to, but stronger than, that of Van Unnik, op. cit. n. 2 above, 167 f.

[30] See particularly Moule, op. cit. n. 2 above.

[31] So Collange, op. cit. n. 2 above, 122 f.

[32] Or καθώσπερ (B): this reading, if correct, would make the point a shade stronger again.

spoke,[33] has now written the new covenant on the hearts of all those who believe in Christ (v. 3). This has come about through the paradoxical and bold ministry of Paul, because Christians are transformed by beholding, in each other, the glory of the Lord (that is, the Spirit) as in a mirror. This interpretation ties the threads of the chapter together more tightly than any other known to me.

III

Up until now it may have seemed that our passage, understood in this way, had to do with the glory not of Christ (as in the title of the present volume) but of the Spirit, and of the Church. This, however, is not so. The exegesis I have offered is strikingly confirmed, and firmly located within Paul's Christology, in the continuation of the argument in ch. 4. First, it is clear from 4: 1 ff. that Paul, at least, has not been side-tracked from the discussion of his ministry. That, clearly, is why he introduced the subject of glory, and of Moses, in the first place. He continues now by answering the objection that, since not all believe his gospel,[34] it must, like Moses' ministry, be veiled. He repeats the shift already made between the veil on Moses' face and that on the hearts of the people (3: 14 f.): 'those who are perishing' have their minds blinded by the God of this world, so that they may not see the light which consists of the gospel of Christ's glory (4: 4). Paul's ministry is therefore not called into question by the phenomenon of continuing unbelief.

Second, 4: 5–6 explains further just what is involved in the 'beholding' of 3: 18. The creator God has shone 'in our hearts' (4: 6, picking up 3: 3: in other words, the act referred to is that which brings people into the new covenant), with the result that the knowledge of the glory of God, now seen in the face of Jesus Christ, can shine as a light to all around.[35] This, in other words, explains the mutual beholding of 3: 18: God shines, with the light of the gospel of Jesus Christ, into the hearts of his people, who then reflect his light, becoming mirrors in which others can see God's glory.

Finally, and most strikingly, this glory, into which Christians are being changed, because of which they reflect God's glory to one another and so enable an honest and open-faced ministry to take place, is indeed seen in the face of Jesus Christ—the Jesus who suffered and

---

[33] Indeed, it is the pre-existent *Spirit*, not the pre-existent Christ as Hanson suggests, that is the striking feature of vv. 13–18: compare 4: 15.

[34] Cf. Rom. 10: 16 for a similar objection.

[35] See Barrett, 135 for this sense of πρὸς φωτισμὸν.

died and rose again.[36] In 4: 7–11 Paul shows how it is that he, at least, is being changed into glory:

But we have this treasure in jars of clay to show that this all-surpassing power is from God and not from us. We are hard pressed on every side, but not in despair; persecuted, but not abandoned; struck down, but not destroyed. We always carry around in our body the death[37] of Jesus, so that the life of Jesus may also be revealed in our body. For we who are alive are always being given over to death for Jesus' sake, so that his life may be revealed in our mortal body . . .[38]

In other words, the glory which is seen, as in a mirror, in Paul's ministry is the glory whch shines through suffering. This glory consists in the fact that Paul does not despair in his sufferings, is not abandoned although persecuted, is not destroyed even when struck down. It is not a glory which enables him to avoid the suffering, just because it is the glory of the Messiah who is Jesus, the one who was crucified and raised. The pattern Paul is acting out is the pattern of Phil. 2: 6–11 or Rom. 8: 17–25, and it gives him confidence that God will in the end vindicate both him and his ministry (4: 13–15). Although in one sense the full glory is yet to be revealed (4: 14, Rom, 8: 18, 23–5), in another sense it is already being accomplished by God in his people: that is the force of the present tense ($\kappa\alpha\tau\epsilon\rho\gamma\acute{\alpha}\zeta\epsilon\tau\alpha\iota$) in 4: 17, which is not to be reduced to 'is preparing'.[39] And this, I suggest, is the full meaning of 3: 18: that the glory of God, at which Christians look with unveiled face when they behold their fellow Christians in whom God is inaugurating the new covenant by the Spirit, is seen precisely in the paradoxical pattern of Christ, that is, the pattern of suffering and vindication.

On the one hand, then, Paul is defending the boldness, the straightforward proclamation of the truth, which characterizes his ministry. On the other hand, he is demonstrating that suffering and persecution do not pose question marks against his apostolic claims, but on the contrary vindicate them. It is enough that the servant be like the master.

---

[36] This is the sense in which Dunn's point, that the mark of the eschatological Spirit is that relationship 'which makes the believer more like Jesus' (J. D. G. Dunn, *Jesus and the Spirit* (London, 1975), 320), ceases to be (as he says) 'simple, pietistic language' and takes on the typical character of Pauline paradox.

[37] Better, the 'killing': see Barrett.

[38] NIV translation. I take v. 12 ('So then, death is at work in us, but life is at work in you') as ironic: Paul is issuing a characteristic rebuke to those who, boasting in a life which has risen above suffering, are ashamed of him or consider him unworthy of apostolic status because of *his* suffering.

[39] *Contra* AGD 421, who cite only this reference in Hellenistic Greek: the classical parallel suggested in Herodotus 7. 6. 1 is not to the purpose, since there $\chi\rho\acute{o}\nu\omega$ $\delta\grave{\epsilon}$ $\kappa\alpha\tau\epsilon\rho\gamma\acute{\alpha}\sigma\alpha\tau\acute{o}$ $\tau\epsilon$ $\kappa\alpha\grave{\iota}$ $\grave{\alpha}\nu\acute{\epsilon}\pi\epsilon\iota\sigma\epsilon$ $\Xi\acute{\epsilon}\rho\xi\eta\nu$ $\ddot{\omega}\sigma\tau\epsilon$ $\pi\iota\acute{\epsilon}\epsilon\iota\nu$ $\tau\alpha\hat{\upsilon}\tau\alpha$ is surely most naturally taken in the sense 'in time he *succeeded in* persuading Xerxes to do this': see LSJ ad. loc., also citing the other classical passage adduced in AGD (Xenophon, *Mem.*, 2 . 3. 11). It is precisely this inaugurated eschatology which is then picked up in v. 5: God worked this very thing in us, giving us the Spirit as a down-payment.

The Corinthians, looking at the Spirit's work in Paul and seeing there
the revelation of God's Christ-like glory, are being changed into 'the
same likeness': that is why they are themselves Paul's 'letter of recommendation'. Paul thus issues both a rebuke and a challenge, anticipating the final challenge of 13: 5–10: if this is how the new covenant
glory is revealed, perhaps your attitude towards my suffering and
ministry shows that you have never shared in that glory at all. The
glory of God is seen in the face of Jesus Christ, the crucified and risen
Messiah: where the Spirit renews the covenant, this glory will be seen in
the lives of Christians. To have the face unveiled does not mean that the
glory is, like that on Moses' face, the sort of thing that can (so to speak)
be seen with the naked eye. That is the mistake the Corinthians, or
those among them whom Paul is opposing, are tempted to make (v.
12). The true glory is in the heart, and provides the real apostolic commendation (3: 1–3, 5: 12). This is the theme which is expressed com-
pactly in 3: 18, and it is this theme too that is picked up at the climax of
the whole section (6: 3–10), which provides a fitting climax also for this
tribute to a great scholar who had well understood the paradoxical
meaning of 'glory', and who lived it out by following his independent
search for the truth, untroubled by scholarly fashions:

As servants of God we commend ourselves in every way . . . by purity, knowledge, forbearance, kindness, the Holy Spirit, genuine love, truthful speech,
and the power of God . . . as unknown, and yet well known; as dying, and behold we live.

11. The Christology of Hebrews 1 and 2

L. D. HURST

'THERE is nothing in which deduction is so necessary as in religion.' This declaration from an unlikely source—Sherlock Holmes of 221B Baker Street—was intended by the creator of the famous detective to introduce readers of *The Strand Magazine* to Holmes's faith in the surety of Providence. Discussing an abstruse case involving national security, Holmes seems to lose his concentration, and to the bewilderment of all shifts his attention to a nearby rose. He then advances an apparently irrelevant thesis. Religion, he says,

can be built up as an exact science by the reasoner. Our highest assurance of the goodness of Providence seems to me to rest in the flowers. All other things, our powers, our desires, our food, are really necessary for our existence in the first instance. But this rose is an extra. Its smell and colour are an embellishment of life, not a condition of it. It is only goodness which gives extras, and so I say again that we have much to hope from the flowers.[1]

An obscure episode from the pages of English detective fiction may seem an odd place to begin a scholarly essay. Somehow, however, it captures for me in a glimpse the life and work of George Caird. It did so in the first instance not because he was best known as a New Testament scholar (and Holmes's premiss reminds one of Matt. 6: 28–34), or because his work on the Bible was characterized by a 'Holmesian' luminescence and precision, or even because he so loved mystery stories. All of these reflections are true, and make the digression hopefully more forgivable. I was at first reminded, however, of one whose love of the flora and fauna of this world suffused and enriched everything he did, and who never came to natural objects without a childlike sense of wonder.

My purpose, however, is not to record my admiration for one of Oxford's better known amateur naturalists, still less to support Holmes's claim that a belief in Providence is logical. My idea is to observe that the connection which Conan Doyle makes between deduction—reasoning from the known to the unknown—and religion is an idea which George Caird almost restated when he enunciated what for him is the biblical theologian's 'first rule of scholarship': 'to

---

[1] From 'The Adventure of the Naval Treaty', by Sir Arthur Conan Doyle.

start from the ascertainable and to allow that to determine the exegesis of the problematical'.[2]

One might justifiably call it 'Caird's Law', so thoroughly did he make it his own and allow it to dominate his exegetical work, although the suspicion lingers that it arose originally from a deep-seated love for crossword and jigsaw puzzles. Whatever the source, it was a principle more than evident in the essay he wrote over twenty-five years ago entitled 'The Exegetical Method of the Epistle to the Hebrews'.[3] He argued, with logic both compelling and iconoclastic, that, far from being outmoded and far-fetched, the exegesis of the epistle asks the very modern question of what the Old Testament, *in its original meaning*, had to say about the Christian faith. Starting with the clearest example of this—the use of Jeremiah 31 in Heb. 8: 6–13—he worked backwards to what he regarded as the most misunderstood (and important) Old Testament passage in the epistle, Psalm 8 in Heb. 2: 5–10. This exercise in simple logic (simple, however, only to those familiar with Columbus's egg) had at least one lasting effect on him and his students: for the rest of his life he taught passionately that Heb. 2 points to the destiny of mankind, which he also felt is the overall theme (2: 5) of the epistle. One of the last essays he wrote, 'Son by Appointment',[4] employs the same relentless logic in advancing the thesis, however surprising, that the first two chapters of Hebrews are not concerned primarily with a pre-existent figure who lowers himself to *become* man; they focus rather upon a human being who is *raised to* an exalted status. This belief grew on him partly as a result of the irritation he felt from reading modern writers who casually toss the term 'pre-existence' about with the assumption that it is self-explanatory, and partly from his awareness that 'the literature contains many discussions of the origin of the concept, very few analyses of its meaning'.[5] Eventually he arrived at the view that to make such an idea *the starting-point* of one's exegesis is to violate the laws of deduction: it is to let the unknown dictate the understanding of the known.

Caird's work on Hebrews has yet fully to be appreciated. It is sad to think that at the time of his death he was under contract to write the new ICC on this most important epistle, and that much of the knowledge, expertise, and logic he would have brought to the task he took with him. The best way to ensure that what he did contribute will be

---

[2] G. B. Caird, 'Son by Appointment', from *The New Testament Age: Essays in Honor of Bo Reicke*, i, ed. William C. Weinrich (Macon, Georgia, 1984), 73.

[3] *Canadian Journal of Theology*, 5 (1959), 44–51.

[4] Op. cit., 73–81.

[5] Ibid., 74.

remembered is for students and friends to take up the discussion where he left it and, if possible, to move it a stage further.

I

> What is man, that you remember him,
> or the son of man, that you care for him?
> You made him for a little while lower than the angels;
> you crowned him with glory and honour;
> you put all things in subjection under his feet. (Heb. 2: 6–8.)

From the amount of time spent discussing it, Ps. 8 may be said to be the author's first main scriptural text. Taking up his exposition, he says in 2: 8a, 'now in subjecting all things to him he left nothing that is not subject'. He then adds, 'Yet we do not yet see all things subject to him. But we see Jesus, who for a little while was made lower than the angels, now crowned with glory and honour because of the suffering of death, so that, by God's gracious will, he might taste of death for every man.'

Since Ps. 8 in its original setting was a psalm concerning the glory of man in God's original intention, and since it was not considered 'Messianic' in the LXX or in rabbinic Judaism,[6] one might normally take Jesus in 2: 8 as proleptically fulfilling what is as yet unfulfilled for man, that is, he represents man in the ideal state for which he was created, a state identified as 'glory'. As a direct consequence of the view that the author of Hebrews disregards the historical settings of his Old Testament passages,[7] however, many have claimed that the author of Hebrews takes Ps. 8 as a 'direct prophecy' of Jesus, meaning by that that for the author, throughout the psalm, Jesus is the *only* one in view.[8] 'Son of man' in the psalm is even taken to be a Christological title.[9] This interpretation has been accepted uncritically for too long a time.

The evidence that the author takes 'son of man' in 2: 6 in any other sense than as a periphrasis of man, for instance, is non-existent. Had he taken it as a Christological title he would have certainly seized it and explicated it elsewhere. The conjunction of Ps. 8 with Ps. 110: 1 in Hebrews, as in the rest of the NT, involves Jesus' enthronement as the

---

[6] Cf. O. Michel, *Der Brief an die Hebräer*[12] (Göttingen, 1966), 70 f., who, citing 3 *Enoch* 5: 10, says it was made Messianic in apocalyptic Judaism.

[7] Cf. n. 13 below.

[8] Cf., among the many who could be cited, G. W. Buchanan, *To the Hebrews. Anchor Bible Commentary* (New York, 1972), 26; O. Cullmann, *The Christology of the New Testament* (Philadelphia, 1963), 188; Pauline Giles, 'The Son of Man in Hebrews', *ET* 86 (1975), 328–32; A. T. Hanson, *Jesus Christ in the Old Testament* (London, 1965), 163, 166; and S. G. Sowers, *The Hermeneutics of Philo and Hebrews* (Zurich, 1965), 80 f.

[9] Cf. Buchanan, 27.

representative of glorified humanity.[10] That the fulfilment of the psalm is said to be 'for all' ($\dot{v}\pi\dot{\epsilon}\rho$ $\pi\alpha\nu\tau\acute{o}s$, 2: 9), furthermore, could not make it clearer that Christ's role is a representative one. The plan of God to which the psalm is called as a witness is defined as 'leading *many* sons to glory' ($\pi o\lambda\lambda o\dot{v}s$ $vio\dot{v}s$ $\epsilon\dot{\iota}s$ $\delta\acute{o}\xi\alpha\nu$ $\dot{\alpha}\gamma\alpha\gamma\acute{o}\nu\tau\alpha$), indicating that 'glory' ($\delta\acute{o}\xi\alpha\nu$) picks up the phrase 'crowned him with glory and honour' ($\delta\acute{o}\xi\eta$ $\kappa\alpha\grave{\iota}$ $\tau\iota\mu\hat{\eta}$ $\dot{\epsilon}\sigma\tau\epsilon\phi\acute{\alpha}\nu\omega\sigma\alpha s$ $\alpha\dot{v}\tau\acute{o}\nu$) of v. 7. The angels mentioned in the psalm, it should also be stressed, to whom God subjected the present age and under whose authority Jesus himself lived 'for a little while',[11] are defined in 1: 14 as 'ministering spirits sent out to serve on behalf of those who were to inherit salvation'. This indicates that the reversal of conditions in the future age will result in the supremacy over these angels by redeemed humanity rather than exclusively by a single individual.[12]

II

It is only when an appreciation of the meaning and significance of Ps. 8 in chapter two is developed that one is in a position to understand the argument of chapter one. The first chapter consists largely of a catena of OT texts designed to prove the superiority of Christ to the angels. The reason for this concern has often been felt to be far from obvious, and, as with the use of Ps. 8 in chapter two, it has been attacked as arbitrary.[13] It has been assumed, in addition, that chapter one is simply a

[10] The author shows little or no interest in developing his understanding of 'the enemies', but they are probably the enemies of man in general, 'spiritual enemies' as Lindars (*New Testament Apologetic: The Doctrinal Significance of the Old Testament Quotations* (London, 1961), 50) would put it ('His presence at the right hand necessarily entails the conquest of the spiritual powers'), or 'dämonischen Mächten' (Michel, 59). Michel considers the possibility that the enemies are the (human) enemies of the community to which the author is writing, but since there is virtually nothing said in the epistle about the persecutors, he rightly rejects it.

[11] The author takes $\beta\rho\alpha\chi\acute{v}$ $\tau\iota$ not as an expression of degree but as a period of time according to the Jewish two-age theory.

[12] Cf. the excellent summary of the author's point by R. N. Longenecker, *Biblical Exegesis in the Apostolic Period* (Grand Rapids, 1975), 181:

The process which will culminate in the fulfilment of this promise has been inaugurated in the person and work of Jesus. Jesus has taken upon himself man's full estate in order that by means of his own redemptive work he might bring the anticipation of the psalmist to full consummation. The Old Testament's teaching about man avowedly points forward into the future, and that future is inextricably bound up with Jesus—the pioneer of man's salvation, who has come to lead *many sons* to the full realization of their destined glory [italics mine].

[13] Cf. H. A. A. Kennedy, *The Theology of the Epistles* (London, 1919), 204 n. 1, who calls his method 'altogether foreign'; Michel, op. cit. n. 6 above, 47, and Käsemann, *Das wandernde Gottesvolk*[4] (Göttingen, 1961), 122 f., who feel that one is here dealing with a 'proof-text' method not suitable for modern thought. Sowers, op. cit. n. 8 above, 84, asks 'how is it that the writer can defy the contexts of these texts and apply them all instead to Christ?' C. Mackay, 'The Argument of Hebrews', *CQR* 168 (1967), 326, calls the argument 'convincing only to the convinced, hardly a helpful start unless as carry-over from agreed exegesis', while G. H. Gilbert, 'The Greek Element in the Epistle to the Hebrews', *AJT* 14 (1910), 528 f., decries the 'unspeakable confusion' created

preface to the rest of the epistle, with little relation to chapter two or the following chapters.[14] One of the values of Caird's essay 'The Exegetical Method of the Epistle to the Hebrews' was his undeveloped suggestion to the contrary that the use of Ps. 8 in chapter two 'controls the argument of the preceding chapter, for from the first mention of angels at 1: 5 throughout the formidable catena of texts in chapter one the author's one aim is to illustrate the theme of the psalm. . . .'[15] Perhaps because space did not allow him adequately to pursue this idea, what he said did not at first appear helpful. The theme of Ps. 8 in chapter two is God's plan for mankind; if, however, chapter one describes the unique prerogatives of a heavenly being who becomes man, it is difficult to see how the two chapters could be talking about the same thing. The apparent dichotomy gains strength from the author's reference in 1: 3 to the Son as 'the effulgence[16] [ἀπαύγασμα] of the glory of God and the very stamp of his nature', language normally thought to be drawn from Wisd. 7: 26—a passage dealing with God's pre-existent wisdom. If so, it would be difficult to find in 1: 3 a reference to man.[17] Stated differently, the epistle contains language which, as proper to God's pre-existent wisdom, can be seen as the beginning of a process which will end at Chalcedon.

Notwithstanding this, there is a case to be made that the *emphasis* of Heb. 1 lies elsewhere, and that the entire chapter has too often been read in the light of Nicea and Chalcedon. Has the author been allowed to speak for himself? The question needs to be asked, if only to consider whether—and to what extent—chapter one may originally have been read from the point of view of the humanity of Jesus. Laying aside for the moment the problematic, the amount of information which is ascertainable is surprising. That chapter one is mainly about the historical Jesus is obvious from the opening of the epistle (1: 2) where God speaks through a 'Son'. When did he speak? It could not have been through

by the author's lack of a 'historical sense of the Scriptures'. For an alternative (and refreshing) view, cf. S. Kistemaker, *The Psalm Citations in the Epistle to the Hebrews* (Amsterdam, 1961), 78, who points out numerous verbal links between *the contexts* of passages such as 2 Sam. 7: 14 (Heb. 1: 5) and Ps. 45: 6 (Heb. 1: 8), something which would have been impossible via the 'proof-text' model.

[14] David M. Hay, *Glory at the Right Hand. Psalm 110 in Early Christianity* (Nashville, 1973), claims that 'much of the content of Heb. 1: 5–14 is not closely related to the rest of the epistle. If the author was using a traditional collection of quotations, the length and partial irrelevance . . . would be more comprehensible'.

[15] 'The Exegetical Method of the Epistle to the Hebrews', 17.

[16] ἀπαύγασμα may be rendered either actively, 'effulgence', or passively, 'reflection', but most feel that in 1: 3 a reference is being made to Wisd. 7: 26, where it definitely has the active meaning.

[17] Longenecker, *The Christology of Early Jewish Christianity* (London, 1970), 55, claims that Heb. 1: 3 is 'only a paraphrase of the concept of "image" (εἰκών)', which could indicate it to be a high-flown restatement of Gen. 1: 26. But a reference to 'the effulgence of everlasting light' would make an allusion to Gen. 1: 26 unlikely. For a discussion of Heb. 1: 3 as pointing to *divinity*, cf. R. G. Hamerton-Kelly, *Pre-existence, Wisdom and the Son of Man* (Cambridge, 1973), 244.

the pre-existent Logos, since 'in these last days' clearly points to the
work of the Jesus of history. The same figure is said to be *appointed*
(τίθημι, v. 2b) 'heir of all things', to have become (γίνομαι, v. 4) 'greater
than the angels', and to have inherited (κληρονομέω, v. 4) 'a name more
excellent than theirs'. The opening paragraph closes with a reference
again to the work of the historical Jesus ('purification for sins', v. 3c).
Thus, even if it is maintained that the writer made no mental distinction between the heavenly Son and the human Son, there is prima facie
a case for saying that if one reads the chapter *from the beginning*, the
figure in view is essentially a human one. Taken in this light, the
language of 1: 3 would be seen as appropriate to one who is the bearer
of the divine wisdom.

The suggestion gains strength when it is noted that the OT texts in
chapter one constitute a strange choice for association with a heavenly,
pre-existent being. The first passage, Ps. 110: 1 (1: 3c), which also closes
(1: 13) the series, probably was chosen because of its similarity to Ps. 8:
4–6, a psalm which, as has been seen, concerns the destiny of man.
Thus what appears to be an anti-climactic concern with Christ's
superiority to *angels* in what follows is perfectly appropriate in any
treatment of man's role in the cosmos. While some have supposed that
the readers had fallen prey to a form of angel worship,[18] there is no
need to look outside the epistle to understand the logic. In 2: 2 is mentioned the belief, widespread in the Jewish world, that angels mediated
the Law at Sinai and were thus in some sense guardians of the old
order.[19] It would be necessary, in mounting any case that the old order
was obsolete, to show the inferior status of these mediators to one who
mediates the superior covenant. Thus the angels to whom Jesus
becomes superior in chapter one appear to be the same angels in
chapter two who, connected with the giving of the Law (2: 2), are
superior to man 'for a little while' (2: 7a). This raises an important
question. If the theme of chapter two is the subjection of the world to
come (v. 4) to man (vv. 6–9) and the leading of the 'many sons' to their
appointed glory (v. 10), and if chapter one *opens* with a reference to the
Son's entering into the possession of the 'all things' promised to man-

---

[18] Cf., e.g. T. W. Manson, 'The Problem of the Epistle to the Hebrews', *Studies in the Gospels and
Epistles* (Manchester, 1962), 242 ff.; G. Delling, 'τάσσω', *Theological Dictionary of the New Testament*,
viii (Grand Rapids, 1972), 42; M. de Jonge and A. S. van der Woude, '11Q Melchizedek and the
New Testament', *NTS* 12 (1965–6), 310–26; F. Schröger, *Der Verfasser des Hebräerbriefes als Schrift-
ausleger* (Regensburg, 1968), 75 f., gives a list of references of those who argue for an angel polemic.
O. Kuss, *Der Brief and Die Hebräer* (Regensburg, 1966), 47, notes the absence of such a polemic in
Hebrews.

[19] Cf. Deut. 33: 2 LXX, Gal. 3: 19, Acts 7: 53, and Jub. 1: 29. The LXX of Deut. 32: 8, Dan. 10:
20 f. and 12: 1, furthermore, indicates an angelic government of the nations (cf. Caird, *Principalities
and Powers* (Oxford, 1956), 5 n. 1).

kind, does the *intervening* material in 1: 3–13 relate as well to the theme of mankind's destiny? The question is made even more pressing when it is remembered that in chapter two the superior status of Christ *to the angels* is rooted in his fulfilment of a psalm concerning mankind.

Christ's superiority to the angels in chapter one is seen in his inheritance of certain 'names' which are better than theirs: 'Son' (v. 5), 'God' (v. 8), and 'Lord' (v. 10). It has often been assumed that these names are drawn from OT texts *pesher*-fashion, with no regard for their original significance. The texts, however, are largely royal psalms, which raises the possibility that the author chose them precisely because he believed that, in their original meaning, they spoke of the dignities of an ideal king. Such a supposition has many advantages, not the least of which is its compatibility with the main emphasis of the opening paragraph. In fact, no matter how idealized is the language concerning the figure in chapter one, he appears to remain quite human. In this case the emphasis of chapter one is the same as that of chapter two: it concerns a figure who, *qua* man, is exalted above the angels and leads those whom he represents, as their ideal king, to an appointed destiny.

Taken in this light the quotation of Ps. 2: 7 and 2 Sam. 7: 14 in 1: 5 is straightforward. A problem, however, begins with the next verse (v. 6). Once again language which appears proper to deity is transferred to Jesus. Nairne tried to get around this by making the original object of the angelic homage the people of Israel, with an underlying typology of the repeated humiliations of Israel during which she was withdrawn and then reintroduced (πάλιν εἰσαγάγῃ)[20] into the world (οἰκουμένη), for instance following the Egyptian bondage.[21] This would then, according to Nairne, point to the subsequent humiliation and exaltation of the ideal man, Jesus.[22] The problem with such a view is that

---

[20] The vexed question of whether πάλιν is to be attached to λέγει or εἰσάγαγῃ is not crucial here. The commentaries are equally divided.

[21] A. Nairne, *The Epistle to the Hebrews* (Cambridge, 1917), 32 f.

[22] The 'repeated humiliations which make the paradox of their spiritual history . . . [were] prophetic of a far more transcendent glory through humiliations still to come'. 'The quotation is apt', he adds, 'since this nation, itself too, bore the title "Christ"' (ibid., 30). Cf. also J. A. T. Robinson, *The Human Face of God* (London, 1973), 160 f., who argues that the point of the term πρωτότοκος in 1: 6 is the drawing of a parallel with 'Israel whose vocation he embodied', and F. F. Bruce, *The Epistles to the Hebrews* (London, 1964), 16, who sees the homage directed to 'the last Adam'. The problem is not eased by Lindars' suggestion (op. cit. n. 10 above, 211 n. 3) that because God has been speaking in the previous verse (v. 5), it is reasonable to take him as the speaker of v. 6, thus requiring the 'him' of Deut. 32: 43 to be another person, i.e. 'the Messiah', or by T. F. Glasson's idea ('"Plurality of Divine Persons" and the Quotations in Heb. 1: 6 ff.', *NTS* 12 (1965–6), 271) that the order of words in the Greek (translated 'let worship *him* all the angels of God') implies another person. Jean Héring, *The Epistle to the Hebrews* (London, 1970), 9, asking 'who is meant by "autō"', says 'in the context of Deuteronomy it can only be descendents of Moses', but offers no explanation of how our present LXX texts could allow this.

most scholars take the text quoted in Heb. 1: 6 to be Deut. 32: 43,[23] and, according to all LXX texts of Deut. 32: 43, the worship is to be directed to God, not men.[24]

Much of the study of this passage has focused on the nature of the LXX text here quoted, since in LXX$^{A/B}$ the subject of προσκυνησάτωσαν is υἱοί, and it is only in the odes appended to the Greek psalter that a reading identical to that of Hebrews is found.[25] It is here that a fragment from Qumran Cave 4 (4Q) is of help.[26] 4Q Deut. 32: 43 not only shows that the form found in the odes is not an interpolation, but has a Hebrew antecedent which may underlie the Greek text preserved in Heb. 1: 6;[27] it shows that Nairne's interpretation is not without basis. In the Qumran version of the text it is easy to read the object of the angelic prostration as *Israel*:

1. Praise his people, O heavens
2. And fall down before him, all gods;
3. for he avenges the blood of his sons

[23] It is sometimes suggested that Ps. 97: 7 has influenced 1: 6 (c.f., e.g., de Jonge and van der Woude, 315, and James Moffatt, *A Critical and Exegetical Commentary on the Epistle to the Hebrews* (Edinburgh, 1924), 11). Moffatt cites Justin Martyr (*Dial.* 130), who reflects the same reading as Heb. 1: 6, as evidence that 'this may have been the text current among primitive Christians'. But due to the popularity of Deut. 32 in the early church (cf., e.g. Longenecker, *Biblical Exegesis*, 179), together with the closeness of wording, the majority view is probably correct.

[24] Nairne's erroneous statement (*Hebrews*, 32) that in the B text of Deut. 32 the subject is 'the whole people of Israel' is hard to explain, unless he confused the B text with the first verse of the MT.

[25] Cf., e.g. Lindars, 244, and K. J. Thomas, 'The Old Testament Citations in Hebrews', *NTS* 11 (1964–5), 304, and Kistemaker (op. cit. n. 13 above), 20 ff.

[26] It is well-known that the LXX mistranslates the Hebrew in the opening clause by taking God as the one in view and rendering עַמּוֹ ('his people') as if it were pointed עִמּוֹ, leaving the cumbersome 'together with him' (line 1) and 'with his people' (line 3). The MT is of no help, for it reads 'nations' (גּוֹיִם) instead of שָׁמַיִם ('heavens') and totally omits the parallel clause about prostrating. Thus, the LXX has the wrong object but preserves the crucial clause; the MT has the right object but omits the crucial clause. It is only 4 QDeut. which preserves both the noun עַמּוֹ in line 1 (as in MT) and the worship offered by 'gods' (אֱלֹהִים) in line 2 (as in LXX). To appreciate the differences best, cf. Buchanan, op. cit. n. 8 above, 15 f., who places the texts in parallel columns for comparison.

[27] Apart from the greater chronological proximity to Hebrews (when compared with our earliest LXX texts), 4Q Deut. 32: 43 provides the most likely term (אֱלֹהִים) to underlie the ἄγγελοι of the odes and Heb. 1: 6. For a discussion of the significance of the Qumran fragment, cf., e.g. P. W. Skehan, 'A Fragment of the "Song of Moses" (Deut. 32) from Qumran', *BASOR* 136 (1954), 12–15; Longenecker, *Biblical Exegesis*, 169; K. J. Thomas, op. cit. n. 25 above, 304; P. Katz, 'The Quotations from Deuteronomy in Hebrews', *ZNW* 49 (1958), 219; F. C. Fensham, 'Hebrews and Qumran', *Neotestamentica*, 5 (1971), 15; G. Howard, 'Hebrews and the Old Testament Quotations', *NT* 10 (1968), 208 ff.; and F. M. Cross, *The Ancient Library of Qumran* (London, 1958), 134–7. In his treatment of Heb. 1: 6 (21 ff.), Kistemaker follows Moffatt (11), who points to the odes of Codex A as evidence that the citation does not come from Deuteronomy but from the psalms, hence from a liturgical context. But, although writing after Skehan had published his findings, he makes no mention of them in his comments on Heb. 1: 6. Lindars, op. cit. n. 10 above, 211 n. 3, claims that 4Q Deut. 32: 43 'is not actually relevant' to Heb. 1: 6, but he provides no argumentation for this.

4. and visits retribution on his enemies
5. and recompenses those who hate him
6. and makes atonement for the land of his people.

In this case the parallelism of 'praise . . . fall down' and 'heavens . . . gods' seems to demand an identification of 'him' in line 2 with 'his people' of line 1. But the interpretation is only possible if the first two lines are taken *in vacuo*. In the larger context it leaves the 'he' of line 3 (which *must* refer to God) hanging in the air. It thus seems that the *original* object of line 2 was God (picking up the 'his' of line 1). It is, nevertheless, quite easy to read the text the other way, and even modern scholars have read line 2 as referring to *the people* rather than to God.[28] 4Q Deut. 32: 43 provides, therefore, a plausible text underlying Heb. 1: 6 in which the writer supposed Deut. 32: 43 to be one more scriptural witness to God's decree concerning the destiny of his people over against that of the angels. 'Firstborn' is a royal term from Ps. 89: 28 (which was given Messianic import by the rabbis),[29] but it also occurs in Exod. 4: 22 (a text which occurs in the Exodus account culminating in the song of Deut. 32).[30] There is no competition here, since the king embodies the people, the 'firstborn' of Exod. 4: 22. The author may well have had both passages in mind.

The next OT text, Ps. 45: 6 (1: 8), is almost universally taken to be a royal psalm.[31] One need not enter into elaborate arguments as to whether or not the Son is addressed here as 'God'.[32] Ps. 45: 6 (interpreted vocatively) could have been a straightforward address to the

[28] Buchanan, op. cit. n. 8 above, 16, for example, claims that 'in Heb. texts of Deut. 32: 43, the object of adoration was probably intended to be "his people", with the "heavens", "nations", "Gods", "sons of God" or "angels of God" doing the worshipping'. Cf. also P. C. B. Andriessen, 'La Teneur Judéo-Chrétienne de HE I 6 et II 14B–III 2', *NT* 18 (1976), 293–313. This is the way I read the text until George Caird pointed out the difficulty of such an interpretation in the light of the larger context of Deut. 32.

[29] So e.g., Lindars, op. cit., 211; Caird, 'Son by Appointment'; and Bruce, op. cit. n 22 above, 15.

[30] Buchanan (op. cit., 16 f.), speculates that line 1 of *the author's* text of Deut. 32: 43 read 'praise his *firstborn*' (i.e. Israel).

[31] Cf., e.g. Bruce, op. cit., 18 ff., and the references he cites there.

[32] As is well known, 1: 8a, ὁ θρόνος σου ὁ θεός, can be translated either as 'my throne is God' or 'thy throne, O God'. The latter translation has had many powerful supporters (e.g. Michel, op. cit. n. 6 above, 55), but K. J. Thomas has recently argued strongly for the former (op. cit. n. 25 above, 305). Whichever rendering is adopted, the conclusion of Thomas that the idea is that of 'closest association with God the Father, reigning with the power and authority of God over all, including the angels' (ibid.) is to be preferred to that of Cullmann, op. cit. n. 8 above, 310 f. and others, who see the verse as an ascription of exclusive deity. If it is taken in the vocative, a parallel may be drawn with the quotation of Ps. 82 in John 10: 32 ff., where the point is that *men* are called 'gods'. In fact, Stephen Neill finds a direct parallel between the Johannine passage and our author, although he does not elaborate further: 'Is it not clear that the nearest parallel to this [John 10: 32 ff.] is in the Epistle to the Hebrews, where we find the same sensitive and imaginative attitude to the earlier writings?' (*The Interpretation of the New Testament, 1861–1961* (New York, 1966), 321 f.).

Hebrew king at some point in his career, an idea which would have caused the Hebrew mind no difficulty. No threat to monotheism was implied, nor was there any divinization of the king as has been claimed for surrounding cultures. The author could rightfully see Christ as the inheritor of the royal title 'God' precisely because, as ideal king, he represents God to the people.[33]

The sixth citation (Ps. 101: 25–27 LXX) in 1: 10–12, however, could be seen as the second pointer away from a human emphasis. Although it is one of the most peculiar passages in the NT, it is often used to argue that 'the first Christians without hesitation transferred to Him [Christ] what the Old Testament says about God.'[34] It is the gain of the work of B. W. Bacon,[35] and more recently C. F. D. Moule,[36] that we now know that in the LXX it is *not* God to whom this oracle is spoken: in the LXX the phrase in v. 24, 'he weakened' (עִנָּה) is translated by 'he answered him' (ἀπεκρίθη),[37] implying that *two* persons are involved. Who is this other 'person'? Moule, following Bacon, thinks it probable that behind Heb. 1: 10–12 lies a non-Christian, Hellenistic Jewish belief, *built into the LXX*, that in Ps. 102: 24b–29 God was addressing an appeal by the Messiah to shorten the appointed days. Moule argues that 'in what is a manifestly apologetic sequence' this is the only explanation which accounts for its presence in the argument of chapter one. The view of Bacon may or may not be correct, but at least he has brought to the fore a crucial point. Whoever was responsible for the interpretation of Ps. 102 as an address by God to some other party, it was *not* the writer to the Hebrews; the idea was already built into his Bible. Moule searches for an explanation for the motive of the LXX translators in introducing a second speaker. Following Bacon, he suggests the insertion at this point of a Messianic motif into the text. God, in other words, is addressing his Messiah. This may be the only reasonable explanation of what is transpiring here,[38] and would be similar to the insertion of a Messianic interest into the LXX of Hab. 2: 3 f.

[33] Note also that the point which the author wishes to make is made quite well by 1: 8a. That he *continues* with the second half of the citation (which speaks of the addressee as having a 'God' and 'fellows'—μέτοχοι) would only make sense if the emphasis of his argument is upon a human figure. The author could have easily left this out; but its inclusion makes sense if what is in focus is the king, elevated above his comrades to be their representative.

[34] Cullmann, op. cit. n. 8 above, 234 f.; cf. also G. E. Ladd, *A Theology of the New Testament* (Grand Rapids, 1974), 577.

[35] B. W. Bacon, 'Hebrews 1: 10–12 and the Septuagint Rendering of Ps. 102: 23', *ZNW* 3 (1902), 280–85.

[36] C. F. D. Moule, *The Birth of the New Testament* (London, 1962), 78 f. Cf. also Glasson, op. cit. n. 22 above, 271 f.; Bruce, op. cit. n. 22 above, 22; and Kistemaker, op. cit. n. 13 above, 79 f.

[37] ἀποκρίνομαι is usually a reply (cf. Matt. 3: 15, 8: 8, 11: 4, etc.). Although occasionally it *can* mean 'continue a discourse', (e.g. Matt. 11: 25, 22: 1, etc.), the presence of αὐτῷ in the phrase ἀπεκρίθη αὐτῷ seems to indicate a reply.

[38] Glasson, op. cit., 272, has questioned Moule's introduction of a 'messianic' motif here, claim-

But what kind of 'Messiah' would this be? It could be said to refer to the pre-existent figure which has become familiar through subsequent Christian interpretation, and the extravagant language of the psalm makes such an interpretation difficult to dismiss casually. To the Jew, however, 'Messiah', if it was understood as a 'title' at all, would have meant the expected agent of God through whom he would fulfil his purposes, and frequently this is envisaged as a coming, idealized *king*. Goodenough has shown to what an amazing extent royal figures in antiquity were assigned divine attributes while remaining human figures. Discussing the concept of Hellenistic kingship prevalent in Alexandria when the LXX and Book of Wisdom would have been produced, he observes that 'the king was deity, and deity king. The identification led to the *most extraordinary mutual borrowing*. What was said of God must somehow be said of the king—so the king is νόμος ἔμψυχος because God's nature is νόμος τῆς φύσεως.'[39]

While to moderns such an interchange may seem surprising, if not shocking, it had a long history in the ancient world. When the Book of Wisdom, which the author probably knew, says (6: 21) 'if, therefore, you value your thrones and your sceptres, you rulers of the nations, you must honour Wisdom, so that you may *reign forever* [εἰς τὸν αἰῶνα],' it is reflecting Near East court protocol (compare, for instance Dan. 2: 4: 'O king, live forever'). That such language is probably not far removed in principle from the more elaborate propositions of Heb. 1: 10–12 (compare this with 'they will perish, but you will remain', and 'you are the same, your years will never come to an end') is made more credible by Goodenough's point. It is the next proposition which appears to cause the real trouble, however. Could one really attribute a creative function to the king, even granting full sway to what Goodenough says? 'You, Lord, founded the earth in the beginning, and the heavens are the work of your hands' is language which seems unlikely for any human being, however exalted. *Or is it?* Looking again to the Book of Wisdom, there pseudo-Solomon is said, drawing on the story in 1 Kings 3, to have petitioned the 'God of my fathers and Lord of mercy, who has made all things by thy word and by thy wisdom has formed man'. The king then asks for 'the wisdom that sits by thy throne' (9: 1–4). He prays, in other words, for the divine wisdom[40] (which he acknowledges as the vehicle

ing that it does not come elsewhere in the letter. This, of course, ignores the Messianic use of Hab. 2: 3 f. in 10: 37 f., and Glasson's substitution of a 'plurality of divine persons' throughout chapter 1 runs counter to the 'human' emphasis I am suggesting controls the first two chapters.

[39] E. Goodenough, *By Light, Light: The Mystical Gospel of Hellenistic Judaism* (New Haven, 1935), 38 f., 40 (italics mine).

[40] On the difficulties of whether or not to capitalize the term wisdom in Jewish literature of the period, cf. Caird, 'The Development of the Doctrine of Christ in the New Testament' in *Christ for Us Today*, ed. N. Pittenger (London, 1968), 76.

of creation), hoping to possess her. In 7: 27 this process of possession is spoken of as wisdom's 'entering into holy souls'. Such a background should not be underestimated, particularly if it is held that the author of Hebrews was familiar with the Book of Wisdom. In fact, if we view Wisd. 7–9 as the missing key which unlocks the mysterious inclusion of Ps. 102: 25–27 in chapter one, we are given for the first time a means of fitting Heb. 1: 10–12 into an overall pattern: it becomes the author's final witness in the catena to an address by God to an ideal human (royal) figure, who, as Israel's representative, possesses and enshrines in this world the divine, creative wisdom. God could then be seen as addressing his own wisdom in its earthly receptacle,[41] the Messiah-king. Those still unconvinced should note that (1) the peculiar inclusion of a second speaker in the LXX of Ps. 102, (2) the inclusion of a text originally spoken to Yahweh in an apologetic sequence consisting of royal psalms, and (3) the identification of the figure of 1: 10 ff. with the figure who in 1: 8, 9 is said to have a 'God' and 'fellows' are indexes which point precisely to an explanation which is out of the ordinary.

The catena of texts closes at 1: 13 with the second reference to Ps. 110: 1. It could be argued, again, that the figure in view is a divine being who, as uniquely privileged, has little to do with mankind's general lot. Fitzmeyer,[42] on the other hand, has correctly stressed that in Ps. 110: 1 the king is 'a religious figure who incorporates in himself' the kingdom of Israel and its hope for a future in which the kingship of Yahweh will become universally effective. This is, in other words, an inclusive and representative role.

A case can thus be made that the king who embodies the people in chapter one paves the way for the presentation in chapter two of the *larger* concept of the one who fulfils God's will for mankind. To what extent notions of a pre-cosmic figure are *also* present may have to remain a delicate matter of judgement. This idea is almost always presupposed for chapter one,[43] and it cannot be denied that there are at

[41] Cf. also Ecclus. 24: 7 f. ('I looked for a home and God said, make your home in Jacob; so I took up residence in the sacred tent').

[42] J. A. Fitzmyer, '"Now This Melchizedek . . ." Heb. 7: 1; Ps. 110: 4; Gen. 14: 8 ff.', in *Essays on the Semitic Background of the New Testament* (London, 1971), 224. It is, of course, true that in all of these references in chapter 1 the author never uses the term 'king' (although see the use of 'king-dom' later in the epistle, 12: 28); but it could be that a previous exegesis of these passages as refer-ring to *enthronement* would make this unnecessary. For the idea of enthronement in ch. 1, cf. Michel, op. cit. n. 6 above, 116 f.; F. J. Schierse, *Verheissung und Heilsvollendung* (Munich, 1955), 96 f.; C. Spicq, *L'Épître aux Hébreux*, ii (Paris, 1952), 23; and J. H. Hayes, 'The Resurrection as Enthrone-ment and the Earliest Church Christology', *Int* 22 (1968), 333 ff.

[43] Cf., e.g. R. P. C. Hanson, *Allegory and Event* (London, 1959), 91 ('In Hebrews Jesus Christ is a heavenly being who has taken human nature upon himself'); J. W. Thompson, 'The Conceptual Background and Purpose of the Midrash in Hebrews VII', *NT* 19 (1977), 217 ('Jesus is considered a heavenly being whose earthly life as υἱός is only a fixed period'); E. F. Scott, *The Epistle to the*

least the starting-points for such a doctrine in Hebrews.[44] As noted, however, evidence exists that the attribution of a creative function to the Son in 1: 2b and 1: 10 ff. would not be inappropriate for one destined by God to be the bearer of his wisdom in this world.[45] That two types of Christology (known by the labels 'low' and 'high' and 'functional' and 'ontological') developed side by side within early Christianity must be remembered. We may be too far removed from the original setting to be sure that language which the Church has taken to be of the one type did not originally represent the other. What is ascertainable, however, is that the writer of Hebrews, whatever his approach to the other type, has no aversion to 'functional' or 'adoptionistic' language. 'Nowhere, in fact,' says J. A. T. Robinson, 'in the New Testament more than in Hebrews do we find such a wealth of expressions that would support what looks like an adoptionist christology—of a Jesus who *becomes* the Christ.'[46] It looks, in other words, as though the author's *main* interest was not in a uniquely privileged, divine being who becomes man; it is in a human figure who attains to an exalted status.

The tendency to homogenize the thinking of the New Testament writers and to read later theological concerns into their statements has been with us always. It is, however, a temptation which the New Testament theologian must resist if the purity of the discipline is to be preserved. I have suggested (1) that the first chapter of Hebrews is concerned with the status of one who is appointed to a 'glory' greater than that of his 'comrades' and/or the angels, (2) that no motif provides a better background to this concern than that of the coming, idealized royal figure like David or Solomon who incorporate the many, and (3) that the point of the extravaganza of chapter one is to lead the readers

Hebrews, Its Doctrine and Significance (Edinburgh, 1922), 151 ('His earthly life is . . . nothing but an interlude in a larger, heavenly life'); F. C. Synge, *Hebrews and the Scriptures* (London, 1959), 1 ff.; and Glasson, op. cit. n. 22 above, 270 ff. The latter two writers see Hebrews 1 as an 'intertrinitarian conversation' between the eternal Father and Son. For a view which makes much more sense of the evidence, see Caird's 'Son by Appointment'.

[44] Aside from 1: 2b and 1: 10–12, cf. 10: 5, which speaks of Christ's attitude 'at his coming into the world', a statement often taken to *imply* pre-existence—cf. J. D. G. Dunn, *Christology in the Making* (London, 1980), 54. Dunn, however, draws attention to the rabbinic description of all men as those 'who come into the world' (ibid., 288, n. 215), and it is hard to think of the writer actually picturing the infant Jesus in the manger uttering the words. A more likely paraphrase of his point would be 'these would have been the appropriate words for him to have spoken at his birth'. 3: 3, 7: 3, and 11: 26 should all be rejected as references to pre-existence.

[45] Caird, 'Son by Appointment', 78, suggests that 1: 2b reflects a popularized version of Aristotle's final cause operating as efficient cause (cf. Aristotle, *Metaphysics* 983ª 24–32; 1013ª 24–35; *Phys.* 195ᵇ, etc.). In this case God creates the cosmos 'through Jesus' because he is the end of the entire process. H. W. Montefiore, *The Epistle to the Hebrews* (London, 1964), 60, commenting on 2: 10, also admits Aristotelian notions into *Auctor's* argument, although there it is *God* who acts as 'final and efficient cause of the universe'.

[46] Robinson, op. cit. n. 22 above, 156.

of the epistle to the glory of mankind foretold in Psalm 8 and explored
in chapter two. This premiss will undoubtedly prove difficult for some,
largely because it disturbs long-held notions, enjoyed comfortably and
without question, concerning a pre-existent figure in Hebrews who
holds an exclusive status. Fortunately, for the late Dean Ireland's Professor, comfort was never a criterion for truthfulness. There were
undoubtedly those who contributed to the Christological debates of the
fourth and fifth centuries who likewise believed that such questions
must be asked,[47] irrespective of how difficult or disturbing they may be.
Did their antagonists, on the other hand, always pursue religious truth
in a manner which would have summoned the approval of the occasional theologian of 221B Baker Street? It might be a question worth
asking from time to time.

[47] Cf. e.g., M. Wiles, 'Person or Personification? A Patristic Debate about Logos', below,
281–9.

12. Who Were the Heroes? An Exercise in Bi-testamentary Exegesis, with Christological Implications

STANLEY FROST

THERE are two passages, one Old Testament and one New Testament, so alike in purpose and structure that it is difficult to think that the one was not consciously chosen as the model for the other. They are the panegyric of the heroes of Israel's past history in Ecclesiasticus, otherwise known as the Wisdom of Jesus ben Sirach, chapters 44–50, and the homily on faith in the Epistle to the Hebrews, chapters 11 and 12. When considered together, the writings raise some deceptively simple questions: 'Why are the persons named not identical? What was the criterion of choice? What changes of religious stance and cultural climate are shown in the New Testament composition when compared with the Old?' The answers lead, as we shall see, to a very difficult question: what if any are the christological implications of these developments?

It will be noted that with reference to the Old Testament, I am concurring in the opinion that Ecclesiasticus deserves to be included within the term. I think that, not because of conciliar decisions, but because the book so patently exhibits the attitudes and convictions of the Old Testament. It is an anthology of proverbs, teachings, and poems, some collected and some composed. It has been suggested that the contents of the book derive from the lecture-notes of a teacher who regularly addressed a disciple-group. Among the poems, the one which engages our attention is a roll-call of 'Heroes of Israel's Past' (44: 1–50: 24).

The New English Bible, taking due account of the rediscovered Hebrew texts, gives a generally acceptable translation, despite a tendency to paraphrase, but some points call for comment. The opening passage (44: 1–15) is introductory to the poem as a whole and is the key to its interpretation.[1] The first line gives us reason to pause: 'Let us now sing the praises of famous men'. The Hebrew is אַנְשֵׁי חֶסֶד [2]. חֶסֶד is one

---

[1] The suggestion (e.g. *Jerusalem Bible, in loc.*) that in this passage there is a reference to Gentile rulers in contrast to Israelite misreads its intent.

[2] In addition to I. Levi, *Hebrew Text of Ecclesiasticus* (Leiden, 1904), see Y. Yadin, *The Ben Sirach Scroll from Masada* (Jerusalem, 1965) and H. P. Rüger, *Text und Textform im Hebräischen Sirach* (Berlin, 1970).

of the pivotal ideas of the Old Testament. In the course of the centuries, it moved from its primary notion of loyalty to a covenant, to the concept of the concern which is continued even after the covenant has been broken, and then to more general ideas of kindness, mercy, and even love.[3] But the primary meaning of 'loyalty within a covenant relationship' was never wholly lost, and 'famous men' (KJV, RSV, NEB) or 'illustrious men' (JB) do not rightly convey the sense. 'Let us now praise covenant-loyal men' is not poetry: 'steadfast men' is a little more acceptable, and it does point in the right direction. This is made clearer in succeeding verses. After dwelling on the differing virtues of honoured persons of the past, ben Sirach continues:

> All these won fame in their own generation,
> and were the pride of their times.
> Some there are who have left a name behind them,
> to be commemorated in story.
> There are others who are unremembered;
> they are dead, and it is as though they had never existed,
> as though they had never been born,
> or left children to succeed them.
> Not so our own forefathers; they were men of loyalty,
> whose deeds have never been forgotten.
> Their prosperity is handed on to their descendants,
> and their inheritance to future generations.
> Thanks to them their children are within the covenants.

Here the dominant idea of staying loyal to an inheritance is clearly brought out; the contrast between the אַנְשֵׁי חֶסֶד and those who never acquired their enduring renown is a deprecatory one; those who did not remain loyal have proved insubstantial and transient.[4] It is the same thought as that expressed in Psalm 1. But the point of contrast is more than one of persistence in communal memory—it derives from the elective nature of the relationship of God and man. God has chosen some men to be joined with him in a covenant relationship; those who are loyal to that covenant acquire a persistence that derives not simply from human memories, but from God's own timeless being. Nevertheless, this persistence is given form and substance by the descendants who stand firmly within the same covenant. חֶסֶד and בְּרִית (covenant) are inextricably joined in Old Testament thought: the Old Testament heroes are patently those who keep the covenant.

---

[3] The significance of חֶסֶד was explored at length by N. H. Snaith, *Distinctive Ideas of the Old Testament* (London, 1944), 94–130.

[4] The popular misapplication of 44: 9 at Remembrance Day services is not likely to be corrected by more accurate exegesis.

The problem with lists is that others are tempted to improve them by adding further names, often not perceiving the original criterion of choice. In a manuscript work this is fatally easy to accomplish. Enoch has wandered in at 44: 16 but is not included there in some Hebrew texts; at 49: 14 he with Shem, Seth, and Adam appears to be equally misplaced and intrusive.[5] For the rest of the heroes named, the point at issue is that 'they stand within the covenants'. God made a covenant with Noah, which persisted for his descendants. He also made a covenant with Abraham, which was inherited by Isaac and Jacob, renewed by Moses, and lived out (or shamefully deserted) by the twelve tribes of Israel, as exemplified by their leading personalities. Joshua and Caleb are very pertinent instances; out of a generation of six hundred thousand, they alone survived to enter the covenant inheritance:

> So all Israel could see
> how good it is to be a loyal follower of the Lord.

Within this larger covenant there are two derived covenants, both of which have particular significance for ben Sirach—the covenant establishing kingship for the house of David, and the covenant establishing priesthood for the house of Aaron. On the latter he expatiates with unrestrained enthusiasm, for he is himself a Sadducee. He ends with a prayer—

> Come, then, praise the God of the universe,
> who ... deals with us in mercy (חֶסֶד).
> May he confirm his חֶסֶד towards us,
> and in his own good time give us deliverance.

We sum up the poem as a whole: 'God has made a covenant with Israel, and enduring are they who are loyal to it; our prayer is that God may also be loyal to his covenant, for with him loyalty is mercy'—the major meanings of חֶסֶד at this point run together. *The Wisdom of Jeshua ben Sirach* would in fact have made a fitting conclusion to any canon of the Old Testament, for while patently representative of the Wisdom School, it exalts the Law (identifying it with wisdom), endorses messianism (in its older, dynastic form), pays homage to prophecy, and glorifies the priesthood, sacrifice, and Temple. It is because the book so faithfully represents the Old Testament that it chooses as heroes of the past men of covenant loyalty.

---

[5] See Yadin, op. cit., 38. For the extra-biblical association of Enoch with covenant, which might explain his insertion into the listing, see P. G. Davis, 'The mythic Enoch: New light on Early Christology', *Studies in Religion* (Toronto) XIII (1984), 335–43.

I choose the opinion that the Epistle to the Hebrews was prepared for the edification of a congregation of Hellenic Jewish Christians, probably with a Gentile component.[6] The recipients were expected to be well versed in the Old Testament in its Septuagint version and in the nature of the Levitical Law, since the document bases many of its arguments on Mosaic ordinances and rituals. On the other hand, the reader becomes quickly aware of a considerable Hellenic influence, both in language and concepts. As in the instance of the Ecclesiasticus, there is a probability that the contents represent the teachings, or at least the homilies, of a recognized instructor—the tone is rather more authoritative than a preacher would normally adopt. Our concern is with a homily now reckoned as 11: 1–12: 14; it is a little difficult to tell where it ends. The sensible end is 12: 14, but the teacher-preacher of the epistle would not be the first or last homilist to continue talking after the efficient ending had been reached. At any rate, the break at 12: 14 is sufficient for our purposes.

In this passage the homilist has taken 'the Song of the Fathers' from ben Sirach to serve as his model, but whereas in the Old Testament book the quality that distinguishes memorable persons is loyalty to the covenants, in the New Testament version the distinctive quality is πίστις, faith, and the homilist's understanding of faith is made clear at the outset. To have πίστις is to believe that the universe was created by God, but following upon that understanding (and this is the more specialized perception), πίστις is an awareness of God's presence and purpose in his universe. Having that perception, Abel was able to foresee the kind of offering that would be acceptable to such a God; Enoch perceived what manner of life would be pleasing to this God, and was so apt in his response that God took him to himself; Noah could tell the difference between right and wrong in a divinely ordered universe, and bravely chose the right; Abraham glimpsed an eternal city created by God, and set out in search of it without reckoning the consequences; Sarah willed to devote even her maternal functions to the enterprise, and so miraculously provided the heir who could inherit the quest. That quest is for a better city than can be found in this world—it is, in fact, a heavenly city that the descendants of Abraham seek, and God has already prepared it for them. 'Heavenly' in this context plainly means 'ideal' in the Platonic sense; 'eternal' means transcendent of place and time. At these points, as at so many others, in the Epistle to the Hebrews, Hellenistic influences are clearly manifest.

In the homilist's reading of history, the perception that man, alerted

---

[6] See the discussion in F. F. Bruce, *The Epistle to the Hebrews* (Grand Rapids, 1964), XXIII–XXV.

to God's presence and purpose in this world, must seek a heavenly city, motivated all the heroes of Hebrew tradition. This was the continuing endeavour from Abraham through Moses, Joshua, the Judges, David, Samuel, and the prophets. Time was indeed too short for the homilist to dwell on each one, but πίστις was in each instance the criterion of choice. Significantly, he or (if as some have attractively suggested, our homilist was a woman, perhaps Priscilla[7]) she found time to include Rahab the harlot. At first, it seems a strange choice, but if one shares the homilist's viewpoint, it is in some ways the most telling illustration of all—an abandoned woman (abandoned in both the moral and social sense) catching the idea of an eternal purpose, revealed in the unlikely event of two spies hiding up in a whore-house, and risking her all on the possibility it might come true. We can understand why the reference would make its appeal: in the drab circumstances of life in a Near Eastern town or a Roman slum, to be motivated in daily living by a sense of eternal inheritance would require a faith as ready to glimpse the invisible as that of Rahab herself. Moreover, she was not Israelite born, but an alien. If as is possible there were Gentile women among the members of the homilist's congregation (we recall their presence at Philippi and Thessalonica), the choice of Rahab would have a particular relevance for them. If someone such as she could have faith, how much more they, who were respectable women?

The supreme illustration of πίστις is, however, Jesus. Just as ben Sirach had dilated on Simon ben Onias, so the homilist makes Jesus the cynosure of all eyes. We are surrounded by all these other participants in this faith but our gaze is fixed on him who is the Architect and Finisher of our faith—that is, the one who first inspired this faith in us, and who will bring us to its fulfilment. He himself lived unswervingly faithful to the hope set before him, even though it meant enduring crucifixion, and he has inherited his reward and now sits in the eternal city, at the right hand of God. If we persist in seeking peace with all men, and living the holy life, we too shall 'see the Lord'. Faith will be realized in experience.

The similarities and the contrasts in these two catalogues of the heroes of a sacred past now explain themselves. Ben Sirach chose his examples because he was devoted to the concept of חֶסֶד, loyalty to the covenants. What he looked for was the improvement of the status quo: Jerusalem should be delivered from the annoyance and indignity of alien rule (he was living before the rigour of the Antiochene proscriptions) and the city and people should prosper in order that the Temple

---

[7] The suggestion was made by A. von Harnack; see Bruce, op. cit., XL.

rituals should continue forever, in all their beauty and reassuring significance. God would be visibly in covenant with his people and all
would be well with the world. It was a powerful but static concept. By
contrast, the author of Hebrews had little sense of the status quo. For
the homilist, a bygone age and a vanished world supplied a wealth of
images, parallels, metaphors, but the hope was for an unknown, unfor-
seeable, but truly believable future. That future was equally the reality
of the present, because Jesus has already inherited it. He has passed into
the heavens, and therefore for us also life is a race to be run and the
prize to be won is the same reward: to enter the eternal city. In contrast
to the static concept of ben Sirach, the thinking of the Epistle to the
Hebrews is dynamic.

If these are the answers to our initial queries, there remains the much
more difficult question: what has this change of expectation done to the
Christian understanding of Jesus? He too was a Teacher, and he too
had a student-group. He began by sitting where ben Sirach sat, and he
used a similar variety of materials—proverbs, riddles, admonitions,
legal arguments, poems, parables (מְשָׁלִים) and short stories. His version of חֶסֶד was keeping the commandments: love God and your
neighbour. He began as a Galilean teacher, and that is how the earliest
accounts depicted him, but he ended where the author of Hebrews
placed him—in the ideal world of the eternal. What that phraseology
means in Hebrews is clearly indicated in Chapter 9: 'now Christ has
come, high priest of good things already in being. The tent (tabernacle)
of his priesthood is a greater, more perfect one, not made by men's
hands, that is, not belonging to this created world' (v. 11) ... 'for
Christ has entered, not the sanctuary made by men's hands, which is
only the symbol of the reality, but heaven itself' (v. 24). Jesus the
Teacher of Nazareth has become the eternal Christ. The riddle of the
New Testament, to use Hoskyn's phrase, is this: how did one who,
given the historical adjustment, would have qualified eminently for
inclusion in ben Sirach's stirring but this-worldly catalogue of heroes,
become in the parallel passage in Hebrews the supreme illustration of
other-worldly reality?[8]

Time would indeed fail us as much as it did the homilist to detail the
whole story, but the major achievement of twentieth-century biblical
scholarship, in which George Caird so fully participated, has been, in
the present writer's judgement, to make clear the lines of development
which point towards an answer. The method employed was to evaluate
the different titles accorded to Jesus in the New Testament writings.

[8] Hoskyns and Davey, *The Riddle of the New Testament* (London, 1931), 14: 'What was the relation between Jesus of Nazareth and the Primitive Christian Church? That is the riddle.'

The work had to begin, however, in the royal psalms of the Psalter, move to the messianic passages in the prophets, ponder the Servant Songs of Deutero-Isaiah, unravel the complexities of Daniel and Enoch and so arrive at a fresh investigation of the Synoptic Gospels, the Acts of the Apostles, the writings of Paul, Hebrews, and the Gospel of John.[9] It was early recognized that a word or phrase in one context might mean something other elsewhere, and that each title undoubtedly underwent its own individual development. The result has been the discernment of major stages in a very complex, but by no means uniform or synchronous development, of which a great many details are as yet still unclear. To state that development in a few words is to run grave risk of distortion, but it is necessary to make the attempt if the line of descent from the heroes of Ecclesiasticus to the faithful of the Epistle to the Hebrews is to be made apparent.

The one major Old Testament characteristic lacking from ben Sirach is eschatology, and even that is implied in his orthodox reading of Israel's history and in his prayer:

> May God grant us a joyful heart,
> and in our time send Israel lasting peace.
> May he confirm his חֶסֶד towards us,
> and in his own good time grant us deliverance.

Old Testament eschatology involved a looking forward to a desirable end of the historical process. It was that expectation which among the Hebrews opened the door to the revived influence of Mesopotamian mythology, which in turn resulted in the efflorescence of apocalyptic. Despite significant anticipations, the phenomenon only reached full flowering beyond the natural confines of the Old Testament. Even though the classic production of apocalyptic, the Book of Daniel, was written only some twenty years later than Ecclesiasticus, the one belongs characteristically to the inter-testamental literature as clearly as the other does to the Old Testament.[10] Within less orthodox circles, such as may have existed in Galilee at the beginning of the Christian era, the kind of material which eventually found its way into the Enoch anthologies may have been equally if not more popular than Daniel. Even so, the scholarly consensus appears to be that the teaching of Jesus had a considerable element of eschatology, but was remarkably free from the mythological elements of apocalyptic.[11]

[9] See for example S. Mowinckel, *He that Cometh* (Oxford, 1956) and Vincent Taylor, *The Names of Jesus* (London, 1962).

[10] Dogmatic and linguistic considerations happened to take Daniel into the Hebrew canon and excluded Ecclesiasticus; but those facts are among the anomalies of history.

[11] Cf. G. R. Beasley-Murray, *A Commentary on Mark 13* (London, 1957), 11: 'We should require

From the writings of New Testament authors, especially Luke and Paul, we can see that this self-discipline was largely carried over into the preaching of the earliest church. Apocalyptic gained ground in some Christian circles, but not many: the surprising fact is not that the New Testament contains apocalyptic writings, but rather how small is their extent. As the Christian community established itself in numerous centres of Hellenistic culture, and as the *eschaton* was progressively delayed, so the general concepts of Platonist idealism, mediated to some extent by Hellenistic Judaism, infiltrated Christian thinking to respond to questions which the distaste for apocalyptic had left unanswered. In a word, the majority of the adherents of the new movement preferred the Gospel of John to the Apocalypse of John. The result was to transform a future *eschaton* in time into a transcendent eternity beyond time—as truly 'now' as ever 'will be'.

In this way, as the present writer reads the evidence, a teacher of Galilee became the eschatological Son of Man (an identification which most scholars would agree took place in Jesus' own thinking), and then among the first Jewish Christians (who in general preferred the Old Testament to apocalyptic) he became the messianic, exalted (but still human) Son of God, and finally in the Hellenistic congregations (as witnessed by the Epistles to the Hebrews, Ephesians, and Colossians and the fourth Gospel), the eternal Lord, one for whom the category of divinity would not be inappropriate. Jesus of Nazareth and the kingdom of God which he set out to proclaim are inseparable, but as Bultmann insisted, in the Synoptic Gospels it is not Jesus who brings the kingdom, but the kingdom which brings him.[12] In the same way, we may comment that it was not Jesus who transformed an historical kingdom into a spiritual ideal, but the transcendentalizing of the *eschaton* which made Jesus of Nazareth the timeless and eternal Christ.

Jeshua ben Sirach and the homilist of the Epistle to the Hebrews both looked back into the past to gain encouragement for the present, and resolve for the future. Ben Sirach saw heroes of covenant-loyalty, and the homilist saw witnesses to a transcendent faith. Both recognized that they stood in a tradition reaching back to the days of Abraham and beyond. Those who today use words like 'loyalty' and 'faith' with the connotations characteristic of our own generation, stand in the same long line of witnesses to an ever more comprehensive truth.

stronger reasons that have been given to accept the suggestion that resort has here (Mark 13) been made to an apocalyptic fiction. To what extent the discourse is a unity and to what extent composite is another matter'. He quotes (18) C. C. Torrey: 'there is nothing in any part of it that can justify the use of the term "apocalyptic"'.

[12] R. Bultmann, *Jesus and the Word* (London, 1935), 27–30.

PART III

METHODS AND THEMES

13. Academic Scepticism, Spiritual Reality and Transfiguration[1]

DONALD EVANS

A FEW years ago at a theological conference I heard a paper in which a scholar said something like this: 'And St Paul, following the traditional metaphor already used by Jeremiah and Ezekiel, spoke of a spirit of love dwelling in the heart.' As I heard these words I wanted to jump to my feet and protest: 'Surely it's possible that St Paul spoke of a spirit of love dwelling in the heart because that's where he *experienced* it—as countless others have in many different religious traditions, and as I have myself, especially during meditation, and as people have in secular psychotherapies such as bioenergetics. It's no metaphor. It's a literal truth.'

It is increasingly obvious to me that spiritual reality—and by this I do not mean God—has an objective structure which human beings can discern, just as they can discern the colours of the rainbow. This objective structure has shaped our human language and concepts, though these in turn have developed independently of that structure in varying degrees, shaping our awareness of spiritual reality in ways which may clarify or distort.

Imagine a blind scholar in a blind community saying, 'And Paul, following the tradition established by Jeremiah and Ezekiel, located the colour orange between red and yellow.' Such an explanation of the location is unnecessary if Paul could actually see colours. But if a linguistic tradition, unlike other traditions, included no word for the colour orange, or if it included a dozen species of orange colours, such variations would of course be open to various explanations—cultural, historical, geographical, etc. It is not the case, however, that we can *never* justify and explain our linguistic distinctions by reference to non-linguistic experience.[2]

---

[1] This essay is a revised version of an article published in *Commonweal* (13 July, 1984) entitled, 'Can we know spiritual reality?'

[2] As J. L. Austin pointed out in a lecture at Oxford during the 1950s, since psychological experiments show that people can distinguish colours even when they have no words to mark the distinction, philosophers should qualify their claim that we only experience reality *through* language and thus can never justify our linguistic distinctions by reference to non-linguistic experience.

The speaker at the theological conference exemplified an epistemological perspective which was evident in nearly every paper that I heard at the conference and which pervades academic thought in general. This perspective excludes the possibility of any direct awareness of spiritual reality. Accordingly it is sheer superstition, supposedly, for me to claim to experience myself as spirit, to discern loving life-energy around my heart, to detect harmful or helpful spiritual influences at work between people at a distance, to see auras or feel vibrations around other people, to contact discarnate spirits of the dead to help them or be helped by them, or to become aware of angels and archangels and all the company of heaven. Why are all such spiritual claims so obviously false and fantastic for most contemporary intellectuals, including theologians? Because their perspective combines what I will call a relativistic Kantianism and a common sense empiricism. Let us consider each of these briefly in turn.

Kant's agnosticism concerning reality, including spiritual reality, is well known. All we can know, according to Kant, is how the human mind *must* shape sense-experience: the forms of space and time and the very general concepts or categories such as cause and substance which we humans impose on sense-experience, giving it an intelligible structure. What is really out there we cannot know. We only know reality on our terms, and what these terms are we can deduce in a 'transcendental' way. Since Kant many diverse thinkers have followed him in emphasizing what the human mind brings *to* our awareness of the world, but differing from him in focusing, not on what we must bring to this awareness, but on what we do bring. What we do bring varies from person to person and group to group, so our alleged knowing is relative to this. The variations in what we bring to our awareness of the world depend on a variety of factors, any one of which can be selected for emphasis. Some epistemologies stress sociological influences, others select psychological influences or cultural-historical influences. And some epistemologies following Wittgenstein depict our knowing as shaped by linguistic practices within a social 'form of life'. What all these perspectives have in common is a rejection of any allegedly direct way of knowing reality.

In so far as contemporary *theology* is governed by this neo-Kantian relativism, we have a variety of approaches to epistemological questions, but they all agree in assuming that we can only study the human conceptual or linguistic framework which is brought *to* an alleged reality, not the reality itself, for it can only be discerned *through* the framework. This relativism may be either sceptical, fideistic, or conservative. The sceptical version, a 'hermeneutics of suspicion', exposes ideology by means of insights drawn from Freud or Marx or sociology of knowledge. Knowledge-claims are thus radically undermined. If the stance is fideistic the theologian makes an explicit leap of faith, putting his trust in a particular conceptual framework or 'language-game' as the authoritative vehicle through which to know and by which to live. To be a Christian means to opt for Christian words and symbols. Where the stance is an unreflective conservatism, there is no sense of choice in the matter. Being a Christian means thinking as a member of a reliable historical-traditional community: 'If Jeremiah and Ezekiel and then Paul spoke of a spirit of love dwelling in the heart, that is what I will think too.' But whether one is sceptical, fideistic, or conservative the common assumption is that I cannot directly know reality—especially spiritual reality. The issue is whether to trust any conceptual or symbolic framework which includes spiritual *terms*. The sceptic refuses to do so, the fideist opts for a framework, and the conservative does not question his or her framework.

In relation to spiritual reality, relativistic Kantianism is often accompanied by a common-sense empiricism. What I mean by this is simply the assumption that experience is limited to sense-experience and that sense-experience of any alleged objective reality is limited to the publicly observable world—which is accessible to virtually everyone. Concerning this publicly observable world, common-sense empiricism may be qualified by Kantian caution concerning claims to know what is really there. Usually, however, empiricism and Kantianism are in conflict concerning knowledge of physical reality. But concerning spiritual reality Kantian and empiricist forget their quarrels and agree in rejecting any possibility that you and I can know directly, by experiencing or discerning what is there. Both tend to reject as sheer superstition any alleged spiritual awareness. To a common-sense empiricist the real world is the publicly observable world, plus perhaps the human mind or centre of consciousness inside each human body. The mind sometimes imaginatively creates fantasies of spiritual entities during abnormal states of consciousness such as dreams, reveries, trances, and meditations; but to regard these fantasies as realities is a reversion to a pre-enlightened, subhuman primitivism and superstition—so the empiricist assumes. Or, less harshly, an empiricist can take up a form of relativistic Kantian perspective on beliefs and practices pertaining to spirit and spirits. Their origins can be explained sociologically, psychologically, or in terms of historical-cultural influences. In such a very typical combination of relativistic Kantianism and common-sense empiricism Kant's own agnosticism concerning physical reality is forgotten and is confined to spiritual reality. Such an empiricist has no resort to neo-Kantian explanations when someone claims to see a stone. The explanations are called in when someone claims to see a spook.

If theologians are reluctant to accept any knowledge-claims concerning spiritual reality, it is not surprising to find that social scientists are also reluctant. Several years ago I attended a conference in Berkeley, California on new religious movements. The central issue was why people join these movements and remain in them. A wide variety of psychological and sociological explanations were proposed, but one kind of explanation which seems to me at least equally relevant was almost totally overlooked: a spiritual explanation. In my association with some of these groups I have often observed people becoming aware of themselves and others as *spirit*, perhaps for the first time in their lives. This is an exciting and momentous discovery for most post-Enlightenment Westerners. It may even be mistakenly identified as an experience of God. Often people continue in the new religious movement mainly because they know they can continue this awareness of spirit in the movement, whereas outside—they assume or are taught—it is unavailable. Being naïve in such matters, they do not realize that similar experiences can occur in many other groups, with different leaders, belief-structures, and communal practices. (And they do not realize that elementary spiritual awareness can occur even though a leader is immoral or crazy, a belief-structure is fanatical or irrational, and a communal practice is manipulative or dangerous—as is the case in some, but not all, new religious movements.)

Whether or not a group is, in its overall character, positive or negative, individuals who join and remain usually have both non-spiritual motives and spiritual motives. The former are open to investigation by secular psychology and sociology, but the latter are not. To say, 'John and Mary sought and found an awareness, however minimal or distorted, of spiritual reality' is alien to social science. Such a spiritual explanation presupposes that there really is a spiritual realm which people sometimes discover. The most that a typical social scientist can assume here is that one important motive may be a person's *conviction* that he or she has found spiritual reality. The conviction itself must be explained by reference to non-spiritual factors. For example, a person might believe that he felt a spirit of love in his heart because that is what the religious tradition taught, or because he was deprived of love in infancy and needed to believe this. What I would insist, however, is that there *is* a spiritual realm and that some forms of meditation enable a person to begin to be aware of this realm. And if a social scientist will not test my claim by taking up meditation himself, he should be more genuinely agnostic concerning such claims, never assuming that non-spiritual explanations are adequate in accounting for people's convictions concerning spiritual reality.

Thus far we have looked at theological and social scientific assumptions concerning the question, 'What can I know about spiritual reality?' A typical philosophical approach can be seen in a recent book by the distinguished philosopher, Susanne Langer. In volume three of her trilogy on the origins of the human mind,[3] she explains the evolutionary origins of human belief in a spirit-world; gods and goddesses, devils and angels, souls of dead people and animals, spirits inhabiting not only persons but also animals and trees. She is amazed that human beings who are intelligent enough to carry on the practical affairs of life can possibly have imagined such absurdities and asserted them as facts. Since for her, as for most academics today, such beliefs are false, their explanation must be sought in how the human mind works. Langer's account of the human mind resembles Kant's in that at its core it is a claim concerning how the human mind *must* work. Since Langer's claims arise from reflections on biology and evolution, we could call it an 'evolutionary-transcendental' deduction. In her view our mind must work as a feeling-response to our environment. This feeling-response is such as to be expressed in symbolism, and the symbolism is a way of understanding whatever is experienced in nature as having a life-like form.

To this fundamental claim concerning mind as feeling Langer adds several ingenious and insightful theories concerning why human beings have had beliefs and practices concerning spiritual reality. Her explanations are very illuminating in accounting for why the spirit-world alleged by various individuals and communities differ, and in understanding some of the motivations of people both past and present who have come to believe in spirits and in life after death. But for Langer the spirit-world is always and entirely a human creation, a fantastic delusion.

What if she is mistaken in this? What if human *discoveries* of supersensible realities are mixed in with the imaginative projections which she astutely describes? Then, although her explanations are still relevant, they are inadequate. What the human mind brings to spiritual reality is not the whole story, for the human mind sometimes discerns spiritual reality, especially during meditation. The whole investigation becomes much more complex. It requires investigators who practice the relevant forms of meditation or who are at least open to study testimonial material from those who do. I readily concede that various non-

---

[3] Susanne K. Langer, *Mind: An Essay on Human Feeling*, iii, (Baltimore, 1982). My remarks concerning Langer are selected from a lengthy review in *Commonweal*, 15 July, 1983.

spiritual explanations are still relevant. Kant and Marx and Freud and Langer and Wittgenstein cannot be ignored. But we also cannot ignore the testimony concerning spirit from most human beings in human history prior to the so-called 'enlightenment' in the West.

Thus far I have questioned a theologian's non-spiritual account of why St Paul located a spirit of love in the heart, a group of social scientists' non-spiritual account of why people join new religious movements, and a philosopher's non-spiritual account of why most human beings in the past have believed in spirits. Now I am going to question some accounts provided by non-fundamentalist biblical scholars and theologians concerning the Transfiguration of Jesus. In general, the story is not interpreted literally, that is, in terms of an objective spiritual reality which people can sometimes discern. My own first impulse to interpret it literally was evoked thirty years ago when I first saw a fresco of the Transfiguration by the great Florentine artist Fra Angelico. In depicting the change in the appearance of Jesus' face and clothing, he painted a literal oval-shaped aura which is analogous to those which I now realize is discerned by people whom we today call 'psychics'. But liberal New Testament scholars today typically do not believe in auras. Nor are they at ease in interpreting what happened when Moses and Elijah allegedly appeared as two discarnate spirits communicating with Jesus on the mount of Transfiguration. Such an event would be entirely intelligible and unsurprising to modern spiritualists and to participants in various non-Christian meditative paths. But most non-fundamentalist biblical scholars seem to be sceptical not only concerning the Transfiguration story but concerning spiritual reality in general. Or if they are not sceptical, they are puzzled and confused.

One notable exception was George Caird. Concerning the various spiritual 'principalities and powers', both good and evil, which St Paul saw as being subjugated by Christ, Caird wrote, 'Paul is using mythological language but his language has a rational content of thought; he is working with ideas which have had a long history, but he is describing *spiritual realities* with whom he and his fellow Christians have *personal* acquaintance'.[4] And in his commentary on the Transfiguration story, he wrote:

The transfiguration cannot be understood simply as a stage in the education of the disciples; it must also have been a crisis in the religious life of Jesus. Luke draws our attention to this point in his usual manner: Jesus, he tells us, was

---

[4] George B. Caird, *Principalities and Powers* (Oxford, 1956), x. Caird's non-fundamentalism is evident in many parts of the book, for example his commentary on 1 Cor. 11: 10f. (17–21) where he criticizes St Paul's 'faulty logic and equally faulty exegesis' and his 'spurious arguments'.

praying; and his comment is borne out by the researches of Evelyn Underhill and others, who have shown that the intense devotions of saint and mystic are often accompanied by physical transformation and luminous glow. . . . Many scholars, past and present, have treated the transfiguration story with suspicion, regarding it either as a misplaced resurrection story or as a legendary product of later Christian piety. But the account may be accepted as literal truth.[5]

It would be a monumental task to show that, in contrast with Caird, most non-fundamentalist scholars seem to be sceptical or cautiously agnostic or confused in their comments concerning the Transfiguration story. But I can at least invite readers to consider as a representative example a book entitled *Transfiguration*[6] by a relatively conservative Anglican theologian, J. W. C. Wand. In this study, published in 1967, he draws on many biblical scholars, comparing and appraising their accounts. He himself suggests that probably Jesus' facial appearance did change as he prayed.[7] After all, a person's face can 'light up', as we say, on seeing his beloved. How much more so for Jesus in prayer to God. But perhaps the disciples' report of this was amplified by them or by others so as to include talk about a change in Jesus' clothing.[8] Why? Partly because hints of the miraculous tend to be exaggerated as a story is passed along; partly because there was a prevalent traditional notion that such a change can affect the clothing; partly because the Hebrew concept of 'glory', linked with the Transfiguration by Luke,[9] includes the notion of a shining garment-like substance. Wand also notes that early Christian apologists arguing with the Jews could have been moved to depict Jesus as a new Moses being transfigured on a mountain-top and as a fulfilment of the Law and the Prophets who conversed there with Moses and Elijah.

Wand is not entirely sceptical. He is convinced that the Transfiguration narrative has a core of historicity, and that something significant happened. He notes that St Matthew refers to the event as a 'vision' and that St Luke emphasizes the trance-like sleepiness of the disciples, so probably the event was not physical but only mental.[10] But for Wand this mental status does not make the event unreal. Indeed he ends by calling the Transfiguration a 'veridical vision' which Jesus

---

[5] George B. Caird, *Saint Luke*, Pelican Gospel Commentary (1963), 132. Cf. G. B. Caird, 'The Transfiguration', *ET* 67 (1955–6), 291.

[6] J. W. C. Wand, *Transfiguration* (London, 1967).

[7] Ibid., 24, cf. 26.

[8] Ibid., 27–8.

[9] Cf. Caird's early work 'The New Testament Conception of Doxa' (unpublished D.Phil. thesis, Oxford, 1944).

[10] Wand, op. cit., 40, 31–2.

somehow shared with his disciples.[11] But how a veridical vision differs from a private fantasy he does not indicate.

What Wand lacks is a metaphysical and epistemological framework in which one can distinguish between (i) publicly observable physical events, (ii) private fantasies, and (iii) objective spiritual events which are partly discerned through what we today often call 'psychic' awareness. Wand does briefly consider an approach which might have led him in this direction, viewing the Transfiguration as a 'mystical phenomenon' alongside other alleged paranormal events in the lives of both Christian and non-Christian holy persons: clairvoyance, levitation, telepathy, and so on. I quote:

Such alleged incidents are generally viewed with dislike by minds trained only in the exact sciences. So far from regarding them as helps to faith we drape them 'in the decent vestments of symbol and myth'. Losing the humble sense of wonder, we only find queerness in the phenomena which our conceptual systems refuse to accommodate.' The difficulty about these alleged experiences is that they are individually so difficult to prove, and that, even when accepted as proven, they are almost always capable of a naturalistic explanation.[12]

Wand does go on to say that it is by no means impossible some such unusual experience may lie behind the narrative of the Transfiguration, but his comment about 'naturalistic explanation' remains. What does he mean by this expression? If he means an explanation which requires no reference to special divine intervention, I would agree with him. The spiritual realm has its own 'natural' structure and characteristics. But I suspect that what he means by a 'naturalistic explanation' is a non-spiritual explanation, for example, one in physical and/or psychological terms. If so, I would simply assert that he is mistaken. No such explanations are available and adequate with reference to telepathy, clairvoyance, spiritual healing, spiritualistic phenomena, or transfiguration. Instead, we have 'naturalistic' assumptions which rule out various paranormal events. It is these assumptions which dictate the conclusions, not only for secular thinkers but also for many Christian theologians. And often the assumptions are unacknowledged. It just seems obvious that some non-spiritual explanation must be possible and that the onus of proof is entirely on the person who makes a claim concerning spiritual reality to show that every possible non-spiritual explanation has been ruled out.

My own personal conviction is that the Transfiguration of Jesus did take place and that it involved both what we now call 'paranormal' changes discernible to 'psychics' and also, more importantly, a total

---

[11] Ibid., 62.
[12] Ibid., 51.

surrender and transparency of a human being in body, passions, mind, and spirit to the divine Spirit. Nobody can discern such surrender and transparency unless they are at least beginning *both* spiritual awareness and personal surrender to the divine Spirit. I do concede the remote historical possibility that the Transfiguration of Jesus may not have happened at all, or that we may have only a simple story about a happy face in prayer which was amplified into a fantastic piece of religious propaganda. But although I concede this is possible, for me the onus of proof is on those who hold that the story is not true as it stands. [13] Here I resemble a fundamentalist, but not because I believe in the literal inerrancy of Scripture. Rather I have no initial reason to disbelieve the story because of the assumption that such things cannot or do not happen. There may be other reasons to disbelieve the story, or to see it as a composite, a kernel of truth plus a subsequent elaboration. Maybe, for example, a story about a resurrection-appearance was somehow transferred back into the earthly life of Jesus. But that is a different kind of issue. The main issue for me is whether a transfiguration can occur, as an objective spiritual event which also involves surrender to the divine Spirit, not only for Jesus but also for us. [14] Similarly problems of scriptural exegesis raised by biblical stories of allegedly objective spiritual healing raise issues concerning the possible reality of such healing for us. Is it all superstition, or at best a kind of 'faith-healing' in which our beliefs can somehow help us to get well—the placebo effect? Even more radically, when St Paul tells us in Romans 8: 16: 'The Spirit itself bears witness with our spirit that we are the children of God', is he assuming that we are aware of our spirit? Is such awareness possible? My own view is that such awareness is not only possible but necessary for an adequate awareness of the divine Spirit.

Few Christians today are clearly aware of themselves as spirit. There are various reasons for this. I have stressed the intellectual climate of

[13] Some form critics take the opposite view. For them the story is so obviously false that they see the authors of the Gospels as here writing a legend so as to *create* an aura or halo around Christ! For an outline and rejection of this perspective see Eugène Dabrowski, *La Transfiguration de Jésus* (Rome, 1939), 36–42.

[14] W. R. F. Browning allows that some saints may have been transfigured: 'It cannot be irrelevant that a similar radiance, transforming the whole bodily appearance is recorded of some of the saints and other persons of sanctity . . . If the Transfiguration of Jesus had no natural cause, it is credible that a similar radiance should be experienced by the saints, for "the glory which thou hast given me I have given unto them" (John 17. 22),' *The Gospel According to St Mark, Introduction and Commentary* (London, 1960), 100–1. For Browning such phenomena are either supernatural or paranormal. The latter may seem to resemble the former but they are 'imitative and merely universal'. Indeed, he implies that paranormal phenomena are 'explicable *psychologically* without recourse to the supernatural' (101, my italics). Browning has only two pigeon-holes: supernatural versus natural-paranormal-psychological. He has no intermediate category, that is no place for a natural event which is not merely psychological because it is objectively *spiritual*. Such an event may, or may not, involve a supernatural surrender to, and transfiguration by, the divine Source.

our age, with its combination of Kantian agnosticism and common-sense empiricism. I should also note, briefly, two other features of the intellectual climate which have deeply influenced Christian theology, and which also impede awareness of oneself as spirit. I am thinking of existentialist theology and liberation theology. Both of these have deeply biblical roots and emphasize important truths, which must be retained in spite of anything I say here. But existentialist theology tends to exclude, or at best blur, spiritual awareness, because it proposes only two metaphysical and epistemological pigeon-holes: scientific investigation and personal discovery or creation of meaning. Discernment of objective spiritual reality fits neither of these. And liberation theology, while rightly recalling Christian thought and practice to the communal justice-commitment of the Hebrew prophets, sometimes rejects all concern with the spiritual as an escapist sanctioning of the oppressive status quo: 'You may be enslaved and hungry now, but there is pie in the sky by and by.' But what if there is such pie in the sky, spiritual consolation in both this life and the next? Does the political misuse of a truth make it false?

Both existentialist theology and liberation theology are post-Enlightenment developments. They share with neo-Kantian relativism and common-sense empiricism a rejection of pre-enlightenment spiritual awareness as 'superstition'. Charismatic Christianity, too, is partly post-Enlightenment—not concerning God, but concerning spirit, and in a different way. It tends to attribute all positive paranormal phenomena directly to God, provided that the 'correct' doctrinal beliefs accompany them, and the rest to the Devil. Hence many experiences of human spirit are misinterpreted as divine or diabolical intrusions. A person's new and exhilarating experience of himself as spirit is often mistakenly assumed to be a visitation by the Holy Spirit, and an eruption from the emotional unconscious or a psychic invasion from another human being is mistakenly seen as a visitation by the Devil. And a genuine surrender of the whole self to God, amply evidenced not only by positive paranormal phenomena but also by an abundance of the fruits of the Spirit, is dismissed, or—the ultimate blasphemy—it is attributed to Beelzebub, because the correct Christian beliefs are absent.

Thus in various ways the intellectual climate of our age imposes severe intellectual constrictions on any Christian exploration of spirit. But there is a specifically Christian constriction as well, which emerged long before the Enlightenment. This constriction is, in my view, a distortion of a legitimate pastoral caution which goes back to St Paul, whom I hear saying something like this: 'Don't be egoistically preoccupied with spiritual phenomena such as visions or tongues or prophecies or ascents to the third heaven. What matters is your openness to the Holy Spirit of love, your being lived by God in Christ as you surrender your old self-centred self.' I totally agree with this, but a distorted outcome of this has been that there is little practical or theoretical teaching concerning the human spirit and the spiritual realm in western Christianity. When I asked a Benedictine monk and scholar why this is so, in contrast with, say, the tantric traditions of the East, his reply was that there has been a fear that Christians would become attached to the consolations of God at the expense of their focus on the God of consolations. This caution arises from a realistic sense of the subtlety and strength and pervasiveness of human narcissism, which can pervert all advances in spiritual awareness. Even Jesus was tempted in the wilderness after the splendours of his baptismal experience, which could have been twisted into an egoistic power-trip and even a pact with the Devil. Today, however, most Christians avoid spiritual pride in the same way that a pauper avoids material pride, by having little to be proud about. For St Paul's caution against a sinful stance towards spiritual phenomena has become, in practice, an effective caution against the phenomena themselves. This is a tragic error. If Christians are to learn how to surrender the whole self to God, to be lived by God, they must have an awareness of self as spirit or spiritual body in complex interdependence with self as physical body, emotions, and mind. We should realize, of course, that spiritual awareness, especially at the lowest or purely psychic level, is no more intrinsically religious than awareness of physical body or emotions or mind. And we should also realize that there are many levels of spiritual awareness, from the psychic, which is merely sensational and fascinating, to the sublimely loving, which is transforming. But a transfiguring surrender of the whole self can only occur if we are aware of our whole self, which includes our self as spiritual body. And spiritual self-awareness has a special importance in all this because a minimal element of it seems to be necessary if we are to *experience* what surrender means in any of our aspects, not only the spiritual but also the physical, emotional, and mental. Spiritual self-awareness is an essential part of the process by which eventually a person surrenders the whole self to the divine Source, so that he or she becomes a transparent channel for the divine Spirit, a luminous human being outshone by the divine Light. For Christians, this transfiguration happens through contemplative identification with Christ: 'All of us, gazing on the Lord's glory with unveiled faces, are being transformed from glory to glory into his very image by the Lord who is the Spirit. . . . For God, who said, "Let light shine out of darkness" has shone in our hearts, that we in turn might make known the glory of God shining on the face of Christ.'[15]

But these words of St Paul can be read as little more than a pious inspirational pep-talk unless, at the very least, we are aware of ourselves as spirit in a spiritual realm. How can we begin to have such an awareness? Concerning this, contemporary Christianity provides little counsel. Yet if we draw on some of the largely lost resources within our Christian tradition and if we have the humility to sit at the feet of teachers from non-Christian traditions who do provide wise counsel, we can readily come to know in our own experience a great deal concerning spiritual reality. Indeed for many people the initial process is relatively easy: becoming aware of the various energy centres of the physical body, beginning to see or to feel other people's energy fields or spiritual bodies, learning how to channel healing energies to others, getting into contact with discarnate spirits who can help us or whom we can help, discovering the blurred boundaries between self and others in the spiritual realm plus the blurred agencies ('I yet not I'). None of this by itself leads to God, and all of this, like any human endeavour, can be perverted into a mere ego-trip. Yet it provides the necessary though elemental basis for what can follow: the arduous process of radical transformation or transfiguration in which we gradually uncover and surrender whatever prevents our being lived by God, resonating and channelling the divine love.

In such a process we Christians can draw on resources of spiritual wisdom from both our own heritage and non-Christian traditions. What distinguishes our path is the privilege of identifying with the risen Jesus Christ in his completed Transfiguration and thereby in his healing and liberating identification with the sick and the poor and the oppressed—other dimensions of Christian life which I have neglected in this necessarily one-sided essay.

---

[15] 2 Cor. 3: 18–4: 6, New American Bible translation. Concerning a luminous human being *outshone* by the divine Light, see the non-Christian spiritual teacher, Da Free John: 'I surrender body and mind and all self-attention to the Living God ... Who Shines above the heads of those who are Awake, Transforming every part of them with Heart-Light, Who is the Transcendental Heart, the Eternal Mystery, the Wonderful Truth, the Unyielding Paradox that finally Outshines the souls of all beings, every part of the body-mind of Man, and all the possible places in the worlds of experience' (*Compulsory Dancing* (Clearlake Highlands, Calif., 1978), 141).

14. The Historical Jesus and the Theology of the New Testament

ROBERT MORGAN

WHEN George Caird died suddenly on Easter Eve 1984, he had written only a part of his eagerly awaited *New Testament Theology*. How well the rest can be constructed from lecture notes and other sources remains a matter of hope.[1] Meanwhile, one way in which friends and former colleagues can honour his memory is by continuing a discussion in which his own last word is not yet public: on the scope and character of a New Testament theology, as this is illuminated by the central structural decision whether to include a historical reconstruction of the ministry or teaching of Jesus. Major recent and reprinted New Testament theologies diverge sharply in shape and proportions. Some evoke the traditional 'Lord and apostle' shape of the canon with an entire first volume on 'the history of the Christ' (Schlatter), or 'the proclamation of Jesus' (Jeremias), or 'the ministry of Jesus in its theological significance' (Goppelt). At the other end Bultmann and Conzelmann in principle exlude the historical message of Jesus from New Testament theology, though Bultmann includes a brief sketch as a 'presupposition' and Conzelmann brings it back (also briefly) as part of 'the synoptic kerygma'.

New Testament theologies have generally tried to summarize those of their authors' scholarly conclusions which are considered most directly relevent to the life and faith of the contemporary Christian Church. For all their attempts to do justice to the historical distance of the New Testament, these textbooks have also been guided by the religious concern of their authors and readers to speak of God through their interpretation of their Scriptures. The phrase New Testament *theology* both reflects that aim and highlights the tension between historical critical scholarship and Christian *theology* which has been characteristic of the mediating discipline. When Wrede proposed renaming it 'the history of early Christian religion and theology',[2] he exposed his generation's tendency to abandon the tension and surrender theology

---

[1] At the time of Caird's death less than half of the first draft of his *New Testament Theology* had been written. The Oxford University Press and Mrs V. M. Caird have commissioned Professor L. D. Hurst with the task of editing and completing the work posthumously.

[2] *Über Aufgabe und Methode der sogenannten neutestamentlichen Theologie* (Göttingen, 1897), ET in *The Nature of New Testament Theology* (London, 1973), 116.

to history. The master of historical theology, F. C. Baur, had been able to set it on its 'purely historical' foundation because for him the history of religious ideas was the disclosure of divine reality. But once this consistently historical conception was cut loose from Baur's Hegelian metaphysics it drifted into a positivistic historiography which had no intrinsic connection with theology. Wrede was only acknowledging and calling for clarity about what had happened in biblical scholarship.

But most German biblical scholars still thought of themselves as theologians. Working in theological faculties with ecclesiastical responsibilities they were under some pressure to forge connections between their historical scholarship and the responsible leadership in the Church for which their students were preparing. The challenge implicit in Wrede's position was therefore taken up after the First War in renewed efforts to do *theology* through the interpretation of Scripture. Bultmann accepted Wrede's criticisms of the historical flaws in Holtzmann's classic, but himself renewed Baur's attempt to do *theology* through his own rather different way of penetrating the meaning of Christian origins.[3] His synthesis of New Testament scholarship (linguistic, literary, and historical), Dilthey's philosophy of history, Heidegger's language for analysing human existence, and a recognizably Lutheran type of kerygmatic theology, constituted a New Testament *theology* properly so called, with all the systematic and philosophical underpinning that theology requires.

Baur and Bultmann both rooted their New Testament theologies in major philosophical and theological options of their day because like many modern theologians they accepted Kant's account of the impossibility of traditional ways of speaking about God. Not all New Testament scholars have shared Baur's or Bultmann's (or Schlatter's) philosophical and theological competence in addition to their necessary linguistic, literary, and historical skills. Neither have they been persuaded about the propriety of introducing a modern philosophical apparatus into their New Testament theologies. This has always been a factor pressing the discipline toward's Wrede's 'purely historical' programme. Doing *theology* through one's interpretation of the New Testament involves these wider questions, once the difficulties of simply repeating traditional doctrinal language are recognized. Only very unmodern theologians can do New Testament *theology* today without attention to philosophical theology, because only they can naïvely as-

---

[3] He indicates the close relationship of his own existential interpretation to Baur's in 'Zur Geschichte der Paulus-Forschung,' *TRu* NS 1 (1929), 26–59, reprinted in K. H. Rengstorf (ed.), *Das Paulusbild in der neueren deutschen Forschung* (Darmstadt, 1964), esp. 310.

sume that the New Testament assertions coincide with their own beliefs. Once the distance between the ancient and the modern world is fully acknowledged, hermeneutics becomes essential for any theological interpretation of Scripture. Naïve theological use of Wrede's purely historical view of the discipline, common in the heyday of the 'biblical theology' movement, could in any case only be sustained where Wrede's critical conclusions were resisted. When the historical dyke built by learned conservative scholars against radical criticism began to crack, and historical differences between Jesus and even early Christology were accepted, the theologies this had protected were an endangered species. Their vulnerability was exposed by biblical scholarship itself and could therefore not be ignored so easily as earlier philosophical criticism had been. Hermeneutics has now been taken up by conservative as well as by radical biblical theologians.

On the other hand, Wrede's purely historical view of New Testament theology remains attractive to the positivist and empiricist mindset of both liberals, who are impatient of the claim of ancient texts to instruct them in anything that ultimately matters, and of conservatives who prefer their revelation tangible—if not in clearly formulated propositions then in hard historical facts. It has also been encouraged by a secularism that wanted university theology restricted to the history of theology and (incongruous alliance) by the deep-rooted English optimism about the apologetic potential of historical research.

There are also more sophisticated reasons for preferring Wrede's conception. Krister Stendahl's restriction of biblical theology to its historical and descriptive dimensions,[4] assigning the normative aspects of scriptural interpretation to subsequent applications, was theologically motivated in part by the concern to preserve Scripture's capacity to surprise the Church by saying something different from what was expected. Whether or not it is an adequate theory for interpreting religious, philosophical, or literary texts, this two-stage model, which distinguishes sharply between what the text once meant and what it means to me now, was a healthy corrective to both the conservative ecclesiastical bias of the 'biblical theology' movement and the equally ideological tendencies of existentialist theology, not to mention materialist and psychoanalytic theologies. Finally, partly for lack of any comparable synthesis, even New Testament theologians most sympathetic to Bultmann's aims have lately placed more emphasis upon the historical than upon the hermeneutical dimensions of their discipline. Nevertheless, as these various uses of Wrede's position show, the

---

[4] 'Biblical Theology, Contemporary' in the *Interpreter's Dictionary of the Bible*, i (Nashville, 1962), 418–32. Reprinted with some further comments in *Meanings* (Philadelphia, 1984).

practical theological interest of this mediating discipline has remained a defining characteristic.

It follows from this practical aim that the decision about what to include depends upon what the theological interpreter considers religiously important, as well as on what the texts are thought to be saying. Disagreement over whether to include a section on the historical Jesus stems from a difference of opinion about the theological importance of the 'historical Jesus' which runs deep through contemporary Christianity.

It is possible to argue quite simply that an interpretation of the New Testament documents which aims to further their theological witness should be guided by the fact that the 'historical Jesus' is a modern construction not envisaged by the evangelists, and that one should not be sidetracked or 'introduce into the text any alien problems'.[5] Admittedly the four accounts of Jesus' ministry form an important part of the New Testament and must be given due weight in any interpretation of this collection of writings. The ministry of Jesus is also important for most Christians' understanding of their faith, and this is a further reason for giving it prominence in a New Testament theology which seeks some correspondence between the interpreter's own theological interests and the texts given in the tradition. But precisely here lies the central problem of a modern New Testament theology, which may be summarized as the necessity and the impossibility of including the 'historical Jesus'.

Even though the modern historical quest was unknown to the evangelists and remains unimportant to most believers today, the necessity of theologians attending to anything that historians can say about Jesus is widely recognized. However uncritical they may have been, believers have always known that the ministry of Jesus was a historical fact, and once the question is raised most insist that it does broadly matter what really took place, even if the historical details are now lost. They would admit to some perplexity if it could be shown that Jesus had never existed, or that he was a bad man; or that the post-Resurrection proclamation of the disciples was a fraud, as Reimarus suggested. It is not easy to specify how much historical truth Christians require, nor even precisely why it is important to them. The saying that the Son of man *must* suffer was probably an early Christian inference from what *had* happened. Similarly, there is no a priori reason why salvation had to be achieved through a real human life and death, as opposed to a myth. But since Jesus *was* a historical figure, and Christians find salvation in this life and this death, they *are* interested in the actual history, and can

---

[5] H. Conzelmann, *An Outline of the Theology of the New Testament* (London, 1969), xviii.

reasonably expect a textbook which answers to their theological interest in the New Testament to include such good historical information
about Jesus as is currently available. Several recent New Testament
theologies have therefore reverted to some form of the older liberal
model classically exemplified by Holtzmann who began his presentation with a historical reconstruction of Jesus' teaching.

The objection to this procedure, and what some would call its theological *impossibility*, is that it substitutes a religiously indeterminate
historical presentation of Jesus for the Gospels and most Christians'
theological evaluation of him. That is not an objection to historical research as such, neither does it excuse theologians from facing the results
of this, but it poses a question about the propriety of including them in
a textbook which aims to interpret and advance the theological witness
of these classical Christian writings.

There would be no problem if the history of Jesus somehow included
Christology, or even if the history led smoothly into theology. But 150
years of liberal theologians' attempts to relate their historical reconstructions of Jesus to the Christian Church's faith in him give reasons
for doubting whether historical research leads smoothly into an adequate Christ of faith.[6] Historical constructions contain information
which a modern Christology must include, and may thus be admitted
by Christians to contain part of the truth about Jesus. The problem is
that they constitute not partial but complete interpretations of him,
and that these tend to compete with Christological interpretations. In
the ensuing clash between faith and historical reason the latter inevitably proves victorious, at least in the context of rational theological
argument.

In what remains the most interesting attempt to resolve the difficulties and exploit the opportunities posed for Christian thought by
modern history and philosophy, D. F. Strauss threw a lifebelt to the
sinking religion of his childhood. In the concluding dissertation to his
misnamed *Life of Jesus* ('critically examined', that is, destroyed) of 1835
he suggested that his cognitively strong Hegelian 'idea' could keep
theology afloat after historical criticism had torpedoed patristic Christology. But nobody wanted to rescue the dogmatic hull at the expense of
the person which it enshrined. In proposing a substitute for Jesus as the
subject of Christological predication, Strauss was abandoning Christian faith. If the metaphysical hull of classical Christian doctrine was
indeed beyond repair, it was better to preserve the human figure at the

---

[6] On their tendency towards a Christological dualism see my 'Historical Criticism and Christology: England and Germany', in S. W. Sykes (ed.), *England and Germany: Studies in Theological
Diplomacy* (Frankfurt, 1982), esp. 104.

heart of it all, if necessary in an idiom all but forgotten in the religious haze that surrounded his death. The 'historical Jesus' was thus the next move in theology, Strauss having failed to strangle the quest at birth by replacing the Christian affirmation of God in Jesus with a quite different suggestion of God in humanity as a whole. This novelty was naturally rejected, but it had the merit of recognizing the scale of the Church's Christological affirmation. Strauss could not apply 'God' language which spoke of reality as a whole to a single individual; he therefore substituted for Jesus of Nazareth what seemed to him a more appropriate subject for these metaphysical claims. His successors, by contrast, kept Jesus as subject, but reduced the Christological predicates to expressions of believers' faith. That was not quite such a break with traditional Christianity, but a break it certainly was.

In rejecting the modern 'historical Jesus' Strauss (with Hegel) may be said to have reminded his successors of the scope of Christology even as he abandoned the subject of Christian faith and clung instead to the 'idea' of the God-man. The refusal of subsequent liberalism to hear his warning marks a deep division in contemporary Christianity, and this is the issue in our problem of the structure of a New Testament theology. Those who place a historical reconstruction of Jesus at the head of their presentations are wittingly or unwittingly placing a question mark against all traditional Christian ways of understanding Jesus. Anyone who wishes to maintain some essential continuity with historic Christianity is bound to look for alternative ways of integrating modern historical knowledge of Jesus into New Testament theology, and so avoiding this head-on collision between Christological faith and historical reason.

The tension between a 'historical Jesus' and New Testament theology only became acute with the widespread acceptance of a fairly radical Gospel criticism. So long as conservative conclusions are maintained, a historical presentation of Jesus can remain more or less in tune with the synoptic evangelists and Christian consciousness. Schlatter's first volume is appropriately called 'The History of the Christ'. But once the full extent of the gap between the historical Jesus and the evangelists' witness is perceived, the Christological problems faced by nineteenth-century Protestant liberalism confront modern New Testament theology also. The issue has not been much discussed in relation to the structure of a New Testament theology, but it has always been present and provides the key to Bultmann's celebrated (or notorious) opening sentence, that 'the message of Jesus is a presupposition for the theology of the New Testament rather than a part of that theology itself'.

The brief argument with which Bultmann supports his structural decision sidesteps the important theological question of the significance of Jesus' earthly ministry, and the consequent relevance of the critical historical quest, for Christianity. But when, in the 1950s and 1960s, some of his pupils reopened the question of the historical Jesus, the central issue was again the theological significance of New Testament scholarship's historical investigation of Jesus. Bultmann's polemical stance in both contexts reflected Martin Kähler's protest against the liberals' 'so-called historical Jesus'.[7] He had himself sharpened Kähler's supporting argument about the speculative character of all these constructions, but for him as for Kähler the decisive objection was theological, not historical: constructions which stripped off the post-Resurrection Christology that the evangelists and their precursors and successors considered necessary for understanding Jesus aright inevitably conflict with what most Christians consider essentially Christian. Once the full difference between the historical reality of Jesus and the early Church's and evangelists' theological interpretations is acknowledged, purely historical reconstructions are inevitably at odds with traditional Christianity.

So much the worse for traditional Christianity, responded the liberals and their Enlightenment predecessors. The Incarnation has become incredible in the modern world and had better be replaced with a historical view of Jesus as a religious teacher pointing mankind to God. In retrospect, that judgement was at best premature—as the title of this memorial volume implies. Some apologetic arguments for the divinity of Christ were destroyed by historical criticism, and some traditional ways of understanding and expressing the doctrine were shown to be inadequate and dated, as Schleiermacher had already insisted. Kähler himself was critical of 'Byzantine' Christology and appreciated the clarification of Christian belief in Jesus' humanity brought by historical study. But what the fourth evangelist expressed in the confession of Jesus as 'my Lord and my God', what Christians have narrated in mythical terms ('he came down from heaven'), defined doctrinally ('true God, true man'), learned through legends (some of the miracle-stories of the Gospels, and the birth narratives), and from discourses placed on Jesus' lips ('he who has seen me has seen the Father'), what they have confessed in Christological hymns and enacted in rituals— the point of all this remains the heart and centre of Christian belief: that in having to do with Jesus we have to do with God.

This Christological belief is constitutive and definitive for orthodox

---

[7] Even his more constructive *Jesus* (1926) contrived to avoid Kähler's strictures. Bultmann interprets the teaching of Jesus kerygmatically as a call to decision, and leaves open the question of how adequately these earliest Christian traditions represent Jesus' earthly ministry. Outside the theological context, *Das Urchristentum* (1949) correctly sets Jesus historically in Judaism, but distorts primitive Christianity by underestimating its interest in Jesus.

Christianity, and in a sense its only 'dogma'. To replace it with a historical statement about Jesus, however true in its own terms, is no mere modification but a radical break with historical Christianity. Kähler did less than justice to the historical insights of the liberals, and Bultmann to the importance of these for Christology, but both recognized the startling novelty of the Enlightenment proposal and were surely right to resist it on account of its lack of essential continuity with what had hitherto been called Christianity. Like Ritschl, they recognized the potential of purely historical accounts of Jesus for subverting Christian faith. There was no reason to argue that the historical quest is impossible, nor that its results are theologically irrelevant; nor was Bultmann justified in assuming that any interest in this represented an attempt to prove the kerygma.[8] But they were surely right to insist that Christian faith and theology are concerned with the Christ of faith, whatever further questions then arise about the relationship of this to the historical reality of Jesus and (what is not the same thing) to such approximations as historical research can provide.

If that is true for Christology generally, it is doubly true for New Testament theology, since this is bound faithfully to reflect the documents it aims to interpret theologically. Christians who resist presentations of Jesus which remove all post-Resurrection theological interpretation can find rational support for rejecting such presentations from New Testament theology: namely, in the character and aims of the text being interpreted. The difference between historians' reconstructions of Jesus and theologians' interpretations of the New Testament is that the latter reflect the intentions of the texts whose witness they seek to advance.

Bultmann's argument for excluding the message of Jesus in any form from the theology of the New Testament is admittedly unsatisfactory. We have seen the necessity for including the ministry of Jesus and respecting the historical truth about it. The only question is how to present this in a way that avoids the liberals' repudiation of the evangelists' Christologies. Even Bultmann's argument is correct in that context and against those opponents. He points out that Christian faith did not exist until there was a kerygma of Christ crudified and risen. That is not a reason for excluding from Christology the historical ministry of Jesus, but it is a good reason for not substituting this for Christology. Even his misleading espousal of Wellhausen's tendentious (though historically true) dictum that Jesus was not a Christian but a Jew, can be defended as polemic against the Enlightenment proposal. It is necessary (against Bultmann) to relate Christian belief in the living Lord

---

[8] So E. Käsemann, *New Testament Questions of Today* (1964; ET, London, 1969), 35–65, esp. 47.

Jesus to the earthly reality investigated by historical research. But that is not a reason for removing what traditional Christology expresses and replacing it with a historical construction devoid of (and so in effect opposed to) Christology.[9] In resisting the 'historical Jesus' Bultmann and Conzelmann emerge as *fidei defensores*.

These considerations reflect Käsemann's theological criticism of Jeremias's continuation of the liberals' historical Jesus theology.[10] Those criticisms have even greater force against the form of Jeremias's New Testament theology (1971), however valuable its content may be. They apply also to Kümmel's inclusion of the historical Jesus as a 'major witness' to the theology of the New Testament (1972). Kümmel agrees with Käsemann that a historical portrait of Jesus is both possible and theologically significant. But, unlike Käsemann, Bornkamm, and Conzelmann, he writes a New Testament theology which includes a section on the historical Jesus. He apparently fails to see that the corrections to Bultmann and Kähler made by the 'new quest' do not weaken the theological reason for excluding historical reconstructions of Jesus from Christology and New Testament theology. It is one thing to be interested in the historical reality of Jesus, and to see there the criterion of the kerygma (Ebeling), but quite another matter to substitute a purely historical for a kerygmatic presentation of Jesus in this context.

Goppelt's attempt (1975) to meet Kähler's objection by refusing to separate the history of Jesus from the theological significance it had for those who followed him during the ministry also fails to solve the structural problem of including a historical picture of the ministry without subverting the Church's Christological confession. His criticism of the nineteenth-century quest misses the main point, which is not the trivial one that all reconstructions involve presuppositions, but the substantive one that any view of Jesus which abstracts from his saving death and Resurrection is theologically inadequate. That is true even of the

---

[9] *Editors' note*: George Caird's own approach to this perennial problem is worth mentioning. As he asks in the introduction to his *New Testament Theology*—

'But what of Jesus himself? Is he not our primary witness? According to Bultmann 'the message of Jesus is a presupposition for the theology of the New Testament rather than a part of that theology itself'. If by the theology of the New Testament we mean the ideas held by the various authors, this statement is obviously true, since Jesus lived, thought, taught and died before any of them set pen to paper. But if by the theology of the New Testament we mean the modern academic research into the ideas of the New Testament writers, then his statement puts the cart before the horse. *The message of Jesus is not one of the data of New Testament study; we have only the message of Jesus according to Mark, Luke, Matthew or John.* Research must begin with the documents and their theology and arrive *only at the end of its course* at the teaching of Jesus' [Editors' italics].

Caird's decision to place Jesus' message *last* in the outline grew out of a sensitivity to the problems of relating Christological considerations to the Jesus of history.

[10] Op. cit., 24–35.

disciples' pre-Easter perceptions (so Mark, rightly!). Goppelt's new factor, the pre-Easter reponse of the disciples, is only indirectly relevant to
New Testament theology. The discipline is concerned with the Christian truth about Jesus. That includes historical information, but above
all elucidates how Jesus is understood in the New Testament itself. This
was no doubt partly dependent upon how he was understood by his followers during the ministry, but that has no independent importance or
theological (as opposed to historical) interest today. Goppelt's presentation is more illuminating in practice than it is in theory, because his
conservative historical judgements bring an element of post-Resurrection
perspective into his account of the ministry. But including theological
interpretation in his 'historical' account of the ministry and (unlike
Kümmel) including a chapter on the death and Resurrection of Jesus
in this same section yields suspect history and inadequate theology, as
well as depending upon an improbable assessment of what is authentic
material. It also reduces the impact of each evangelist's witness, though
that must also be accounted to the uncompleted state of Goppelt's
manuscript when he died. Finally, the critical task of assessing each
evangelist's theology by reference to the historical reality of Jesus is
impeded by Goppelt's structure.

The importance of this critical function of historical knowledge of
Jesus in Christology and New Testament theology will be considered
below. The point to note here is that a theological criticism which uses
historical research as its instrument[11] presupposes the legitimacy of the
theological perspective which it seeks to correct. It is thus very different
from the historian's rationalist criticism which replaces Christological
interpretation of Jesus with its own description in purely human terms.

The reason why historical accounts of Jesus threaten Christology is
summed up by the opening sentence of Conzelmann's encyclopaedia
article, 'Jesus Christ': 'The historical and substantive presupposition
for modern research into the life of Jesus is emancipation from traditional Christological dogma on the basis of the principle of reason.'[12]
This declared hostility to traditional Christianity neither invalidates
the quest nor excuses theologians from taking it seriously—if only for
apologetic reasons. Since Reimarus produced a historical account of
Jesus and Christian origins which (if accepted) would falsify Christian
faith, theologians have had no choice but to meet him on his own
ground of rational investigation. They have had to write better, more
rational accounts which show that what can be known about Jesus by

[11] On this see M. Pye and R. Morgan, *The Cardinal Meaning: Buddhism and Christianity in Comparative Hermeneutics* (The Hague, 1973), esp. 90–100.
[12] *RGG*[3] (1959), ET, *Jesus* (Philadelphia, 1973), 5.

historical research is at least compatible, perhaps even congruent, with Christian faith. Bornkamm's *Jesus of Nazareth* shows that this can be achieved even where the Gospels are treated fairly sceptically, and even Bultmann claimed that the proclamation of the historical Jesus implied a Christology. But neither Bultmann nor his pupils saw this as reason for doing Christology 'from below'. There are strong reasons for *not* including such defensive apologetic constructs in positive Christian theological attempts to say who Jesus is and was. Purely historical constructions of Jesus are theologically at best defective and probably misleading. The historical information which (against Bultmann) must be included in Christology and New Testament theology has to be presented in those contexts in a way that does not undermine the faith that is being expressed.

This argument only sharpens the problem of how to include the historical information that must be included. But even this first step of excluding from a New Testament theology all reconstructions of the 'historical Jesus' may cause unease. A historical description of Jesus admittedly falls short of Christian confession because it mentions neither the Incarnation (in the broad Christian sense of a claim that Jesus represents God finally and uniquely) nor the Resurrection (vindication by God). But to call conscientious historical reconstructions of Jesus 'non-Christian', as is implied by our contrasting Christian (Christological) interpretations of Jesus with historical ones, must arouse the suspicion of pitching faith against reason, which good theology seeks to avoid. Most Christians would assume that whatever historical truth about Jesus can be unearthed ought to illuminate their faith. So far as it goes such information is valuable; to *contrast* it with Christian belief is counter-intuitional. This reaction can be supported by the testimony of many Christians whose faith has been nourished by historical accounts of Jesus.

This last observation suggests that Christians typically read these books through the lens provided by their own Christology. Since both history and Christology refer to the same Jesus, historical accounts can be read from the perspective of a religious pre-understanding. Information quarried from the Gospels and pieced together into a historical narrative is again taken piecemeal by believers and built into their own symbolically heightened mosaic. Christology is thus enriched or challenged by historical insights without being replaced by a rival perspective.

The legitimacy of Christian apologists assisting this process by writing histories which relate Jesus positively to post-Resurrection faith is not our present concern. Provided these are open to rational assessment by other historians there can be no objection in principle, though some theologians will prefer to keep their history free of apologetics.[13] But whatever one thinks about these historical accounts of Jesus, how Christians read them implies a solution to the structural problem of a New Testament theology.

The solution is for a New Testament theology to retain the evangelists' own Christological frameworks, but to build into its interpretations further historical information. This piecemeal insertion of reliable historical information does not aim at a complete historical account of Jesus, for which the data is in any case too fragmentary, but remains subject to the aims of theological interpretation. It is motivated and can be justified as the necessary second part of the theological interpretation of each evangelist. Firstly the interpreter must summarize the content of an evangelist's presentation of Jesus' ministry and teaching, elucidating the Christological framework within which it is set. This summary will contain some good historical information about Jesus, but will not identify it as such by separating it from what is historically less reliable. However, a critical New Testament theology cannot stop at a presentation of each author's thought. If it is *theology*, and not simply the history of early Christian theology, it must go on to assess each author's contribution. This task of critical evaluation provides the theologian with a theological reason to bring in further historical information. For one way that an evangelist's theology can be criticized is by reference to the historical reality of the man the evangelist is seeking to interpret.

This cautious use of historical criticism as an instrument of theological criticism, or critical theological interpretation, introduces further historical information about Jesus into what remains a Christologically oriented picture. It does not substitute a purely historical interpretation of Jesus for what remains a christologically orientated picture. It interprets the evangelists, but interprets them critically, where necessary challenging their interpretations by reference to the modern theologian's own understanding of Jesus, which is dependent upon the larger theological tradition and upon rational historical thought.

This process of theological evaluation and appropriation presupposes the validity of the evangelists' theological interpretations of Jesus in principle, even though it challenges them with the help of public historical information at particular points. Historical reconstructions of Jesus, by contrast, challenge the evangelists' Christological presentations wholesale and substitute a historian's Jesus. The intellectual prestige of historical research has tempted some to assume that this

---

[13] See L. E. Keck's criticisms of Bornkamm's *Jesus of Nazareth*, *JR* 49 (1969), 1–17.

'historical Jesus' is the real Jesus. That is a mistake fostered by the ambiguity of the phrase which can mean either the now largely inaccessible historical reality of Jesus, or the historians' approximations whch are as close as human reason can come to that on the basis of public evidence and inference. But these approximations are as surely interpretations of Jesus as the prescntations of the evangelists are, and they contain a large element of hypothesis and guesswork, as well as some 'hard' historical information.

These historians' constructions are in some circles preferred to those of the evangelists on the grounds that they remain within the limits of reason alone. Modern European rationalism judges them cognitively superior. Christians, however, continue to assert the presence of God in Jesus, disputed though this Christological claim is, and one task of theology, including New Testament theology, is either to defend these claims of faith from rationalist attacks or, if that is impossible, to advise the Church to alter or abandon its claims.

The present proposal is a defence of the Christian claim and a criticism of the liberals' surrender of Christology. The proposal depends upon distinguishing between the good historical information which is true and must be included in a New Testament theology, and the highly speculative reconstructions of modern historians, which can make no such high claims to truth or knowledge. These constructions are legitimate, indeed necessary, in historical research. But they are as fragile as Christological assertions, though for quite different reasons, and as they confront Christians' understandings of the influential reality of Jesus they are not necessarily more persuasive.

It once appeared that rational accounts of Jesus must overcome faith's interpretations because the theological interpretations of the evangelists actually contradicted what could be rationally known about Jesus. But the approach suggested here builds all this good historical material into modern Christology and critical interpretations of the evangelists. The conflict is thus no longer between faith and reason but between a reasonable faith and a faithless reason. The outcome will depend not on historical evidence, now respected by both sides, but on a total view of reality and one's own place within it.

To repeat: in the early days of modern historical study historians' interpretations of Jesus seemed more true than the evangelists' interpretations because at many particular points the history that these purported to relate was inaccurate. But these vulnerable points which once discredited the truth of the Gospels have now been covered. The Gospels are agreed to contain both historical information and the results of subsequent Christological reflection; the resulting amalgams sometimes contradict human reason's best approximations to the historical reality. Historians and theologians alike therefore now distinguish between the historical information they can quarry from the Gospels and the secondary, generally Christologically motivated developments. Historians also make the distinction, important to our proposal, between what they can know with some certainty and where they can only guess.

What the historian judges secondary, Christologically motivated, developments of the tradition are of primary importance to the Christian theologian, who shares the faith of the evangelists and aims to communicate this. New distinctions are necessary, to avoid unwarranted historical claims. Whereas the Gospels were once read as an accurate account of what happened, much of their material has now been reclassified as the vehicle and expression of post-Resurrection faith. But Christian theologians continue to assert what this material is saying: that in Jesus we have to do with God. The truth of this claim cannot be established by historical research. But finding God in Jesus was no more rationally defensible when Paul wrote 1 Cor. 1: 18–25 than it is today, whatever the additional problems faced by theistic belief in a secular culture. Interpretations of Jesus which speak of reality as a whole and make serious moral claims upon their hearers (and speakers) naturally come harder than historical interpretations which profess metaphysical agnosticism. But New Testament theology has to articulate what Christian faith is, not replace it with what modern positivists and empiricists might prefer it to be.

Historical research cannot establish Christology. It might even erode or conceivably destroy it. If Jesus were discovered to contradict anything that Christians can believe about God[14] (beyond what has always been implied by the fact of his humanity), then traditional Christianity would be falsified, and depending on what the historians discovered there might be a case for basing a new religion on the historical Jesus. Since this has not happened, and only some historically conditioned Christological formulations have been discredited by rationalist criticism, it is possible to retain the traditional Christian framework for understanding Jesus, and to incorporate the new historical information into that.

An orthodox New Testament theology[15] must therefore reject the

[14] Even the doctrine of God might be modified as a result of historical study. The Christian understanding of God is partly shaped by how the story of Jesus is heard, which varies somewhat from age to age. This small element of plasticity allows developments in faith's understanding of Jesus to be incorporated without abandoning the fundamental Christian assertion of the presence of God in Jesus.

[15] Alan Richardson's much criticized remark about some New Testament theologies being

liberals' break with historic Christianity and retain the New Testament writers' Christological frameworks, introducing modern historical knowledge piecemeal, in and through critical assessment of each evangelist. This approach enables us to include relatively secure historical knowledge while excluding the more speculative constructions necessary for writing a historical narrative. These hypotheses which bind the fragments of evidence into a meaningful whole belong to the historian's art, but cannot claim to be more than possibly true and therefore have no particular claim to be included in a Christology or a New Testament theology. This does not mean that they are unimportant. New Testament theologians need some provisional historical sketch of Jesus' ministry in their minds as they interpret the Gospels. It helps them to make sense of the material and to assess each evangelist's use of it. But it is mental scaffolding, helpful in the construction of a critical theological interpretation of each evangelist, not part of the final product, which includes only those pieces of hard historical information which the scaffolding enabled the theologian to place.

The Christological accounts of Jesus contained in a critical New Testament theology differ from the interpretations of historians while including their good historical information. But these differently motivated constructions speak of the same Jesus. They therefore confront and challenge one another in contemporary New Testament scholarship. The New Testament theologian's first task here is to demolish the historian's claim to possess 'the truth' about Jesus, and so to make room for Christological claims which assert a fuller and obligatory truth about Jesus, not simply an optional preference of believers. The aim of this essay in prolegomenon to New Testament theology is to propose a shape for the discipline once purely historical reconstructions of Jesus have been banished from its domain.

The argument thus far has accepted the main point of Kähler and Bultmann against the liberals, but also that of the 'new quest' against Bultmann. Kähler's kerygmatic emphasis upon 'the preached Christ' (of faith) was taken over by the early Barth and by Bultmann to stress the divine act in Jesus. But they achieved this at the expense of its human content. Barth and Bultmann recovered the grammar of traditional Christology (truly human, truly divine) at the price of 'no longer knowing Christ according to the flesh' (misusing 2 Cor. 5: 16). Barth subsequently corrected this Christological deficiency and indirectly influenced Käsemann, Bornkamm, and Fuchs, who later sought to cor-

orthodox and others heretical has the merit of indicating that a New Testament theology is a theological interpretation, and so is open to such description. But Richardson misplaced the labels when he judged Bultmann heretical.

rect their still too Kierkegaardian teacher by renewed attention to the
Synoptic Gospels and the historical ministry of Jesus. However, these
properly kerygmatic theologians had no desire to revert to the liberals'
displacement of Christology. It was actually rather appropriate that
their discussion petered out when it had established that the historical
investigation of Jesus was both possible and theologically necessary.
Bornkamm wrote a fine book and Conzelmann an article, but both
ensured that these would not replace Christology. Engaging in historical research and reaching some fragmentary conclusions is part of the
work of Christology. Total success in this (were it possible) would presumably remove all mystery from the historical figure and so weaken
the pressure towards symbolic heightening (expressed in Christology)
experienced by the earliest disciples and their successors.

But why should a New Testament theology begin with the kerygma
theology, and he did not place his encyclopaedia article on Jesus at its
head. But neither did he relegate it to the presuppositions of the discipline. By including it as part of his section on the 'synoptic kerygma' he
respected Bultmann's injunction that 'theological thinking—the theology of the New Testament—begins with the *kerygma* of the earliest
church, and not before' (Bultmann, i, section 1).

But why should a New Testament theology begin with the kerygma
of the earliest Church, rather than with its proper business of interpreting the New Testament writings? In including the necessary preparatory work in their finished products Bultmann and Conzelmann both
continued to pay tribute to Wrede's purely historical conception. But
Wrede was discussing a different (though overlapping) discipline. He
disowns both parts of the phrase, 'New Testament' and 'theology'.

Including the necessary historical scaffolding in the finished product
is most clear in Bultmann's inclusion of extra-canonical witnesses,
namely the Apostolic Fathers. It is true that the New Testament theologian must be a historian, and cannot understand the New Testament
adequately without paying the close attention that Wrede devoted to
the Apostolic Fathers. It is also true that Bultmann does not introduce
the Apostolic Fathers in their own right, but to build up a picture of the
development after Paul. Nevertheless, this has the effect of focusing on
the period rather than on the canonical texts. That is reminiscent of
Wrede's quip about no New Testament writing being born with the
predicate 'canonical' attached (op. cit., 70). Wrede's remark was relevant to 'the history of early Christian religion and theology', but is
quite irrelevant to New Testament theology, which (as the name
implies) focuses on the collection of writings designated canonical by
the Christian community.

This same canonical principle, which does not limit the range of material to be studied historically, but does prescribe what documents the theologian has to interpret as guidance for the contemporary Church, rules out independent sections on 'the kerygma of the primitive community and the Hellenistic community' (Conzelmann's Part I) and 'the synoptic kerygma' (his Part II).[16] Again, the historian inside every New Testament theologian attends closely to all this. No historically responsible study of the New Testament today can avoid trying to reconstruct the history of early Christian religion through the history of traditions. But this is no reason for including such preparatory work or scaffolding in one's theology of the New Testament. The task of this theological discipline is to interpret the canonical witnesses theologically, and so inform the life and thought of the Christian Church. The evangelists cannot be adequately understood or assessed apart from their prehistory. But it is Matthew, Mark, Luke, and so on, or rather the New Testament documents bearing their names, which constitute the New Testament. The material of Q, M, L, and so on, has been incorporated into the writings of the evangelists, and our understanding of the evangelists is enriched by identifying (however hypothetically) the traditions they used, and studying their redactional activity. But the theology of Q and the rest is not itself part of the theology of the New Testament. These pre-canonical stages belong to its historical presuppositions.

The beginnings of Christian theology are of interest to the historian, and thus indirectly relevant to New Testament theology. But to make these hypothetically reconstructed early experiments normative for Christian faith and life today would be an extraordinary novelty.

The canonical principle leaves a few loose ends, such as textual variants (notably Mark 16: 9–20, John 7: 53–8: 1) which may be considered canonical but are not part of the canonical evangelists' compositions and therefore at best peripheral to New Testament theology.[17] The same principle of identifying the witness applies where the probabilities are more finely balanced. Thus scholars who believe there are redactional additions in the fourth Gospel, or glosses in Romans, are right to exclude these from their interpretations of John and Paul. New Testament theology is based on the canon, but does not read it uncritically. However, its task of interpreting the canonical documents excludes both their prehistory and their textual post-history, even

---

[16] Some brief account of these will appear in the exposition and criticism of Luke's narrative theology.

[17] This proposal thus stops well short of the canonical criticism of B. S. Childs, while sharing its ecclesial orientation.

where (Mark 16: 9–20) this post-history probably belongs to the process of canon formation. The canon has a harmonizing effect within Christian consciousness, but theological interpretation instructs the community by attending to the individuality of particular witnesses. If a witness is judged theologically defective the critical theological interpreter can express this judgement without the help of earlier ecclesiastical redactors.

A more important 'loose end' left stranded by the approach advocated here is the Old Testament. Orientation to the canon must face the objection that there never was a New Testament scripture without the Old. A New Testament theology must therefore become a Christian biblical theology. But contrary to current proposals for this a Christian biblical theology can only be a New Testament theology. Christian interpreters' understanding of the Old Testament should ideally be built into their theological interpretation of the New. The practical difficulties and architectural problems cannot be elaborated here. Mention of the canonical principle in New Testament theology simply arose, in passing, out of the case for excluding the 'historical Jesus' from this discipline.

In the structure proposed here all the available historical information about Jesus is found in the same places as in the New Testament itself: buried in the theologies of the four evangelists and exposed by the critical interpreter. Since the evangelists constitute four of the (arguably) seven major witnesses that should dominate any New Testament theology, their accounts of Jesus' ministry and Passion, and particularly his teaching according to the Synoptic Gospels, will receive due prominence in an interpretation that respects their narrative character and content. But critical theological interpretation involves assessment, and it is here that a theological role for historical knowledge has been identified and a method for inserting it without cutting across the Christological grain of the documents being interpreted proposed. The Gospels are interpreted and evaluated in terms of their Christological aims. But since they aim to speak Christologically of the man Jesus their interpretations can be criticized by reference to independent information (gained by historical methods) concerning Jesus. Thus John's alleged docetism can be criticized through reference to his astonishing freedom with the tradition, or Matthew's alleged legalism by denying the authenticity of certain material. Both these evangelists must be criticized for their treatment of the Jews, and this can be done by criticizing their history at certain points.

This piecemeal approach allows modern historical judgements to be introduced individually and with due awareness of their often uncertain character, whereas a historical reconstruction necessarily includes more than can be known. But, above all, this approach avoids substituting a non-Christian interpretation of Jesus for a Christian one. The canonical emphasis in our proposal for a New Testament theology might seem to give Scripture priority over the Lord. In fact it is designed (as is Scripture itself) to protect Christology, which is lost if a 'historical Jesus' is preferred to the Lord of faith. The method of introducing critical historical judgements at the secondary stage of assessment, after the evangelist's message has first been interpreted in its own terms, allows that when necessary 'urgemus Christum contra Scripturam' (Luther). But it does not begin by substituting a human historical interpretation of Jesus for Jesus the Christ. Understanding a document precedes criticism in principle, though in practice they interpenetrate; most theological interpreters have a provisional historical idea of Jesus in their minds from the start. More importantly, like their readers they approach these texts with a theological view of Jesus which may be challenged or reinforced by further study. The most religiously valuable historical accounts of Jesus are very sparing in their appeal to historical causality. They can be absorbed piecemeal and integrated into their readers' Christological frameworks because they are written somewhat piecemeal. They are perhaps not intended to be so 'purely historical' as they appear. Goppelt repudiates the phrase, and Jeremias refers to 'the mystery of the mission of Jesus' (76). Even if Jeremias intended to refer to its historical obscurity he has been read with a fuller religious seriousness. There is a place for such apologetic books, as well as for historical works like those of Caird's Oxford colleague Dr Geza Vermes, and his successor in Dean Ireland's chair, Professor E. P. Sanders, which abjure all apologetic interests.

But there is no room for either (*pace* Jeremias) as part of a New Testament theology.[18] Our argument has been that this discipline should

[18] *Editors' note:* George Caird was sympathetic to this twofold warning. While he was less attracted than some to the lure of historical scepticism (he believed firmly that the task of the modern scholar who tries to reconstruct the original message of Jesus is not hopeless), he maintained that a New Testament theology should be sensitive to the problems of recreating past events on the basis of testimony. It should seek rather to set up a *dialogue* ('apostolic conference') between the New Testament writers which allows each, in his turn, to give his own understanding and interpretation of the event. This 'conference' model likewise allowed little room for apologetic concerns. As he says in the introduction—

'It is one thing to ask what the New Testament teaches, and quite another to ask whether that teaching is credible to ourselves or to others. The nineteenth century writers of lives of Jesus assumed that if they could strip from the gospel story the accretions of ecclesiastical dogma they would find a Jesus in whom it would be possible for a rational person to believe. More recently Bultmann, believing that even the earliest gospel was couched in thought forms and language which make it unacceptable to 'the modern mind', has demanded the demythologizing of the New Testament. But to make the New Testament intelligible is not the same thing as making it credible.'

follow the logic of the New Testament authors and their ancient and modern Christian readers. The reason is that, contrary to Wrede's conception, New Testament theology, like other forms of theology, is a matter of faith seeking understanding of its object, using whatever rational instruments are available to help it. Historical criticism is one such *Hilfswissenschaft*. Generations of Oxford undergraduates have learned how to use these instruments but have also learned of the New Testament theologian's witness to the glory and the humility of Christ as this was expressed in the work and in the life of George Bradford Caird.

15. An Orthodoxy Reconsidered: The 'End-of-the-World Jesus'

MARCUS BORG

IN an essay written to honour the memory of a mentor, one is perhaps permitted to be more personal than in other scholarly essays. In this tribute to Professor George Caird, I wish to reminisce briefly and then to speak of a central emphasis of his thought which has greatly influenced my own work on the historical Jesus.

I first met Professor Caird at the beginning of Michaelmas Term in the autumn of 1965 in Oxford. For the duration of that academic year, I and another twenty-three-year-old American student, Hugh Macmillan, met with him twice weekly in his study on the Mansfield College quad. Each time, one of us presented a twenty- to thirty-minute paper, and Dr Caird then responded for the remainder of the hour. The experience was both exhilarating and intimidating. From it we learned much, especially two things: the difference between receiving immediate verbal criticism from a senior scholar compared to the safe anonymity of turning in a written piece of work and the difference between reading secondary sources (which is what I had learned to do as an undergraduate) and working with primary sources. Or, to put the last point differently, we learned that there is a major difference between concentrating on what the history of scholarship says compared to listening to what the primary sources themselves say.

Professor Caird could be formidable. One day my compatriot reported that Homer had said 'Zeus is the rain', and Professor Caird rose quickly from his chair, dashed to a bookshelf high on the wall, his academic gown fanning out behind him, pulled down a volume from which dust literally flew as he opened it, instantly pointed to a passage and said, 'No—Zeus *is raining*.' Or perhaps the passages went the other way around; but I remember the scene vividly. We were impressed.

My indebtedness to Professor Caird is great, both for that year and for the three years from 1969 to 1972 when I wrote my doctoral thesis under his supervision. One of his persistent interests was the historical Jesus, even though much of his published work concerned other subjects. His interest, seen especially clearly in his lectures and in some of his briefer writings, was marked by two emphases. First, there was the rigour with which he insisted that the political and historical dimensions of Jesus' ministry be taken very seriously. In a letter to one of his former students, he wrote: 'We have failed in the quest for the historical Jesus precisely because we have left out of consideration all those factors which would enable us to see him as a genuinely historical figure.'[1] From this concern emerged the question, 'What was the *historical intention* of Jesus?' How was he related to the affairs of his time, and how were those affairs related to his purpose and intention? In his published work, perhaps this concern is best seen in his essay *Jesus and the Jewish Nation*.[2]

Second, he frequently called into question one of the prevailing orthodoxies of New Testament scholarship in this century: the widely shared conviction that Jesus proclaimed the imminent end of the world. This view of Jesus, which we may call the 'end-of-the-world-Jesus', is basically the Schweitzerian Jesus stripped of its more specific details (for instance, that Jesus deliberately sought death in order to 'compel' God to transform him into the Son of man and bring about the supernatural Kingdom of God), and transmitted to us through such giants as Bultmann, Kümmel, Jeremias, Käsemann, Conzelmann, and Bornkamm. Though the orthodoxy is expressed in a number of ways, the variations have a single claim in common: Jesus thought the end of the world was near, and this expectation accounts for the tone of urgency and crisis in his ministry.

Professor Caird never tired of sparring with this view, whether found within the walls of Oxford or in its German and North American variations. Among other jabs, he noted the inconsistency in the modern view which most frequently combined the 'end-of-the-world Jesus' with an extreme historical scepticism by giving priority to what it called the 'criterion of dissimilarity': one must exclude from the authentic teaching of Jesus elements which reflect interests or beliefs of the early Church or Judaism. If one uses this criterion, he stressed, then one of the elements most clearly slated for exclusion is the expectation of the end of the world, for that was obviously a belief of many in the early Church.

His challenge was, to a large extent, a lonely one. The orthodoxy remains firmly entrenched; the introductions to the New Testament most widely used in North American colleges and universities affirm it. Indeed, it is impossible, or nearly so, to find a textbook intended for a non-sectarian university or college audience in which this orthodoxy is

[1] Quoted from a letter written in 1972 to David Rhoads, now a professor of religious studies at Carthage College. His *Israel in Revolution: 6–74 CE* (Philadelphia, 1976) is an important study of the political and social setting of the first century in Palestine. Rhoads studied with Caird in 1964–5.

[2] G. B. Caird, *Jesus and the Jewish Nation* (London, 1965).

not assumed: the obvious exceptions are in fundamentalist and evangelical works, which are often marred by inadequately critical historical methodologies. It has become one of the 'assured results'. All disciplines need such orthodoxies, of course, in order to avoid always needing to begin at square one. However, developments within New Testament studies over the past several years together with my own exploration of paths upon which Professor Caird set me suggest that the time may have come for seriously reconsidering that orthodoxy. In this essay written in memory of Professor Caird and deeply indebted to him, I wish to continue the challenge which he mounted by drawing together three major elements into a single argument: the relationship between Jesus and his socio-cultural milieu, the virtual disappearance of the exegetical base for the 'end-of-the-world Jesus', and, thirdly, when once the orthodoxy is set aside, the more satisfactory *Gestalt* of the historical Jesus which emerges.

The first element is the increasingly detailed picture of the way the ministry of Jesus was related to his social and political environment which has emerged in recent years. This picture is the product both of having more data about the environment through the accumulation of specialized studies, synthesized in a number of important works in the last decade;[3] and of looking at the data in a new way, namely from an interdisciplinary perspective shaped by the wedding of the historical approach to the social sciences.[4]

The application of this approach with the greatest relevance to historical Jesus studies is Gerd Theissen's *Sociology of Early Palestinian Christianity*.[5] Theissen does not focus on the historical Jesus himself, but on the 'Jesus movement' in Palestine in the years between AD 30 and 70, that is on the followers of Jesus closest in time and space to the same Palestinian environment in which he carried on his activity. From the characteristics of that movement in its environment, it is but a short step to affirming that such were also characteristic emphases of Jesus himself, of the 'movement' during his lifetime. From Theissen's study emerges a picture of the Jesus movement as competing with other Jewish renewal movements for the allegiance of the Jewish people, each of them with its own response to the major social/political/economical/

---

[3] S. Safrai and M. Stern, eds., *The Jewish People in the First Century: Compendia Rerum Iudaicarum ad Novum Testamentum*, 2 vols. (Assen, 1974); the revision of Emil Schürer's classic *The History of the Jewish People in the Age of Jesus Christ*, ed. Geza Vermes *et al.* (Edinburgh, 1973, 79, 86). Also very important are the numerous works of J. Neusner and M. Hengel.

[4] For surveys, see Robin Scroggs, 'The Sociological Interpretation of the New Testament: The Present State of Research' *NTS*, 27 (1980), 164–79; Paul Hollenbach, 'Recent Historical Jesus Studies and the Social Sciences', SBL 1983 Seminar Papers, (Missoula, Montana), 61–78; Bruce Malina. 'The Social Sciences and Biblical Interpretation', *Int* 37 (1982), 229–42.

[5] Gerd Theissen, *Sociology of Early Palestinian Christianity* (Philadelphia, 1978).

cultural issues of the day. The Jesus movement, Theissen argues, was the 'peace party' and the 'inclusive party' within Palestine, concerns which most plausibly stemmed from Jesus himself. Thus his teaching was integrally related to the historical issues of his day.

In my own recently published book, which had its origin in the thesis I wrote under Professor Caird's supervision, I argue that the central controversies of Jesus' ministry concerned the historical shape and future of his own people.[6] The claim is grounded in a perception of the central cultural dynamic at work in the other Jewish renewal movements, the quest for holiness understood as separation from all that is impure. Systematically, in the controversies about table fellowship, the sabbath, tithing, purity laws, and the Temple and in parables and teachings related to those issues, Jesus criticized the quest for holiness as blind, as well intentioned but unable to see that its programme for Israel was contributing to Israel's destruction, to its division into mutually hostile groups, and to a catastrophic collision with Rome. He deplored the rejection of the outcasts and embraced them; regarding the Romans, he rejected the path of armed resistance. In his entry into Jerusalem and his expulsion of the merchants from the Temple, he carried on the practice of prophets in his own history, who often performed 'prophetic acts' to symbolize or vivify their message. The first action pointed to the path of peace, the second to non-exclusion and rejection of the path of violence. So also his table fellowship with outcasts may have been a prophetic action with not only religious but also political-cultural significance. Moreover, like Jeremiah some 600 years earlier, he warned his people of the historical consequences of continuing on their present path: revolt, war, the destruction of Jerusalem and the Temple. In place of the quest for holiness as the content of the *imitatio dei* and the paradigm for Israel's corporate life, he called his people to the path of compassion: 'Be compassionate, even as your Father is compassionate' (Luke 6: 36).

Quite apart from particular conclusions, an often overlooked result of these and similar studies is a claim of considerable importance: the more we know about Jesus' environment, the more connections we can see to that which he emphasized in his teachings and actions. That is, from the fuller picture of the environment emerges a clearer glimpse of Jesus' own historical intention—what he himself intended, what he saw his mission to be. What did he intend? The increased attention to the socio-political setting increasingly suggests that he intended the trans-

[6] Marcus Borg, *Conflict, Holiness and Politics in the Teachings of Jesus* (New York and Toronto, 1984). For the quest for holiness as the cultural dynamic of first-century Palestinian Judaism, see 51–72; for Jesus' ministry in this context, see 73–200.

formation of Israel, not the preparation of a community ready for the imminent end of the world. Of course, the two intentions (transformation of Israel, preparation of an end-time community) need not be exclusive of each other; even millenarian movements may relate themselves to society. But the kinds of concerns present in the ministry of Jesus, both in his teaching and actions, suggest a continuing historical community rather than the abolition of historical community through apocalypse.

Although the clearer picture of Jesus' environment and of his relationship to historical issues of his day does not in itself necessarily require the abandonment of the 'end-of-the-world Jesus', a second major element in the argument directly attacks the exegetical basis for the orthodox view and sketches a different picture of the crisis which faced Israel. According to the scholarly orthodoxy, the crisis was the imminent end of the world. What has become the 'orthodox view' rightly saw the element of crisis running throughout the synoptic tradition, which its nineteenth-century predecessors had largely overlooked, and then identified that crisis as the coming of the 'end events' of resurrection, last judgement, the transformation of all things—a supernatural Kingdom of God to be brought in by a supernatural Son of man coming on the clouds of heaven. Jesus believed this was imminent. But the textual basis for this view is very seriously undermined by recent research on the 'Son of man' sayings and by an examination of the synoptic 'threat' tradition.

Increasingly within New Testament studies, the 'coming Son of man' sayings, on which the orthodox view is largely based, are no longer seen as part of the authentic teaching of Jesus and instead are seen as the product of a process of Christian reflection and interpretation after Easter. A number of elements have contributed to this emerging consensus. In England, the formidable Aramaic specialist Geza Vermes (like Caird, also at Oxford) has argued convincingly that the phrase 'son of man' in Aramaic had no pre-Christian titular usage and indeed, given its common idiomatic use, could not have been heard by the hearers of Jesus as having a titular meaning. Jesus therefore could not have used it as a 'title', either to refer to himself or to a supernatural figure other than himself (though he may have used it idiomatically as a common circumlocution to refer to himself).[7]

In addition to Vermes's argument on linguistic grounds, there is the lack of evidence for its titular usage among the manuscripts discovered at Qumran, including the continuing absence of any fragments of the

---

[7] Geza Vermes, *Jesus the Jew* (New York, 1973), 160–91; and *Jesus and the World of Judaism* (Philadelphia, 1983), 89–99.

Similitudes of Enoch, where the phrase appears in any apocalyptic context. In the United States, Norman Perrin, in many ways the authoritative voice in North American historical Jesus scholarship in the decade before his death in 1976, argued that the 'coming Son of man' sayings are the product of Christian scribal interpretation of Dan. 7: 14.[8] These strands of evidence and argument have converged in the growing conviction that the 'coming Son of man' sayings are not part of the teaching of the historical Jesus. Yet these are precisely the sayings which link the Son of man to the 'end of the world', which speak of a supernatural figure coming on the clouds of heaven, of judgement, of the 'collapse' of the created order. Without them, the basis for saying that Jesus expected the end of the world becomes very slim.

Such is also the conclusion pointed to by a comprehensive examination of the synoptic threat tradition, which I have done in detail elsewhere.[9] The procedure is very straightforward and yields striking results: one simply reads through the synoptic tradition and collects all the threats, that is all the warnings about the future. Discounting parallels, there are sixty-seven such threats, found in a variety of forms and in all strands of the synoptic tradition: ten in Mark, twenty-five in Q, twelve in L, and twenty in M.

Of these, the threats peculiar to Matthew have a distinctive quality that sets them apart from the rest of the synoptic tradition. They regularly point to the eternal fate of the individual: he will be liable to judgement, liable to hell, condemned on the day of judgement, thrown into the furnace of fire where there will be weeping and wailing and gnashing of teeth, cast into the outer darkness. Unique to Matthew, this emphasis is presumably due to Matthaean redaction. The exceptions to this pattern in Matthew are found, interestingly enough, in the parables peculiar to Matthew.

Thus, excluding special Matthew but including the Matthaean parables, fifty-four threats remain in the synoptic tradition. These fall into two major groups. Twenty-two are threats of unidentifiable content, in which the threat is either expressed in very general terms (for instance 'wrath to come', 'will not be forgiven') or left in the imagery with which the saying or parable began (for instance salt will be thrown out, the ruin of the house will be great, the fig tree will be cut down, and so on). None of these threats provides any basis for saying *what* the danger or crisis is. That can be decided only be examining the other major group, the threats of identifiable content. There are thirty-two of these, falling into three roughly equal categories: nine have a

---

[8] Norman Perrin, *Rediscovering the Teaching of Jesus* (New York, 1967), 164–206, esp. 173–85.

[9] Borg, op. cit. n. 6 above, 201–21. The threats are tabulated in the appendix, 265–76.

'taken away/given to others' pattern, eleven warn of a future filled with historical destruction, and twelve speak (apparently) of a final judgement.

Neither of the first two categories contains any evidence for saying that Jesus expected the imminent end of the world; indeed, both (especially the second) suggest that the crisis which animated the ministry concerned the historical future rather than the end of all things. The second set speaks of historical catastrophe, apparently still seen as contingent, rather than of an inevitable imminent end of the world: invasion, war, the destruction of Jerusalem and the Temple by military siege. The first set, 'taken away/given to others', need not necessarily point to a continuing historical order, but perhaps most plausibly does.

Thus the exegetical base for saying that Jesus expected the *imminent* end of the world resides in the third category of threats of identifiable content. Of these twelve sayings, half are 'coming Son of man' sayings. In the other six sayings, though they speak of one or more of the end events of final judgement, resurrection of those long dead, hell, and so on, *it is not said that this is imminent*. Especially illustrative here are four Q sayings:

Luke 10: 12 = Matt. 10: 15: I tell you, it shall be more tolerable on that day [the day of judgement] for Sodom than for that town [which rejects the message of Jesus].

Luke 10: 13–14 = Matt. 11: 21–2: Woe to you, Chorazin! Woe to you, Bethsaida! For if the mighty works done in you had been done in Tyre and Sidon, they would have repented long ago, sitting in sackcloth and ashes. But it shall be more tolerable in the judgment for Tyre and Sidon than for you [Capernaum is then similarly threatened.]

Luke 11: 31 = Matt. 12: 42: The queen of the South will arise at the judgment with the men of this generation and condemn them; for she came from the ends of the earth to hear the wisdom of Solomon, and behold something greater than Solomon is here.

Luke 11: 32 = Matt. 12:41: The men of Nineveh will arise at the judgement with this generation and condemn it; for they repented at the preaching of Jonah, and behold, something greater than Jonah is here.

These sayings indicate that there is a 'cosmic' strain in Jesus' eschatology: he did see history as having a final judgement at its boundary; like many of his Jewish contemporaries, he believed in the resurrection of the dead and the last judgement. Noteworthy, however, is the absence of imminence in these sayings. None of them says that judgement is *near*. Rather, *when* that judgement occurs, *when* the resurrection of people long dead—the queen of the South and the people of Nineveh—

occurs, at that judgement the verdict will fall with particular severity upon the people of 'this generation'. The connection to imminence is missing.

Thus the exegetical base for saying that Jesus expected the *imminent* end of the world becomes very slender: what remains are a few 'coming Son of man' sayings. Among the six which are threats (Luke 12: 8–9; Mark 8: 38; Luke 12: 39–40; Luke 17: 23–4, 37; Luke 17: 26–7; Luke 17: 28–30), the element of imminence is not unambiguously present. The element of imminence is most clear in two other 'coming Son of man' sayings, neither of which is a threat but which must be taken into account. In its context, Mark 13: 26–7 speaks of the coming of a supernatural Son of man on the clouds of heaven, to be expected in that generation. So also in its context does Matt. 10: 23, the passage which was so pivotal for Schweitzer: 'When they persecute you in one town, flee to the next; for truly, I say to you, you will not have gone through all the towns of Israel before the Son of man comes'.

But it is precisely the 'coming Son of man' sayings which modern scholarship increasingly views as not coming from Jesus. In short, the exegetical base for saying that the crisis animating the ministry was the expected imminent end of the world virtually evaporates. Only a small percentage of the synoptic threat tradition speaks of 'end-of-the-world' events, and even then most often does not mention imminence; the element of imminence is clearly present only in a few sayings, no longer commonly attributed to Jesus. Almost without realizing it, recent mainstream scholarship on the 'Son of man' has undermined the foundation of the 'end-of-the-world Jesus'.

In order for this undermining to be complete, one further element must be considered: the fact that many in the Church did expect the end and the judgement to be imminent. To speak personally for a moment, this was for years the most compelling reason for my accepting the orthodoxy. It seemed reasonable (to me, and presumably to many) to assume that, if people in the early Church believed the end of the world to be near, they must have obtained that conviction from the preaching of Jesus. But the assumption is both unnecessary and unlikely. Not only is the imminent end of the world absent from the synoptic threat tradition, but a more likely explanation of the Church's expectation can be found. It was, in all likelihood, the Easter event that triggered the belief that the end of the world was at hand. Within Jewish thought, resurrection (as opposed to resuscitation) was an event associated with the end of time. The Easter event, coupled with the outpouring of the Spirit, easily led to the inference that the rest of the 'end events' were at hand.

Moreover, it is worth noting that the Church did not expect the end of the world in an abstract way; they expected specifically *the imminent return of Christ*, which would, of course, include the final judgement. Their belief in the return of Christ most plausibly comes from the Easter event, not from any teaching of Jesus about the coming Son of man. The victim who had been elevated to God's right hand, known even beyond his death as a still-living reality, would return as the king and judge. It is also worth noting that the two major figures of the New Testament other than Jesus, Paul, and the author of the fourth Gospel, put the emphasis elsewhere. Though expressions of the expectation of the return of Christ are found in their writings, that is not the centre of their message. The picture of the early Church as a radically eschatological and therefore disappointed community goes beyond the sources.

In the history of scholarship, the narrow exegetical base of the 'end-of-the-world Jesus' became very broad through a series of extensions. The element of imminence was added to all those sayings which speak of judgement or of the coming Son of Man; the threats of unidentifiable content were filled with the picture of an imminent final judgement; the language of crisis running throughout Jesus' teaching was because of the nearness of the end; and the elements in the Gospels which imply a continuing historical order were attributed to the creativity of the early Church as it dealt with the non-arrival of the Parousia. From this emerged a *Gestalt* of Jesus: the eschatological prophet, calling his hearers to repent in the face of the end. His historical intention was to warn his hearers of the end or, alternatively, to invite them to ground themselves in God because the world was passing away. But when one sees how narrow the exegetical base is and reflects upon the actual content of the synoptic threat tradition, a different picture of the crisis and a more comprehensive *Gestalt* of the historical Jesus develop. If Jesus was not the eschatological prophet who proclaimed the imminent end of the world, who then was he, and what was his intention?[10]

To begin with the element of urgency, the Synoptics speak clearly about a deep crisis facing Jesus' contemporaries in particular. The synoptic threat tradition suggests that the crisis concerned the collective path of his people and the collective consequences of that path. In the divisiveness and violence and spiritual blindness which, from his point of view, had beset many of his contemporaries, he saw a path leading to historical catastrophe and suffering. Like an Old Testament prophet, he saw the crisis as simultaneously (to use what is at best an heuristic dichotomy) spiritual and historical: upon the ability to see, to

---

[10] The *Gestalt* which follows is sketched in the concluding chapter of my previously mentioned book, and is the subject of a manuscript in preparation.

be transformed, depended the fate of a generation. The spiritual condition of a generation (or of the religiously and politically powerful among them) had collective and historical consequences. This essentially 'prophetic' understanding of the crisis is more satisfactory both because it has a firmer and broader textual base than the 'end-of-the-world Jesus' and because it makes better sense of Jesus' words and actions, which frequently had a pointed connection to Israel's collective shape and course. With the intensity of consciousness characteristic of the prophets of Israel, Jesus sought to redirect his people's course, warning them of the consequences of their present one.

There has been a strong sense both within the Church and among New Testament scholars that one should not 'reduce' Jesus to a prophet. The reluctance is well founded, for the tradition reports that he was more than a prophet. To use categories drawn from the history of religions (which, like the social sciences, is increasingly contributing to a multidisciplinary view of the historical Jesus), he was also a holy man and sage.

The term 'holy man' refers to a person experientially in communion with 'the holy', the numinous, the power of the 'other realm'. Such a person not only intimately knows 'super-ordinary reality', but becomes a channel between 'the holy' and ordinary reality, a medium or mediator through whom the power of the holy flows into quotidian reality. Known in virtually every culture, they were also known in Jesus' tradition, pre-eminently in the ancient figures of Moses and Elijah, and also among his contemporaries in figures such as Hanina ben Dosa and Honi the Righteous (or 'Circle-Drawer'). As a holy man, he was a charismatic, a 'spirit-filled one', and a healer/exorcist. It is in the context of his activity as a holy man that the 'coming of the Kingdom' is to be understood, as one of the foundational Kingdom of God sayings suggests. Located in the context of an exorcism, the saying states:

Matt. 12: 28 = Luke 11: 20: If it is by the Spirit of God that I cast out demons, then the Kingdom of God has come upon you.

Rather than pointing to the imminent end of the world, the coming of the Kingdom of God refers to the power ($\delta \acute{v} v a \mu \iota s$) of the other realm active through Jesus the holy man. (In other contexts, the phrase may also refer to a community created by that power, or in which that power is known.)

He was also clearly a sage, a teacher of wisdom, with great insight, power, and artistry. Not only did he use the forms of the wisdom tradition (the proverb, parable, beatitude, and so forth), but he treated the central themes of the wisdom tradition. Most basically, he spoke about the two ways—the narrow way and broad way, the wise way and foolish way—and the path of transformation, of the need to ground oneself in God rather than in possessions, status, familial or national or religious identity. The heart needed to be transformed from having its treasure on earth to having its treasure in God.

This threefold understanding of the historical Jesus as a holy man, sage, and prophet is the third and final element in the argument against the 'orthodox' position. Compared to the portrait of Jesus as the eschatological prophet proclaiming the imminent end, this *Gestalt* provides us with a fuller picture, one which more comprehensively incorporates what we find in the synoptic texts themselves. In its picture of Jesus as a holy man, it accounts for the vivid awareness in the Synoptics of the 'nearness of the other world' (as opposed to the *end* of the world), for Jesus' authority as a teacher, and for his deeds of power. (Here again, the role of disciplines outside of New Testament studies may be noted: our awareness of the 'world' of holy men, of the content and texture of their experience, is due largely to studies in anthropology and phenomenology of religion). In its picture of Jesus as a sage, it accounts for the relatively 'timeless' character of some of his teaching; he did speak about the quality of God, the nature of the heart, and the path of transformation. In its picture of Jesus as a prophet, it accounts for the passionate concern with the historical path and future of his own people. Though he was more than a prophet, he was not less than one, urgently concerned with his people's corporate life, direction and future.

Professor Caird would, I think, be excited about some of the things in this essay and perhaps cautious about others. I do not know. In any case, this essay is offered as a tribute to my mentor, as an account of what I have come to glimpse about the historical Jesus because of paths whose direction he initially pointed.

16. Reflections on So-called 'Triumphalism'

C. F. D. MOULE

WHEN Haydn heard about the Battle of Aboukir Bay, he is said (probably apocryphally) to have added an entry of trumpets to the Benedictus of his D Minor Mass, the *Missa in angustiis*, now popularly known as the Nelson Mass. Subsequently, the composer and the Admiral exchanged gifts: Haydn gave Nelson his pen, and Nelson gave Haydn his gold watch. Eucharist and paean seemed to be in the same key. By contrast, the note of triumph was studiously kept out of the service in St Paul's Cathedral at the end of the campaign to recover the Falkland Islands, to the disgust of some of the public who wanted to sing militant hymns and shout 'hurrah!' (It was then that the same public discovered for the first time the existence of a 'peace version' of the National Anthem, though Churchmen had had it in their hymn books for decades.) The difference between the two occasions marks a revulsion in the Christian conscience from the idea that success in warfare is necessarily a gift from God. It registers a decisive repudiation of jingoism by Christians. Essentially, this is only the recovery of what has been at the heart of Christianity from the beginning; but at least it is a new awakening.

Awakening has come on a still deeper level also. It is not merely a matter of realizing that Yahweh of Hosts, the God of battles, is not the Father of our Lord Jesus Christ. More profoundly, it is a recognition that 'triumph' and 'success' may themselves be disastrously misleading words to describe love's endeavour. If, by definition, love takes ultimate risks, passionately throwing itself away in the dark, with no guarantee of success; if the very essence of love is to love with no certainty of being loved in return, if it means dying without any certainty of life, then the language of victory and success is in danger of trivializing that which it is supposed to acclaim. This consideration is thrust home by W. H. Vanstone's two fine books, *Love's Endeavour, Love's Expense* (London, 1977) and *The Stature of Waiting* (London, 1979 and 1982). Facile notions of the success of goodness, shallow presentations of Easter as a triumphant reversal of Good Friday, have come to be called by the regrettable but convenient name of 'triumphalism', and the thoughtful Christian is keenly on guard against it.

Rightly so; but when human language gropes for words to describe the indescribable, there is no expression that does not have its attendant drawbacks; and in resiling from 'triumphalism' there is a danger of losing the proper note of triumph from the Christian gospel. This essay, dedicated to the memory of a scholar whose precision and intellectual courage have set the highest standards, is intended to draw attention to two considerations which, though familiar, are perennially important in the face of this dilemma. The first consideration, to which George Caird's own book, *The Language and Imagery of the Bible*, is relevant, not least in its suggestive discussion of anthropomorphism, is this. The language of warfare, of conquest and victory, belongs among the many metaphors applied by Christians, from New Testament times onwards, to the work of God in Jesus Christ and, like the metaphor that it is, it must not be pressed beyond its proper function. The same applies to the biblical metaphor of washing and cleansing. The abolition of dirt ('Out, damned spot!') is a good analogy for what a guilty conscience longs for: 'though your sins are scarlet, they may become white as snow'. But the actual processes of forgiveness, repentance, and reconciliation—the mysterious work of God's love which engages the sinner's whole person with its relentless but gentle demands—are in the end not adequately matched by the action of an omnicompetent detergent. Impersonal metaphors can go only so far and no further towards illuminating personal realities. Therefore, we shall escape 'triumphalism' not by moderating the language of military success or royal dignity or radical cleansing. On the contrary, when used it should be used with abandon and zest. But what we must do is to recognize its function and so observe its limited scope, using the metaphor but not abusing it. Victory is a metaphor for success; but if it is allowed to imply success by main force, it hinders the presentation of a Christian gospel. If love 'wins', it is not by flattening the opposition, but by eliciting the good that is buried under self-concern, by redirecting the perverted, by liberating a person to be his true self.

The other consideration is this. While of course it is true that the deepest realities of life are incapable of proof—how could anyone prove that 'love never fails'?—nevertheless it is possible to point to very strong grounds for believing that the love of God in Jesus Christ did in fact create life out of death and love out of hatred. There is a sense in which 'success', that dangerous word, may with reason be applied to the outcome of the life and ministry of Jesus of Nazareth. He did see of the travail of his soul, and was satisfied.

I

When Christians began to look for words with which to express their faith, they naturally drew upon the Scriptures. These Scriptures—which Christians subsequently came to call the Scriptures of the Old Covenant—are full of battle language to describe the work of God, and they unashamedly ask for and proclaim success. Not only are there certain levels of Old Testament thought on which it is assumed that Yahweh will win literal and material victory for his people if they remain loyal to him, and that defeat in war must mean that their loyalty has failed. There are also the familiar passages where the language of conquest is applied metaphorically—for instance, to the work of creation. God the Creator, the God of light and order, is depicted in creation myth as subduing the monsters of chaos—Tehom, the great deep, Rahab the rager, Leviathan and Tannin, those primeval dragons. It is a theme of ancient religions generally, and Babylonian epic correspondingly has its battle between Marduk and Tiamat. When light and order overcome darkness and chaos, this is victory, this is success. So the New Testament represents Jesus as saying that he has witnessed the fall of Satan like lightning from heaven, and that he gives his disciples authority, like the psalmist in Psalm 91, to tread upon serpents (Luke 10: 18 f.). Paul looks forward to a time very soon when the God of peace will crush Satan under his people's feet (Rom. 16: 20), and when all other government and authority shall be abolished (1 Cor. 15: 24).

Revelation uses a spate of victory-language. It depicts war in heaven, when the dragon is thrown down (12: 7); and a climactic battle in which the triumphant Word of God rides forth with his white-clad armies to conquer the forces of evil (19: 11 ff.). Of the martyrs it is said that they conquered by the blood of the Lamb (12: 11). Disturbingly, the victory of Christ seems even to be depicted as a blood-bath (14: 20), though G. B. Caird, and, after him, J. P. M. Sweet, in their commentaries, argue powerfully that here the blood is not the blood of opponents but the blood of Christ and of the martyrs, which will ultimately be creative and constructive.

The same conquest-language, condensed from myth to metaphor, is exploited in the Johannine Gospel and First Epistle. Indeed, these, with Revelation, almost have the monopoly of words from the νικ-group. Outside this group of writings these words are sparse: Matt. 12: 20, quoting from Isa. 42, has 'leads justice on to victory' (νῖκος); Luke 11: 22 has 'when someone stronger comes upon him and overpowers him', in a parabolic saying; Rom. 3: 4, quoting from the LXX of Ps. 51, has 'conquer', in the sense of win in a law-suit (compare

Hebrew 'come out clean'); Rom. 8: 37 has 'overwhelming victory is ours' ($ὑπερνικῶμεν$) and Rom. 12: 21 has 'do not let evil conquer you, but use good to defeat evil'. All the rest belong to John, 1 John, or Revelation, and all, in one way or another, refer to the triumph of good or faithfulness or right belief over evil and falsehood. It is a metaphor not uncommon in Philo (for instance *All.* 2. 108 (metaphor from the Olympic Games), 3. 190, *Abr.* 244).

To the actual use of words of the $νικ$-group must be added, of course, all the expressions for power or authority which are applied to God or Christ or their followers. Such—besides those already quoted—are the promise to Peter that the gates of Hades shall not prevail (Matt. 16: 18), and the profusion of power-words in Ephesians, leading up to the Christian warrior's mastery and firm stand (Eph. 6: 13). J. S. B. Monsell's hymn, 'Fight the good fight', so beloved by militants who have not altogether come to terms with its metaphorical nature, is a pastiche of phrases of this sort, mingled with the competitive language of the Olympic games. As it happens, the opening phrase itself is the Authorised Version's mistranslation of what is not a military but an athletic metaphor in 1 Tim. 6: 12. Unambiguously military, however, is the campaign language of 1 Tim. 1: 18 and 2 Cor. 10: 3 f., as are 'soldier' and 'fellow-soldier', used metaphorically, in Phil. 2: 25, 2 Tim, 2: 3 and Philem. 2. Finally, the actual word $θριαμβεύειν$ occurs twice in the New Testament—at 2 Cor. 2: 14 and at Col. 2: 15. In both instances there is controversy over the exact meaning of the verb (lead *as captives* in his triumphal procession, or *as fellow-conquerors?*); but certainly the image is that of a victor's triumphal procession, and it is paradoxically applied to the strange work of God through the cross and through those who accept it.

All in all, the New Testament is not shy of the language of coercion, and a study of the word $ἐξουσία$ is instructive, for it points unequivocally to the conviction that God's authority is successfully exerted over authorities. In the temptation, Christ rejects the spurious $ἐξουσία$ offered him by Satan (Luke 4: 6, and the same sense in Matt. 4: 8 f., though without the word $ἐξουσία$). As a result, he can declare at the end of the story that all $ἐξουσία$ has been given him in heaven and on earth (Matt. 28: 18). So, too, the disciples are given authority over the unclean spirits (Matt. 10: 1, Mark 3: 15, 6: 7, Luke 9: 1). The Lucan saying (10: 19) about authority to trample on serpents has already been mentioned. In Col. 1: 13, the $ἐξουσία$ of darkness from which Christians are rescued is contrasted with the kingdom of God's beloved Son into which they are transferred. The language is that of a commando raid to free hostages.

The 'warlike language' of the Johannine writings, says R. E. Brown in his commentary on the Johannine Epistles (304), 'is at home in a dualism where the forces of darkness seek to overcome or to kill the forces of light ... The Johannine Community could have addressed to Christ the praise addressed to God in the Qumran *Scroll of the War between the Sons of Light and the Sons of Darkness* (1QM 11: 4–5): "The battle is yours and the power comes from you, not from us. Our strength and the power of our hands accomplish no mighty deeds except by your power and the might of your valor"'—a theme already familiar in the Old Testament. This warlike language, whether in a dualistic context or not, stands not only for man's dependence on divine help but also for the success of the divine forces: 'God does win in the end', it affirms. And in the New Testament such assertions are sometimes cast in the form of a peripeteia, to emphasize the surprise and paradox of God's road to triumph: what seemed defeat turned out to be victory; what seemed humiliation ended in glory. 'God has made this Jesus, whom you crucified, both Lord and Messiah' (Acts 2: 36); 'he died on the cross in weakness, but he lives by the power of God' (2 Cor. 13: 4); 'he humbled himself ... Therefore God raised him to the heights' (Phil. 2: 8 f.). Not seldom the New Testament adopts what might be called the victory-sign—a V-shaped pattern of descent to the depths followed by exaltation to the heights: a peripeteia from defeat to victory is woven into the texture of the gospel. But it is only a metaphor, with a strictly limited validity. If it stood alone, it would misrepresent the gospel, for the simple reason that the language of the reversal of fortunes from adversity to triumph suggests brute force, whereas the Christian good news is constructive and is concerned with personal relations into which coercion may not enter. Indeed, all the biblical metaphors relating to the processes of reconciliation suffer from some such limitation because they belong in sub-personal realms: conquest, cleansing, emancipation, acquittal, cancellation of debts, sacrifice, ransom—all are analogies borrowed from below the level of the fully personal. Applied metaphorically to the deeply personal reality of reconciliation between estranged persons, each of the metaphors performs some particular function in affirming God's ultimate success, in emphasizing the costliness of the process, in magnifying the sheer generosity of God, or in underlining man's inability to save himself. But to press them beyond their limited function is to court doctrinal disaster.

To safeguard against this, there are checks and balances built into the New Testament itself. What saves all expressions of victory from 'triumphalism' is not a sparing or muted use of them. It is the recognition that peripeteia—a story about the reversal of fortunes, and, as such, about chronologically successive circumstances—is only a device to illuminate one aspect of a reality in which there is no successiveness, for it is eternal and all its aspects coexist simultaneously. The 'descent' in the V-shaped story, and the apparent failure or humiliation, are not really preliminary to ascent and exaltation, for the eternal graciousness of God holds all together and simultaneously. The New Testament itself does not fail to make this point. C. K. Barrett (*A Commentary on the Second Epistle to the Corinthians* (London, 1973), 336), commenting on 2 Cor. 13: 4 ('. . . died on the cross in weakness . . . lives by the power of God') writes:

the weakness shown in his crucifixion, being a mark of his grace, is not an unfortunate lapse from strength but one aspect of the action God intended in his Son. Historically, he preferred crucifixion to the exercise of some kinds of power; he preferred crucifixion to the abandonment of the outcast groups of Palestinian society, with whose social and religious weakness he identified himself. Similarly, though it is true it is also inadequate to say that the resurrection was a signal manifestation of divine power . . . Christ is both weak and strong.

Similarly, the inadequacy of a one-sided statement is recognized in the well known *double entendre* used by the fourth evengelist when the word 'exalt' signifies both the uplifting of Jesus on the shameful cross and his uplifting in glory (John 3: 14, 8: 28, 12: 32, 34). In other words, the New Testament itself as it were flattens out the V-pattern. If the V-pattern helps to bring home the marvel of Christ's humility, a straight line puts the humiliation on the same plane as the glory, as though to say 'Marvel not, for the two are one'. It has even been proposed to interpret Phil. 2: 6 f. in a 'rectilinear' way, so as to mean: 'Christ did not reckon equality with God to mean grasping: instead, he emptied himself.' (See my 'Further Reflexions on Philippians 2: 5–11', in W. W. Gasque and R. P. Martin, eds., *Apostolic History and the Gospel* (Exeter, 1970), 264 ff., in which I revived a suggestion made by J. Ross in *JTS* 10 (1909), 573 f.). Subsequent research seems to have established that ἁρπαγμὸν ἡγεῖσθαί τι means, rather, 'to regard as *something to be taken advantage of*' (see R. W. Hoover, 'The Harpagmos Enigma: a Philological Solution', *HTR* 64 (1971), 95 ff.). If so, the sense of the passage remains 'rectilinear', though this sense is reached by a different route: it means that Christ interpreted God-likeness in terms of self-emptying rather than of *glorying* (see the full and illuminating discussion in N. T. Wright's article '*Harpagmos* and the Meaning of Phil. 2: 5–11', *JTS* 37 (1986)). But supposing that this is what Phil. 2: 6 f. was intended to mean, then it is significant that one would find the 'straight line' pattern there 'bent', only a few verses later, into the V-pattern, in 'therefore God has more than exalted him'. So it is that, in human thinking, the two patterns need to alternate.

Again, it is noteworthy that, in St John's Gospel, the word ἐξουσία, which has already been mentioned as affirming the divine authority, is subtly handled so as to fall into the same pattern as is indicated by the *double entendre* of uplifting on the cross and in glory. For what is the authority given to those who accept Christ? It is the authority, the right, simply *to be chidren of God* (1: 12, cf. 1 John 3: 1). What is Christ's own authority? It is *to lay down his life*, as well as to take it again (10: 18). Christ has authority to judge (5: 27) and exercise authority over everybody (17: 2), but it is clearly a moral authority, in contrast to Pilate's authority to sentence him, which is only a derived and secondary authority (19: 10 f.).

Again, one of the themes that runs through the teaching of Jesus as far as it is discernible through the Gospel traditions is that of 'the Son of man'. If it is correct to treat this phrase as a genuinely dominical reference to Dan. 7, then it is noteworthy that the human figure in that vision represents the martyr loyalists whose strength was in their obedience and their submission even to the length of death, and that the 'success' of this way looks like failure, being vindicated only beyond death and in heaven. There it is that they are given favourable judgement and a kingdom. Thus, the adoption of this symbol by Jesus is one more way of declaring that for him the way to royal glory is the way of the cross. (Does Barnabas Lindars, in *Jesus Son of Man* (London, 1983), in regarding the Danielic reference as post-dominical, pay sufficient attention to the evidence provided by the definite article, and to the suitability of the phrase, not as Messianic nor apocalyptic nor titular, but as a symbol of martyrdom vindicated beyond death?)

Thus, the New Testament itself reminds the reader that, in preaching the gospel, the metaphorical nature of the analogies and their limited function need to be observed. No analogy from a sub-personal level can ultimately do justice to the whole of a personal relation; but what it can do is to affirm some aspect of it. 'Glory follows humility'— that is a way of affirming faith in the glory; but 'the humility is the glory' represents a deeper insight, closer to the level of personal relations and very close to the cross. It is along the *via dolorosa* that the triumphal procession moves. If the preacher knows what he is doing he will not modify the triumph; yet neither will he fall victim to 'triumphalism'.

II

But if love never coerces, must not its triumph be at the mercy of the beloved? If love wins not by winning a victory over the other but by winning the other over, must not our gospel forever be an expression only of hope without certainty? Is it possible to point to any argument on which to rest such brave affirmations as the following, taken at random from contemporary theological writing? 'The Gospel is that Jesus's God is King, that the source of all things and the meaning of all things is what Jesus called *Abba* ...' (R. Williams, *The Truce of God* (London, 1983), 77). Describing the message implicit in the life and work of Jesus, Ben F. Meyer (*The Aims of Jesus* (London, 1979), 250) writes:

Divine salvation would be nothing short of total victory over evil. Such was the *a priori* which evoked and linked the repulse of Hades, the ordeal and its resolution, the reversal of the lot of the depressed, the ransom for many, the destruction and raising of the temple, the banquet of the saved in God's reign. These themes incarnated the message that good would prevail, that the vicious circle of disorder and decline would be broken.

Once more, L. Newbigin, in *The Finality of Christ* (London, 1969), speaks of 'the infinite power and resourcefulness of God to use men's rebellion as the means to his victory' (86). On what is it legitimate to rest such confidence? Can we point—not of course, to proof, but—to considerations that at least constitute good grounds for such assertions? We can.

A starting-point is offered by the genesis of the Easter-belief. How came the friends of Jesus to believe that, after his Crucifixion, they saw him alive with life transcendent, the life of the age to come? 'Judaism', said the late J. Jeremias (*New Testament Theology* i (English trans., London, 1971), 308 f.), 'did not know of any anticipated resurrection ... to δόξα as an event of history. Rather, resurrection to δόξα always and without exception means the dawn of God's new creation ...' In other words, it is not possible to account for the Easter faith from any already existing Jewish expectations which might have been entertained by the friends of Jesus. Then what did generate their Easter faith? Notoriously attempts to rationalize it as the result of psychological aberrations or subjective visionary experience fail to reach plausibility. They do not make sense of the sober, tenacious conviction which squeezed this Jewish sect out of the synagogue and compelled them eventually to know themselves as a *tertium genus*. Then what did generate this faith? It is not unreasonable, given the poverty of alternative explanations, to conclude that what they seemed to see did indeed correspond with reality: in Jeremias' words in the same context, 'the disciples must have experienced the appearances of the Risen Lord as an eschatological event, as a dawning of the turning point of the worlds.'

But this turns out to be no isolated or rootless revelation. Despite its overwhelming novelty, it became clear, on reflectiòn, that the Jesus whom his friends had known was just such a one as to fit this new dimension. As C. K. Barrett observed (as already quoted), Jesus had in his lifetime identified himself with the social and religious outcasts, insisting that what he was doing in fraternizing with such persons was what God does. Constantly, the Jesus who emerges from critical scrutiny of the traditions is one whose work is God's work, in whose presence God's sovereignty becomes a reality, who shows God's mind directly, without appeal to antecedent authority. This immediacy, this directness, this embodying of the divine presence is the sort of thing, it appears, that made Jesus intolerable to his own religious contemporaries; but now, in the resurrection appearances, his self-identification with God's way and his being the vehicle of the immediate presence of God are confirmed, and from such apprehension there springs, eventually, the articulation of a distinctive doctrine of the cross, a Christology and a gospel. The belief that the strange and gentle way of love is ultimately the only valid way is firmly based on historical events.

III

If so, then the aliveness of Jesus is good news which may be confidently proclaimed. It is a well-authenticated triumph; it is a victory for which no language of conquest can be too positive. Yet it is a victory on that mysterious level of personal relations, for which the language of victory is too small, and the language of coercion simply not appropriate. So far from being a reversal of the cross, this triumph is part and parcel of it and only endorses the absolute risk, the unqualified self-offering, of love's endeavour, love's expense. There is every reason why Christian triumph must on no account be 'triumphalist'; yet neither should a Christian, rightly rejecting 'triumphalism', be betrayed into singing the Easter hymns in a minor key: the evidence is strong enough for confidence. Love may be blind, but it will find out the way:

> Some think to lose him
>   By having him confined;
> And some do suppose him,
>   Poor thing, to be blind;
> But if ne'er so close ye wall him,
>   Do the best that you may,
> Blind love, if so ye call him,
>   Will find out his way.

17. Christ the Sacrifice: Aspects of the Language and Imagery of the Bible

COLIN GUNTON

I

IT is a mark of great and stimulating teaching that by it seeds are sown which germinate and continue to bear fruit many years later, often in fields of interest very different from the original. One memory, now nearly twenty years old, is of George Caird's insistence that to describe the Church as the body of Christ is to use a metaphor. Those who held that it is literally a body he rightly asked to indicate the arms, legs, fingers, and toes. And yet he did not take such an insistence as any concession to subjectivism or to the view that to use a metaphor is to use a *mere* picture. The Church is *really* the body of Christ, and to acknowledge the metaphorical character of the claim is in no way to endanger the doctrine. The realistic theory of language underlying such an example recurs in *The Language and Imagery of the Bible*. 'Any statement, literal or metaphorical, may be true or false, and its referent may be real or unreal.'[1] Caird's achievement was to have long said what is now coming widely to be accepted, and its importance lies in the fact that the opposite is often believed or assumed. Early modern philosophers like Hobbes and Locke, who have done so much to form our attitudes to language, were deeply suspicious of metaphor, and until recently it was widely held that to find the truth, if any, in a metaphorical statement one must first find a way of translating it into literal terms.

The rejection of such dogmas has become a commonplace of recent studies. It is now almost unanimously believed, for a variety of reasons that cannot be rehearsed here, that the truth is the reverse of the old view, and that metaphor is one of the central means by which truth is discovered and expressed. One feature of a very complex topic in the philosophy of language will take us to the heart of the theme of the paper. It comes from a classical source, and is Aristotle's teaching that metaphor is what happenes when a term is transferred from one context to another (*Poetics*, 1457^b 7–8). It is this feature of language which makes the expression of new truth possible, for without the new use of old language there could be no new knowledge and discovery. Dis-

---

[1] G. B. Caird, *The Language and Imagery of the Bible* (London, 1980), 131.

covery is not only dependent on change of language; it comes to be by means of it. New linguistic usage is what brings discovery to birth, for it is only by such means that once hidden features of reality come within the grasp of human conceptualizing. This is nowhere more evident than in the history of science, where metaphorical words like *force, gravity, machine, field*, and *charm* have all been vehicles of advance in human understanding of the way things are. Far from being the enemy of scientific truth, metaphor is one of the means by which, according to an important article by Richard Boyd, the sciences are able 'to cut the world at its joints'. Such new linguistic usages are what give 'epistemic access' to the world, and so enable us to accommodate our language to the structures of reality.[2] This is a very important point indeed, for it throws light not only on our language, but on the nature of our universe. It means that the world is the kind of place that can come to expression in language, not in the narrow and limited way supposed by logical empiricism but in an open and dynamic way. Words have to change their meaning in order to, so to speak, mould themselves to newly discovered aspects of reality. On such an understanding there is no one way in which a word must be used, but language is successful as it adapts itself to things. Accordingly, we have to understand metaphor as one of the means by which reality is able to speak. In this respect we must say—using the word in a general and not specifically theological sense—that it is a vehicle of revelation.

This doctrine has important implications for our understanding of the way our world is ordered and the way the human mind comes to apprehend that order. The world on this understanding is a rational yet mysterious place, which gives itself to be understood only indirectly and partially: metaphor is both the sign and the vehicle of what we can call the world's open rationality. It is the sign of it because it indicates at once the success and limits of our endeavours to grasp reality in language. It is its vehicle, because it is a way of expressing truth which is appropriate to the combination of mystery and openness which marks all human expressions of value, truth, and beauty.

Metaphor is significant also in another way. In some of its instances, it shows how the mind can understand the world by being prepared to allow one part of its experience to illuminate another—as when, to use an example cited by George Steiner, someone first saw autumn in a man's face[3]—and so to allow a transfer of meaning from one sphere to

---

[2] Richard Boyd, 'Metaphor and Theory Change: What is "Metaphor" a Metaphor for?' *Metaphor and Thought*, ed. Andrew Ortony (Cambridge, 1979), 356–408 (esp. 358, 363 f., 381, 392, 399 f.).
[3] George Steiner, *After Babel: Aspects of Language and Translation* (London, 1975), 23.

another. It is in this way that metaphor reorders the way things are perceived. The history of culture, religion, and science is in one major respect a history of how this has happened. No wonder Aristotle believed that the employment of metaphor required genius, for it is here that new features of order are discerned and new efforts are required of the one who would understand and make known. In the next section we shall see something of how this briefly sketched theory of language enables us to make sense of one central theological metaphor.

II

In the West, we have very nearly come to believe that there is only one real way of 'cutting the joints', and that is the way of the natural scientist. It was not always so and is in any case a mistake. The artist and musician bring us into contact with reality in ways different from, but not entirely unrelated to, those of the sciences. (After all, scientific and literary uses of metaphor often have a good deal in common.) The situation in theology is complicated by the fact that many practitioners of its various disciplines have capitulated to the view best described as scientism, which holds that only scientific ways of finding out truth are valid, and that everything else is located merely or largely in the human response to the world—in emotion, in experience, or in the choice of a certain way of life. The points made in the previous section about metaphor should make us cautious about accepting any such dogmas. In this section, we shall examine a particularly difficult test case in order to see whether any life remains in an old and apparently dated metaphor.

A verse from the Epistle to the Hebrews both sets the problem and orientates this essay to the theme of the book. '[Christ] has appeared once for all at the end of the age to put away sin by the sacrifice of himself' (Heb. 9: 26c). It does not require pointing out that the description of Christ as a sacrifice is central to the New Testament's presentation of him. It is also clearly a metaphorical use of language: there is no altar, but a cross; he is killed by soldiers not (directly—see John 11: 50!) by priests and there is no provision in the sacrificial regulations as they appear in the canon of the Old Testament for the sacrifice of a human being. Christ's death both is and is not a sacrifice. The metaphorical nature of the language is also manifest in the fact that the writers conflate and adapt different aspects of the Old Testament background, as in the use of Leviticus 16 in Hebrews and in the combination of Passover and sin offerings in the imagery of the Johannine tradition. As

Frances Young has shown, various strands of the Old Testament language of sacrifice are applied to Jesus in different ways.[4] That is archetypally metaphorical, as it involves the central Aristotelian activity of transferring language from one context to another. It is also worth noting that the language of sacrifice rarely appears as the sole metaphor, even in Hebrews. It is always supplemented by metaphors taken from other areas of human experience: the law court, the battlefield, and the slave market.

But that introduces our major problem. Legal and military imagery is alive and well in our culture, too much so, we might say. By contrast, sacrifice appears to be almost a paradigm case of a dead metaphor. The difficulty is well expressed by J. S. Whale:

In our modern world sacrifice has become a mere figure of speech. Parents sacrifice themselves for their children; a politician may sacrifice a career for a principle; ... In the ancient world sacrifice was no figure of speech but stark fact; the solemn taking and surrendering of the warm blood of life itself; the ritual slaughter of bullock or goat, lamb or pigeon at an altar. It asserted the powerful religious efficacy of shed blood. Ancient man took the necessity of blood-sacrifice for granted. Indeed, sacrifice is as ancient and universal as religion itself; it expresses the ultimate concern of the human race. ... But modern man finds this very idea revolting, on more than one ground.[5]

In view of such an observation—which, it must be noted, appears at the head of a chapter proposing to give some positive account of the matter—can we continue seriously to use such language of Christ? To phrase the question in ways which echo the progress of the paper so far: Does the metaphor of sacrifice enable us to cut the world at its joints, to bring to expression the way things really are? There is undoubtedly a serious problem. But could it be that it is as much ours as the language's, and that if we are to live in our world as it really is we need the insights and realities mediated by this and similar imagery?

The first need in attempting an answer to such questions is some appreciation of the function of sacrifice in what has come to be called primitive religion. Here we must beware of modern theories dominated by assumptions of the superiority of contemporary enlightenment. As Mary Douglas has shown, we must assume neither the intellectual immaturity of earlier cultures nor the enlightened maturity of ours. To some extent, the 'primitives' have the advantage over us, for 'in the primitive culture the rule of patterning works with greater force and more total comprehensiveness. With the moderns it applies to dis-

---

[4] Frances Young, *Sacrifice and the Death of Christ* (London, 1983).
[5] J. S. Whale, *Victor and Victim: The Christian Doctrine of Redemption* (Cambridge, 1960), 42.

jointed, separate areas of experience'.[6] In her book, Professor Douglas is speaking chiefly of purity and defilement rather than of sacrifice, but the parallel is clear. Ancient and modern ideas of purity are, like ancient notions of sacrifice, concerned with dimensions of human living in the world. But far from being irrational concerns, their primary focus is to be found in their occupation with the order of creation. Thus, where Old Testament scholars have regularly found themselves perplexed at, or dismissive of, the classifications of clean and unclean creatures in Leviticus, Professor Douglas indicates a crucial key. 'Holiness means keeping distinct the categories of creation ... It therefore involves correct definition, discrimination and order' (53). If we take the notion of order—of wholeness, completeness, particularly in relation to God—as a first clue to the significance of a sacrifice, we shall have a foundation on which to build. Sacrifice has to do at least in part with the ordering or reordering of human life both in relation to God and in the cosmos. We may now be bound to use the term metaphorically, but this need not be at the expense of this feature of the former usage. Part of the connotations carried over from old to new usage may be the continuity of this concern with the rightness of the way life is ordered in the cosmos.

Another related matter which we should take with due seriousness is the apparent universality, or near universality,[7] of sacrifice either as rite or as metaphor. May not the very pervasiveness of the phenomenon point to a fundamental feature of human experience without which we shall not understand ourselves? George Caird again: 'Deep in the heart of mankind there is an instinctive aversion to dirt, disease and death; and in almost every language the words which convey this abhorrence are used metaphorically to express and evoke a similar loathing for sin, and especially for sins of fraud, sensuality and violence' (17). Like the metaphors of justice, redemption, and victory, this one goes very deep. George Steiner has commented on the fact of 'the quality of genius in the Greek and Hebrew statement of human possibility' and that certain of their metaphors 'reorganize our habitation in reality' (21–3). Similarly, as Frances Young has shown, the language of sacrifice appears at the heart of important modern novels (13–15). There seems little doubt that a feeling of the rightness and necessity of a sacrificial dimension to human living runs very deep in much human consciousness. Such a consideration takes us only a short way, of course. It may be simply an

[6] Mary Douglas, *Purity and Danger: An Analysis of the Concepts of Pollution and Taboo* (London, 1984) (1st edn., 1966), 40.
[7] See the note by Stephen Sykes to p. 61 of 'Sacrifice in the New Testament and Christian Theology', in *Sacrifice*, ed. M. F. C. Bourdillon and Meyer Fortes (London, 1980).

atavistic survival, to be eradicated when enlightenment finally triumphs. And in any case, it gives little reason why we should treat the sacrifice of Christ as particularly interesting or important. To this central question of the paper we now turn.

III

New Testament talk of Christ as a sacrifice comes to us only after the language has already undergone considerable metaphorical transformation in the course of history. Here it does not seem necessary to enter the debate about whether or how far the Old Testament prophets rejected cultic sacrifice. Two facts seem to be clear. The first is that the cult continued, and that Jesus is portrayed as on occasions acquiescing in it (Mark 1: 44, compare Lev. 14: 2 ff.). The second is that alongside this there developed a tradition of metaphorical usage, which did not necessarily contradict the literal cultic meaning: 'The sacrifice acceptable to God is a broken spirit . . .' (Ps. 51: 17, compare 27: 6, 107: 22). The duality is repeated in the New Testament, which can speak of the death of Christ in sacrificial terms and recommend that believers 'present your bodies as a living sacrifice' (Rom. 12: 1). In the New Testament, both of these usages are metaphorical: the sacrifice of Christ is metaphorical not in the sense that it is unreal, but in the sense already noted; that of the believer, in that the mode of life enjoined is transferred both linguistically and as a matter of living practice from the primary sacrifice on which the manner of life depends.

Before, however, we leap to traditional conclusions about the fact that the sacrifice of Christ both completes and abolishes the old sacrificial system, more time should be spent on exploring the parallels between the way the language works in the two dispensations. All the talk of metaphor so far has been designed to demonstrate the flexibility of language. A word changes its meaning as it is used in different contexts and as it is used to express different aspects of human response to the world. Therefore it can never be assumed that, however ubiquitous a word, it will always have the same meaning. When different cultures and religions do the same *kind* of thing—ritually slaughtering animals—they are not necessarily doing the same thing. Even when the expression of the matter seems quite similar, as when the Homeric gods enjoy the smoke of the heroes' holocaust and 'the Lord smelled the pleasing odour' of Noah's sacrifice (Gen. 8: 21), the particular and general contexts indicate that we are whole worlds apart in the meaning given to the institution.

Here a point made by Professor Rogerson is relevant, 'that, ultimately, all sacrifices in the Old Testament depend for their context upon the story of God's deliverance of his people from Egypt at the Exodus'.[8] The point can be expanded. Sacrifice only means what it does in the context of the giving of the law, and all that it implies for the life of the covenant people. Similarly, the prescriptions for sacrifice in Leviticus cannot merely be understood anthropologically in terms of a system of pollution and taboo, but must be seen theologically in terms of the holiness of Israel's God. The exploration of the notion of sacrifice ultimately leads us not only to the notion of a story, but to that of a world of relationships. The relations of person to person in Israel are comprehended within the relations of them all to God, and the sacrifices are to do with the ordering of those relationships: with the establishing and re-establishing of the focus of Israel's life as a people. On such an understanding, the prophetic critique takes its place within that same network of relationships, anticipating the theology of the Letter to the Hebrews by highlighting the inadequacy of the sacrificial forms in themselves to secure true order in divine-human and consequently human-human relations.

If we extend Professor Rogerson's point to the New Testament language of sacrifice, we can draw two related conclusions. The first is that the Old Testament provides the matrix within which the language works. Metaphor, as we have seen, involves transfer, and its use requires a context from which to transfer. And with the transfer, some of the old connotations are carried over into the new usage. At the very least, we shall expect to find taken up into New Testament usage some of the relational considerations that operated so centrally in Israel's institutions. The second is that the referent for the language is changed: not now a dead animal but a human being whose life and more particularly death becomes that from which the transferred meaning takes its centre. This means that the metaphor is successful if it achieves its end of bringing to expression, with the help of such associations brought from the old context, aspects of the reality of Jesus Christ. In order to show how this happens, we shall look at the matter of relations in general before moving to a conclusion.

IV

It is of the essence of relationships to be particular, and yet to be classifiable into types, to be in some way intelligible and expressible in language. Thus, marriage is one type of relationship, of man to woman,

[8] J. W. Rogerson, 'Sacrifice in the Old Testament: Problems of Method and Approach', in *Sacrifice*, ibid., 57.

while actual marriages are always of particular men to particular women. It is also of the essence of relationships that, although particular, they take up into themselves other, different relationships. A marriage is in one sense an exclusive relationship, but in another it is an open one, in that its very existence shapes and determines other sets of relationships to society and to the wider world: to children, parents, friends, colleagues, but also to the world whose resources are differently used by a couple than by two people living in a differently ordered network. Changes in this relationship—childbirth, breakdown, death—necessarily effect changes in all the others. Conversely, changes in the wider social network effect changes in the particular relationships within it.

By analogy, we can come to understand the extrapersonal world as a network of relationships, in which any one part of our universe is only what it is in virtue of its relatedness to all other parts. An atomic explosion affects in different degrees the weather throughout other parts of the world. The first section of this essay was designed to show how metaphor in particular and language in general can be conceived to bring to expression aspects of this interrelated world: to 'cut the world at its joints'. Language is at once the means by which we indwell our world and by which our world comes to be understood. General terms which in one way or another express relationship—'cause', 'marriage', 'gravity', 'symphony', 'mother'—are accordingly the means by which salient features of our interrelated universe are brought to expression. The growth of culture, science, and knowledge in general comes about as language is expanded and stretched so as to be able to encompass a grasp of greater intricacies and extent of relationships. The growth of technical languages, often highly metaphorical, is one of the fruits of specialization and the growth of knowledge. (That it is sometimes the fruit of less admirable tendencies is not here the point.) As more is understood of the relationships of things and people to each other, so language takes on greater complexity and subtlety.

Theological language is that language in which the relations of God with his world are expressed. The relations are many sided, partly because of the all-encompassing reality expressed by the word *God*, partly because of the richness and diversity of relationships experienced in human religious history and partly because of the inadequacy of any one word or group of words to express the reality of the divine-human encounter. But salient features of the relationship are abstracted by the use of a variety of central terms. *Sacrifice* is one of these, and has served to express not just a salient feature of the network of relationships, but a number of similar features which it is appropriate to designate by the same word. We have already seen that there are important differences not only between the Old Testament and other ancient religions, but also between Old and New Testament. It now remains to outline some of the hallmarks of the way the New Testament uses this central term of relation metaphorically in order to express some of the salient features of the realities brought to be by what happened with Jesus of Nazareth. Here a full theology of sacrifice is not being essayed, merely some remarks intended to show what is being achieved in this transfer of language to a new context.

At the centre is the notion of order. Old Testament sacrifice was concerned with the ordering and reordering of Israel's relation with the Covenant God. The claim that Christ is a sacrifice implies that he is now the source of the relationship with God, as once the sacrificial system had sought to be, but in such a way that the old system is at once fulfilled and superseded. How may the life and death of a man—for part of the transfer of meaning requires that we include the life and not just the death in our interpretation—be conceived to reorder human relationships with God? The Epistle to the Hebrews (8: 8–12) argues that such a reordering has in fact been achieved, and claims the fulfilment of Jeremiah 31: 31–4, 'I will put my law into their minds, and write it upon their hearts, and I will be their God, and they shall be my people.' He claims, that is to say, that something real happens in the divine-human relationship, such that there is achieved what was not achieved by the slaughter of bulls and goats.

How may this be conceived to happen? Here we witness a major instance of metaphorical reordering. One of the chief ways of understanding sacrifice is as gift: in some religious systems as gift in which to appease or 'buy off' the deity, in the Bible more as a gift to the God who by virtue of what he is cannot be bought. When Christ is conceived of as sacrifice, the notion of gift remains, but both the nature of the giver and the means of its giving are radically changed: transferred from one context to another. The most radical aspect of the change is that there is a complete reversal of roles, in that the primary giver is God and not man. This is particularly evident in many Pauline expressions, perhaps notably the much debated 'whom God put forward as an expiation by his blood' (Rom. 3: 25), but it is everywhere the implicit or explicit assumption of New Testament expression. In turn, this has moulded what is in many ways the chief difference between ancient and modern uses of the word *sacrifice*. To say, for example, that a politician sacrificed his career for a principle is to concentrate on sacrifice as a cost of some kind to the sacrificer, which is the kind of point Paul is making when he sees God through Christ as paying the price of human rebellion against himself.

The stressing of God's sacrificial giving up of his Son could have, and has had, unfortunate theological consequences, especially if it is construed, with the aid of penal imagery, in terms of God's visiting upon the human Jesus the penalties owed by others. A theologically intolerable doctrine of penal substitution can be avoided if the other shift in the meaning of the sacrificial gift is also stressed. A New Testament expression of the second metaphorical transfer is given in Eph. 5: 2: 'Christ loved us and gave himself up as a fragrant offering and sacrifice to God.' The gift, as the Letter to the Hebrews stresses so strongly, is not the imposed death of a beast, but the voluntary self-giving of Jesus. And the giving is not simply the death, but the death as the completion of a life in obedience to God. Jesus offers to the Father the human life that the others of us have failed to live. But to what end? We return to the point made earlier by George Caird's remark about human abhorrence for sin considered as pollution. 'It is for this reason that the New Testament so constantly employs the language of sacrifice to declare the benefits of the Cross . . .' Hence 'the imperative need of those whom sin has defiled is that which can cleanse the conscience from dead works (Heb. 9: 14)' (17). But how can this be conceived to happen? We return to the matter of relationships.

Two relationships in particular are under consideration here. The first is that between God and his rebellious people, broken by the sin that erects a barrier between the two and so disrupts fellowship or communion. The second is that between Jesus and his Father. The second, particular, relationship is that which reorders and so takes up into itself the first. How can this human life, this sacrificial career, take other human beings up into its reality? A full answer would involve detailed attention to the claim that the life of Jesus is also and at another level, so to speak, the life of the recreating Word, but that is the work of another whole paper. Suffice it to say here that the crucial link is to be found in the doctrine of the Holy Spirit. It is the Spirit that is the source of Jesus' self-giving humanity, and that same Spirit which enables believers to share in the one reordering sacrifice. Indeed, does not Paul use sacrificial language of the Spirit also: 'We ourselves, who have the *first-fruits* of the Spirit . . .' (Rom. 8: 23); my emphasis)?[9] The sacrifice of Christ is to this end: that God should, in him and through the Spirit, reorder to himself his alienated creation. That is the glory of Christ, both in the New Testament and in eternity.

---

[9] I owe this point to C. Brown, 'Sacrifice', *New International Dictionary of New Testament Theology*, vol. 3 (Exeter, 1978), pp. 415–38 (417).

18. Christ as Agent

A. E. HARVEY

THE study of Christology has traditionally concentrated on the implications of the *titles* by which Jesus was most commonly addressed or designated in the New Testament, such as Messiah, Son of God, or Son of man. Less frequently, attention has been given to words or concepts which occur only occasionally or by implication in the New Testament, such as λόγος, mediator, or *victor*. Very occasionally, a word makes its appearance whch appears to have no basis in Scripture but which may be held to be implied by it. In ancient times such a word was ὁμοούσιος. Recently, another newcomer has made its appearance: Christ the *Agent*.

The word 'agent' seems attractive to modern theological writing because it appears to offer a way of describing the person and work of Christ without the encumbrance of theological jargon. To say that Christ was 'God's agent' is to use a language that is familiar to people living in the modern world, that bypasses traditional theological embarrassments, and yet enables the unique claims of Jesus to be understood. At this level, the term works as an analogy, or 'model', and those who use it need not be pressed to offer a precise definition. But it has recently been argued that the use of the term has historical justification, in the sense that the concept of 'agency' can be discerned as underlying some of the language used of Jesus in the New Testament, and that therefore a study of the institution of agency in that culture can actually throw light on the early history of Christology. If this project is successful, it might have the further implication that the word 'agent' should be more systematically explored in Christological thinking today.

It is important at the outset to distinguish between ancient and modern conceptions of 'agency'. In contemporary English, the words 'agent' and 'agency' refer as much to a field of activity as to a legal relationship. In current parlance a 'land agent' is one who is professionally occupied with the buying and selling of land. Admittedly he will normally do this on behalf of a client, and consequently will act as someone else's 'agent' in the strict sense; but the connotations of 'land-agency' are less to do with the procedures by which he is authorized to act for his clients than with his professional knowledge about the value of land and buildings. But in ancient agency the terms we are concerned with—שָׁלִיחַ and ἀπόστολος[1]—have a different connotation. Here, all the emphasis is on the 'sending out', that is, the authorization of the agent. His field of activity is not indicated (though it may have to be defined for legal purposes). The question raised by a שָׁלִיחַ is, 'Whom does he represent?'—not (as with a modern agent), 'What is he expert in?'

A further significant difference lies in the definition of an agent's function. To us, the essence of an agent is that he should *act*. We appoint an agent to do something on our behalf which otherwise we should have to do for ourselves. What we do *not* need an agent for is to *say* things for us: we can do this ourselves by letters or messages. An agent is required only when actions or procedures have to be carried through on our behalf. Communicating our intentions through another person (a messenger) is something different from having our interests promoted by an agent. But in the Jewish culture this distinction was less important;[2] indeed the legal refinements which were placed upon the practice of agency in the post-biblical period[3] embraced the activities of the messenger as well as those of the agent; for there were many occasions on which the utterance of a word or words by the principal's representative might incur legal consequences just as much as the performance of an act. This point becomes particularly important when these categories are applied to religious phenomena. On the modern western model of agency it would be natural to think of a spokesman for God (a prophet) as doing something essentially different from an agent of God (such as a miracle worker or healer); and this distinction underlies all but the most recent scholarly work on the subject.[4] But in fact it can be shown that 'the secular concept of "messenger", which influenced the concept of prophecy, underwent further development in post-biblical Judaism and became juridically defined in terms of Representation. The result was a new interpretation of the nature of prophecy as communication from God.'[5]

The book from which this quotation is taken is *Der Gesandte und sein*

[1] The fundamental, and extremely influential, work on these terms was done by K. H. Rengstorf in his article on ἀποστέλλω κτλ. in Kittel's *Wörterbuch*, i (Stuttgart, 1933), 397 ff.

[2] J. A. Bühner, *Der Gesandte und sein Weg im 4. Evangelium* (Tübingen, 1977), 271–5, contrasts the Roman distinction between *nuntius* and *mandatarius*. But this appears not to be correct: a *nuntius* could pronounce words for his sender which created contractual obligations; and in any case *mandatarius* is not strictly an 'agent' (R. W. Lee, *Elements of Roman Law* (London, 1944), 351). The appropriate term in commercial transactions would be *institor*, cf. Max Kaser, *Römisches Privatrecht*[8] (Munich, 1974), 59 (Ulpian D. 14. 3.1a).

[3] Bühner, op. cit., 181 ff.

[4] Which has followed Rengstorf's distinction between certain individual *sheluhim*, such as Moses or Elijah, and prophets in general (art. cit., 419).

[5] Bühner, op. cit., 190–1.

Weg by J. A. Bühner, published in 1977. This book is the first major study to have been devoted to the Jewish law of agency in relation to the New Testament, and in my opinion it makes a conclusive case for understanding much of the language used of Jesus in the Fourth Gospel as drawn from juridical practice. Jesus is 'sent' by the Father under conditions which clearly imply his authorization; the sphere of his authorized activity on behalf of his Father is clearly defined (that is, those activities, such as creation and judgement, which are peculiarly God's sphere); his activity conforms to the maxim that 'a man's agent is like himself',[6] and also to the (lesser known) maxim that an agent cannot work to his principal's disadvantage;[7] and he returns (as an agent must) to his Father-principal at the discharge of his agency. Again and again the Johannine Father–Son terminology is illumined by this agent-model; in particular, the 'oneness' predicated of the Father–Son relationship is convincingly (in my view) explained in terms of a functional identity of authority rather than of a personal or mystical relationship;[8] and though it is recognized that the origins of this emphasis on Father and Son may well lie further back in the tradition represented by the Synoptics, the presentation of the Son as the Father's agent *par excellence* (which was empirically the case in ancient Middle Eastern commerce) is likely to be the product of the evangelist's innovative mind.

This conclusion is one to which (though after far less extensive research) I had tentatively come myself[9] before Bühner's book was published, and had incorporated in my own thinking on Christology[10] before I had the opportunity to study his arguments in detail.[11] I therefore greatly welcome his results as confirmation of my own thinking, though I recognize that it would be premature to regard them as fully established until further scholarly discussion has taken place. However, it is not too soon to explore some of its wider implications. These have to do, ultimately, with the way in which language which appears to have a precise reference to human institutions may be used in a much looser and more figurative sense with respect to the things of God—a topic to which I am privileged to make a small contribution in a

[6] *m. Ber.* 5. 5 and many Talmudic texts.
[7] Qid. 42b etc.
[8] As against the 'juridical mysticism' suggested by Théo Preiss, *Life in Christ* (London, 1954), 25 and P. Borgen, 'God's Agent in the Fourth Gospel' in *Religions in Antiquity: Essays in Memory of Erwin Ramsdell Goodenough*, ed. J. Neusner (Leiden, 1968), 137–48.
[9] A. E. Harvey, *Jesus on Trial* (London, 1976), 88–92.
[10] A. E. Harvey, *Jesus and the Constraints of History* (London, 1982), 161 ff.
[11] I do not of course claim any originality in this: Preiss and Borgen (see above, n. 8) had already pointed the way, though without sufficient attention to the refinements of the legal institution.

memorial volume to one who wrote about it so lucidly in the last of his books that was published in his lifetime.

The first requirement is to meet the obvious objection to this whole line of argument that there is apparently no reference to 'agent' or 'agency' in the entire New Testament, and therefore that to regard the concept of agency as a factor in New Testament Christology is artificial if not actually misleading. To this the following points can immediately be made:

(1) the Hebrew word שָׁלִיחַ is well attested in Mishnah and Talmud as the correct name for the person bound by the legal conditions of agency;[12]

(2) the Greek equivalent for שָׁלִיחַ was ἀπόστολος;[13]

(3) John 13: 16: 'the slave is not greater than his master nor is the ἀπόστολος greater than he who sent him.' The two clauses are parallel, and require that ἀπόστολος should refer to a secular institution as familiar as slavery. The correct translation is therefore 'agent'—and this is in fact how it was taken by Origen,[14] Chrysostom,[15] and (in his paraphrase) Nonnus.[16] It is true, of course, that there may be a deliberate ambiguity: the Christian ἀπόστολος ('apostle') is not greater than he (Christ) who sent him. But in its context the primary reference must be to the familiar institution of agency.

It must be allowed therefore that the word 'agent' was used by the author of the Fourth Gospel, and in such a way as to prove that he was familiar with the concept of agency. The work of Bühner has offered a strong case for believing that he was also familiar with the basic technicalities of the Jewish law of agency, and that he exploited this terminology in order to clarify the relationship of Jesus with his heavenly father. But we have now to face the question why he did not go so far as to *call* Jesus an agent, ἀπόστολος.

Bühner himself suggests two answers to this question.[17] First, by the time the Gospel was written the term ἀπόστολος had already been adopted into the Christian vocabulary to refer to those who have ever since been known as 'apostles'. Secondly, the term suffers from that restriction of meaning which follows from the emphasis we noted at the outset on the moment of 'sending'. That Jesus had been sent and auth-

---

[12] Rengstorf art. cit. n. 1 above, 414 ff. For a bibliography on the Jewish law of agency, cf. Bühner, op. cit., 181 n. 1.

[13] Eus. *Is.* 18: 1–2 etc.

[14] *Jo.* 32: 17.

[15] *Is. interp.* 1: 1.

[16] *par. Jo.* 13: 16.

[17] pp. 265 f.

orized by his Father was indeed an important feature of his agency, but it was by no means the only one or even the most important one: his 'works', his teaching, his judging, and the prospect of his return to his sender were equally important, and the word ἀπόστολος would not have seemed appropriate to convey the full range of this agent's activity. These answers may well be correct; but I would myself take them a stage further, and in so doing indicate certain lines of enquiry which lie well outside the scope of Bühner's pioneering study.

I would suggest, first, that the model in the evangelist's mind was not just any agent, but the agent who is the principal's son. A son, after all, was the best agent a man could ever have, and the one whose credentials were most likely to be accepted.[18] If moreover he was an only son (μονογενής) who could expect to receive the entire inheritance, and if he was in good standing with his father (ἀγαπητός), so that there was no risk of his father disinheriting him, then he could be relied on absolutely to promote his father's interests ('to seek his glory'), for in the long run these interests were the same as his own: he would inherit them all. Such a son, speaking and acting in his father's absence and claiming his father's authority to do so, would be assumed without question to be his father's agent (indeed in law, if his actions were to the advantage of his father, this would constitute him an agent whether he had been formally appointed or not). It follows that simply by calling Jesus 'son' in relation to his Father's work and purposes the evangelist made it perfectly clear that he was also the Father's agent. It was not necessary to spell the matter out; and there were many reasons (not least the pressure of the existing tradition) for preferring 'son' as a *title* to agent.

But this leads on to some wider questions. What could have been the *religious* reasons for calling anyone God's 'agent' in the first place? The essence of agency is that it provides a means by which business can be done in the absence of the principal. And why should the principal be absent? The usual reason is practical. My business is growing, I want to open a subsidiary in another town, but I cannot be in both places at once. So I must find an agent whom I can trust (and who will be trusted by my customers) to run my subsidiary for me. Or the reason may be physical disability. Tobit has a debt to collect in a distant country, but is too old to make the journey himself; so he sends his son Tobias as his agent. But whatever the reason, the agent is needed to carry on business when his principal is necessarily absent.

What then is implied by the use of the agency model in respect of God? That God is absent! In one sense this is surely illegitimate. Again and again in the Bible we read that God is 'with' his people, he is

[18] Mark 12: 6. Cf. Harvey, op. cit. n. 10 above (1982), 160 ff.

'present' at certain times and places, and through his Spirit he intervenes in human affairs without any need of the services of an agent. But in another sense some agent or intermediary is absolutely necessary, if God is to be *God*—that is, a devouring fire, one whom to see is to die, the Lord of heaven and earth whose holiness is such that his creatures, for their own sake, cannot encounter him face to face. 'No man has seen God at any time': this is not just an unfortunate shortcoming of human history, to be made good at some time in the future. It is a necessary attribute of God that his creatures cannot see him and expect to survive. Such interventions as he makes in the affairs of men, and such manifestations as he offers of his nature and power, have to be adjusted to the capacity of human beings to witness them without being overwhelmed. God must therefore make use of intermediaries in his dealings with us. These might occasionally be supernatural—angels, or freakish phenomena in weather and firmament. More often they were men, acting and speaking in one way or another as God's representatives, God's 'agents'. They were employed because God was absent, and must necessarily be so lest he should burn us up by his unveiled presence.

We may best approach this aspect of the matter by way of the Letter to the Hebrews. Of all the New Testament writers, the author of Hebrews had the most intense perception of the unapproachable majesty and terror of God. The image which possessed his mind, and to which he returned again and again, was of the dark mysterious chamber in the Temple, the Holy of Holies, where God was deemed to be more nearly present than anywhere else on earth, and to which even the priests in their state of ritual purity had no access, but only the High Priest, once a year, and that without any permanent change being effected for the general body of worshippers. How then could Christians claim to have a new intimacy with this awesome God? How could they dare to stand in his presence when the entire Mosaic dispensation seemed designed to keep them at a safe distance from that electric presence within the sanctuary? Could it be that Jesus had done what the High Priest could never do, had 'gone through' that final curtain into the Holy of Holies, and taken his new brothers with him so that they could now have *confidence*—παρρησία—in the very presence of God?

The author, as we know, found his answer in the notion that Christ is the High Priest to whom the whole of Scripture points. God remains in principle majestic, unapproachable, but Christ has enabled us to traverse the distance and enter his presence. The importance of this for our purpose is that it is one of the solutions—but not the only one—which the New Testament offers to the problem of the necessary distance between God and man. God cannot draw too close to human beings lest he should annihilate them; humans cannot draw too close to God in his holiness because of their sin. Yet Christians have this extraordinary intimacy with God, this sense of assurance in his presence. One way of explaining it is by the High Priest model. In the old dispensation, the High Priest was the one human being who, after a period of isolation and elaborate purification, was permitted to enter the Holy of Holies and stand in the presence of God. But this dread privilege was ineffectual: the essential sinfulness which separates man from God remained, the people were still kept as far as ever from the Presence, and the whole procedure had to be gone through all over again the following year. Yet it was not to be imagined that an institution validated by Scripture was purposeless and obsolete. Could it be that its true meaning and intention was now revealed by one who had achieved the purpose for which it was instituted—who had penetrated permanently into the divine presence, decisively going through the curtain which separated man from God, and enjoying such solidarity with his own people that he could take them with him and impart to them the confidence they needed to stand before God?

The author to the Hebrews was the only New Testament writer to approach the problem in terms of the High Priesthood; but the conception of Christ as one who overcomes the necessary distance between God and man is not confined to this epistle. The question, after all, was an old one; and it was often asked in the context of our future destiny. We shall all stand before the judgement seat of God, and nothing we sinners have done for ourselves can avail to give us confidence at that dread moment. If we are to survive, we shall need someone to speak for us, and this is the function of the 'paraclete' who might represent the merits of the patriarchs, our own good deeds, or simply some heavenly being whom God will have designated for the purpose.[19] It should occasion no surprise that Christians should have sensed that they have such a 'paraclete' in Jesus (1 John 2: 1). But the real problem comes, not so much with man drawing near to God, but with God drawing near to man. How can God make his will and his nature known to human beings without coercing them into obedience or annihilating their moral freedom? How can he both reveal himself as God and protect his creatures from the ultimate sin of blasphemy which they will commit if they do not instantly acknowledge him?

There is a passage of Josephus which bears closely upon this question. In a speech of Herod to his Jewish troops, reference is made to the

---

[19] Cf. Harvey, op. cit. n. 9 above (1976), 108–9.

disgraceful act of their Arab enemies, who put to death the Jewish
envoys who had come to sue for peace,

even though the Greeks have declared heralds to be sacred and inviolable, and
we have learned the noblest of our doctrines and the holiest of our laws from
the messengers [δι’ ἀγγέλων] sent by God. For this name can bring God's presence to men and reconcile enemies one to another.

(Ant. 15. 136, tr. R. Marcus (Loeb, 1963).)

This passage has been the subject of scholarly discussion with regard to
the question of the ἄγγελοι:[20] did Josephus know of the doctrine that the
Law was mediated by angels, or does the word here simply mean
'messengers' and refer to the prophets? More important for our purpose
is the following sentence: τοῦτο γὰρ τὸ ὄνομα καὶ ἀνθρώποις θεὸν εἰς
ἐμφάνειαν ἄγειν ... δύναται. The context is admittedly rhetorical: Herod
is being made to use all the arguments at his disposal to stir up animos-
ity against 'the Arabs'. But Josephus is undoubtedly drawing upon his
own perceptions when he suggests, as a ground for the Jewish abhorrence of violence done to a messenger, that 'this name' (that is, that of
the office of herald or messenger) 'can bring God into manifestation for
men'. What kind of 'manifestation' is this? Clearly, for Josephus, there
could be no question of any person, or even an angel, presenting a
visual impression of God. In another place (Ant. 15. 425) he uses the
word ἐμφάνεια for signs of God's intervention, such as freakish variations of the weather. In the case of messengers of God, he is evidently
referring to those who speak or act with divine authority. We are in the
world of Deut. 18: 18–20, the prophet like Moses whom to disregard is
to disregard God himself; or of the יְהֹוָה מַלְאַךְ, a heavenly being with
whom God identifies himself for the purpose of carrying out a particular intervention in the affairs of men. Whether the intervention is by
word or deed is immaterial; it is thus (in this culture) that God is
'brought into manifestation'. In either case (according to subsequent
rationalization[21]) we have to do with 'God's agent'.

For the Greeks, the sacrilege (ἱερούς καὶ ἀσύλους εἶναι τοὺς κήρυκας
φαμένων) of killing envoys was easily identified and avoided: heralds of
peace bear visible marks of their sacred office. For the Jews it was a
more dangerous matter. Anyone might come forward and claim to be
speaking with the authority of God. Amittedly, the penalty for making
such a claim falsely was death, and this would certainly eliminate the
likelihood of frivolous impersonations. But the mere assertion of the
claim entailed the necessity of judgement. If the claimant was genuine,

---

[20] Cf. W. D. Davies, HThR 47 (1954), 135–40, who argues that ἄγγελοι can mean 'prophets'.
[21] Bühner, op. cit. n. 2 above, 275 ff.

he must be obeyed; if false, he must be punished. Failure to react one way or the other was tantamount to blasphemy.[22] It was thus an important matter to know how to assess a man's claim to be 'God's agent'. But how could this be proved? In civil matters, the appointment of an agent does not appear to have been a formal or public act:[23] the agent could not point to the moment of his authorization as evidence for his power to act on behalf of his principal. Rather it had to be asked what 'sign' the agent had of his authority (such as the bill to be presented to the debtor, compare Tobit 5: 3), and how far his character and 'works' were consonant with his alleged mission. The same principles applied in the case of an agent of God. Intimate knowledge of his principal's affairs and methods would be a 'sign' of authenticity—he must be, in some sense, a 'man of God'; and he must be working to God's advantage (his 'glory'). If he was a true agent, then he had a right and a duty to do what God would be doing; if false, he would be committing blasphemy. To put it another way: the entire question would turn on his 'authority' to say and do things in which God had an interest. And this, in the synoptic as well as the Johannine traditions, was the question raised again and again by the utterances and actions of Jesus.

As soon as an agent's credentials were authenticated, he became (so far as the transaction in hand was concerned) 'like' the principal himself: it was *as if* the principal was present. So with God's agent: as soon as one was convinced that he was really authorized by God, it was *as if* God was present—and there could be no limit to the transactions which the agent might undertake on God's behalf; he would certainly be involved in those which were specifically associated with God, such as forgiving, healing, and judging. To do other than acknowledge and yield to God's presence in his agent would therefore be nothing less than blasphemy, and presumably attract instant punishment from God himself—we are back with the problem of how God can draw near to us without annihilating us. How can God's agent *prevent* instant 'judgement' taking place at the moment of his appearance?

We have seen that in the case of a man's agent there were certain procedures to be gone through in order to establish his credentials. Until that had been done, there was no obligation to treat with him as if his principal were present; only when his authorization was established would legal consequences follow from his words and actions. The same would apply to God's agent. His appearance would force a third party to come to a decision on his credentials. Time must be allowed to ask appropriate questions—to challenge his 'authority' or ask for

---

[22] Harvey, op. cit. n. 10 above (1982), 59, 170 f.
[23] Bühner, op. cit. n. 2 above, 181 ff.

'signs'. His claims would be open to discussion; in the nature of the case
it would be difficult to define what would count as decisive proof. Indeed it would be in everyone's interest to keep the question open for a
while. To accept the claims meant to acknowledge the agent's authority over the whole of one's life; to reject them placed one under the
obligation to procure the death of the blasphemer.[24] An interval of test-
ing offered a merciful respite. It is (at least in part) under the scheme of
such an 'interval' (between the making of the claim and its recognition
or rejection) that the Fourth Gospel presents the appearance of Jesus—
God's 'agent'.

But not only (I believe) the Fourth Gospel. In Josephus's perception
(as we have seen) the same principle of communication/agency applied
both to 'bringing God into manifestation' and to 'reconciling enemies
with one another' ($\pi o \lambda \epsilon \mu i o v s \ \pi o \lambda \epsilon \mu i o i s \ \delta \iota a \lambda \lambda a \tau \tau \epsilon \iota v$). When therefore we
ask what model of activity Paul had in mind when he wrote that 'God
was in Christ, reconciling [$\kappa a \tau a \lambda \lambda a \sigma \sigma \omega v$] the world to himself' (2 Cor.
5: 19), or that God was pleased to 'dwell in him and to reconcile
[$a \pi o \kappa a \tau a \lambda \lambda a \xi a \iota$] everything to himself through him' (Col. 1: 19–20), it
is only reasonable to think that the agency model was the one which
occurred most naturally to him: God was 'in' Christ in the sense in
which the principal is in the agent, bringing about reconciliation
between hostile parties. But the same model offers (I believe) the best
explanation for the significant reserve with which, throughout the
synoptic tradition, the title Son of God is used of Jesus in his lifetime. If
I may be allowed to repeat the conclusion I have argued for elsewhere,[25] 'To have said of a person who appeared to speak and act with
absolute authority that he was "Son of God" was to say much more
than that he was innocent or pious; it was to acknowledge him to be
God's actual representative on earth, to whom the same homage and
obedience would be due as if one were suddenly in the presence of God
himself.' Just as a man's son, in the father's absence, once his credentials had been established (such as that he was not in dispute with any
brothers over his inheritance, or that he was in good standing), would
be assumed to be speaking and acting as his father's agent, so to
acknowledge Jesus as the only and beloved 'Son of God' during his lifetime would have been to accept him as God's authorized agent,
entitled to homage and absolute obedience. For the most part only
heavenly beings or demons would have been in a position to draw this
conclusion. It was a sure instinct of the evangelists that human beings
would hardly have taken the risk. It was only after his death and

[24] Deut. 18: 18–20.
[25] Op. cit. n. 10 above (1982), 165.

resurrection to the right hand of God that a safe 'distance' was restored across which Jesus could be acknowledged by believers as Son of God— God's plenipotentiary agent, whose enemies are now being abased beneath his footstool, while those who acknowledge him seek (with his aid) to conform their lives to the pattern which he has been authorized to lay down for them.

How far will this concept of 'agency' take us? In the end, perhaps it all depends on what we mean by 'God'. For the Jews, the term was highly exclusive: only one being could possibly be called 'God', and since that being was lord of the universe no casual intercourse with him was conceivable. Elaborate safeguards were necessary in situations where human beings might find themselves in close proximity to God, whether here and now in the Temple (or in sanctified daily living) or after death. It is instructive (and important for understanding the development of Christology) to compare the use of the term 'God' in Greek culture. Here, far from being an exclusive name, it was a predicate with a wide range of application.[26] There were already many 'gods', and no difficulty was felt about adding to their number a human being—an emperor or a philosopher—who seemed particularly worthy of the description. Such 'gods' hardly needed an 'agent': they could move about themselves among the affairs of men, and only flagrant dishonour to their persons attracted serious penalties: human beings need not be mortally afraid of meeting a god in the street.

It was between these two poles in the understanding of the term 'god' that Christology underwent its early development. From the Greek side there was no problem about calling Christ θεός: it was the natural thing to do, indeed the problem was rather that this familiar word did not say *enough* about Jesus. To distinguish him from all other 'gods', it was necessary to define his divinity in relation to the one God in whom the Jews believed. From the Jewish side, on the other hand, the problem was rather that to call Jesus 'god' would have been to say far too much. In their culture, the term could not refer to any being other than the one God. Jewish Christian writers and later Greek theologians therefore started from totally different linguistic conventions. The Greeks needed to refine the general term 'god' in order to say something uniquely significant about Jesus. The Jewish Christians could not match this by seeking to *extend* their exclusive use of 'god'; instead, I have suggested that they leaned towards a kind of functional identity between Jesus and God, and that some of them found in the concept of 'agency' a useful model for doing so. Their efforts were soon submerged in the flood of Greek speculation, which took it for granted that Jesus

[26] Cf. S. Price, 'Gods and Emperors', *JHS*, 104 (1984), 79 ff.

should be called 'god' and sought to define the precise sense in which this should be done. The Fourth Gospel itself was promptly enlisted in this task, and the functional origin of much of its Christological language was lost to view. But today, when the supremacy of Greek philosophical categories in Christian theology is beginning to be called into question, the possibilities of an agency Christology may once again be found to be a stimulus in the endless search to find human words adequate to express the nature of Christ.

19. 'A Light to the Gentiles': the Significance of the Damascus Road Christophany for Paul

JAMES D. G. DUNN

I

ONE of the most striking, and at the same time most puzzling features of Paul's writings is the way he speaks of his conversion. The fact that he thinks of it as his *commissioning* rather than as a conversion has of course often been noted. So, for example, John Knox: for Paul 'its major significance lay in the fact that the experience made him a witness of the Resurrection and thus qualified him to be an apostle (referring to 1 Cor. 9: 1, 15: 8 and Gal. 1: 11–17). But he never cites it as the explanation (although it was undoubtedly the occasion) of his Christian life.'[1] What is even more striking, however, is the fact that he understood his commissioning from the first as having the Gentiles in view. This is not presented as a deduction or a corollary which Paul drew from some *other* conviction given to him in or brought home to him by the encounter on the Damascus road. It belonged to the central conviction itself. The primary purpose of the risen Christ's appearance was to send him to the Gentiles.

The evidence on the point is quite clear. Gal. 1: 15–16—ὅτε δὲ εὐδόκησεν (ὁ θεὸς) ... ἀποκαλύψαι τὸν υἱὸν αὐτοῦ ἐν ἐμοί, ἵνα εὐαγγελίζωμαι αὐτὸν ἐν τοῖς ἔθνεσιν .... The force of the ἵνα should not be diluted. So far as Paul was concerned, God's purpose in revealing his Son in Paul (that is, on the Damascus road) was to commission Paul as apostle to the Gentiles. And though it has often been argued that this full significance of the Damascus road Christophany may only have come to him later or grown within Paul's conscious thought over a period,[2]

---

[1] J. Knox, *Chapters in a Life of Paul* (London, 1954), 117; see also e.g. J. Munck, *Paul and the Salvation of Mankind* (London, 1959), 11–35; Wilckens (below n. 12), 12; M. Hengel, *Between Jesus and Paul* (London, 1983), 53; K. Stendahl, *Paul Among Jews and Gentiles* (London, 1977), 7–12; J. Blank, *Paulus: Vom Jesus zum Christentum* (München, 1982), 20; Kim (below n. 17), 56; H. Koester, *Introduction to the New Testament* (Philadelphia, 1982), ii. 100. The perennial attraction of speculation on the psychology of Paul's conversion, though renounced regularly in the above, is attested by J. G. Gager, 'Some Notes on Paul's Conversion', *NTS* 27 (1980–1), 697–704, who suggests that Paul's compulsion to engage in Gentile evangelism was part of Paul's attempt to reduce 'post-decision dissonance'; but here as elsewhere Paul's own assertions should be given greater weight than our speculative reconstructions.

[2] e.g. Dupont (below n. 11): 'He did not claim that Christ had given him the command to evangelize the Gentiles and there is nothing to allow us to imagine that this injunction was given

Paul's own claim is that it was there in the beginning, already clear to him before he first met the other apostles, a well-formed conviction which owed nothing to them (1: 16–17) and everything to that initial revelation (1: 1, 11–12).[3]

Elsewhere Paul speaks in more general terms: Christ appeared to him to make him an apostle (1 Cor. 9: 1; 15: 8–9). But for Paul that always meant 'apostle to the Gentiles' (Rom. 11: 13). It is most unlikely that Paul ever thought of himself as called to be an apostle (without further specification), and only later concluded that his apostleship was to the Gentiles.[4] So far as he was concerned what he received from the risen Christ was grace and apostleship εἰς ὑπακοὴν πίστεως ἐν πᾶσιν τοῖς ἔθνεσιν (Rom. 1: 5; so also 15: 15–16).

Similarly with Paul's use of the μυστήριον motif. Clearly the mystery for Paul was the divine purpose to bring in the Gentiles into the people of God (Rom. 11: 25), the mystery 'made known to all the nations, to bring them to the obedience of faith' (16: 25–6—εἰς ὑπακοὴν πίστεως εἰς πάντα τὰ ἔθνη γνωρισθέντος).[5] According to Col. 1: 26–7 it was precisely this ministry which Paul was given (by implication, in the initial commissioning which constituted and shaped the rest of his life): to make known 'the riches of the glory of this mystery among the Gentiles'. The same point is made more explicitly in Eph. 3: he (Paul) had been given the stewardship of God's grace (compare Rom. 1: 5), by means of revelation (κατὰ ἀποκάλυψιν—compare Gal. 1: 12, 16), the mystery of the Gentiles being fellow-heirs, members of the same body, partakers of the promise in Christ Jesus through the gospel; it was of this gospel Paul

him explicitly at this time' (193); even more emphatically, M. S. Enslin, *Reapproaching Paul* (Philadelphia, 1972), 64–5: cf. H. Schlier, *Galater*⁴ (Göttingen, 1965), 56; but also F. Mussner, *Galaterbrief*³ (Freiburg, 1977), 87–8. However the fact that Paul here clearly evokes the commissioning of Isa. 49: 1–6 ('... formed me from the womb ... a light to the nations ...') and Jer. 1: 4–5 ('Before I formed you in the womb ... I appointed you a prophet to the nations') should not be so lightly ignored. Paul at least intended it to be understood that his commission came to him directly from and in the Damascus encounter. See further Munck especially, 24–9.

[3] On the significance of the verbs used in 1: 16 and 18 see my 'The Relationship between Paul and Jerusalem according to Galatians 1 and 2', *NTS* 28 (1982), 462–6. The strength of Paul's assertions in Gal. 1: 1, 11–12 seem to tell against the view that Paul inherited the Gentile mission from the Hellenists. How far the Hellenists had already gone in opening the gospel to the Gentiles is not clear either from Galatians or from Acts (Hengel, *Between Jesus and Paul*, 53–4). On the question of whether the universal mission originated further back, with Jesus himself, see now E. Best, 'The Revelation to Evangelize the Gentiles', *JTS* 35 (1984), 1–30; C. H. H. Scobie, 'Jesus or Paul? The Origin of the Universal Mission of the Church', *From Jesus to Paul*, F. W. Beare FS, ed. P. Richardson and J. C. Hurd (Waterloo, Ontario, 1984), 47–60.

[4] Cf. M. Dibelius and W. G. Kümmel, *Paul* (London, 1953): 'The supposition that Paul was converted a second time—from missionary to the Jews to missionary to the Gentiles—is untenable, for he speaks too clearly of one radical conversion (Phil. 3: 7–11). He began the mission to the Gentiles not more than some weeks or months after the occurrence, and his decisive motive for doing so must have lain in the experience of conversion' (50).

[5] Although these words were added later to the letter they succeed in summing up a central theme of Romans.

had been made a minister by the gift of God's grace to preach to the Gentiles ... (3: 2–9).

If final confirmation is necessary we need simply refer to the accounts of Paul's conversion in Acts. In each case, though in strikingly different ways, the same point is made. The purpose of the risen Christ in stopping Paul short on the road to Damascus was to send him to the Gentiles. And in each case the statement of this purpose is an integral part of the story itself. To Ananias the Lord says, 'He is a chosen instrument of mine to carry my name before the Gentiles' (9: 15). Ananias informs Paul: 'you will be a witness to all men of what you have seen and heard' (22: 15). Most striking of all, in the third account it is the Lord himself in the Damascus road encounter itself who tells Paul that he is sending him to the Gentiles (26: 17–18).[6] Clearly what is being preserved here is the same conviction to which Paul himself gave expression in his own letters: that his calling to become apostle to the Gentiles was not merely rooted in the Damascus road epiphany but constituted its chief content and its most immediate as well as most lasting impact.[7]

II

In view of the emphasis which Paul (and the earliest Christian traditions) placed upon this point, and the consistency of that emphasis, the treatment of Paul's conversion-commissioning by successive commentators is somewhat surprising. For even where there is a recognition of this Pauline emphasis, the tendency generally has been to place the focus of the Damascus road encounter elsewhere, with the call to the Gentiles understood, implicitly or explicitly, as a secondary corollary, a deduction which Paul may not have drawn for some time. The temptation to attempt to spell out the rationale of the conclusion, 'therefore to the Gentiles', has rarely been resisted, but almost always the reasoning process envisaged seems a good deal more circuitous, even tortuous, than can be easily encompassed by the rather bald statements of Paul and the other traditions.[8]

[6] G. B. Caird, *The Apostolic Age* (London, 1955): 'The third account agrees more closely than the other two with Paul's own description, and it is best to follow this version and to assume that the Gentile mission was an integral part of Paul's original call to apostleship' (123); see also Munck (above, n. 1), 27. For more cautious assessments of the Acts evidence see G. Lohfink, *The Conversion of St Paul* (Chicago, 1976); C. W. Hedrick, 'Paul's Conversion/Call A Comparative Analysis of the Three Reports in Acts', *JBL* 100 (1981), 415–32.

[7] The different accounts in Acts and Galatians of Paul's activities following his conversion at least agree to the extent that they show him active in evangelism (Acts 9: 19–30; Gal. 1: 23).

[8] This is not an appeal to an auditory element in the Damascus road encounter, as though it would suffice to say Paul heard the words 'I am sending you to the Gentiles' (Acts 26: 17–18). Even were that to have been the case (and an auditory element in visionary experiences can

One possibility has been to depict the main impact of the Damascus epiphany in *Christological* terms. So, for example, H. G. Wood and Philippe Menoud have argued that the scandal for Paul the persecutor was the earliest Christian claim that the crucified Jesus was the expected Messiah. Consequently the Christological fact of Jesus' Messiahship is the first thing that his Damascus road experience brought home to him, with the soteriological significance seen as secondary, and the call to the Gentiles barely considered.[9] Certainly there must be something of this involved in Paul's radical rethink. As a devout Jew the cross would have been a scandal to him (1 Cor. 1: 23), and the fact that 'Christ' has become such an established referent for Jesus, not least in such formulations as 'Christ died' and 'Christ crucified',[10] clearly implies that this was part of the base-rock faith of the first Christians to which Paul was converted. But it is hardly enough to explain the rationale of Paul's commissioning: the conviction 'Jesus is Messiah' hardly leads immediately to the corollary, 'therefore to the Gentiles'. More damaging is the fact that Paul himself never seems to trace out or imply such a progression of thought. The recognition of Jesus' Messiahship is insufficient explanation of Paul's apostolic self-understanding.

In recent years the more popular explanation has focused on the *soteriological* aspects of the Damascus epiphany. The argument here generally runs as follows: that already before Paul's conversion the first Christians (or at least the Hellenists) had posed the alternatives, salvation through Christ rather than through the law. This was why Saul the Pharisee persecuted them so fiercely—out of zeal for the law (Phil. 3: 6). Paul's conversion therefore was conversion to this understanding of salvation. The conviction 'to the Gentiles' then follows as an immediate corollary: since faith in Christ, or the gospel of Christ, is now seen to have replaced the law in God's scheme of salvation, it follows that

---

hardly be ruled out on *a priori* grounds), the words heard must have spoken to some established understanding or train of thought in Paul. It is the rationale of that movement in Paul's thought, however achieved, which is the subject of investigation.

[9] H. G. Wood, 'The Conversion of Paul: Its Nature, Antecedents and Consequences', *NTS* 1 (1954–5), 276–82; P. H. Menoud, 'Revelation and Tradition: The Influence of Paul's Conversion on his Theology', *Interpretation* 7 (1953), 131–41. A link could be made through Isa. 49: 1–6, on the assumption that the first Christians had already attributed Messianic significance to it, except that Paul refers the passage more to *himself* (above n. 2), or by arguing that the conviction that the Messianic era had already come carried with it a cosmic or world-wide perspective (cf. Blank op. cit. n. 1 above, 21 ff.), except that the typical Jewish eschatological hope was for the Gentiles to come *in* to Israel (Mt. Zion) rather than of a mission *out to* the Gentiles (Ps. 22: 27; Isa. 2: 2–3; 56: 6–8; Zech. 14: 16; Tob. 13: 11; *Ps. Sol.* 17: 33–5; Matt. 8: 11/Luke 13: 29).

[10] See e.g. G. Bornkamm, *Das Ende des Gesetzes: Ges. Aufs. I* (München, 1952), 40; W. Kramer, *Christ, Lord, Son of God* (London, 1966), 26–8; J. D. G. Dunn, *Unity and Diversity in the New Testament* (London, 1977), 42–3.

this gospel must be open to all men and not just Jews.[11] The most forceful and influential exposition along these lines in recent years has been offered by Ulrich Wilckens. Paul's conversion to the gospel of Christ and his commission to the Gentiles are linked because Christ appeared to him as 'the end of the law' (Rom. 10: 4); his appearance to Paul indicates that in Christ there has been a decisive transition in the terms of salvation-history; 'Christ ὑπὲρ ἡμῶν', rather than the law (of the Jews), means 'for us', both Jew and Gentile.[12]

Here too there must be at least some truth in this explanation, as Phil. 3: 5–9 surely indicates. But is it so clear that a sharp antinomian antithesis between law and Christ had already been drawn prior to Paul? The testimony of Acts 6–8 indicates more a break with temple and cult rather than with the law as a whole, or the law in principle. And even Paul's zeal for the law probably speaks more of the Pharisee's high evaluation of the law in all its outworking (Gal. 1: 14) than of a complete breach with the law on the part of the Hellenists. The difficulty here is this: the more complete we see the breach between law and gospel to be *before* Paul's conversion, the more difficult is it to explain why the sort of confrontation described in Gal. 2: 1–10 and 11–14 did not occur sooner; and the more difficult is it to understand why it was Paul who came to be regarded as the chief arch-heretic and apostate in Jewish Christian tradition (*Epistula Petri* 2: 3; Clem. *Hom.* 17: 18–19).[13] The more obvious line of reasoning is that Paul was so remembered because he was in fact the one who brought the tension between law and gospel (already present in Jesus' own ministry—Mark 7: 1–23/ Matt. 15: 1–20) to its sharpest and indeed antithetical expression. At the very least the neat link forged by Wilckens ('the end of the law', therefore 'to the Gentiles') must stand in question. Certainly Paul himself never poses such an argument or justification for his mission to the Gentiles. Rather, the *immediacy* of his conviction, 'to the Gentiles', and the *delay* before Paul's and Gentile Christian practice was seen as a threat to Jewish Christian self-understanding, together suggest that Paul's calling to the Gentiles may have been the *primary* feature of the Damascus road encounter for Paul, with the implications for the law and its bearing on the gospel being more the *corollary*, worked out with

[11] See e.g. J. Dupont, 'The Conversion of Paul, and its Influence on his Understanding of Salvation by Faith', *Apostolic History and the Gospel*, F. F. Bruce FS, ed. W. W. Gasque and R. P. Martin (Exeter, 1970), 176–94. This has been the dominant view in German scholarship—see e.g. P. Stuhlmacher, '"Das Ende des Gesetzes": Über Ursprung und Ansatz der paulinischen Theologie', *Versöhnung, Gesetz und Gerechtigkeit* (Göttingen, 1981), 176 and n. 22.

[12] U. Wilckens, 'Die Bekehrung des Paulus als religionsgeschichtliches Problem', *Rechtfertigung als Freiheit: Paulusstudien* (Neukirchen, 1974), 11–32 (particularly 15, 18, 23–5). So Stuhlmacher 179–86.

[13] Further details in Dunn, *Unity and Diversity*, 241.

increasing sharpness over the early years of his work as a missionary of
the church at Antioch.

The variation of this view, that it was the Damascus road experience
itself whch posed the sharpness of the antithesis to Paul, can also claim
some support. Either we could say that Paul's own experience of grace
in that encounter (accepted by Christ despite his persecution inspired
by zeal for the law) brought home to him 'the bankruptcy of the law
and the all-sufficiency of Christ' there and then and therefore the
accessibility of that grace to Gentile as well as Jew (compare 1 Cor. 15:
10).[14] Or we could argue that Paul's confrontation with a Jesus crucified and cursed by the law (Gal. 3: 13), but now obviously vindicated
by God, convinced him there and then that the law could no longer
function as God's instrument of salvation,[15] and that therefore the gospel of this Jesus should go to Gentile as well as to Jew. But the problem
remains the same in each case: nowhere does Paul himself develop or
even hint at this line of argument. Moreover, Jewish Christians before
Paul must surely have been confronted by the same charge, that the
crucified Jesus was accursed by God (Deut. 21: 23); yet there is no
suggestion that their recognition of Christ's vindication caused them to
pass a negative judgement on the law.[16] Once again both exegetical
base and the necessary rationale seem to be inadequate to sustain the
case argued.

III

In recent years the work of Seyoon Kim has brought the question of the
importance of Paul's Damascus road experience for the understanding
of Paul's faith and theology back to the forefront of discussion.[17] His
thorough and well-argued thesis marks a significant step forward in the
discussion. His claim is that crucial emphases of Paul's gospel, both
soteriological *and* Christological, were derived directly from the
Damascus event. Indeed he is prepared to argue that central features of
Paul's Christology and soteriology were formed to a considerable
extent in that encounter itself.

So far as its soteriological significance is concerned, Kim adds little to
the main thesis already argued by Wilckens and others. 'Rom. 10: 2–10
corresponds with Paul's autobiographical statements especially in Phil.

[14] So F. F. Bruce, *Galatians* (Exeter, 1982), 93–4.
[15] See e.g. those cited by Sanders and Räisänen in n. 16 below.
[16] E. P. Sanders, *Paul, the Law and the Jewish People* (Philadelphia, 1983), 25–6; H. Räisänen,
Paul and the Law (Tübingen, 1983), 249–50.
[17] S. Kim, *The Origin of Paul's Gospel* (Tübingen, 1981).

3: 4 ff.', so that Rom. 10: 4 can be attributed directly to Paul's conversion: 'in the Christophany on the road to Damascus Paul received the knowledge of Christ as the end of the law'.[18] This affirmation made with minimal argument in the opening pages of the book is already a statement of his conclusion on the point.[19] Its main elaboration comes in his section on 'Paul the Persecutor', in which he ties together the evidence of Phil. 3: 5–6 and Gal. 3: 13: the former indicating that Christians' criticism of the law was the main reason for Paul's persecuting zeal, the latter that Paul himself must have used Deut. 21: 23 when persecuting the Christians. 'The two offences, the criticism of the law and the proclamation of the crucified Jesus as the Messiah, belonged together: the Christians criticized the law in the name of Jesus the Messiah. ... So Paul was confronted with the alternative: either the law or the crucified Christ.'[20] Kim's later treatment of 'Justification' in his chapter on 'Soteriology' is simply a restatement of this earlier finding. Paul's own experience of grace on the Damascus road is the basis of his doctrine of justification. 'Paul perceived the revelation of the Son of God on the Damascus road as the revelation of God's righteousness apart from the law (Rom. 3: 21) immediately.' 'At the Damascus revelation Paul came to understand that "no man is justified by (works of) the law" and so to see the fundamental problem of the law itself.'[21]

The Christological thesis grows out of 2 Cor. 3: 4–4: 6, particularly 4: 4 and 6, and again is already stated *in nuce* in the opening pages: 'the risen Christ must have appeared to Paul accompanied by the radiance of light which was perceived by him as the divine glory'.[22] The elaboration of this thesis develops partly out of the preceding argument about Christ and the law. 'This Corinthians passage indicates not only that at the Damascus revelation Paul realized that Christ had superseded the Torah but also that *at the same time* he perceived Christ as the true Wisdom' (since the Torah had previously been identified with divine Wisdom).[23] But the main elaboration and principal contribution of the book focuses on the use of εἰκὼν τοῦ θεοῦ in 2 Cor. 4: 4. The phrase itself carries great weight: 'the conception of Christ as the εἰκὼν τοῦ θεοῦ both in 2 Cor. 4: 4 and Col. 1: 15 clearly conveys the sense that Christ is the (visible, therefore material) manifestation of (the invisible) God, and therefore his likeness to God is strongly implied in it'.[24] This is

---

[18] Ibid., 3–4.
[19] See particularly ibid., 126, 307–8.
[20] Ibid., 46–8.
[21] Ibid., 269–311, quotations from pp. 271 and 283.
[22] Ibid., 8.
[23] Ibid., 128–36, quotation from 128 (my emphasis).
[24] Ibid., 219. See also particularly J. Jervell, *Imago Dei* (Göttingen, 1960), 214–8; followed by C. K. Barrett, *2 Corinthians* (London, 1973), 132–5.

filled out by reference to the epiphanic visions in Jewish apocalyptic, particularly Ezek. 1: 26 and Dan. 7: 13: what Paul saw (or understood himself to be seeing) was Christ as 'the physical embodiment of divinity';[25] 'Paul's Damascus experience must have led him immediately to Dan. 7: 13 because he saw a heavenly figure "like a son of man" just as Daniel did.'[26] Into this already complex pattern Kim weaves a further strand by identifying the concepts Son of God (Gal. 1: 16) and image of God (2 Cor. 4: 4): 'to see the risen Christ as appearing "like a son of God" is the same as to see him as having the εἰκόνα of God'.[27] This εἰκών-Christology provides a further root for Paul's Wisdom Christology (Wisd. 7: 26), and it develops also into his Adam Christology (compare Gen. 1: 26 f.). 'Thus, both Paul's Wisdom-Christology and Adam-Christology are grounded in the Damascus Christophany.'[28] The latter conclusion in addition allows Kim to elaborate the soteriological significance of the Damascus encounter for Paul beyond the claims about justification inherited from Wilckens and others. If Christ is the Son and image of God, then God has restored in him the divine image and glory lost by Adam: hence Paul's concepts of believers' being adopted as sons of God, being transformed into Christ's image and made a 'new man' in him, the last Adam.[29]

What of Paul's own conclusion, 'therefore to the Gentiles'? Kim fully recognizes that 'for Paul the Christophany on the Damascus road constituted . . . his apostolic commission for the Gentile mission'.[30] He is quite clear that the decisive revelation of the 'mystery' of Rom. 11: 25 f. came to Paul on the Damascus road, and he goes on to argue that Paul was probably decisively influenced on this point by Isa. 6 and 49: 1–6.[31] But how does this tie in to Kim's main Christological and soteriological thesis? Unfortunately he does not address this question at any length.[32] Such rationale as he does offer lists the conviction of 'universal mission' as a corollary to the 'new creation' corollary of his Adam Christology, itself derived from the Damascus Christophany.[33] But that 'therefore to

[25] Kim, 226; the phrase is from C. C. Rowland's thesis, 'The Influence of the First Chapters of Ezekiel on Jewish and Early Christian Literature' (Cambridge, Ph.D., 1974), to which Kim acknowledges his indebtedness. See now Rowland's own publication, *The Open Heaven* (London, 1982).

[26] Kim, 251.   [27] Ibid., 257.

[28] Ibid., 257–67, quotation from p. 267 (italicized).

[29] Ibid., 315–29, 332.   [30] Ibid., 57.

[31] Ibid., 74–99; note also 10, 23–4. See also above n. 2.

[32] One of the unfinished tasks to which Kim alludes in his closing paragraph (335).

[33] Ibid., 268. Kim makes a distinction between the commission for the Gentile mission and Paul's conception of a world-wide mission (which took time, 'perhaps more than a decade', for its full development—60–1). But does Paul make such a distinction? Cf. Gal. 1: 16 with Rom. 1: 5— ἐν πᾶσιν τοῖς ἔθνεσιν; also Isa. 49: 6—'I will give you as a light to the nations, that my salvation may reach to the ends of the earth'. See also above nn. 2 and 4.

the Gentiles' does not seem to have the immediacy it had for Paul, so that the question about the correlation of these different emphases in Paul's response to and understanding of the Damascus Christophany remains open. How did it all hang together or tie up in Paul's thinking?

IV

As the most recent and most thorough study in the area of our concern, Kim's monograph deserves to be given the main focus of attention. Its central thesis can be questioned at a number of points.

1. 2 Cor. 4: 4, 6 can very properly be taken as a reference to Paul's Damascus road experience, even though Paul expresses himself in more generalized terms. But to what extent can this passage be taken as a description of what Paul *saw*? He certainly uses the language and imagery of light shining, which naturally suggests some correlation with the description in Acts (9: 3—αὐτὸν περιήστραψεν φῶς ἐκ τοῦ οὐρανοῦ; similarly 22: 6 and 26: 13), but the talk is of the impact of the event on Paul rather than a description of the event itself: God has shone his light ἐν ταῖς καρδίαις ἡμῶν; the light is 'the light of the gospel', 'the light of knowledge' (τὸν φωτισμὸν τοῦ εὐαγγελίου ..., φωτισμὸν τῆς γνώσεως ...). And the fact that Paul makes it a generalized description of Christian conversion confirms that he cannot be thinking particularly of the features which *distinguished* his conversion from those which followed (compare 1 Cor. 15: 8—'last of all'). In fact the whole passage is still influenced by the Midrash on Exod. 34 (2 Cor. 3: 7–18),[34] with Moses' entrance unveiled into the presence of God seen as the type of *all* Jewish conversion from old covenant to new; and the theme of divine glory (δόξα) is drawn more from there than anywhere else (2 Cor. 3: 7–11, 18; 4: 4, 6).[35]

2. Whatever we make of 2 Cor. 4: 4, 6 in particular, the question still stands, what did Paul see on the Damascus road? Christ 'clothed in glory', could be deduced from 2 Cor. 4: 4, 6 (cf. 1 Cor. 15: 43; Phil. 3: 21).[36] But Kim also deduces from the important role played in early Christology by Ps. 110: 1 that Paul 'saw him exalted by God and enthroned at his right hand',[37] saw him as the εἰκὼν τοῦ θεοῦ, as "one like

---

[34] See e.g. my '2 Corinthians 3. 17—"The Lord is the Spirit"', *JTS* 21 (1970), 309–20.

[35] Rowland, *Open Heaven*, like Kim, treats Gal. 1: 12, 16 as a reference to what Paul saw, but does not draw 2 Cor. 4: 4, 6 into the discussion (376–9). Somewhat misleadingly he compares 2 Cor. 3: 18 when speaking of ascents to heaven which involve separation from the earthly body (384).

[36] Kim, 7, 228.

[37] Ibid., 108, 111, 225; cf. Rowland, *Open Heaven*, 378.

a son of man"' (Dan. 7: 13), 'one like a son of God'.[38] But this is now reading a tremendous amount into the few very allusive references Paul makes to the Damascus road itself. Does it follow that because Paul uses the titles 'Lord' and 'Son' in 1 Cor. 9: 1 and Gal. 1: 16 we should conclude that Paul *saw* Jesus as enthroned, as 'Son' (however that would be expressed visually)? May these titles not simply be referents rather than descriptions, Paul's way of saying 'The one I encountered then I know (now) as "Lord" and "Son of God"'? Is it even so clear that the ὅς ἐστιν εἰκὼν τοῦ θεοῦ is a description of what Paul saw, rather than a confessional formula attracted by association of ideas to what has gone before, in the style of a liturgical coda?

3. Assuming that Jesus appeared to Paul as a glorious figure, do the parallels cited by Kim support the view that Paul must at once have jumped to the conclusion that this was a divine figure, the figure of hypostatized Wisdom, properly speaking a *theo*phany, as Kim clearly wants to infer?[39] But the same range of evidence indicates that the glorious figures seen in some visions were frequently identified as angels (Dan. 10; *Apoc. Zeph.* 6: 11–15; 2 *Enoch* 1: 5; *Apoc. Abr.* 11; *Asc. Isa.* 7: 2), or as dead heroes of the past now transfigured or exalted in some degree (Samuel—1 Sam. 18: 13–14; the righteous—Wisd. 5: 5; Jeremiah—2 Macc. 15: 13–14; Enoch—*Jub.* 4: 23; 2 *Enoch* 22: 8; Adam and Abel—*Test. Abr.* A 11–13). Kim's assumption that the man-like figure of Daniel 7's vision is a divine figure,[40] is highly questionable, since the man-like figure seems rather to represent the saints of the Most High over against the beast-like figures who represent the enemies of Israel.[41] Even more questionable is Kim's attempt to merge different elements of different visions into a composite form of theophanic vision (in a manner disturbingly similar to the *religionsgeschichtliche* constructs of the 'pre-Christian Gnostic redeemer myth' or the 'divine man')— particularly Ezek. 1: 26, Dan. 7: 13, and the identification of the figure

[38] Ibid., 193, 224, 251, 257.

[39] Ibid., 198, 214, 222–3.

[40] Ibid., 208, 246; but clouds of heaven denote a mode of transport through or to heaven, rather than determine the status of the one so carried as divine (cf. 1 Thess. 4: 17; Rev. 11: 12).

[41] See further M. Casey, *Son of Man* (London, 1979); J. D. G. Dunn, *Christology in the Making* (London, 1980), 67–82; B. Lindars, *Jesus, Son of Man* (London, 1983), 1–16. Kim's complete failure to reckon with any of Casey's work is regrettable, and all the more surprising in his sequel, '*The "Son of Man"' as the Son of God* (Tübingen, 1983). The flimsy possibilities which he draws from 4QpsDan Aᵃ and variant readings of the Greek text of Dan. 7: 13 are scarcely sufficient to overthrow the clear indications of the NT writings, that in the beginnings of Christianity 'son of man' had no titular significance or heavenly referent outside Christian circles. Since both the Similitudes of Enoch and 4 Ezra are to be dated after the time of Jesus and Paul (as Kim accepts—n. 44 below), and since they both present their conception of the heavenly figure (Son of Man, Man) as though it were a fresh interpretation of the Dan. 7 vision (see Casey, *Son of Man* and Dunn, *Christology*, above), they can scarcely be called as evidence for the pre-Christian Jewish understanding of Dan. 7.

seen as Messiah and Son of God.[42] Some partial merging of this sort is evident in the Similitudes of Enoch (1 *Enoch* 46) and 4 Ezra 13; and it has certainly occurred in the vision of Rev. 1: 13–14.[43] But can we assume that the whole composite was already in play in Paul's mind at the time of his conversion, simply on the basis of the 'image' language used in 2 Cor. 4: 4? Where the whole point of the argument is to demonstrate that a Christology, which is certainly evident later, actually emerged in Paul's thought following (or even at) the Damascus encounter, a more carefully delineated exposition is necessary.[44]

4. Kim's thesis is strongest when he is able to argue that Paul was converted to a view he had previously fought against. But in this case his thesis is that it was Paul who first made the identification of Christ as divine Wisdom.[45] Again we must ask whether the use of $\epsilon i\kappa\grave{\omega}\nu \tau o\hat{v}$ $\theta\epsilon o\hat{v}$ in 2 Cor. 4: 4 is strong enough evidence that Paul traced this identification back to the Damascus Christophany.[46] The fact that the talk of 'wisdom' features so prominently in the Corinthian correspondence suggests more strongly if anything that a greater stimulus for Paul was the misuse of 'wisdom' ideas in Corinth itself.[47]

5. Since the argument turns so much on the use of $\epsilon i\kappa\grave{\omega}\nu \tau o\hat{v} \theta\epsilon o\hat{v}$ in 2 Cor. 4: 4, it is worth enquiring more closely whether the thought is not more of Adam than of Wisdom.[48] The allusion to creation in 4: 6 does not tell either way. More to the point is the fact that in other occurrences of $\epsilon i\kappa\acute{\omega}\nu$ in the undisputed Paulines the thought is of Adam not of Wisdom (1 Cor. 11: 7; 15: 49; compare Rom. 1: 23). More significant is the eschatological thrust of the most closely parallel passages—the transformation of believers into the image of Christ or of God as the goal of the whole process of salvation which climaxes in Resurrection (2 Cor. 3: 18–5: 5; compare particularly Rom. 8: 29; 1 Cor. 15: 49; also

[42] Kim, *Origin*, 214–15, 246, 248. One should hesitate more than Kim does before taking the phrase 'one like a son of man' out of the context of Dan. 7, where it has a clear function in contrast to creatures like extraordinary beasts, and where it is distinguished from the figure on the throne, and linking it to Ezek. 1: 26, where it is the occupant of the throne itself who is referred to and who is described with the greatest tentativeness and reserve as a 'likeness like the appearance of a Man'.

[43] See particularly C. Rowland, 'The Vision of the Risen Christ in Rev. 1. 13 ff.', *JTS* 31 (1980), 1–11.

[44] Kim accepts Black's view that the Similitudes of Enoch stem from 'the same period and vintage' as 4 Ezra (*Origin*, 247).

[45] Kim, *Origin*, 114–17, 127–36, 258–60.

[46] '... grounded *ultimately* in Paul's Damascus experience' (Kim, ibid., 114, my emphasis) leaves more scope for other input.

[47] See further my *Christology* §24, especially 179.

[48] See e.g. M. Black, 'The Pauline Doctrine of the Second Adam', *SJT* 7 (1954), 174; R. Scroggs, *The Last Adam* (Oxford, 1966), 68, 96–9; A. T. Lincoln, *Paradise Now and Not Yet* (SNTSMS 43, Cambridge, 1981), 190. Jervell also regards 2 Cor. 3: 18–4: 6 as an exposition of Gen. 1: 27 (173–6), but is distracted by his belief that Paul's 'image of God' language is influenced by 'the Philonic-gnostic conception of the divine Anthropos' (217)—a thesis which Kim rightly rejects (*Origin*, 162–83).

Phil. 3: 21). In this motif the image which Christ bears (or is) is that of the last Adam, Christ as fulfilling the original purpose God had in making man to be his image (Gen. 1: 26).[49]

6. By way of corollary it should be noted that the affirmation of Christ as 'Lord' also ties back into Adam Christology, by virtue of the integration of Ps. 110: 1 with Ps. 8: 6—Christ as Lord fulfilling God's original purpose for Adam's domination over 'all things'.[50] This development is too widespread to be attributed solely to Paul and it could even predate his own contribution to Adam Christology (Mark 12: 36; 1 Cor. 15: 25–7; Eph. 1: 20–2; Heb. 1: 13–2: 8; 1 Pet. 3: 22).[51] If so, it suggests that the thought of the risen Jesus as eschatological man, as the one beginning a new form of humanity in which God's image and glory is fully expressed, was quite a prominent feature of earliest Christian thinking, and that in using the εἰκών language of the exalted Christ in 2 Cor. 4: 4 Paul was more likely to have had that emphasis in mind.

It should not go unnoticed that this shift in emphasis helps to resolve the problem from which we have started. For if indeed the εἰκών τοῦ θεοῦ in 2 Cor. 4: 4 speaks primarily of Christ as Adam, then the immediate corollary is that in 2 Cor. 3–4 Paul deliberately transforms the matrix of salvation-history from Israel and Sinai to man and creation. The rationale of Paul's thought would then have been more direct: if with Christ now raised from the dead God's purpose for man (and not simply Israel) has been realized, it must follow that the object of his concern is mankind as a whole and not merely the Jews; God's purpose (not least in stopping Paul short in his full flight as a persecutor on behalf of Israel's prerogatives and law) must be to realize through Christ his purpose of creation and not simply of election. The puzzling 'therefore to the Gentiles' thus becomes a more immediate deduction from the Damascus Christophany than even Kim allows. Conversely, since 'to the Gentiles' is so central in Paul's recollection of his conversion, it probably confirms that Paul intended the εἰκών language of 2 Cor. 4: 4 to evoke Adam rather than Wisdom motifs, and that the Wisdom Christological corollary may have taken longer to develop than Kim envisages.[52]

[49] Scroggs: 'Christ as image of God clearly describes eschatological humanity' (99). D. J. A. Clines, 'The Image of God in Man', *Tyndale Bulletin* 19 (1958), 53–103, points out that Gen. 1: 26 is better translated 'Let us make man as our image' or 'to be our image' (75–80). On the significance of Adam Christology in Paul see my *Christology*, 105–113, 126–7.

[50] See further my 'Was Christianity a Monotheistic Faith from the Beginning?' *SJT* 35 (1982), particularly 327–8.

[51] Dunn, *Christology*, 108–9.

[52] Dunn, *Christology*, §24, especially 194–6.

V

Kim's restatement of the soteriological significance of the Damascus encounter for Paul is open to the same critique offered above of the earlier formulations of the same thesis (above part II). In particular, the more significance one reads back into the Damascus event (Christ at once seen as the end of the law), the less easy is it to understand why the confrontations of Gal. 2 did not take place earlier. Kim himself recognizes that he may be pushing his thesis too hard. In his final re-statement he contents himself with the claim: 'it is probably better to think that Paul saw the full implications of the Damascus revelation and more or less completely formulated the main lines of his theology soon after the Damascus revelation—certainly, at latest by the time of the Apostolic Council . . .—than to posit a long period of slow develop-ment'.[53] But since the Apostolic Council took place about fifteen years after his conversion, probably more than half-way through his life as a Christian, this qualification only serves to undermine the boldness of the earlier claims and to pose once again the issue of what was the *immediate* impact of the Damascus Christophany and what was its theo-logical rationale in Paul's mind.

I suspect in fact that the sharpness of the antithesis, *either* Jesus *or* the law, was indeed a later development, at least in the sharpness with which Paul poses it explicitly or implicitly in Gal. 3, Rom. 10, and Phil. 3; moreover that the antithesis as antithesis was more the corollary of 'therefore to the Gentiles' than vice-versa.

(a) This would certainly accord best with the sequence of Gal. 1–2. There the commission 'to the Gentiles' is clear from the first (1: 16), whereas circumcision only emerges as a clear issue some fourteen or seventeen years later (2: 1–10), and 'covenantal nomism' (the food laws and purity standards which regulated daily life and all social inter-course) only emerges as an issue after that (2: 11–18). What becomes evident from the latter episode is precisely that the great bulk of Jewish Christians did *not* see an antithesis between faith in Christ and a life regulated by the Torah. So the question cannot be avoided: when and how soon did it become an either-or antithesis in earliest Christian thought (including Paul's)? Certainly the simple assumption that Paul read Rom. 10: 4 straight off from his experience on the Damascus road does not seem to accord too well with the testimony of Gal. 1–2.[54]

(b) Wherever Paul poses the antithesis in his writings (explicitly or implicitly), he does so within the context of and as part of what

[53] Kim, *Origin*, 335; so earlier 102–3.
[54] See further Dunn, 'Relationship' 303–36; also 'The New Perspective on Paul', *BJRL* 65 (1983), 95–122.

amounts to a redefinition of the people of God. In Gal. 3 the question is, who are Abraham's offspring? The definition is reworked in terms of promise rather than law—the promise which had the Gentiles in view from the first (particularly vv. 8, 14). In Rom. 9–10 it is Israel's failure as a nation which is in view (9: 31), the assumption of Paul's kinsmen that righteousness is something which is peculiarly theirs and not anybody else's (10:3). In Phil. 3 the contrast is drawn between the before and after of his conversion where the 'before' all has to do with Paul's previous self-definition of himself as a loyal and devout Jew (3: 4–6). In each case the clear implication is that his own conversion involved a shattering of his self-identity as a member of the people of God (Israel). Not any striving for self-achievement, not even the possibility of fulfilling the whole law (compare Gal. 5: 14), but his devoutness *as a Jew* was what was called in question. A reassessment of the role of the law was of course bound up with this, but not the law as a revelation of God's will (compare Rom. 13: 8–10), rather the law in its function of marking the boundary between the righteous and the sinner, between Jew and Gentile.[55] The clear implication of all this is that the insight, 'therefore to the Gentiles also', was a much more fundamental part of Paul's conversion rethink, and not simply a corollary to some other principle independently arrived at.

(c) The clue for this rationale may lie in Gal. 3: 13 with its citation of Deut. 21: 23, 'Cursed is everyone who hangs on a tree'. It is now generally agreed that Deut. 21: 23 had already been referred to crucifixion at the time of Jesus (4QpNah. 1: 7–8; 11QTempleScroll 64: 6–13).[56] So the probability must be ranked as high that it had been used in the earliest Jewish polemic against the first expression of Christian faith in Jesus as Messiah—probably by Paul himself. If so, then we may fairly conclude that the line of thought behind Gal. 3: 13 was part of the reversal which Paul experienced in the Damascus Christophany. The point is this: that for Paul the loyal Jew, the curse of Deut. 21: 23 was the opposite of the blessings of the covenant (particularly Deut. 27–8); to be cursed by God was to have the covenant revoked, to be put out of the covenant (27: 58–68)—that is, to be put in the position of the Gentile sinner. The crucifixion of Jesus meant that God had rejected him, numbered him with the Gentiles, reckoned him as outside the covenant. The Damascus Christophany must obviously have turned such a line of reasoning completely on its head, for it indicated clearly

---

[55] See further my 'Works of the Law and the Curse of the Law (Gal. 3: 10–14)', *NTS* 31 (1985) 523–42.

[56] See particularly J. A. Fitzmyer, 'Crucifixion in Ancient Palestine, Qumran Literature and the New Testament', *CBQ* 40 (1978), 493–513.

that God had accepted and vindicated this one precisely as the crucified. The *immediate* corollary for Paul would be that God must therefore
favour the cursed one, the sinner outside the covenant, the Gentile.[57]
And thus it can be easily seen how the conclusion 'therefore to the
Gentiles' could follow directly from the Damascus Christophany and
not at some further remove as a corollary to more elaborate Christological and soteriological schemes.

VI

To sum up and conclude.

1. Paul's own testimony, that his commissioning to preach Christ to
the Gentiles was given him in his encounter with the risen Christ on the
road to Damascus, ought to be accorded greater importance in discussions of Paul's conversion and of the origin of his characteristic and distinctive theological emphases. Paul's conclusion, 'therefore to the
Gentiles', seems to lie closer to the root of his theology than has generally been recognized.[58]

2. Although all attempts to 'get inside' the rationale of Paul's
thought processes at the time of his conversion are inevitably speculative, Paul's own assertions make most sense when we see the primary
Christological significance of the Christophany for Paul in terms of
Adam Christology and the primary soteriological significance in terms
of a radical redefinition of the boundary marking out membership of
the covenant people of God. In other words, he saw Christ as the
'image of God' as the risen embodiment and therefore eschatological
fulfilment of God's plan from the beginning to share his glory with the
man he had created. And he understood this glorious vindication as a
reversal of the curse of Deut. 21: 23, and therefore as implying God's
covenant concern to embrace both outsider and insider, sinner as well
as blameless, Gentile as well as Jew.

3. The corollary to this is that other important emphases of Paul's
theology as we now have it may have to be regarded as the product of
further reflection on Paul's part, rather than an immediate deduction
from the Damascus Christophany. In particular, Paul's Wisdom Christology seems to owe a good deal to the stimulus of responding to the
vigorous wisdom theology which he encountered at Corinth. And the
sharpness of his antithesis between Christ and the law must certainly

[57] See again n. 55.
[58] Cf. Hengel, n. 1 above: 'This calling forms the basis of his whole theology' (53); Stendahl, n.
1 above: 'Again and again we find that there is hardly a thought of Paul's which is not tied up with
his mission ... The "I" of his writings is not "the Christian" but "the Apostle to the Gentiles"'
(12).

owe a good deal to the debate about circumcision at Jerusalem (Gal. 2: 1–10) and the confrontation about covenant restraints on social intercourse at Antioch (Gal. 2: 11–18).

4. The thesis argued here has the further value of showing how Paul's earliest theological impulses as a Christian may well have been related to and even to some extent dependent on a central feature of the Jesus-tradition. Paul the persecutor would presumably have regarded the cross as the inevitable outworking and consequence of Jesus' disregard for the rules of the covenant during his ministry (particularly his association with 'sinners'—Mark 2: 15–17; Matt. 11: 19/Luke 7: 34).[59] The reversal of the Damascus road would then carry with it a radical revision in attitude to this feature of Jesus' ministry: God accepts sinners, including 'Gentile sinners', as did Jesus when on earth (an echo of this may be implicit in Gal. 2: 17). If this is so we have a further valuable link between Jesus and Paul.

I gladly dedicate this essay to the memory of George Caird. His *The Apostolic Age* was one of the first books I read as a young student of theology. Its careful scholarship provided a model from which I greatly benefited then and since.

---

[59] See further my 'Pharisees, Sinners and Jesus' in the forthcoming M. C. Kee Festschrift, *The Social World of Formative Christianity and Judaism*, ed. P. Borgen *et al.* (Philadelphia, 1988).

20. Some Comments on Professor J. D. G. Dunn's *Christology in the Making*[1] with Special Reference to the Evidence of the Epistle to the Romans

C. E. B. CRANFIELD

THE publication of any new book of serious scholarship on the subject of NT Christology is an important event. When the book is arrestingly written and is capable of provoking to activity even sluggish minds and compelling them to work over afresh questions of the greatest importance, it will be no surprise if it stirs up a considerable flurry of reactions. Such a book is Professor Dunn's *Christology in the Making*. It undoubtedly requires and deserves careful and critical attention. The resolute application and sheer physical stamina of one who can write so substantial a book, requiring so much hard thought and at the same time involving the vast amount of research which the bibliography attests, in so short a time (on p. x Professor Dunn observes that the project 'has filled most of my research time for the past three years') command unbounded admiration. It is an astounding achievement— all the more so, as it is written with a light touch and is free from the reek of small hours' oil, though a great deal of that substance must surely have been expended on it. And it does not stand alone, but is flanked by a number of articles supporting and supplementing it, which Professor Dunn has published in recent years.[2]

To respond at all adequately to so important and already influential a book within the space which I can take is beyond my powers. What I shall attempt to do is first to make some general comments, then to refer to the exegesis of passages from Romans contained in the book, and finally to consider some features of that epistle which seem to me to have been given too little attention in it or to have been ignored.

I

Professor Dunn tells us that he has deliberately refrained from attempting 'to define "incarnation" at the outset' because of 'the considerable

[1] *Christology in the Making: A New Testament Inquiry into the Origins of the Doctrine of the Incarnation*, London, 1980.
[2] e.g., 'Was Christianity a monotheistic faith from the beginning?', in *SJT* 35 (1982), 303–36; 'In defence of a methodology', in *ET* 95 (1983–4), 295–9.

risk that any such definition would pre-set the terms and categories of the investigation and prevent the NT authors speaking to us in their own terms' (9). Had he been intending to consider all, or, at any rate, as much as possible, of the evidence which could be relevant, this procedure might have been feasible. But, since he was going to be highly selective with regard to the evidence to be considered, the method has (so it seems to me) a serious defect. For, though he does not give his readers a definition of 'incarnation' at the outset, he must of necessity have had a working definition of it in mind, by which to determine what material had to be examined and what might be ignored; and a definition, undeclared to the reader but present all the time in the author's mind controlling his selection of the evidence to be considered, was surely likely to 'pre-set the terms and categories of the investigation and prevent the NT authors speaking to us in their own terms' (9) at least as effectively as, and potentially much more damagingly than, one shared with the reader from the start. So the working definition, by which Professor Dunn selected his evidence, should surely have been declared from the beginning.

Moreover, he was not concerned with a general idea of incarnation, but was conducting '*a historical investigation into how and in what terms the doctrine of the incarnation first came to expression*, an endeavour to understand in its original context the language which initially enshrined the doctrine of the incarnation or out of which the doctrine grew' (10). Presumably the definite articles placed before 'doctrine' and 'incarnation' each time the words occur in this sentence and also in the subtitle of the book are meant to indicate that the reference is quite specifically to the historic Christian doctrine of the Incarnation. But, if that is so, would it not have been wise to state near the beginning briefly but clearly that historic Christian doctrine so as to save the readers from any doubt or confusion as to what precisely it is, the first coming to expression of which the author is seeking to investigate? Certainly the attempt must be made to understand the language used for this expression 'in its original context' (10), to 'let the NT evidence speak in its own terms and dictate its own patterns' (9), and to bear constantly in mind the danger of our misunderstanding the original intentions of the earliest Christian writers through reading back into what they have said the thoughts of later times (with none of this is any competent NT scholar likely to quarrel). But at the same time we ought to recognize the possibility of our mistaking a vision distorted by reaction against the orthodoxy of later times for an authentic seeing with the eyes of the earliest Christians. That the omission of a brief but clear statement of the sort indicated above has really facilitated an objective understanding of the

NT evidence in its own historical context seems to us highly unlikely. Is it not more likely that it has resulted in failure to recognize the relevance to the subject of inquiry of some NT material, and so has led to the exclusion from consideration of some things which ought to have been considered?

Professor Dunn himself is well aware that the Christian doctrine of the Incarnation cannot be properly understood except in the context of the Christian doctrine of the Trinity. He is also conscious of the fact that an insufficiently informed and thoughtful zeal for maintaining the doctrine of the Incarnation can betray people into tritheism.[3] Yet, while his index of subjects contains a few references under 'Trinitarian tendency', such a prime Pauline passage for the doctrine of the Trinity—and surely also for the doctrine of the Incarnation—as 2 Cor. 13: 13 (RV: 14) does not seem to be mentioned at all in the book. Reading *Christology in the Making* led me to reread once again that part of Karl Barth's *Church Dogmatics* i/1 which is concerned with the doctrine of the Trinity, and I cannot help thinking that, had Professor Dunn reread those pages when he was engaged with his book, he might have been persuaded of the relevance to his subject of some NT material which he has excluded from his discussion and also encouraged to be more precise in his use of language with regard to the pre-existence of Christ than he has been. But there is only one reference to Barth in his index of authors.

II

In the second place, we turn to a consideration of Professor Dunn's exegesis of passages in Romans. There are in all thirteen passages of Romans, of which, according to the index of NT references, some exegesis is offered; but we shall here consider only those five of them which bear directly on the question whether or not the doctrine of the Incarnation can be discerned in Paul's Epistle to the Romans.

The first is 1: 3–4. On pp. 33–5 Professor Dunn is attempting to draw out the meaning, not of these verses in their present context, but of the pre-Pauline formula which he thinks Paul has incorporated. While I am inclined to agree that the suggestion that Paul is making use of an already existing formula is probable, I do not share Professor Dunn's confidence that we can be sure of the sense it carried originally, not knowing its original context. I cannot see how his statement that it is 'clear . . . that *there is no thought of a pre-existent sonship here*' (that is, in the presumed pre-Pauline formula) can be justified. That this thought

---

[3] See *ET* 95 (1983–4), 299.

could have been present is surely not inconceivable, particularly if 'in power' was part of the original formula (an alternative he admits as possible). There are other statements in these pages which seem to me questionable. But, as I am now concerned with the sense of the passage in its context in Romans, I pass on to his suggestion on p. 138 f. that 'it is possible that Paul meant [by the "according to the flesh / according to the Spirit" antithesis] that Jesus' installation as Son of God (in power) "according to the Spirit" was in part at least the consequence of his having lived "according to the Spirit"'.[4] Paul's κατὰ πνεῦμα ἁγιωσύνης is notoriously difficult and has been very variously interpreted. Professor Dunn's explanation seems less probable than that which takes the phrase to refer to the presence of the Holy Spirit, which, as resulting from Christ's exaltation, is the guarantee of his having been appointed Son of God in power since his Resurrection. For one thing, it is surely preferable to understand the times referred to in the two phrases κατὰ πνεῦμα ἁγιωσύνης and ἐξ ἀναστάσεως νεκρῶν as the same, rather than to assume a temporal disjunction between them, as does Professor Dunn. What is most important for our present purpose is that Professor Dunn does not consider anywhere in *Christology in the Making* (as far as I can see) the possibility that κατὰ σάρκα is intended to limit the application of τοῦ γενομένου ἐκ σπέρματος Δαυίδ to the human nature which the One, who has already been described as God's Son at the beginning of v. 3, assumed, or, to put it in other words, that the point of κατὰ σάρκα is, in fact, to indicate that, true though it is—and it is indeed of real importance—that, as far as his manhood is concerned, the Son of God is the legal descendant of David, his manhood is not coextensive with the fullness of his person. The use of κατὰ σάρκα here may be compared with its use in 9: 5. While it is true that, treated as an isolated scrap of evidence, these verses do not afford any incontrovertible proof that the writer believed in the pre-existence of Christ and in his Incarnation, understood in their context and in the light of the rest of Romans, they are significant support for the view that he did so.

The second passage is 8: 3. Professor Dunn's treatment of this key verse is scattered over several places (in particular, pp. 44 f., 111 f. and 126 f.), but there is no really thorough discussion of it. The reference of πέμψας to the sending into the world of the pre-existent Son is not to be dismissed so lightly. It is true that the use of πέμπειν (as also of ἐξαποστέλλειν in Gal. 4: 4) does not in itself require such a reference; for the language of 'sending' is often used in the Bible of the divine commissioning of prophets. But the fact that the reference to the divine sending

[4] Cf. J. D. G. Dunn, 'Jesus—Flesh and Spirit: an exposition of Romans 1. 3–4', in *JTS*, NS 24 (1973), 40–68.

and the description of the One sent as God's Son (note here the specially emphatic τὸν ἑαυτοῦ υἱόν) are followed both here and in Gal. 4: 4 by words which are naturally understood as indicating the consequence of the sending for the One sent, namely, that he comes to have a human existence (in Rom. 8: 3 the words ἐν ὁμοιώματι σαρκὸς ἁμαρτίας and in Gal. 4: 4 the words γενόμενον ἐκ γυναικός, γενόμενον ὑπὸ νόμον), surely makes it very difficult to avoid the conclusion that in both places we are up against strong evidence of the presence of the doctrine of the Incarnation in Paul's thought.[5]

But more must be said about 8: 3. An obvious problem is: why did Paul not just say ἐν σαρκὶ ἁμαρτίας? Why did he insert ὁμοιώματι and put the genitive σαρκός instead of σαρκί? This has been much discussed and various explanations have been offered. Professor Dunn simply assumes, without consideration of other views, that the meaning of ἐν ὁμοιώματι σαρκὸς ἁμαρτίας is 'in the (precise) likeness of sinful flesh' (44 and 45) and that Paul wanted to make 'an affirmation of the complete oneness of Christ with sinful man making his death effective for the condemnation of sin by the destruction of its power base (the flesh)' (45). The purpose of Professor Dunn's addition of the word 'precise' is not absolutely clear. Was it perhaps to indicate agreement with the suggestion that ὁμοίωμα here means 'form' rather than 'likeness'? This suggestion can certainly be defended, but its correctness should not be taken for granted. As a matter of fact, much of the attention of interpreters of Romans has been directed towards explaining why Paul should introduce the idea of likeness here. But of this *Christology in the Making* gives no hint. Of the suggestions which might have been discussed the one which still seems to me the most probable is that Paul did it in order to take account of the truth that God's Son was not changed into man, but, while assuming our fallen human nature and becoming truly man, still remained himself. According to this suggestion, the use of ὁμοίωμα was intended to guard against the notion of a 'complete oneness of Christ with sinful man' (45) in the sense of a oneness which is so complete that there is a time when he is fallen man without remainder— not to call in question the reality of his true humanity, the reality of his sharing our fallen human nature, but to draw attention to the fact that in becoming man the Son of God never ceased to be himself.[6] (Here the

[5] Reference should be made to E. Schweizer, in *Theologisches Wörterbuch zum Neuen Testament*, ed. G. Kittel and G. Friedrich (Stuttgart, 1969), 376–8, 385–6.

[6] Professor Dunn's 'wholly' in his sentence, 'it was the first Christians' recognition *both* of the reality of God in Christ *and* that Christ was wholly one with them, a man among men, that determined the course of future orthodoxy', in *SJT* 35 (1982), 335, is to be questioned. Is there not a vital distinction between *vere* and *totaliter*, which must not be blurred, if we are to keep to Christian truth?

ἐν ὁμοιώματι ἀνθρώπων γενόμενος of Phil. 2: 7 is to be compared.) Professor Dunn does not mention this suggestion, as far as I can see. But to assume that Paul could not conceivably have thought in such a way is surely to underestimate his intelligence.

The third passage is 8: 9–11. Professor Dunn has some discussion of these verses on pp. 144–6. He refers to 'the familiar observation that in Rom. 8: 9–11 "Spirit of God dwells in you", "you have the Spirit of Christ", and "Christ is in you" are all more or less synonymous formulations' (145). But he does not consider the possibility that the parallelism between 'the Spirit of God' and 'the Spirit of Christ' in v. 9 is one more evidence of Paul's recognition of the divine dignity, and therefore of the pre-existence, of Christ.

The fourth passage is 9: 5. Professor Dunn gives it less than half a page altogether. This is surprisingly slight treatment in view of the fact that he himself admits 'the very real possibility that *Rom. 9. 5* refers to Christ as God (θεός)' (45). It is also marked by an uncharacteristic looseness, which leaves the reader puzzled if he tries to analyse what exactly is being said. Was Professor Dunn unhappy with this piece of evidence? One sentence states that 'the punctuation intended by Paul and the meaning of the doxology is [*sic*] too uncertain for us to place any great weight on it'; but the very next sentence is: 'The argument on punctuation certainly favours a reference to Christ as "god"'. After the confusing combination of 'too uncertain' and 'certainly', we are told that 'Paul's style is notably irregular and a doxology to Christ as god at this stage would be even more unusual within the context of Paul's thought than an unexpected twist in grammatical construction'. But is Paul's style so 'notably irregular'? And is 'an unexpected twist in grammatical construction' an adequate description of the difficulty involved in taking v. 5b as an independent doxology? Professor Dunn goes on to assert that 'Even if Paul does bless Christ as "god" here, the meaning of "god" remains uncertain, particularly in view of our earlier discussion (above, 16 f.)'; but the material gathered on p. 16 f. seems to have very little in common with Rom. 9: 5. The last sentence of p. 45 ('Whatever the correct rendering of the text it is by no means clear that Paul thinks of Christ here as pre-existent god') would seem to suggest that even in Professor Dunn's own mind there remains sufficient doubt to make imperative a much more serious discussion of the various arguments which have been put forward in connection with this verse than he has given us. It is true that several recent commentators[7] have rejected the reference of v. 5b to Christ; but it is significant that they had not had the chance to consider the extremely careful contribution by B. M.

[7] e.g., E. Käsemann, O. Kuss, U. Wilckens.

Metzger entitled 'The Punctuation of Rom. 9: 5',[8] to which Professor Dunn refers but the detailed arguments of which he makes no attempt to rebut. Other recent commentators have given their support to the reference to Christ,[9] and—what is perhaps the most important recent development in this debate—the editors of the Nestle-Aland Greek New Testament, whose concern for thoroughly objective scholarship will hardly be impugned, have in the twenty-sixth edition (1979) substituted a comma after σάρκα for the colon of the previous edition. It is surely not unreasonable to suggest that at the present time the *onus probandi* rests squarely on the shoulders of those who reject the reference of v. 5b to Christ. We regard as by far the most probable explanation of v. 5 as a whole that which understands it to be affirming that Christ, who, in so far as his human existence is concerned, is of Jewish race, is also Lord over all things and by nature God blessed for ever; and we therefore regard v. 5 as strong evidence of Paul's belief in Christ's preexistence and in the Incarnation.

The fifth passage is 10: 6–10, with which Professor Dunn deals on pp. 184–7. He rejects the common interpretation of v. 6 ('But the righteousness which is of faith saith thus, Say not in thy heart, Who shall ascend into heaven? (that is, to bring Christ down:)') as referring to the Incarnation, arguing instead that Paul is thinking of heaven as the place where Christ is now, since his exaltation ('Christ may seem far away, inaccessible to earth-bound men, but the word of faith is near at hand' (186)). But this interpretation, though Professor Dunn is of course not alone in maintaining it, does seem to be too much of a *tour de force*. One obvious difficulty in the way of accepting it is the order of vv. 6 and 7. The fact that v. 7 refers explicitly to Christ's Resurrection from the dead makes it natural to suppose that what is referred to in v. 6 is likely to be something chronologically prior to the Resurrection. Professor Dunn's reply to this is that the order of the questions in vv. 6 and 7 was determined simply by Deut. 30: 12 f. It is true that in Rom. 10: 9 we get a surprising order (outward confession mentioned before inward belief) and that the explanation of this seems to be Deut. 30: 14, in which 'in thy mouth' precedes 'in thy heart'. But in this case Paul immediately reverses the order in v. 10, so that the awkwardness is straightened out: nothing like this is done for the awkwardness presented (on Professor Dunn's interpretation) by the order of vv. 6 and 7. There is a further difficulty in the way of accepting Professor Dunn's interpretation: even if we can get over the obstacle of the order, there

---

[8] In B. Lindars and S. S. Smalley (ed.), *Christ and Spirit in the New Testament: Studies in honour of C. F. D. Moule* (Cambridge, 1973), 95–112.
[9] e.g., H. Schlier, C. E. B. Cranfield.

remains the difficulty that the parallelism between vv. 6 and 7 strongly suggests that, since what is spoken of in v. 7 has already happened, what is spoken of in v. 6 must also be something which has occurred already. A reference to bringing down the now exalted Christ from heaven combines very oddly with that to bringing up from the dead him whose Resurrection is a fact of the past. The natural interpretation of v. 6 is surely that which understands it to refer to the Incarnation.

III

We turn now, in the third place, to a consideration of some of the features of Romans, the bearing of which on the subject of his inquiry Professor Dunn does not acknowledge but which seem to have a very strong claim to be taken into account.

Professor Dunn refrains from giving a separate treatment of the title 'Lord', on the ground that 'it denotes Christ's exalted (i.e. post-Easter) glory'.[10] But Paul's use of the title can hardly be without some bearing on the question whether he believed in Christ's pre-existence and in the Incarnation or not. That he must have been well acquainted both with the common secular uses of the word κύριος and also with its use in pagan religions is clear. But, if it is right to say that its use in the Septuagint (more than six thousand times) to represent the divine name YHWH is the key to understanding Paul's use of it with reference to Christ (and the fact that he applied to Christ, without—apparently—the least sense of inappropriateness, the κύριος of Septuagint passages in which it is perfectly clear that the κύριος referred to is God himself[11] would seem to be very strong support for this view), then Paul's use of the title with reference to Christ must surely mean that, for him, the exalted Christ shared the name, the majesty, the authority, the deity of the living God himself. But a necessary implication of this is that Paul believed in Christ's pre-existence and in the Incarnation. On any other assumption than this, the use of the title κύριος of Christ in the way in which Paul (someone who lived with, and, as it were, breathed, the OT) used it, would surely be incomprehensible.

Strong confirmation of what has just been said about Paul's use of the title 'Lord' of the exalted Christ is afforded by the fact that he countenanced the offering of prayer to Christ. Evidence of this in Romans is to be seen in 10: 12–14. In each of these three verses reference is made to 'calling upon' the Lord or the name of the Lord. That the Lord

[10] pp. 271 f., n. 33 to ch. I.
[11] e.g., Rom. 10: 13: for other examples reference may be made to my ICC commentary on Romans, pp. 529 and 839.

referred to is Christ is clear from the context. The Greek ἐπικαλεῖσθαι (rendered here in the RV by 'call upon') is a technical term for invoking in prayer.[12] That Paul, who certainly had not abandoned his commitment to the first two commandments of the Decalogue (to have done so would surely have been perceived by him as downright apostasy), could countenance prayer to Christ, is something which has often not received the attention it deserves. Its significance cannot be neatly confined to the subject of how Paul thought about the exalted Christ; for only the one true living God can be rightly invoked in prayer, and, if the exalted Christ is one to whom prayer may rightly be addressed, then he must have been true God from all eternity. The idea of apotheosis was acceptable to pagans of the centuries before and after Christ, but to one who has lived in the light of the OT can it be any thing but a nonsense? To grasp the full significance of Paul's acceptance of the rightness of praying to Christ, one needs to consider Exod. 20: 2–6 and Deut. 5: 7–10, and along with them such passages as Deut. 6: 4 (compare Rom. 3: 30); 11: 16; Isa. 42: 8; Matt. 4: 10; Mark 12: 29, 32.

There is a rich variety of other ways in which Paul associates Christ with God with an uninhibitedness which may easily be passed over unnoticed because it has become so familiar, but which, as soon as we stop to reflect on the implications of what we are reading, can hardly fail to strike us as utterly extraordinary and astonishing. Thus in 1: 7 the source from which grace and peace are desired for the Roman Christians is 'God our Father and the Lord Jesus Christ'; and there is a suggestive parallel between 'The grace of our Lord Jesus Christ be with you', which is the *subscriptio* to the letter (16: 20), and the prayer-wish of 15: 33. 'Now the God of peace be with you all, Amen.'[13] In 8: 35 and 39 'the love of Christ' and 'the love of God, which is in Christ Jesus our Lord' are used, respectively, in two closely corresponding contexts. The phrase 'the churches of Christ' in 16: 16 answers to 'the churches of God' in 1 Cor. 11: 16. There is an interesting parallel between 'the gospel of God' in 15: 16 and 'the gospel of Christ' in 15: 19, though the two genitives are of different kinds, as is also the case in 1: 1 ('separated unto the gospel of God') and 1: 9 ('whom I serve in my spirit in the gospel of his Son'). In chapter one Paul makes it clear that 'the gospel of God' (v. 1), for the proclamation of which he has been set apart, is the gospel 'concerning . . . Jesus Christ our Lord' (vv. 3–4), that it is God's saving power (v. 16), and that, in its being proclaimed, both the

---

[12] Cf. W. Bauer, *Griechisch-deutsches Wörterbuch zu den Schriften des Neuen Testaments* (Berlin, 1971) corrected reprint of 5th edn. of 1958, s.v. ἐπικαλέω 2.b and see also 1.a. Cf. Paul's use of '[those] that call upon the name of our Lord Jesus Christ' as a designation of Christians in 1 Cor. 1: 2.

[13] On the 'God be with' formula reference may be made to my ICC commentary on Romans, p. 780.

gift of a status of righteousness before God (so I understand 'a righteousness of God' here) and also God's wrath are being revealed (vv. 17 and 18). According to 2: 16, 'God' is going to carry out his eschatological judgement of men 'by Jesus Christ'.

Of special interest is the association of Christ with God in relation to faith. There are places where faith is spoken of explicitly as in God. So in 4: 3 Paul quotes Gen. 15: 6, 'And Abraham believed God...' (ἐπίστευσεν ... τῷ θεῷ): that is a giving credence to God's word, God's promise (compare 4: 17–21). In 4: 5 he speaks of one who 'believeth on [ἐπί with the accusative] him that justifieth the ungodly' (that is, of course, God). And in 4: 24 he describes Christians as those 'who believe on [again ἐπί with the accusative] him that raised Jesus our Lord from the dead'. In other places Christ is equally explicitly indicated as the object of faith. Thus in 3: 22 the righteousness referred to is defined as being 'through faith in Jesus Christ', while in 3: 26 God is spoken of as justifying the man 'that hath faith in Jesus': in both these places the noun πίστις is used with an objective genitive. The verb πιστεύειν is used with ἐπί and the dative in 9: 33 and 10: 11 in the Septuagint quotation and with εἰς in 10: 14 (expressly in the first relative clause: εἰς is no doubt also to be supplied in the second question, where οὗ stands for εἰς ἐκεῖνον οὗ). In all three verses Paul is thinking of Christ as the one believed in. There are also many occurrences both of πίστις and of πιστεύειν, where no object of faith is mentioned and yet the existence of an object of faith is surely implied. To attempt to decide in each place whether God or Christ would more naturally be supposed to be the unspecified object would surely be unrealistic and inappropriate. The right conclusion to draw, I suspect, is—and, if this is true, then it is of the greatest importance for the subject of our inquiry—that, for Paul, faith in God and faith in Christ are inextricably bound together. Occurrences of πίστις to be mentioned here are in 1: 5, 8, 12, 17; 3: 25, 27, 30, 31; 5: 1, 2; 9: 30, 32; 10: 6, 8, 17; 11: 20; 12: 3 (if my understanding of μέτρον πίστεως is right), 6; 16: 26; and of πιστεύειν in 1: 16; 3: 22; 10: 4; 13: 11; 15: 13.[14]

Two other matters fall to be mentioned just here. The first is that there is a close relationship between faith and hope in the Bible, and that, though ἐλπίς and ἐλπίζειν occur much less frequently in Romans than do πίστις and πιστεύειν, there is perhaps enough of a hint of the possibility of discerning a similar pattern implicit in the use of the former pair of words in the epistle to that which we have seen in the use of the latter, to be worth noting.

[14] On the various meanings of πίστις and πιστεύειν in the Pauline epistles reference may be made to the ICC on Romans, 697 f. See also pages referred to in index II, under πιστεύειν and πίστις, and in index III, under 'faith'.

The second matter is that there is a great deal of material in the OT which makes the point that only God is the proper object of faith or hope in the fullest and deepest senses of the words. To put absolute faith or hope in anyone or in anything but the one true God is idolatry. Out of many passages which could be cited it will be enough here to mention just a few (in each case indicating the words or expressions used in the LXX for faith or hope): Ps. 22: 4, 5 (LXX: 21: 5, 6): 'Our fathers trusted in thee: They trusted, and thou didst deliver them ... They trusted in thee, and were not ashamed' (ἐλπίζειν three times, twice with ἐπί and dative); 27 (26): 13 (where the LXX has πιστεύω τοῦ ἰδεῖν τὰ ἀγαθὰ κυρίου ἐν γῇ ζώντων); 31: 14 (LXX: 30: 15): 'But I trusted in thee, O LORD: I said, Thou art my God' (ἐλπίζειν with ἐπί and accusative); 38: 15 (LXX: 37: 16): 'For in thee, O LORD, do I hope: Thou wilt answer, O LORD, my God' (ἐλπίζειν with ἐπί and dative); 78 (LXX: 77): 22: (God was wroth with Israel) 'Because they believed not in God, And trusted not in his salvation' (πιστεύειν ἐν and ἐλπίζειν with ἐπί and accusative); 118 (LXX: 117): 8, 9: 'It is better to trust in the LORD Than to put confidence in man. It is better to trust in the LORD Than to put confidence in princes' (πεποιθέναι with ἐπί and accusative twice in v. 8, ἐλπίζειν with ἐπί and accusative twice in v. 9); 146 (LXX: 145): 3, 5: 'Put not your trust in princes, Nor in the son of man, in whom there is no help ... Happy is the man that hath the God of Jacob for his help, Whose hope is in the LORD his God' (πεποιθέναι with ἐπί and accusative, and ἡ ἐλπὶς αὐτοῦ also with ἐπί and accusative); Prov. 3: 5: 'Trust in the LORD with all thine heart, And lean not upon thine own understanding' (εἶναι πεποιθώς with ἐπί and dative); Isa. 7: 9: 'If ye will not believe, surely ye shall not be established' (πιστεύειν: it is faith in God that is in question); Jer. 17: 5, 7: 'Cursed is the man that trusteth in man, and maketh flesh his arm, and whose heart departeth from the LORD ... Blessed is the man that trusteth in the LORD, and whose hope the LORD is' (τὴν ἐλπίδα ἔχειν with ἐπί and accusative, πεποιθέναι with ἐπί and dative, and ἐλπίς).

It seems to me that what is said in Romans about faith (when it is seen in the light of the wealth of relevant OT material of which only a few examples have been given above) is further strong evidence of the author's conviction of Christ's oneness with God, and so of his eternity— and so of the author's belief in Christ's pre-existence and in the Incarnation.

Yet further evidence is provided by the passages concerning Christ's death for us. Its full weight can be measured accurately only when all the relevant passages are seen together,[15] but 5: 8 and 3: 24–6 will, I

---

[15] For a list of these see ICC *Romans*, pp. 826–33.

think, suffice to make the point which has to be made here. The assertion in 5: 8 that God proves his own love for us by the fact that Christ died for us while we were still sinners is not to be explained as merely referring to a specially outstanding instance of the general truth that a man who performs an act of self-sacrificial love for his fellow-men affords a pointer to God's love and care for them. It is so solemnly and emphatically expressed (note the emphatic ἑαυτοῦ and the fact that the subject of the action described in the main clause is God), besides being an integral part of a context dealing with our reconciliation (that is, of God's transforming us from being his enemies into being his friends), that it surely cannot be convincingly explained as implying anything less than that Paul believed that in Christ's giving himself in death God was himself involved not just in sympathy but in person. A clue to the right understanding of the other passage is, I believe, afforded by the recognition that the καί in 3: 26 is adverbial, that is, that it means not 'and' but 'even', so that the latter half of the verse may be translated 'so that he might be righteous even in justifying the man who believes in Jesus'. Paul is indicating that God's object was to justify sinners, who put their trust in Jesus, righteously, that is, in a way altogether worthy of himself as the merciful and loving God, who, because he truly and faithfully loves men, cannot condone their sin or allow it to appear as other than it is. In order so to forgive, without cruelly betraying his whole creation by compromising his own righteousness, God purposed that Christ should be a propitiatory sacrifice (3: 25), that is, surely, purposed to direct against his own very self in his Son the full weight of that righteous wrath which men deserve. If—and only if—Jesus Christ is essentially one with the eternal God (and this carries with it pre-existence and incarnation), this passage makes sense, sense consonant with the character of God disclosed in Scripture.

In the light of what has just been said, must we not conclude that, when he refers to Christ as 'Son of God' in 1: 4, 'his [that is, God's] Son' in 1: 3, 9; 5: 10; 8: 29, 'his [that is, God's] own [ἑαυτοῦ] Son' in 8: 3, 'his [that is, God's] own [ἰδίου] Son' in 8: 32, and to God as 'the God and Father of our Lord Jesus Christ' in 15: 6 (compare 'the Father' in 6: 4), Paul intends to indicate a relationship which involves a real community of nature between Christ and God? The ἑαυτοῦ and ἰδίου in 8: 3 and 32, respectively, seem to be used to underline the contrast between the one true Son of God by nature and the sons by adoption.

But the evidence of Romans seems to take us still farther. There are a number of short passages each containing a combination of references to God (the Father), to Christ, to the Spirit, in close proximity to each other, which, taken together, seem to me to constitute a very strong basis for the affirmation that, though no explicit formulation of a doctrine of the Trinity is to be seen in the epistle, the theology of the author of Romans is essentially Trinitarian. The following must be set out.[16] (i) 1: 1–4 ('Paul, slave of Christ Jesus, ... set apart for *the work of proclaiming* God's message of good news, which he promised beforehand ..., concerning his Son, who was born of David's seed according to the flesh, who was appointed Son of God in power according to the Spirit of holiness from the resurrection of the dead, even Jesus Christ our Lord'). (ii) 5: 1–5 ('... we have peace with God through our Lord Jesus Christ, ... we exult in hope of the glory of God. ... And this hope does not put us to shame, for God's love has been poured out in our hearts through the Holy Spirit who has been given to us'). (iii) 8: 1–4 ('So then there is now no condemnation for those who are in Christ Jesus. For the law of the Spirit of life has in Christ Jesus set thee free from the law of sin and of death. For God, having sent his own Son in the likeness of sinful flesh and to deal with sin, condemned sin in the flesh ..., so that the righteous requirement of the law might be fulfilled in us who do not walk according to the flesh but according to the Spirit'). (iv) 8: 9 ('But you are not in the flesh but in the Spirit, seeing that God's Spirit dwells in you. (If some one does not possess Christ's Spirit, then he does not belong to Christ.)') (v) 8: 11 ('But, if the Spirit of him who raised Jesus from the dead dwells in you, he who raised from the dead Christ Jesus shall quicken your mortal bodies also through his Spirit who dwells in you'). (vi) 8: 16 f. ('The Spirit himself assures our spirit that we are children of God. And if children, then also heirs: heirs of God and fellow-heirs of Christ, seeing that we are *now* suffering with him, in order that we may *hereafter* be glorified with him'). (vii) 14: 17 f. ('For the kingdom of God is not eating and drinking, but righteousness and peace and joy in the Holy Spirit; for he who therein serves Christ is well-pleasing to God and deserves men's approval'). (viii) 15: 16 ('to be a minister of Christ Jesus unto the Gentiles, serving God's message of good news with a holy service, in order that the offering consisting of the Gentiles may be acceptable, having been sanctified by the Holy Spirit'). (ix) 15: 30 ('I exhort you [, brothers,] by our Lord Jesus Christ and by the love of the Spirit to join earnestly with me in prayers on my behalf to God').

But more significant than the simple fact that passages occur in which God, Christ, and the Spirit are mentioned together, is what is ascribed (whether explicitly or implicitly) to Christ and to the Spirit not only in these passages but also in many other places throughout the

---

[16] I quote these passages according to the translation in my ICC commentary, by permission of Messrs. T. and T. Clark.

epistle. It seems to me that Paul is thinking of Christ and the Spirit as effecting (for example, in justification and sanctification) what only the one true God himself can be seriously thought of as effecting—things, which, if they are not done by the eternal God himself (and none other), are just not done at all. If this reading of Romans is correct, then the whole structure of theological thought which has shaped and ordered it must surely be acknowledged to have a Trinitarian character.

The conclusion to be drawn from the evidence of Romans is surely, *pace* Professor Dunn, that its author firmly believed in the pre-existence of Christ, in the sense that as Son of God he has shared the divine life from all eternity, and in the Incarnation, in the sense that at a particular time the eternal Son of God assumed our human nature for the sake of mankind and of the whole creation. My impression is that the author of *Christology in the Making*—for all the valuable provocativeness of the contribution he has made, which is gratefully acknowledged—has not yet got the measure of the sheer intellectual power and alertness of the author of the Epistle to the Romans.

It is with painful awareness of their inadequacy for the purpose that the writer of these comments offers them as an expression of his gratitude to, and affection for, the distinguished scholar to whose memory this volume is dedicated.

21. Person or Personification? A Patristic Debate about Logos

MAURICE WILES

ONE may learn a lot from one's colleagues, as I have done from George Caird, but not usually from hearing them lecture. It is perhaps partly for that reason that I still have a clear recollection of the first of the only two occasions that I heard him give a formal lecture, although it is now nearly twenty years ago. In that lecture, on 'The Development of the Doctrine of Christ in the New Testament',[1] he concluded that 'neither the Fourth Gospel nor Hebrews ever speaks of the eternal Word or Wisdom of God in terms which compel us to regard it as a person'. Our tendency to do so, he suggests, derives from reading those writers in the light of Paul, who, in his judgement, stands alone among New Testament authors in affirming belief in the pre-existence of Christ as a person.

The issue has long fascinated readers and scholars of the New Testament. It is generally agreed that in works like the book of Proverbs or the Wisdom of Solomon the figure of Wisdom herself is to be understood as a personification rather than a person. 'The personified Wisdom of Jewish literature remains from start to finish an activity or attribute of God.'[2] But when New Testament writers make use of the same conception, or of the cognate idea of the Word, do they intend it in the same sense? Or do they envisage a fully personal form of pre-existence? Although (or because) I am on this occasion rashly keeping company with New Testament specialists, I shall not offer a contribution of my own to the continuing debate on that question.[3] I am inclined indeed to think that the evidence may be so ambivalent in character, that no decisive answer can be forthcoming. Nevertheless, however open the exegetical question may be and may have to remain, the Church quite quickly gave a clear and unequivocal answer to the distinct, but related, theological question. Modalist interpretations of the person of Christ, which did not involve the concept of a fully per-

---

[1] Published in N. Pittenger (ed.), *Christ for Us Today*, Papers from the Fiftieth Annual Conference of the Modern Churchmen, Somerville College, Oxford, 24–8 July 1967 (London, 1968), 66–80 (esp. 79–80).

[2] Ibid., 76.

[3] I have in fact done so in discussion with James Dunn in *Theology* 85 (March, 1982, 92–6 and Sept. 1982, 324–32).

sonal form of pre-existence, made little headway in the life of the
Church. The decisive reasons for their rejection had more to do with
devotion and worship than with exegetical argument. Nevertheless exegesis did play its part. Our fullest picture of the exegetical reasoning
involved appears at a late stage in the debate, when the Church's mind
is already effectively made up, namely the debate between Eusebius of
Caesarea and Marcellus in the 330s. Since this particular exegetical
issue is still a live one, a brief account of one aspect of the debate
between them may not be without interest.

Marcellus has suffered the fate of almost all those whose teachings
failed to find favour in the Church. We know him almost entirely
through the polemical witness of his opponents. We need always to remember therefore the partial nature of our evidence (in both senses of
the word 'partial'). Nevertheless Eusebius cites his words directly to a
sufficient degree for us to be able to grasp both sides of the debate with
a reasonable degree of accuracy.

The main point at issue between them can be succinctly put. Both
believe in a pre-existent 'only-begotten-Son-Logos' who becomes
incarnate as Jesus Christ. For Marcellus, Logos is the dominant image
and this means that for him the affirmation of any pre-existent personal
entity, distinct from the Father, is not called for. For Eusebius, Son is
the dominant image, and Logos must be understood in terms of it; for
him therefore the distinct hypostatic existence of the Son before the
Incarnation is of the essence of the faith. Each, as we shall see in more
detail later, accuses the other of treating his dominant image too
anthropomorphically and thereby drawing false implications from it.
Thus the structure of the dispute embodies a classic form of theological
argument. If we are to order the varied imagery of Scripture in some
more coherent way, we are bound to arrange those images in some sort
of hierarchical scheme. Some images will be picked out as particularly
significant and made the key to the appropriate interpretation of the
others. Where one image is so picked out, it will normally be because
we believe that it points more directly to and more nearly represents
the transcendent reality about which we are trying to speak. A natural
retort of anyone wishing to propose some alternative ordering of the
images will be to claim that our way of handling the image we regard as
dominant is an improperly literalistic one.

One feature in this outline account of the central issue at stake in the
debate must be admitted to be problematic. I have said that both Marcellus and Eusebius believed in a pre-existent 'only-begotten-Son-
Logos'. But is that true of Marcellus? Did he speak of a pre-existent *Son*?
The limited nature of our evidence does not allow us to answer that

question with absolute confidence. Eusebius certainly claims that he did not and regards that fact as one of the primary faults in Marcellus's theology that he is determined to expose.[4] Many modern scholars follow Eusebius on this point. Thus Kelly affirms that 'Marcellus restricts the title "Son" to the Incarnate'.[5] The primary evidence on which both Eusebius and the modern writers rely is the statement of Marcellus that before the Incarnation 'there was nothing other than Logos'.[6] But it is noteworthy that when Marcellus contrasts Logos with other titles that belong to Christ incarnate, he never includes 'Son' as an example of that second category.[7] It is thus seriously misleading when Pollard writes: 'He [Marcellus] repeatedly insists that before the assumption of the flesh the Logos was nothing but Logos, and that "*Son*", "Jesus", "Christ", "Life", "Resurrection", and the rest are titles which are properly applicable to the Logos only after the incarnation.'[8] Later followers of Marcellus are quite explicit that the accusation that they separate Logos and Son in this way is one they vigorously deny.[9] So what of Marcellus himself? Other scholars have argued that pre-existent Son is an integral feature of Marcellus's own teaching. Grillmeier draws much of his evidence for such a claim from the pseudo-Athanasian *De Incarnatione et Contra Arianos* and the *Epistula ad Liberium*, which are of very dubious attribution.[10] If we discount this evidence, he can still point to the occurrence of the phrase 'only-begotten-Son-Logos', in the authentic epistle to Julius.[11] It may be that in that letter Marcellus is accommodating his language in some measure to the more general usage of the Church. Certainly it seems difficult to see how Marcellus could have remained within orthodox church life to the extent that he did, had he been wholly unprepared to acknowledge 'Son' as a pre-existent title. Moreover he regularly uses 'Father' in relation with 'Logos' when speaking both of God's eternal existence and of his pre-incarnate activity.[12] More significantly in the actual fragments cited by Eusebius there is one reference to the relationship of the flesh to

---

[4] Eusebius, *Contra Marcellum et De Ecclesiastica Theologia* (GCS, Leipzig, 1906), *Con. Marc.* 1. 1. (p. 7 ll. 3–7 and ll. 34–5). The scriptural evidence adduced by Eusebius is Gal. 4: 4 and John 1: 14.

[5] J. N. D. Kelly, *Early Christian Doctrines* (London, 1958), 240. Cf. J. T. Lienhard, 'Marcellus of Ancyra in Modern Research', *TS*, 43 (1982), 489: 'For Marcellus, the title "Son" applies only to the incarnate Word'.

[6] Frag. 48 (p. 193); (p. 204).

[7] In Frag. 42 (p. 193) the contrast is with 'Jesus or Christ'; in Frag. 43 (ibid.) it is with 'life, way, day, resurrection, door, bread'.

[8] T. E. Pollard, *Johannine Christology and the Early Church* (Cambridge, 1970), 253 (italics added).

[9] Eugenius of Ancyra, *Expositio Fidei ad Athanasium*, 1, 2 and 4, 3. (See text of M. Tetz in *ZNW*, 64 (1973), 79 and 83.

[10] A. Grillmeier, *Christ in Christian Tradition*, 2nd edn. (London, 1975), 279–81.

[11] Frag. 129 (p. 215 ll. 4–5).

[12] e.g. Frag. 52 (p. 194 l. 11); 60 (p. 196 ll. 3, 11–12); 61 (p. 96 l. 13).

'his [God's] true Son, the Logos', which seems to show a clear identification of the two not limited to the incarnate state.[13] All in all it seems safest to conclude that Marcellus did not restrict 'Son' to the time of the Incarnation, but that 'Logos' was for him so dominant an image for understanding the pre-existence of Christ[14] that the term 'Son' had very little part to play in his own theology. At the same time we must remain open to the possibility that the selective nature of our evidence may be misleading us at this point.

What then are the reasons which lead Marcellus to treat Logos as so wholly dominating an image in relation to the pre-existence of Christ? No doubt the most important is his conviction that by doing so he is enabled to maintain a far more convincing account of the unity of God. But he is also able to give his interpretation a more specifically exegetical justification. That justification is based on the fourth Gospel. Logos is the title that John uses in the prologue of Christ's pre-existence; when speaking of the incarnate Christ he uses a great variety of other titles, but not Logos.[15] It is therefore clearly the appropriate category for interpreting Christ's pre-existence. Marcellus further insists that in using it for this purpose it needs to be understood in a strict rather than an indirect sense ($\kappa\nu\rho\iota\omega s$ and not $\kappa\alpha\tau\alpha\chi\rho\eta\sigma\tau\iota\kappa\hat\omega s$).[16]

Eusebius is determined to refute this position on both counts. He marshals a number of ingenious, and sometimes ingenuous, counterarguments. He does not deny that the fourth evangelist uses Logos in the prologue in the prominent way that Marcellus indicates or that he uses it exclusively with reference to pre-existence. But he points out that it is not the only term used in that context in the prologue. John also employs there the designations of God, light, son, and only-begotten.[17] We have already seen reason to believe that, although this is a serious challenge to Marcellus's more extreme and epigrammatic statement that before the Incarnation there was nothing but Logos, it is one which a more measured presentation of his position might not have found it too difficult to meet. Eusebius further insists that these other terms from the prologue (unlike Logos) are also used in the main body of the Gospel by and of the incarnate Christ himself, thus calling into question Marcellus's sharp distinction between pre- and post-incarnate

---

[13] Frag. 20 (p. 188 l. 19). F. Loofs (*Paulus von Samosata* (Leipzig, 1924), 239), who cites this passage as evidence for Marcellus's use of 'Son' as a title with reference to pre-existence, appeals also to Fragments 3 and 64, but both of these are capable of other interpretations.

[14] The term 'pre-existence of Christ' is the normal form of words used in contemporary theology. I shall therefore use it here rather than the more cumbersome 'pre-existence of the only-begotten-Logos-Son', despite the fact that Marcellus would have strongly objected to our modern form of words.

[15] *Ec.T.* 1. 18 (pp. 78–80).

[16] *Ec.T.* 1. 1 (p. 63 ll. 4–8); *Ec.T.* 2. 10 (pp. 110–12).   [17] *Ec.T.* 2. 10 (p. 110 ll. 24–6).

designations.[18] Moreover Eusebius gives a different significance to the distinction that Marcellus had drawn between the prologue and the rest of the Gospel. Where Marcellus had emphasized the difference of content (pre-existence and incarnate existence), Eusebius points to the difference of spokesman (the evangelist and the incarnate Lord). Is it, he implies, right to attach such pre-eminent importance to a title which has only the lesser authority of the evangelist and not that of the Lord himself?[19]

But Eusebius does not, of course, want to deny the validity of the term 'Logos' altogether as a designation of the pre-existent Christ. So he is concerned to reject Marcellus's insistence that the term is to be understood κυρίως rather than καταχρηστικῶς. One objection he raises is that Marcellus's position involves an arbitrary selectivity. If Logos is to be understood κυρίως, why not Son? Since Marcellus's interpretation of Logos is grounded in its similarity to human speech, why does he not similarly interpret the title 'light' on the basis of its similarity to the rays of the sun?[20] As that alleged contrast between Marcellus's understanding of the two terms 'Logos' and 'light' suggests, Eusebius's more fundamental and continually repeated objection is that Marcellus treats the term too anthropomorphically.[21] Sometimes, as when he declares that the divine Logos is 'not like human speech composed of syllables, verbs and nouns',[22] Eusebius uses parody and ridicule to make his point. But it is clear that he is unfair in so doing. Some of his own citations from Marcellus show that it is no crude literalism, but a sensitive use of analogy,[23] with which Eusebius needs to come to terms. And it is vital for him to do so. For he does not appear to dispute that if Marcellus's basic approach were allowed, his conclusions would follow. Logos (in all the various senses that word can bear) exists only in relation to something else; it is not an οὐσία in its own right.[24] When Marcellus says that the human Logos is inseparable (ἓν καὶ ταὐτόν) from the human being, the fault lies not in the statement but in its application to the divine Logos.[25] What Eusebius has to show therefore is that Marcellus's underlying assumption that the designation Logos should be treated κυρίως, on a strict analogy with human speech, is to be rejected. And that is no easy task. It cannot be done on any general

[18] Ibid. (p. 110 ll. 26–30).
[19] *Ec. T.* 2. 9 (p. 110 ll. 15–22).
[20] *Ec. T.* 2. 10–11 (p. 112 ll. 6–17).
[21] *Con. Marc.* 1. 4 (p. 18 ll. 33–5); *Ec. T.* 1. 17 (p. 77 ll. 9, 17); 1. 18 (p. 80 ll. 7–10); 2. 9 (p. 109 ll. 10–11; p. 112 l. 14).
[22] *Ec. T.* 2. 17 (p. 121 ll. 10–11).
[23] Frag. 58 (p. 195 ll. 15–17); 61 (p. 196 ll. 19–20); 62 (p. 196 ll. 25–6).
[24] *Ec. T.* 2. 13–14 (p. 114 ll. 10–35).
[25] *Ec. T.* 2. 15 (p. 118 ll. 21–9).

ground that no imagery is to be taken in that strict way, because
Eusebius is himself committed to doing precisely that in the case of the
title 'Son'. It is true that the word he normally uses in that context is
ἀληθῶς rathet than κυρίως. But the two are frequently used together as
effectively synonymous.[26] On one occasion, indeed, Eusebius uses the
superlative form, κυριώτατον, of the sonship of the only-begotten, and
insists that it is this strong reality of sonship, and not any analogy with
human speech, which is the key to a proper understanding of the divine
Logos.[27] It is not hard to see how easily Marcellus might have turned
back against Eusebius the arguments Eusebius uses against his understanding of Logos. Indeed, even in the fragments preserved by
Eusebius, we have evidence of Marcellus bringing the charge of a false
anthropomorphism against the view that sonship implies hypostatic
differentiation from the Father.[28] It is not the first time, or the last
either, that a theologian has found it difficult to controvert a position
he is sure is false, without rendering his own position vulnerable to the
same line of argument from the other side.

So far I have been trying to describe the debate in terms of the
underlying differences of approach and the broad exegetical justifica-
tions of those approaches. But in all exegetical work there is a continual
interaction between broad approach and the minutiae of specific
exegesis of texts. In this case both interpreters would have claimed that
evidence for their understanding of the pre-existent Christ was to be
found throughout the Scriptures, and in a comparatively detailed and
specific form at that. Uncompromising affirmations of the Old Testament about the unity of God might seem to favour Marcellus's cause.
But these could be accounted for by Eusebius as temporary concessions
to human weakness, like the institution of animal sacrifices, made
necessary like divorce because of the hardness of men's hearts.[29] And
other features of the Old Testament, like the theophanies, could be
used to point in the opposite direction.[30] Moreover Eusebius could
complain further that it was a weakness of Marcellus's position that his
interpretation of the Logos involved no advance on the Old Testament
and would be fully acceptable to a Jew; it failed to do justice to the
newness of the New Testament.[31] So it is a long catalogue of texts from
both testaments that Eusebius adduces in his support in the final
chapter of Book 1 of the De Ecclesiastica Theologia, where he summarizes

[26] e.g. Ec.T. 1. 1. (p. 63 ll. 8–9).
[27] Ec.T. 2. 24 (p. 135 ll. 17–20).
[28] Frag. 36 (p. 190); 63 (pp. 196–7).
[29] Ec.T. 2. 20 (p. 127 ll. 7–27).
[30] Ec.T. 2. 21 (p. 130 ll. 3–17).
[31] Ec.T. 2. 18 (pp. 121–3). Cf. Con. Marc. 2. 4 (p. 57 ll. 16–30).

his appeal to the evidence of Scripture.[32] But clearly it is the New Testament that predominates, and the Johannine prologue (its opening verse in particular) that has pride of place within it for the purposes of this debate. Since it is also only there among the New Testament texts to which Eusebius appeals that we have much prospect of recovering Marcellus's more precise exegesis, it is to that that we will restrict our attention here.

'In the beginning was the Word; and the Word was with God; and the Word was God.' Each writer can claim that in each of the three clauses of that famous text, the precise wording and the intended nuance of meaning are evidence in favour of his interpretation. We will take Eusebius first. The phrase 'In the beginning' shows that the Logos has a beginning other than itself. It is not itself ἄναρχος. And thereby it is differentiated from the Father.[33] The use of the preposition 'with' rather than 'in' in the second clause inhibits the use of the human analogy and indicates the hypostatic as opposed to accidental character of the Logos.[34] The same implication is seen in the fact that the third clause describes the Logos as God rather than as God's.[35] Moreover the anarthrous character of the word for God (θεός rather than ὁ θεός) is further protection against any misunderstanding of the phrase as teaching an identity between the Logos and the supreme God.[36]

Marcellus's interpretation is preserved in Fragment 52.[37] He identifies 'the beginning' with 'the Father', since God is he 'from whom are all things'. Thus for him the first clause directly affirms that the Logos is in God, the very conception that Eusebius claims the author has carefully avoided. But the Logos is also 'with God', so that two distinguishable relations of the Logos to God must be intended. The difference is said to be one of δύναμις and ἐνέργεια. That distinction is one that plays a large part in the thought of Marcellus. ἐνέργεια is regularly described as the only category in terms of which one may speak of any separation of the Logos from God.[38] The reason for such a separation is most commonly described as being for the work of creation,[39] though sometimes for the sake of incarnation.[40] It is the former that is explicitly envisaged here, since the later words of the prologue, 'All things were

---

[32] *Ec.T.* 1. 20 (pp. 80–98). The main Pauline texts cited are 1 Cor. 8: 6; 1 Cor. 10: 4; Phil, 2: 5–8; Gal. 3: 19–20; Heb. 4: 14; Heb. 1: 3; Col. 1: 15–17.

[33] *Ec.T.* 2. 14 (p. 114 l. 35–p. 115 l. 2).

[34] Ibid. (p. 115 ll. 4–19).

[35] *Ec.T.* 1. 20 (p. 80 l. 31–p. 81 l. 3).

[36] *Ec.T.* 2. 14 (p. 115 ll. 2–4).

[37] p. 194.

[38] Frag. 61 (p. 196 ll. 20–2); 71 (p. 198); 116 (p. 209 ll. 27–8); 117 (p. 210 ll. 15 ff.).

[39] Frag. 60 (p. 196 l. 5); 121 (p. 212 ll. 10–12).

[40] Frag. 117 (p. 210 ll. 15 ff.).

made through him and without him was not anything made', are cited by way of elucidation. The words δύναμις and ἐνέργεια are best translated as 'capability' or 'faculty' and 'its exercise in practice', rather than as 'potentiality' and 'actuality'.[41] In its activity as ἐνέργεια, the Logos does not cease to continue as δύναμις. Thus the first two clauses of John 1: 1 indicate the two coexisting forms of the relation of the Logos to God. Finally Marcellus understands the third clause, 'the Word was God', in a way that contrasts sharply with that of Eusebius. The anarthrous character of the word is not commented on, and the phrase is taken to indicate the undivided character of the Godhead.

It is not hard to see how such contrasting approaches to the exegesis of the Johannine prologue could have been carried on consistently throughout. But we do not have the evidence to trace that out in detail. One example from v. 3 must suffice. There the preposition διά is used in describing the role of the Logos in creation. Marcellus appears to have argued that the use of διά supports his less independent, less personal conception of the Logos. Had the author conceived of the Logos in personal, hypostatic terms, ὑπό would have been the natural word for him to have used. Eusebius counters this argument by stressing the mediatorial role of the Logos, and sees the use of the word διά as ensuring our recognition of the Father as the ultimate source of creation.[42]

Neither the position of Eusebius nor that of Marcellus on the pre-existence of Christ established itself as the faith of the Church. For while orthodoxy unequivocally sided with Eusebius on the personal hypostatic character of the pre-existent Son, it eliminated the clearly secondary and subordinate understanding of his status that was an intrinsic element in the teaching of Eusebius. Yet it might be claimed that Eusebius and Marcellus represent, rather better than later orthodoxy, the two basic exegetical options in relation to New Testament teaching about the pre-existence of Christ. As the continuing divergence of views among New Testament scholars today reveals, it is possible to read most of the relevant texts in either way. In relation to the fourth Gospel prologue, for example, on which we have concentrated here, one modern scholar has suggested a history of the text that shows the genuine support that both Marcellus and Eusebius could find there for their particular views. James Dunn, like many other scholars, believes that there was an earlier Christian poem, which the author of

---

[41] The distinction between these two understandings, only the second of which involves a change in the subject, is clearly made by Aristotle (*De Anima* 2. 5: 417[a,b]) with use of the terms δύναμις and ἐνέργεια. For this point I am indebted to the Revd Dennis Minns and the Revd Dr Paul Parvis of Blackfriars, Oxford. The same general point is emphasized by A. Grillmeier, op. cit. n. 10 above, 282–3, citing both T. Zahn and M. Tetz.

[42] *Ec.T.* 1. 20 (p. 81 ll. 13–21).

the fourth Gospel adopted and incorporated as the prologue to his work. Dunn believes that in the original poem 'we are dealing with personifications rather than persons, personified actions of God rather than an individual divine being as such'; it is only by virtue of the conflation of that approach with the Son of God Christology characterizing the main body of the Gospel that 'it becomes clear that for John the pre-existent Logos was indeed a divine personal being'.[43] If that is a true speculation we would have a 'Marcellan' originator and a 'Eusebian' redactor of the Johannine prologue. That would help to account for the way in which both can find reasoned support for their conflicting views in the wording of that text, and would also justify the important role given in the debate to the relation of the prologue to the Gospel as a whole. Indeed this whole debate about how personally the New Testament writers intended their speech about the pre-existence of Christ to be understood appears to be one in which the interests and arguments of the Fathers stand closer to ours than is sometimes thought to be the case.

[43] J. Dunn, *Christology in the Making* (London, 1980), 243–4.

Index of Passages

APOCRYPHA AND PSEUDEPIGRAPHA

DEAD SEA SCROLLS

NEW TESTAMENT

JEWISH WRITERS

RABBINICAL LITERATURE

EARLY CHRISTIAN WRITINGS

GNOSTIC TEXTS

GREEK AND LATIN AUTHORS

Modern Authors

Subject Index